Information Systems: Principles and Practices

Information Systems: Principles and Practices

Edited by Reuben Hammond

CLANRYE
INTERNATIONAL
www.clanryeinternational.com

Clanrye International,
750 Third Avenue, 9th Floor,
New York, NY 10017, USA

ISBN: 978-1-63240-648-4

Cataloging-in-Publication Data

Information systems : principles and practices / edited by Reuben Hammond.
    p. cm.
Includes bibliographical references and index.
ISBN 978-1-63240-648-4
1. Information science. 2. Information technology. 3. Information resources.
4. Information storage and retrieval systems. I. Hammond, Reuben.
Z665 .I54 2018
020--dc23

For information on all Clanrye International publications
visit our website at www.clanryeinternational.com

Contents

Preface

The purpose of the book is to provide a glimpse into the dynamics and to present opinions and studies of some of the scientists engaged in the development of new ideas in the field from very different standpoints. This book will prove useful to students and researchers owing to its high content quality.

Information systems are used for the collection and storage of information. Some examples of information systems are enterprise resource planning, data warehouses, geographic information system, global information system, etc. This book presents the complex subject of information systems in the most comprehensible and easy to understand language. As this field is emerging at a rapid pace, the contents of this book will help the readers understand the modern concepts and applications of the subject. Students, researchers, experts and all associated with information systems will benefit alike from this book.

At the end, I would like to appreciate all the efforts made by the authors in completing their chapters professionally. I express my deepest gratitude to all of them for contributing to this book by sharing their valuable works. A special thanks to my family and friends for their constant support in this journey.

Editor

Topic Level Disambiguation for Weak Queries

Hui Zhang*
School of Library and
Information Science
Indiana University, U.S.
E-mail: hz3@indiana.edu

Kiduk Yang
Department of Library and
Information Science
Kyungpook National University, Korea
E-mail: yangkiduk@gmail.com

Elin Jacob
School of Library and
Information Science
Indiana University, U.S.
E-mail: ejacob@indiana.edu

ABSTRACT

Despite limited success, today's information retrieval (IR) systems are not intelligent or reliable. IR systems return poor search results when users formulate their information needs into incomplete or ambiguous queries (i.e., weak queries). Therefore, one of the main challenges in modern IR research is to provide consistent results across all queries by improving the performance on weak queries. However, existing IR approaches such as query expansion are not overly effective because they make little effort to analyze and exploit the meanings of the queries. Furthermore, word sense disambiguation approaches, which rely on textual context, are ineffective against weak queries that are typically short. Motivated by the demand for a robust IR system that can consistently provide highly accurate results, the proposed study implemented a novel topic detection that leveraged both the language model and structural knowledge of Wikipedia and systematically evaluated the effect of query disambiguation and topic-based retrieval approaches on TREC collections. The results not only confirm the effectiveness of the proposed topic detection and topic-based retrieval approaches but also demonstrate that query disambiguation does not improve IR as expected.

Keywords: Topic Detection, Query Disambiguation, Language Model, Information Retrieval, Natural Language Processing

*Corresponding Author: Hui Zhang
Adjunct Assistant Professor
School of Library and Information Science
Indiana University, U.S.
E-mail: hz3@indiana.edu

1. INTRODUCTION

Information retrieval (IR) has emerged as a central technology in modern society by enabling individuals to extend their ability to discover and obtain knowledge. The quality of queries has a profound impact on retrieval performance because users must formulate their information needs into queries. Queries that produce low retrieval performance on most IR systems are called *weak queries* or *ineffective queries*. In addition to poor query formulation due to the lack of domain knowledge, the problem of weak querying is intensified by the complexities of natural language such as polysemy. For instance, previous research has found that polysemous words in queries can adversely affect automatic query expansion by introducing terms related to incorrect senses of the polysemes (Voorhees, 1994). To address problems of polysemy, IR researchers use techniques developed for word sense disambiguation (WSD) to identify the intended meaning of a given polyseme. However, the effective application of query disambiguation in IR is not a trivial task because the majority of the queries are short and unable to provide the adequate context required by traditional WSD methods.[1] In consequence, previous studies that have examined the issue of query disambiguation report unsatisfactory results (Sanderson, 1994, 2000; Voorhees, 1993).

With the ongoing debate over the benefit of query disambiguation on IR, this study revisits the issue with a new approach that will segment a keyword query into topics and resolve ambiguity only at topic level. The motivation of the study is to examine whether query disambiguation is helpful to IR with the latest developments in machine learning and new knowledge resources such as Wikipedia. In particular, this study focuses on the following research questions,

- Does query disambiguation improve retrieval?
- Do the structural features of a Wikipedia entry (e.g., title, hyperlinks) offer an effective means of establishing context for topic detection and query disambiguation?

with two corresponding hypotheses:

H1. There is no difference in performance between retrieval runs with query disambiguation and baseline retrieval runs without query disambiguation.

H2. There is no difference in performance between retrieval runs with query disambiguation based on Wikipedia knowledge and retrieval runs with query disambiguation based on free text.

The rest of the paper is organized to provide details on the investigation of both questions starting with a brief review of the existing approaches

2. LITERATURE REVIEW

Methods for WSD are characterized based on the approach they adopt to acquire word meanings. Approaches that adopt predefined word senses from existing knowledge structures such as dictionaries, thesauri, and Wikipedia are considered to be knowledge-based, while approaches that extract word sense information from the underlying collections are considered to be corpus-based.

Corpus-based WSD approaches derive knowledge from corpora using machine learning algorithms. Researchers who rely on this approach consider word sense disambiguation a straightforward classification problem that attempts to determine the category of a context based on models learned from examples. A Bayesian algorithm has been widely adopted for corpus-based WSD. Gale, Church, & Yarowsky (1992) applied the Naïve Bayesian approach for WSD using a bilingual corpus for training. They selected as the context the 50 words surrounding an ambiguous word. The correct sense was then determined by selecting the sense with the highest probability based on the con-

---

[1] The average length of a web query is 2.4 terms and important terms that are descriptive of the information needed are often missing from these short queries (Spink, Wolfram, Jansen, & Saracevic, 2001)

text. The authors found six words in the corpus that had only two senses (e.g., *drug* with the senses of *medical* and *illicit*). The disambiguation model was trained on 60 examples of each of the two senses using words surrounding the target polysemes. The trained model was tested on 90 new word instances for each word sense, and Gale et al. reported an accuracy of 92% on all occurrences of six selected ambiguous nouns. The primary challenge of applying supervised learning algorithms for WSD lies in the overhead for building a sense-tagged corpus. In contrast, knowledge-based approaches overcome this problem by adopting predefined word senses from existing knowledge structures such as dictionaries, thesauri, and lately Wikipedia.

There is a growing trend to use Wikipedia[2] as the sense resource for disambiguation because it provides not only a huge lexicon (i.e., the current English version contains about four million articles) but also extensive descriptions of each word sense. Mihalcea and Csomai (2007) disambiguated terms that appeared in text by mapping them to appropriate Wikipedia articles. The whole process involved two steps: term extraction and word sense disambiguation. In the first step, terms were ranked by their likelihood of becoming hyperlinks in Wikipedia, and only those terms with likelihoods that exceeded a predefined threshold were chosen for disambiguation. For word sense disambiguation, the authors derived word senses from hyperlinks found within Wikipedia articles in order to create training data for supervised disambiguation. For every hyperlink in a Wikipedia article, its author must select the correct destination (i.e., another Wikipedia article) that represents the sense of the anchor text. For example, the term *bar* is linked to different articles on bars in the sense of drinking establishments and in the sense of entertainment sources (e.g., music). Hence, when a polyseme is defined as the anchor of a Wikipedia hyperlink with multiple destinations, a machine learning approach can build a classification model for each polyseme by integrating features such as part of speech and context words. The trained classifier is then used to disambiguate selected terms in the text.

Medelyan, Witten, & Milne (2008) developed another disambiguation approach using Wikipedia as a knowledge resource. They used Mihalcea and Csomai's (2007) strategy of collecting word senses from links in Wikipedia articles. To disambiguate a polyseme in the text, the surrounding terms that were unambiguous Wikipedia anchors (i.e., links to only one Wikipedia article) were then chosen as contexts. The disambiguation process was carried out by calculating semantic similarity to the contexts and conditional probability for the polyseme. Semantic similarity was calculated as the average of each candidate article that represented a sense of the polyseme to all context articles. Conditional probability was computed from counts of Wikipedia links; for example, because the word *jaguar* links to the article for the car jaguar in 466 out of 927 links, the probability of the automobile sense is 0.5. Semantic disambiguation was then determined by multiplying the semantic similarity by the conditional probability of each sense and selecting the one that produced the highest score. The approach devised by Medelyan et al. achieved an *F*-measure of 0.93 on automatically mapping terms to correct Wikipedia articles.

The latest development in query disambiguation research emphasizes the integration of natural language technology and knowledge bases. Selvaretnam and Belkhatir (2012) proposed a query expansion framework considering sense disambiguation as an essential step. In particular, the authors suggested that syntactic parsing such as part of speech recognition should be applied at first followed by semantic sense disambiguation. The decision of whether a sense is appropriate will depend on the relatedness of that sense to its occurring context measured in an external knowledge base such as WordNet. Similar to this study, Klyuev & Haralambous (2011) investigated query disambiguation in the context of improving query expansion, with their finding indicating that combining multiple knowledge bases such as WordNet and Wikipedia could bring better retrieval results. The authors also suggested that selecting the Wikipedia articles that are closely related to the query is vital to the success of

---

[2] http://www.wikipedia.org/

query expansion, which affirms the importance of query disambiguation if one query term has multiple matched Wikipedia articles.

Lack of context deepens the ambiguity problem for weak queries. Most current disambiguation approaches demand 20 to 50 context words to produce a relatively reliable prediction. However, weak queries are unable to provide that much context because they usually contain only two or three words. A common solution is to enrich a short query with query expansion techniques such as pseudo relevance feedback and web expansion. The challenge when using these strategies is how to overcome the impact of "noisy" words due to inaccurate query expansion. Both query expansion and query disambiguation can benefit from operating at the level of the topic instead of the word. Query expansion at the topic level will reduce error due to query drift and lead to higher retrieval performance (Bendersky, Croft, & Smith, 2009). One major problem for query disambiguation is how to find the appropriate context for a polyseme. Using query topic detection, it is likely that a polyseme and its most revealing context will be grouped in the same segment based on co-occurrence patterns, and this will help a software agent to improve its disambiguation accuracy (Navigli, 2009). Recognizing boundaries and the correct meanings of query topics is an important step towards understanding a user's search intent and improving the retrieval accuracy of weak queries. The unsupervised approach is efficient, but it has a high error rate. One solution that could lower the error rate would be to use external knowledge for guidance. The research reported here explored this direction by developing an approach to unsupervised query segmentation that utilized the knowledge in Wikipedia to achieve better performance on boundary recognition.

3. METHODOLOGIES

3.1. Topic Detection with Language Model

The first challenge for topic-based query disambiguation is to develop an approach to recognize top-

ics, such as phrases and named entities, from user queries. Given the success of the statistical language model (LM) with tasks involving natural language, including IR (C. X. Zhai, 2008), this study developed an LM-based approach as a solution for the challenge.

Each keyword query will be split into complementary pairs of n-grams, or "chunks," as input for the topic detection process. For instance, the query *new york* and *times square* will be segmented into pairs of chunks as: *[new][york times square]*, *[new york][times square]*, and *[new york times][square]*. This method is effective on weak queries where typically there are fewer topics in each query in consequence of the short query length.

The topic detection algorithm first expands the query with textual contents from the Web to address the problem of lack of context, which is common in user queries. In particular, a Google search can be performed using the original query,[3] and the textual content extracted from the first 20 results of the search can be used to provide context for the query. With this enriched context C and a set of topic candidates S, the question of topic detection is stated as: Given a query q, which candidate s in S generates the highest probability? This question can be formulated as the following:

$$p(s|q) = \frac{p(s,q)}{p(q)} \qquad (1)$$

Because q is random, $p(s|q)$ is only determined by $p(s,q)$. To estimate the value $p(s,q)$, the assumption is that they are drawn from the context collection C:

$$p(s,q|C) = \sum_{d \in C} p(s,q|d).p(d|C) \qquad (2)$$

where $p(d)$ is a prior distribution of documents and is assumed to be uniform across all documents, so the major challenge left is how to estimate the probability of $p(s,q|d)$:

$$p(s,q|d) = p(s|q,d).p(q|d) \qquad (3)$$

where $p(q|d)$ is estimated with maximum likelihood

---

[3] https://www.google.com/

estimation as:

$$p(q|d) = \prod_{w \in q} p(w|d) \qquad (4)$$

A serious problem imposed on LM-based approaches is data scarcity, which is worsened by the textual content because a few words occur frequently while many words appear rarely or are entirely absent in the document collection. Jelinek-Mercer smoothing, which has been proven to be effective for IR tasks (C. Zhai & Lafferty, 2004), is chosen as the method to estimate a "discount" probability to words that are not present. With Jeliner-Mercer smoothing, $p(s|q,d)$ is transformed into:

$$p(s|q,d) = (1 - \alpha_D)p(s|q,d) + \alpha_D p(s) \qquad (5)$$

where $p(s|q,d)$ is estimated as:

$$p(s|q,d) = \frac{f(s,q,d)}{\sum_{w \in q} f(w,d)} \qquad (6)$$

and the background model $P(S)$ is estimated as with Wikipedia titles and anchors:

$$P(S) = \lambda P(S|Wk\_title) + (1 - \lambda)P(S|Wk\_anchor)$$

$$= \lambda \frac{f_{S,title}}{|title|} + (1 - \lambda) \frac{f_{S,anchor}}{|anchor|} \qquad (7)$$

In summary, the generative probability of a query topic s that appears in query q given the context of collection C is estimated as

$$p(s,q|C) = \sum_{d \in C} [(1 - \alpha_D)p(s|q,d) + \alpha_D p(s)]p(q|d) \qquad (8)$$

and the candidate (i.e., query chunk) with the highest probability will be chosen as the query topic.

3.2. Topic Disambiguation

The first task of word sense disambiguation is to build what is known as a "sense inventory" containing all the possible meanings for each polyseme. Follow-

ing the strategy of Mihalcea and Csomai (2007), the approach adopted here collects word senses as hyperlinks (i.e., anchors) in Wikipedia articles. For many hyperlinks in Wikipedia the author manually annotates the intended meaning of an anchor by linking it to a relevant Wikipedia article. Therefore, the sense inventory for any polyseme can be derived by extracting link destinations from all hyperlinks associated with the polyseme. Using this approach, five senses were identified for the polyseme *bar: bar (counter), bar (establishment), bar (landform), bar (law),* and *bar (music).*

The disambiguation approach used in this research is known as a *decision list* (DL), which contains a set of ordered and conjunctive rules that are either hand-crafted or derived by algorithm. For each ambiguous query topic, the algorithm first uses the count of overlapping Wikipedia anchors between the topic and the rest of the query terms to resolve its appropriate meaning. If no overlapping anchor exists, the algorithm will consider the count of co-occurrence words in the definition paragraph (excluding stopwords) between the topic and the other query terms.[4] And the fallback criterion is the frequency of different senses appearing in Wikipedia, where the most common sense is chosen as the disambiguation result. The disambiguation algorithm is illustrated in Figure 1 with details.

3.3. Topic-based Query Expansion

One major problem related to weak queries is the failure to respond to required aspects of a user's information need (Buckley & Harman, 2004); but adding inappropriate expansion terms to a weak query can lead to the problem of query drift and may reduce the performance of query expansion (Ruthven & Lalmas, 2003). To address problems of query drift, this research introduces a query expansion method that would provide for robust retrieval by exploiting the query topics detected in the disambiguation process.

The query expansion method used here relied on terms identified both in Wikipedia and on the Web in order to harvest evidence from two different types of content. Wikipedia is considered a structured resource

---

[4] The first paragraph of a Wikipedia article that is mandatory in order to provide a brief summary of the subject.

1. Build sense inventory: Search the Wikipedia knowledge base to identify all articles (destinations) linked to by the query segment as anchor text and count the total number of each unique destination article; save the count; a query segment is defined as a polyseme if it has more than one unique destination article.

2. Build sense representation:
   a. For sense as page link: For each linked-to page, extract and save all the Wikipedia anchors that appear in the article.
   b. For sense as definition: Extract and save the text of the definition paragraph of each linked-to page.
   c. For sense as count: count the occurrences of every unique linked-to page in Wikipedia.

3. Disambiguation:
   For each query segment
   if it is a polyseme
   · get the senses built in step 2
   · search Wikipedia to find whether the query context matches any article title or anchor text
   · count the number of overlapping linked-to articles between the Wikipedia pages of the query context and each sense of the query segment
      if there are overlapping links
         · identify the sense of the query segment as the Wikipedia page that has the highest overlapping count with the query context page;
      else
         · identify the sense of the query segment as that of the Wikipedia page whose definition paragraph has the highest number of co-occurring words with the query context page;
         if there are no overlapping words
            · identify the sense of the query segment as the one that appears most frequently in Wikipedia based on the results of step 1.

Fig. 1 Disambiguation Algorithm for Query Segment

because the full text of each article was excluded from the process of query expansion: Given that expansion terms were extracted only from the title of a Wikipedia article and its definition paragraph (i.e., the first paragraph of a Wikipedia article) based on the frequency, they are not only concise and accurate but also provide a relatively small vocabulary. In contrast, even though expansion terms extracted from the Web would include terms that were potentially irrelevant, the fact that they are harvested from a large vocabulary and can therefore address aspects of the topic missing in Wikipedia articles was considered an advantage. Thus, this approach is able to exploit the advantages of both sources to offset the weakness of each. The technique chosen for Web-based query expansion is local context analysis (LCA), which selects concepts based on their

co-occurrence with query terms and their frequency in the whole collection.

4. EXPERIMENT DESIGN

4.1. Data

The test collections used in the experiment are AQUAINT and Blog06. The AQUAINT corpus is distributed by the Linguistic Data Consortium (LDC) and has been used in TREC competitions as the test collection for both the HARD Track and the Robust Track in 2005.[5] The AQUAINT corpus consists of 1,033,461 news stories taken from the *New York Times*, the Associated Press, and the Xinhua News Agency newswires between the years 1996 and 2000. The corpus contains

---

[5] The goal of the High Accuracy Retrieval from Document (HARD) Track is to achieve high accuracy retrieval from documents by leveraging additional information about the searcher and/or the search context captured using much targeted interaction with the searcher. The goal of the Robust track is to improve the consistency of retrieval technology by focusing on poorly performing topics.

a total of 284,597,335 terms, 707,778 of which are unique, and the mean document length is 275 words (Baillie, Azzopardi, & Crestani, 2006). The Blog06 collection was developed by the University of Glasgow and consists of 148GB of blog data spanning a time period of eleven weeks from December 2005 to February 2006. The Blog06 collection contains more than 3.2 million permalinks[6] that the Blog Track guideline[7] considers eligible retrieval units and was used as the test collection for the TREC Blog Track in 2006, 2007, and 2008. Both collections were indexed and searched by Indri,[8] a search engine that combines the advantages of a language model and an inference network that allows the formulation of structured queries composed by topics (Metzler & Croft, 2004).

This research used *mean average precision* (MAP) as the measure of IR effectiveness. *Average precision* is a single-valued measure used to evaluate a system's overall performance for a given query. It is calculated by dividing the sum of the precision values obtained after retrieval of each relevant document by the total number of relevant documents in the collection. Because average precision rewards an IR system that ranks a relevant document higher, it is compatible with the overall goal of this research, which is to improve retrieval accuracy. System performance over a set of queries can be evaluated using MAP-the mean value of average precision values over all queries. In addition, pairwise differences between systems can be plotted for each query to indicate relative system performance over queries.

4.2. Retrieval with Query Expansion

The process of query expansion used the detected query topics as input and produced as output a list of weighted expansion terms for each query. The expansion terms were based on the detected query topics and were selected from both the Web and Wikipedia. The final version of the transformed query was formulated according to the Indri format and included three components: the original query, the detected query topics, and the top 20 expansion terms as determined by the weighting. The query topic component was constructed according to the following rules: If topics were detected in the query, then each topic would be formulated as an exact match, and all words in the original query would be included in an unordered match within a window of 12 words (i.e., *uw12*); if no topic were detected, then the words in the original query would be formulated as an unordered match within 20 words (i.e., *uw20*). For instance, given the query *law enforcement dogs* where *law enforcement* is the topic, the query would be transformed into *#1(law enforcement)* and *#uw12(law enforcement dogs)*. In contrast, the query *marine vegetation* would be transformed into *#uw20 (marine vegetation)* because the two words do not constitute a topic. Each component of the final query was manually assigned a weight to quantify its contribution to relevance judgment, and the weights for the original query, the query topic, and the expansion terms were specified as 0.5, 0.2, and 0.3, respectively, based on preliminary results. Figure 2 illustrates the final version of the query *law enforcement dogs*.

4.3. Query Disambiguation Experiment

The first of these experiments (referred to hereafter as experiment #1) investigated the effect of query disambiguation on IR by comparing the retrieval performance of ambiguous queries with and without resolving topic

---

> #weight(0.5 #combine(law enforcement dogs)
> 0.2 #combine(#1(law enforcement) #uw12(law enforcement dogs))
> 0.3 #weight(0.170731707317073 dog 0.146341463414634 police 0.0487804878048781 morphology ...))

Fig. 2 Example of a fully transformed query using Indri syntax

---

[6] A permalink in the blogosphere is a blog post that has a unique URL, which enables visitors to find it even if the post has been moved.
[7] http://ir.dcs.gla.ac.uk/wiki/TREC-BLOG#head-c84eaf4868470d38ed1815b77e8fba909de21f54
[8] The KL-divergence language model was chosen as the retrieval model for Indri.

ambiguity (i.e., H1). Four ambiguous queries from the Blog collection and ten ambiguous queries from the HARD collection were selected based on the criterion that either the query or, at minimum, one topic in the query was a Wikipedia hyperlink referring to one or more Wikipedia articles. For example, the string "black bear" could refer to a minor league baseball team or to a North American animal species. Query disambiguation effects on IR for ambiguous queries from the Blog and HARD collections were analyzed using four different query treatments: *wsd_qe* represents query expansion (*qe*) with disambiguation (*wsd*) based on Wikipedia hyperlinks where the resolved Wikipedia article is used as the source for query expansion terms; *no_wsd_qe* represents query expansion without disambiguation and uses Google search results as the source for query expansion terms; *wsd _ir* represents information retrieval (*ir*) with query disambiguation and formulates the query with the disambiguated segment(s) as the topic;[9] and *no_wsd_ir* represents word-based retrieval without disambiguation.

4.4. Wikipedia for Query Disambiguation Experiment

The other experiment (referred to hereafter as experiment #2) investigated the hypothesis that using Wikipedia structures for query disambiguation would lead to better IR performance (i.e., H2). IR performance was measured by comparing the retrieval performance produced with two disambiguation approaches: results obtained by using Wikipedia knowledge and results obtained by using only textual context. Experiment #3 used only ambiguous query topics that had more than one sense representation derived from Wikipedia. For each ambiguous topic, this experiment attempted to identify the correct sense using two types of contexts: Wikipedia hyperlinks and free text (i.e., terms appearing in the first paragraph of the associated Wikipedia article). The assumption was that the two types of contexts would lead to significantly different disam-

biguation results (i.e., would not resolve to the same Wikipedia article). If a Wikipedia article was found, the polyseme under consideration would be considered a valid topic and the Wikipedia article would become the source of query expansion terms; if a Wikipedia article was not found, the polyseme under consideration would be treated as text without query expansion.

Queries from the Blog and HARD collections were disambiguated using knowledge at two different semantic levels: Wikipedia and free text. These experiments used four different query treatments:

- *wsd_qe_wiki*[10] represents query disambiguation (*wsd*) with Wikipedia knowledge (*wiki*) such as hyperlinks in the articles using the Wikipedia article that expresses the correct sense as the source for query expansion (*qe*) terms; if no associated Wikipedia article was found, the original query was used for retrieval without expansion;
- *wsd_qe_nowiki* represents query disambiguation with text context (i.e., expansion terms acquired by Local Context Analysis from Google search results, or *nowiki*) to identify word sense using the Wikipedia article that expresses the correct sense as the source for query expansion; if no associated Wikipedia article was found, the original query was used for retrieval without expansion;
- *wsd_ir_wiki* represents query disambiguation using Wikipedia knowledge such as hyperlinks in the articles to formulate the disambiguated query segment as a topic for information retrieval (*ir*); if no associated Wikipedia article was found, the query segment in consideration was treated as text;
- *wsd_ir_nowiki* represents query disambiguation using text context (i.e., the rest of the query) to identify word sense and formulate the disambiguated query segment as a topic for information retrieval; if no associated Wikipedia article was found, the query segment was treated as text.

---

[9] For instance, the disambiguated segment *Whole Foods* in the query *Whole Foods wind energy* will be formulated as a topic in Indri query #combine(#1(Whole Foods) #1(wind energy)).

[10] The experiment *wsd_qe_wiki* follows the same procedure as outlined in *wsd_qe* in section 4.3; the additional suffix of _wiki is used to highlight the source of knowledge, which is the focus of the experiment. The same naming patterns also apply to *wsd_ir_wiki*.

Retrieval performance was measured by MAP in both experiments.

5. RESULTS

5.1. Query Disambiguation to IR Improvement

A summary of the results for retrieval with and without query disambiguation are provided in Table 1. The Wilcoxon signed ranks test performed on the results did not reject the null hypothesis (H1) that query disambiguation has no significant effect on retrieval performance for either the Blog queries or the HARD queries. For ambiguous queries from the Blog collection, Wilcoxon tests for two-tailed significance conducted between wsd_qe and no_wsd_qe and between wsd_ir and no_wsd_ir retained the null hypothesis ($p=0.068$, $N=4$) even though, in all experimental runs, disambiguated queries outperformed queries that had not been disambiguated. For ambiguous queries from the HARD collection, Wilcoxon tests for two-tailed significance conducted between wsd_qe and no_wsd_qe and between wsd_qe and no_wsd_ir also retained the null hypothesis, but at a higher p-value ($p>0.2$, $N=10$).

5.2. Wikipedia Effect on Query Disambiguation

Retrieval results for queries from the Blog and HARD collections are listed in Table 2 when disambiguation is carried out using Wikipedia knowledge or free text. For both the Blog and the HARD queries, Wilcoxon's signed ranks test did not reject the null hypothesis (H2) that using Wikipedia knowledge had little effect on query disambiguation. Comparison of the wsd_qe_wiki and wsd_qe_nowiki treatments and the wsd_qe_wiki and wsd_ir_nowiki treatments for Blog queries using Wilcoxon's signed ranks test retained the null hypothesis ($0.2>p>0.1$) with a sample of four values ($N=4$); comparison of wsd_qe_wiki and wsd_qe_nowiki treatments and of the wsd_qe_wiki and wsd_ir_nowiki treatments for the HARD queries using Wilcoxon's test retained the null hypothesis ($0.8>p>0.1$) with a sample of ten values ($N=10$).

6. DISCUSSION

Experimental results indicate that both of the null hypotheses regarding query disambiguation should be retained: Query disambiguation has little impact on IR; and the use of knowledge in Wikipedia documents

Table 1. Query disambiguation effects on IR for ambiguous queries from Blog (denoted B) and HARD (denoted H) collections

	Mean Average Precision			
	wsd_qe	no_wsd_qe	wsd_topic_ir	no_wsd_ir
Fox News Report (B)	0.1363	0.1253	0.1397	0.1253
Business Intelligence Resources (B)	0.0671	0.0464	0.0660	0.0437
Whole Foods wind energy (B)	0.7927	0.6553	0.7928	0.7044
federal shield law (B)	0.6125	0.2514	0.5759	0.1167
Radio Waves and Brain Cancer (H)	0.2854	0.3028	0.0992	0.0982
Black Bear Attacks (H)	0.5066	0.5142	0.5504	0.5181
mental illness drugs (H)	0.0801	0.0790	0.0496	0.0594
Ireland peace talks (H)	0.2318	0.2431	0.2518	0.2568
Legal Pan Am, 103 (H)	0.3830	0.3145	0.2795	0.3682
law enforcement dogs (H)	0.1242	0.0837	0.1132	0.0968
Greek philosophy stoicism (H)	0.4403	0.5220	0.5202	0.5271
Inventions scientific discoveries (H)	0.1173	0.1099	0.0884	0.0966
family leave law (H)	0.6549	0.6702	0.5902	0.5030
tax evasion indicted (H)	0.1197	0.1277	0.053	0.1045

Table 2. Effects of using Wikipedia knowledge for disambiguation of queries from Blog (denoted B) and HARD (denoted H) collections

	Mean Average Precision			
	wsd_qe_wiki	*wsd_qe_nowiki*	*wsd_ir_wiki*	*wsd_ir_nowiki*
Fox News Report (B)	0.1339	0.1253	0.1397	0.1253
Business Intelligence Resources (B)	0.0558	0.0558	0.0660	0.0660
Whole Foods wind energy (B)	0.7927	0.7919	0.7928	0.7928
federal shield law (B)	0.6366	0.1167	0.5759	0.1167
Radio Waves and Brain Cancer (H)	0.0952	0.0952	0.0992	0.0982
Black Bear Attacks (H)	0.5042	0.5181	0.5504	0.5181
mental illness drugs (H)	0.0791	0.0791	0.0496	0.0496
Ireland, peace talks (H)	0.2138	0.2568	0.2518	0.2568
legal, Pan Am, 103 (H)	0.383	0.3682	0.2795	0.3682
law enforcement, dogs (H)	0.1242	0.1058	0.1132	0.1132
Greek, philosophy, stoicism (H)	0.4488	0.4050	0.5202	0.5202
inventions, scientific discoveries (H)	0.1036	0.1036	0.0884	0.0884
family leave law (H)	0.6922	0.6922	0.5902	0.5902
tax evasion indicted (H)	0.1197	0.1197	0.053	0.053

does not produce significant improvement in disambiguation accuracy. Furthermore, this result is found for queries from both the Blog and the HARD collections.

One of the major motivations for this research is to re-examine the ongoing argument regarding the usefulness of query disambiguation in IR in light of relatively new knowledge resources such as Wikipedia. As has been pointed out in the IR literature (Harman, 1992; Salton & Buckley, 1990), disambiguation accuracy and quality of the sense inventory have been thought to make major contributions to disambiguation effects on IR. Given the experimental results indicating that the null hypotheses regarding query disambiguation should be retained for both query collections, it is helpful to examine the influence of each of these two factors in the context of the current findings.

6.1. Correlation between Disambiguation Accuracy and IR Performance

Query disambiguation accuracy has been claimed to be the most important factor affecting the effectiveness of disambiguation in IR (Buckley, Salton, Allan, & Singhal, 1995; Salton & Buckley, 1990). Based on the commonly held assumption that low accuracy in the

resolution of polysemes will hurt retrieval performance, an experiment was designed to examine whether there was a correlation between disambiguation accuracy and retrieval performance: For an ambiguous query term, each of its word senses (i.e., a corresponding Wikipedia article) was represented by three features: anchor links that appeared in a Wikipedia article; the text in the first paragraph of an article; and the count of each sense appearing in Wikipedia. The hypothesis was that there would be discrepancies in disambiguation accuracy across the different sense representations, and the goal was to test whether retrieval performance would be significantly affected by ineffective query disambiguation.

Only one query from the Blog collection (i.e., _Whole Foods_ wind energy) and two queries from the HARD collection (i.e., Ireland, _peace talks_, and _Greek, philosophy_, stoicism) yielded different disambiguation results. A list of retrieved documents was produced for the disambiguated retrieval results for each of these three queries using the corresponding Wikipedia article(s) as the source of query expansion terms. Assuming that only one sense represented by the correct Wikipedia page was appropriate given the query context, it was possible to observe whether disambiguation errors had

Table 3. Retrieval performance of disambiguation accuracy measured as MAP compared to baseline. Wikipedia page ids are indicated in parentheses and correct Wikipedia page ids are presented in bold

	Mean Average Precision			
	baseline	represent_by_link	represent_by_text	represent_by_count
Ireland, <u>peace talks</u> (HRAD)	0.2568	0.2318 (**3021179**)	null	0.2063 (7258068)
Greek, <u>philosophy</u>, stoicism (HARD)	0.5271	0.4403 (**10649725**)	0.4403 (10649725)	0.4002 (171171)
<u>Whole Foods</u> wind energy (Blog) ·	0.7044	0.7927 (**620343**)	0.7927 (620343)	0.7002 (30871513)

an impact on retrieval, as shown in Table 3.

To examine the impact of query disambiguation accuracy on retrieval performance, three statistical significance tests (i.e., t-Test with paired samples) were carried out on the results listed in Table 3:[11] baseline vs. query expansion based on the correctly disambiguated Wikipedia page, which is in bold; baseline vs. query expansion based on the incorrectly disambiguated Wikipedia page; and query expansion based on the correctly disambiguated Wikipedia page vs. query expansion based on the incorrectly disambiguated Wikipedia page. The resulting t values for all three tests were smaller than the critical values for the *0.05* significance level, and the null hypothesis was retained. Although the results of the t-Test with paired samples indicate that disambiguation accuracy does not have a significant impact on retrieval performance, the null hypothesis should not be rejected out of hand due to the small sample size. For instance, the term *Whole Foods* is the title of several Wikipedia pages; but, given the query context of *wind energy*, only the Wikipedia article with the page id *620343* is relevant and leads to better retrieval performance when compared to the baseline retrieval results (i.e., query expansion run without disambiguation). In addition, a mistake in query disambiguation such as pointing to Wikipedia page id *30871513* for the query *Whole Foods wind energy* produced a decrease in retrieval performance when compared to retrieval performance using the appropriate Wikipedia page for disambiguation.

6.2. Wikipedia Effect for Query Disambiguation

Any attempt at resolving natural language ambiguities will depend on the quality and scale of the sense inventory, the repository of terms, and the common meanings for each term. WordNet is an example of a sense inventory and has been used extensively for word sense disambiguation (Jing & Croft, 1994; Qiu & Frei, 1993). However, according to recent studies (Rada Mihalcea, 2003; Prakash, Jurafsky, & Ng, 2007), WordNet has certain major drawbacks that make it unsuitable for query disambiguation in IR:

· Sense granularity is too fine: For purposes of logic reasoning, definitions in WordNet include very fine distinctions between word senses. For instance, the verb *eat* has the two senses *take in solid food* and *eat a meal*. While this fine sense granularity is obviously helpful in areas such as artificial intelligence, it is not necessary in IR.

· Semantic connections are too complete: The number of relationships defined in WordNet produces a huge number of possible semantic connections between two words. Such a large number of semantic connections will overload the IR system, requiring longer processing time without increasing relevance.

· The scale of WordNet is too limited: The latest version of WordNet (i.e., WordNet 3.0) contains a total of 155,287 words and 206,941 word-sense pairs.[12] Such a limited scope is not adequate for

---

[11] If two sense representations yield the same disambiguation results, such as page id 10649725 for query *Greek philosophy stoicism*, only one result is highlighted in bold.
[12] http://wordnet.princeton.edu/wordnet/man/wnstats.7WN.html

modern IR applications.

Given the weaknesses of WordNet, researchers have been looking for other knowledge resources that could be used for query disambiguation. Because of its large scale and the richness of its content, Wikipedia is a primary candidate and was selected for this research motivated by the hypothesis that the coverage and currency of Wikipedia articles would improve query disambiguation accuracy. However, as indicated by the results presented in Table 2, it is evident that using the structural knowledge in Wikipedia (i.e., the anchor links) did not lead to significant improvement in disambiguation accuracy because user queries do not normally contain sufficient context to associate a query with an appropriate Wikipedia page.

To understand the failure of Wikipedia as a knowledge base for disambiguation, it is helpful to assess Wikipedia based on the same criteria that have been applied to WordNet:

· Sense granularity: Word senses are indicated by article topics in Wikipedia. For instance, in Wikipedia, the word *Bush* has various senses ranging from a type of plant, to a surname, and even to an island because there is a Wikipedia article for each of these three senses as discrete topics. Each sense should have adequate context for disambiguation in natural language, which is a decided advantage of Wikipedia. However, sense granularity is still an important issue in Wikipedia because there is no oversight of or planning for the nomination and selection of topics. Anyone can add a new meaning for a word by contributing a new Wikipedia article for that topic; the only constraint on a new page is that it must follow Wikipedia's guidelines for articles. In consequence, a disambiguation program could spend unnecessary processing time on senses that are rarely used or incorrectly identify a sense because terms expressed in the query are either undefined or over-defined in Wikipedia.
· Semantic connections: In Wikipedia, polysemes are generally connected to meanings through one of two methods: through anchor links that point to an article associated with one sense of the term or

through a so-called *disambiguation page* that lists all meanings associated with a term. Harvesting word senses from anchor links has two advantages over a disambiguation page: It associates a meaning within the language context where it occurs, and it offers a count distribution of sense usage in Wikipedia. Experimental results show that distribution of sense usage is effective in query disambiguation since the primary sense (i.e., the sense that appears most frequently) is usually the correct one. However, no matter which sense representation is used, query disambiguation will suffer from the weaknesses of sense granularity.
· Scale: As of December 2012, the English version of Wikipedia contained more than four million articles, with new articles submitted every day. However, it requires significant effort both to extract the knowledge embedded in Wikipedia articles and to build that knowledge into a structural resource for applications such as query disambiguation.

Analysis of the problems associated with granularity, sense connections, and scale in both WordNet and Wikipedia indicate that query disambiguation demands a type of knowledge resource that is very different from what either of these resources offer. For instance, based on the observation that users will correct spelling errors, add context, or change words in original queries to improve retrieval results (Guo, Xu, Li, & Cheng, 2008), large-scale query logs available from commercial search engines could be used to extract a series of queries from individual sessions and build a knowledge base that would not only catch grammatical variations and misspellings but also semantic contexts such as synonyms and co-occurring terms that point to the same topic (i.e., the same document). It would also be possible to construct a sense inventory by harvesting click-through records from query logs. Such a knowledge base built from query logs would not only save the cost of creating definitions and samples manually but might also be more effective for query disambiguation. In fact, using well-developed data mining algorithms, a knowledge base generated from a large and diversified query log, would be a very special kind of mass intelligence produced by user collaboration on a common task.

7. CONCLUSION

To overcome the challenge of ineffective user queries, this research implemented a query disambiguation approach that integrates topic detection and maps the detected topic to the most appropriate Wikipedia page. This research tested two hypotheses for query disambiguation in IR. The experimental results could not reject the null hypothesis that there was no significant difference in performance between retrieval with query disambiguation and retrieval without disambiguation. Furthermore, statistical testing did not support the hypothesis that representing word meanings with structural Wikipedia knowledge such as anchor links would significantly improve disambiguation effectiveness in IR compared to representing meanings with text. Both of these findings suggest that future knowledge bases of word meanings should favor defining word senses by harvesting language usage patterns, probably from large search engine logs, in order to maintain a rich level of diversified contexts for query disambiguation and optimization. However, because the test collections used in this research contained only a limited number of ambiguous queries,[13] the validity of any conclusions regarding query disambiguation based on statistical analysis must be considered preliminary due to the small sample size.

REFERENCES

Baillie, M., Azzopardi, L., & Crestani, F. (2006). Adaptive query-based sampling of distributed collections. *Lecture Notes in Computer Science, 4209*, 316.

Bendersky, M., Croft, W. B., & Smith, D. A. (2009). *Two-stage query segmentation for information retrieval.* Paper presented at the Proceedings of the 32nd international ACM SIGIR conference on Research and development in information retrieval, Boston, MA.

Buckley, C., & Harman, D. (2004). Reliable information access final workshop report. *ARDA Northeast Regional Research Center Technical Report.*

Buckley, C., Salton, G., Allan, J., & Singhal, A. (1995). Automatic query expansion using SMART: TREC 3. *Overview of the Third Text REtrieval Conference (TREC-3)*, 500-225.

Gale, W. A., Church, K. W., & Yarowsky, D. (1992). A method for disambiguating word senses in a large corpus. *Computers and the Humanities*, 26(5), 415-439.

Guo, J., Xu, G., Li, H., & Cheng, X. (2008). *A unified and discriminative model for query refinement.* Paper presented at the Proceedings of the 31st annual international ACM SIGIR conference on Research and development in information retrieval.

Harman, D. (1992). Relevance feedback revisited. *Proceedings of the 15th annual international ACM SIGIR conference on Research and development in information retrieval*, 1-10.

Jing, Y., & Croft, W. B. (1994). An association thesaurus for information retrieval. *Proceedings of RIAO, 94*(1994), 146-160.

Klyuev, V., & Haralambous, Y. (2011). *Query expansion: Term selection using the ewc semantic relatedness measure.* Paper presented at the Computer Science and Information Systems (FedCSIS), 2011 Federated Conference on.

Metzler, D., & Croft, W. B. (2004). Combining the language model and inference network approaches to retrieval. *Information processing & management, 40*(5), 735-750.

Mihalcea, R. (2003). Turning WordNet into an information retrieval resource: Systematic polysemy and conversion to hierarchical codes. *International Journal of Pattern Recognition and Artificial Intelligence, 17*(05), 689-704. doi: doi:10.1142/S0218 001403002605

Mihalcea, R., & Csomai, A. (2007). *Wikify!: Linking documents to encyclopedic knowledge.* Paper pre-

---

[13] These are four ambiguous queries in the Blog collection and ten queries in the HARD collection.

sented at the Proceedings of the sixteenth ACM conference on Information and knowledge management, Lisbon, Portugal.

Milne, D., & Witten, I. H. (2008). *Learning to link with Wikipedia*. Paper presented at the Proceedings of the 17th ACM conference on Information and knowledge management, Napa Valley, CA.

Navigli, R. (2009). Word sense disambiguation: A survey. *ACM Computing Surveys (CSUR), 41*(2), 10.

Prakash, R. S. S., Jurafsky, D., & Ng, A. Y. (2007). Learning to merge word senses. *Computer Science Department, Stanford University.*

Qiu, Y., & Frei, H. P. (1993). Concept based query expansion. *Proceedings of the 16th annual international ACM SIGIR conference on Research and development in information retrieval,* 160-169.

Ruthven, I. A. N., & Lalmas, M. (2003). A survey on the use of relevance feedback for information access systems. *The Knowledge Engineering Review, 18*(02), 95-145.

Salton, G., & Buckley, C. (1990). Improving retrieval performance by relevance feedback. *Journal of the American Society for Information Science, 41*(4), 288-297.

Sanderson, M. (1994). *Word sense disambiguation and information retrieval.* New York, NY: Springer-Verlag.

Sanderson, M. (2000). Retrieving with good sense. *Information Retrieval, 2*(1), 49-69.

Selvaretnam, B., & Belkhatir, M. (2012). Natural language technology and query expansion: Issues, state-of-the-art and perspectives. *Journal of Intelligent Information Systems, 38*(3), 709-740. doi: 10.1007/s10844-011-0174-3

Spink, A., Wolfram, D., Jansen, M. B. J., & Saracevic, T. (2001). Searching the web: The public and their queries. *Journal of the American Society for Information Science and Technology, 52*(3), 226-234.

Voorhees, E. M. (1993). Using WordNet to disambiguate word senses for text retrieval. *Proceedings of the 16th annual international ACM SIGIR conference on Research and development in information retrieval,* 171-180.

Voorhees, E. M. (1994). *Query expansion using lexical-semantic relations.* New York, NY: Springer-Verlag.

Zhai, C., & Lafferty, J. (2004). A study of smoothing methods for language models applied to information retrieval. *ACM Transactions on Information Systems, 22*(2), 179-214.

Zhai, C. X. (2008). Statistical language models for information retrieval: A critical review. *Foundations and Trends in Information Retrieval, 2*(3), 137-213.

2

Publication Trends and Citation Impact of Tribology Research in India: A Scientometric Study

P. Rajendran*
SRM University, India
E-mail: librarian@srmuniv.ac.in

B. Elango
IFET College of Engineering, India
E-mail: elangokb@yahoo.com

J. Manickaraj
SRM University, India
E-mail: manickraj@gmail.com

ABSTRACT

This paper analyzes India's contribution to world tribology research during the period 2001–2012 based on SCOPUS records. India's global publication share, annual output, and its citation impact of Indian contribution, partner countries, leading contributors, leading institutes, and highly cited papers were analyzed. Additionally, a cloud technique is used to map frequently used single words in titles. It is observed that India ranks in the 7th position with a global publication share of 3.83% and an annual average growth rate of 25.58% during the period 2001–2012. The citation impact of India's contribution is 6.05 which decreased from 12.74 during 2001–2006 to 4.62 during 2007-2012. 17.4% of India's total research output was published with international collaboration.

Keywords: Tribology Research, Scientometrics, Word Cloud, India

1. INTRODUCTION

Tribology is the science and technology of two interacting surfaces in relative motion and of related subjects and practices. The term was coined by Jost (1966) in a report and derives from the Greek word *tribos*. Tribology is a multidisciplinary field which incorporates a number of disciplines, including mechanical engineering, material science, mechanics, surface chemistry, surface physics, and a multitude of subjects such as surface characterization, friction, wear, lubrication, thin films and coatings, materials,

Corresponding Author: P. Rajendran
Librarian
SRM University, India
E-mail: librarian@srmuniv.ac.in

lubricants, and the selection and design of lubrication systems and contact properties.[1] The application of tribological principles is essential for reliability of motor vehicles, in order to reduce friction and wear with minimum adverse impact on the environment. A study estimated that the cost of friction and wear in India is Rs.78.67 billion, and 50-60% of equipment damage is caused by poor lubrication and severe wear (Singh, Vimal & Chaturvedi, 2012). Mukhopadhyay (2011) estimated that savings up to 20% of gross national product can be achieved by paying proper attention to tribology especially in the areas of education, research, and application. New areas of tribological studies have been developed at the interfaces of various scientific disciplines, like nanotribology, biotribology, and green tribology (Assenova et al., 2013). BHEL was the first industry in India to start a department of tribology for analyzing its journal and bearings failure used in rotating machines. In the education field tribology is not a subject in the curriculum although some attempts have been made by IITs to introduce tribology course at the masters' level (Biswas, 2007). With this background, the present study is designed to examine the Indian status on tribology research at a global level and to explore the leading Indian contributors (authors and institutes) during the period of 12 years from 2001 to 2012.

2. RELATED STUDIES

Various quantitative studies on different branches of learning analyzing India's contribution have been carried out in the past. Gupta, Kshitij, and Verma (2011) analyzed the Indian contribution in computer science published during 1999-2008 based on the bibliographic records retrieved from SCOPUS. Kaur and Gupta (2010) studied 1380 Indian dental science papers published during 1999-2008 as covered in SCOPUS. They focused on research output and quality, identification of leading authors and institutions, and major collaborating partners. Varaprasad and Ramesh (2011) analyzed the growth of

Indian chemical research published during 1987-2007 based on the SCOPUS records with a focus on quantifying the national contribution and identifying the most productive institutions. Gupta, Kaur, and Kshitig (2011) analyzed the contributions of India in dementia research as reflected in SCOPUS for the period of 10 years from 2002 to 2011. Gupta, Kaur, and Bala (2011) mapped the Indian diabetes research output published during 1999-2008. They focused on pattern of international collaboration and characteristics of highly cited papers. Kademani, Sagar, and Bhanumurthy (2011) conducted a quantitative assessment on materials science publications in India for a period of 10 years from 1999-2008 based on the SCOPUS database. They studied growth of publications, national and international collaboration, highly productive institutions and authors, and highly cited publications.

Karpagam et al. (2011) mapped the nanoscience publications contributed by Indian authors for a period of 20 years from 1990 to 2009 based on the SCOPUS database. They measured the growth rate, pattern of author collaboration, and pattern and impact of Indian institutions contributions by various scientometric measures. Rajagopal et al. (2013) analyzed the growth and development of pheromone biology research output in India based on the Science Citation index for the period 1978-2008. Sinha & Joshi (2012) examined the status of solar PV research in India for the 10 year period 2000-2009. Rajendran, Manickaraj, and Elango (2013) analyzed research output in the field of wireless communication contributed by Indian scientists for the period of 12 years from 2001 to 2012. They focused on growth of literature, collaboration of authors, and pattern of research communication. Gupta and Bala (2011) analyzed the research activities of India in medicine during 1999-2008 based on the SCOPUS database. Their focus was on evaluating the research performance of different Indian medical colleges, hospitals, research institutes, universities, and research foundations. However, we did not find any studies which reported on tribology research in the past from the above research literature.

---

[1] Retrieved from http://www.master-tribos.eu/

3. OBJECTIVES

This study aims to analyze:
- India's global publication share
- Growth of Indian contribution
- Share of international collaborative papers and preferred partner countries
- Productivity of prolific authors and institutes; and
- Analysis of words in title.

4. METHODOLOGY

A total of 1,293 papers contributed by Indian authors to world tribology research during the period of 12 years from 2001–2012 has been considered for the present analysis. The bibliographic records related to the tribology research have been retrieved and downloaded from the SCOPUS (Elsevier) database. The keyword *tribolog* has been used in the combined fields of Title, Abstract, and Keyword.

Further searches were refined to Indian affiliations where the papers were attributed to at least one Indian author. Only articles, conference papers, and reviews (Elango, Rajendran & Bornmann, 2013) have been considered for the present study. The bibliographic details and citations profile were downloaded on April 25, 2013. A straight count method is applied where the corresponding author of a paper receives the full credit (Moya-Anegón et al., 2013; Tellez & Vadillo, 2010). The h-index (Hirsch, 2005; Schubert & Glänzel, 2007) is applied to evaluate publication output along with traditional bibliometric indicators, such as number of papers, share of international collaborative papers, internationalization index, number of citations received, and citations per paper. Additionally a cloud technique is used to analyze the frequency of single words in titles.

4.1. Word Cloud Visualization

A word cloud is a beautiful informative image that communicates much in a single glance. Tagcrowd specializes in making word clouds easy to read, analyze, and compare for a variety of useful purposes. It was created by David Steinbock and is a handy website that allows anyone to create a tag cloud from a file or pasted text (3 MB of data). To visualize the hot topics in Indian tribology research, the word cloud online tool Tagcrowd was used. The controls allow you to add a numerical frequency display, group similar words, and turn off common word filters. To generate a word cloud, the following steps (Zhang, Huang, & Li, 2011) are followed:
- All of the titles from the research output are extracted and entered into an online word cloud generator, Tagcrowd (http://www.tagcrowd.com).
- Set the maximum number of words and exclusion criteria.
- Visualize.

5. RESULTS

5.1. Share of Top Ten Countries

The global publication share of the top ten countries in tribology research varies from 2.13% to 26.31% during the period 2001–2012 (Table 1). The top ten countries together produced 68% of world tribology research output. China tops the list with a share of 26.31% followed by the USA with 16.19% and Japan with 10.27%. These top three countries together produced 53% of world publications. India ranked seventh among the top ten most productive countries with a global publication share of 3.83%.

5.2. Indian Publication Output and its Citation Impact

India contributed 1,293 papers to world tribology research during the period 2001–2012 with an average number of papers per year of 108 (Table 2). Cumulative publications have increased from 227 in 2001–2006 to 1066 in 2007–2012 with a growth rate of 369%. A total of 7,817 citations have been received by these papers from its time of publication up to April 15, 2013. Of 1,293 papers, 863 papers received one or more citations (ranging from 1 to 552) from their publication. Citations per paper were 6.05 during the study period, which has decreased from 12.74 in 2001–2006 to 4.62 in 2007–2012.

Table 1. Research Output and Share of Top Ten Countries in Tribology 2001-2012

Country	TP	World Share	Rank
China	8887	26.31	1
USA	5469	16.19	2
Japan	3470	10.27	3
Germany	2390	7.08	4
UK	1767	5.23	5
France	1552	4.60	6
India	1293	3.83	7
South Korea	952	2.82	8
Italy	723	2.14	9
Russia	721	2.13	10
World	33775	100.00	

TP = Total Papers

Table 2. Annual Output and Citation Impact of Indian Tribology

Year	TP	TC	CPP
2001	21	260	12.38
2002	33	460	13.94
2003	32	660	20.63
2004	39	496	12.72
2005	48	532	11.08
2006	54	484	8.96
2007	70	1285	18.36
2008	98	631	6.44
2009	199	1257	6.32
2010	285	1053	3.69
2011	248	612	2.47
2012	166	87	0.52
2001 - 06	227	2892	12.74
2007 - 12	1066	4925	4.62
2001 - 12	1293	7817	6.05

TP = Total Papers, TC = Total Citations, CPP = Citations per Paper = TC / TP

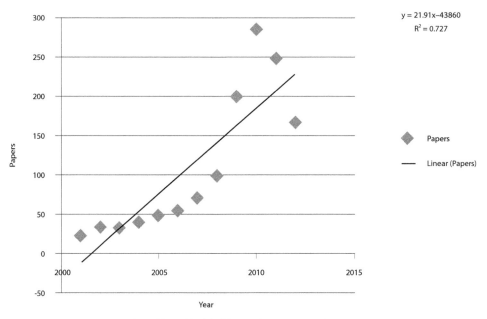

$y = 21.91x–43860$
$R^2 = 0.727$

◆ Papers

— Linear (Papers)

Fig. 1 Linear Model of Papers from 2001–2012

The annual number of papers in tribology research contributed by Indian scientists increased from 21 in 2001 to 166 in 2012 with a peak of 285 in 2010. The coefficient of determination of number of publications is found to be $R^2 = 0.7276$ which indicates that the literature was expanding at a considerable growth rate (Fig. 1). The linear best fit was found to be $y = 21.913x–43860$ where y is number of papers and x is the predicting year. With this, the predicted number of papers is 339 for the year 2017 which is twice that in 2012.

5.3. International Collaborative Papers

India published 17.40% of its total papers with international collaboration during the period 2001–

2012 which has increased from 12.33% in 2001–2006 to 18.48% in 2007–2012 (Table 3).

Major international partner countries are listed in Table 4 and India collaborated with 34 countries during the study period. There were 256 international links in the 225 international collaborative papers, and the internationalization index is 19.80 (=100 x number of international links / total number of papers by India) (Frame & Carpenter, 1979) for tribology research contributed by Indian researchers / scientists. Among the partner countries, the USA had most of the links with 81. Five G7 countries are listed among major partner countries which indicate that India has more frequent partnerships with scientists from G7 countries.

Table 3. Share of International Collaborative Papers

Block period	TP	ICP	% ICP
2001–2006	227	28	12.33
2007–2012	1066	197	18.48
Total	1293	225	17.40

TP = Total Papers, ICP = International Collaborative Papers

Table 4. Major Partner Countries

Partner Countries	No. of Articles	%
USA	81	31.64
Germany	22	8.59
UK	18	7.03
South Korea	15	5.86
France	14	5.47
Austria	12	4.69
Australia	12	4.69
Japan	9	3.52
Portugal	8	3.13
Switzerland	7	2.73
China	6	2.34
Singapore	6	2.34
Others	46	17.97
Total*	256	100

*Since some papers (#28) have international partners from more than one country, this number exceeds the total of international collaborative papers (225).

5.4. No. of Countries by Line and Citation Impact

India published papers with a maximum of three countries during the period 2001–2012 (Table 5). Citation impact of papers with three or more countries received the highest score with 8.33 followed by national output with 6.35. Papers with three countries registered a lowest citation impact of 3.04.

5.5. Prolific Indian Authors in Tribology Research (2001–2012)

Authors contributing more than 0.5% of the country's output during 2001–2012 are considered prolific authors and listed in Table 6. Among the 17 most productive authors, 7 authors are from IIT's and 3 from IISc. B. Basu of IIT Kanpur was the most productive author with 46 papers (3.56%) followed

Table 5. Collaboration Type and its Impact

Description	TP	TC	CPP
Unilateral (India)	1068	6785	6.35
Bilateral (India with another country)	197	931	4.73
Trilateral (India with two other countries)	25	76	3.04
>3 countries (India with more than two countries)	3	25	8.33
TP = Total Papers, TC = Total Citations, CPP = Citations per Paper = TC / TP			

Table 6. Prolific Authors and their Citation Impact

Author	Affiliation	TP (%)	TC	CPP (R)	h (R)
Basu, B.	IIT Kanpur	46 (3.56)	547	11.89 (5)	18.67 (3)
Bijwe, J.	IIT Delhi	44 (3.4)	519	11.80 (6)	18.3 (4)
Kailas, S.V.	IISc	27 (2.09)	129	4.78 (13)	8.51 (12)
Biswas, S.K.	IISc	26 (2.01)	169	6.50 (11)	10.32 (8)
Kumar, N.	Indira Gandhi Centre for Atomic Research	19 (1.47)	20	1.05 (16)	2.76 (16)
Suresha, B.	National Institute of Engineering	16 (1.24)	156	9.75 (7)	11.5 (5)
Balasubramanian, V.	Anna University	15 (1.16)	122	8.13 (10)	9.97 (9)
Menezes, P.L.	IISc	13 (1.01)	29	2.23 (15)	4.01 (14)
Ramesh, C.S.	PES Institute of Technology	12 (0.93)	102	8.50 (9)	9.54 (11)
Gnanamoorthy, R.	IIT Madras	12 (0.93)	105	8.75 (8)	9.72 (10)
Prasad, B.K.	Advanced Materials and Processes Research Institute	10 (0.77)	25	2.5 (14)	3.97 (15)
Sundararajan, G.	International Advanced Research Centre for Powder Metallurgy and New Materials, Hyderabad	10 (0.77)	371	37.10 (2)	23.97 (2)
Sahoo, P.	Jadavpur University	9 (0.7)	111	12.33 (4)	11.1 (6)
Agarwal, A.K.	IIT Kanpur	9 (0.7)	575	63.89 (1)	33.24 (1)
Satapathy, B.K.	IIT Delhi	8 (0.62)	40	5 (12)	5.85 (13)
Jangid, R.S.	IIT Bombay	8 (0.62)	40	5 (12)	5.85 (13)
Dwivedi, D.K.	IIT Roorkee	8 (0.62)	100	12.5 (3)	10.77 (7)

by J. Bijwe of IIT Delhi and S.V. Kailas of IISc. A.K. Agarwal of IIT Kanpur had the highest CPP of 63.89 followed by G. Sundararajan of IARCPMNM Hyderabad (37.1) and D.K. Dwivedi of IIT Roorkee (12.5). The prolific authors had h-index in range from 3.97 to 33.24. The author A.K. Agarwal had the highest h-index value of 33.24 while B.K. Prasad had the lowest at 3.97.

5.6. Prolific Indian Institutes in Tribology Research (2001–2012)

Institutes contributing more than 1% of the country's output during 2001–2012 are considered prolific institutes and listed in Table 7. These 17 prolific institutes contributed 688 publications (53%) of the country's output with a range of 14 and 93 papers. Papers contributed by these prolific institutes re-

ceived 5,437 citations (~ 70%) from their time of publication of a total 7,817 citations. The top five institutes for production (IISc, IIT Delhi, IIT Kanpur, IIT Madras, and Anna University) contributed 391 papers accounting for 30% of the country's output. The CPP of these prolific institutes varies from 1.19 to 29. Among the prolific institutes, the International Advanced Research Centre for Powder Metallurgy and New Materials, Hyderabad received the highest CPP of 29 followed by IIT Kanpur (15.17) and IIT Delhi (8.72). Only two universities, namely Anna University and Jadavpur University, are listed among the prolific institutes. Four research institutes are listed among the prolific institutes. IITs and IISc together published 461 (36% of the country's output) papers related to tribology during 2001–2012 and this suggests that these are the specialized In-

Table 7. Performance of Prolific Institutes

Institute	TP (%)	TC	CPP (R)	h (R)
Indian Institute of Science	92 (7.12)	606	6.59 (10)	15.87 (4)
IIT Delhi	83 (6.42)	715	8.72 (3)	18.4 (3)
IIT Kanpur	81 (6.26)	1229	15.17 (2)	26.5(1)
IIT Madras	69 (5.34)	360	5.22 (13)	12.34 (8)
Anna University	66 (5.1)	408	6.18 (11)	13.61 (5)
IIT Kharagpur	49 (3.79)	341	6.96 (9)	13.34 (6)
IIT Roorkee	46 (3.56)	325	7.07 (8)	13.2 (7)
NIT Trichy	35 (2.71)	192	5.49 (12)	10.18 (11)
Indira Gandhi Center for Atomic Research	32 (2.47)	38	1.19 (17)	3.57 (17)
IIT Bombay	23 (1.78)	82	3.57 (14)	6.64 (14)
International Advanced Research Centre for Powder Metallurgy and New Materials, Hyderabad	19 (1.47)	551	29 (1)	25.19 (2)
IIT Varanasi	17 (1.31)	141	8.29 (6)	10.53 (9)
The National Institute of Engineering, Karnataka	16 (1.24)	120	7.5 (7)	9.65 (13)
Advanced Materials and Processes Research Institute India	16 (1.24)	52	3.25 (16)	5.53 (16)
National Aerospace Laboratories India	15 (1.16)	128	8.53 (4)	10.3 (10)
NITHamirpur	15 (1.16)	51	3.4 (15)	5.58 (15)
Jadavpur University	14 (1.08)	117	8.36 (5)	9.93 (12)

dian institutes in tribology research. The highest h-index was achieved by IIT Kanpur, followed by International Advanced Research Centre for Powder Metallurgy and New Materials, Hyderabad (h-index = 25.19) and IIT Delhi (h-index = 18.4), while the lowest is by the Indira Gandhi Center for Atomic Research (h-index = 3.57) among the prolific institutes.

5.7. Most Preferred Journals

The most productive journals published at least 10 papers contributed by Indian authors are listed in Table 8. These top 22 journals together produced 600 papers contributed by Indian authors comprising 46% of the total Indian output. Only 2 journals originated from India (*Sadhana and Transactions of the Indian Institute of Metals*) and the remaining journals originated from different countries. It indicates

that Indian authors prefer to publish their research findings in international journals more than in Indian ones. *Wear* ranked top with 121 papers in terms of number of papers while this journal ranked third in terms of CPP. *Surface and Coatings Technology* received the highest CPP with 17.1 while it is ranked fourth in terms of number of papers. *Sadhana* ranked fifth in terms of CPP while it is ranked 14th in terms of number of papers.

5.8. Highly Cited Papers

Characteristics of highly cited papers (having >50 citations) of Indian tribology research during the period 2001–2012 are presented in Table 9. 12 papers received 50 or more citations and these 12 papers have been published in 7 different journals. Of these 7 journals, one journal originates from India while

Table 8. Most Preferred Journals

Title	TP	Rank (%)	TC	CPP (R)
Wear	121	1 (9.36)	1324	10.9 (3)
Materials and Design	68	2 (5.26)	615	9.0 (4)
Tribology International	51	3 (3.94)	433	8.5 (7)
Surface and Coatings Technology	38	4 (2.94)	651	17.1 (1)
Tribology Transactions	38	5 (2.94)	108	2.8 (15)
Tribology Letters	35	6 (2.71)	162	4.6 (13)
Advanced Materials Research	21	7 (1.62)	3	0.1 (21)
Journal of Reinforced Plastics and Composites	21	7 (1.62)	135	6.4 (9)
International Journal of Advanced Manufacturing Technology	20	8 (1.55)	107	5.4 (12)
Materials Science and Engineering A	19	9 (1.47)	222	11.7 (2)
Proceedings of the Institution of Mechanical Engineers, Part J: Journal of Engineering Tribology	19	9 (1.47)	30	1.6 (18)
Tribology - Materials, Surfaces and Interfaces	18	10 (1.39)	2	0.1 (21)
Journal of Materials Science	16	11 (1.24)	101	6.3 (10)
Journal of Tribology	16	11 (1.24)	57	3.6 (14)
Materials and Manufacturing Processes	16	11 (1.24)	98	6.1 (11)
Surface Engineering	16	11 (1.24)	29	1.8 (17)
Journal of Materials Engineering and Performance	15	12 (1.16)	33	2.2 (16)
Materials Science Forum	11	13 (0.85)	5	0.5 (20)
Metallurgical and Materials Transactions A: Physical Metallurgy and Materials Science	11	13 (0.85)	76	6.9 (8)
Journal of Materials Processing Technology	10	14 (0.77)	86	8.6 (6)
Sadhana - Academy Proceedings in Engineering Sciences	10	14 (0.77)	89	8.9 (5)
Transactions of the Indian Institute of Metals	10	14 (0.77)	9	0.9 (19)

others are from international locations. Out of 12 papers, two were contributed by a single author while others have collaborators. Cumulative citations of these 12 papers are 1,498 accounting for 19% of all citations. One paper has been published with international collaboration (Israel) while others have domestic collaboration (India). The top-cited paper is "Biofuels applications as fuels for internal combustion engines," authored by A.K. Agarwal for *Progress in Energy and Combustion Science* in the year 2007 which was published as Review Paper. This paper has received 552 citations from its time of publication through April 25, 2013.

Table 9. Most Cited Papers

Authors	TC	DT	Collaboration
Agarwal, A.K. (2007). Biofuels (alcohols and biodiesel) applications as fuels for internal combustion engines. *Progress in Energy and Combustion Science, 33*(3), 233–271.	552	Review	India
Sundararajan, G., & Rama Krishna, L. (2003). Mechanisms underlying the formation of thick alumina coatings through the MAO coating technology. *Surface and Coatings Technology, 167*, 269–277.	222	Article	India
Rama Krishna, L., Somaraju, K.R.C., & Sundararajan, G. (2003). The tribological performance of ultra-hard ceramic composite coatings obtained through microarc oxidation. *Surface and Coatings Technology, 163–164*, 484–490.	136	Article	India
Bijwe, J., Indumathi, J., Rajesh, J., & Fahim, M. (2001). Friction and wear behavior of polyetherimide composites in various wear modes. *Wear, 249*(8), 715–726.	92	Article	India
Tenne, R., & Rao, C.N.R. (2004). Inorganic nanotubes. *Philosophical Transactions of the Royal Society A: Mathematical, Physical and Engineering Sciences, 362*(1823), 2099–2125.	76	Review	India, Israel
Surappa, M.K. (2003). Aluminium matrix composites: Challenges and opportunities. *Sadhana - Academy Proceedings in Engineering Sciences, 28*, 319–334.	73	Article	India
Mishra, R., Basu, B., & Balasubramaniam, R. (2004). Effect of grain size on the tribological behavior of nanocrystalline nickel. *Materials Science and Engineering A, 373*, 370–373.	70	Article	India
Jain, V., & Sundararajan, G. (2002). Influence of the pack thickness of the boronizing mixture on the boriding of steel. Surface and Coatings Technology, *149*(1), 21–26.	62	Article	India
Thakur, S.K., & Dhindaw, B.K. (2001). Influence of interfacial characteristics between SiCp and Mg/Al metal matrix on wear, coefficient of friction and microhardness. *Wear, 247*(2), 191–201.	56	Article	India
Unnikrishnan, R., Jain, M.C., Harinarayan, A.K., & Mehta A.K. (2002). Additive-additive interaction: An XPS study of the effect of ZDDP on the AW/EP characteristic of molybdenum based additives. *Wear, 254*(2), 240–249.	54	Article	India
Bensely, A., Prabhakaran, A., Mohan Lal, D., & Nagarajan, G. (2005). Enhancing the wear resistance of case carburized steel (En 353) by cryogenic treatment. *Cryogenics, 45*(12), 747–754.	54	Article	India
Rajesh, J.J., Bijwe, J., & Tewari, U.S. (2002). Abrasive wear performance of various polyamides. *Wear, 252*(10), 769–776.	51	Article	India

TC = Total Citations, DT = Document Type

5.9. Analysis of Words in Title

Article titles contain information about the whole paper which can express the authors' attitude to the readers, and analysis of words in title gives the exact trend of particular research fields (Malarvizhi, Wang, & Ho, 2010; Sun, Wang, & Ho, 2012; Ma, Ho, & Fu, 2011). Fig. 2 provides information about the frequency of single word in titles of research papers contributed by Indian tribologists. Some preposi-

tions such as *of, and, the,* and *or* are discarded from the display. Common words like *during, analysis, study, performance, investigation, behavior, experiment, tool, characteristics, properties, evaluation, conditions* and *based* were omitted from the analysis. The font size of the text indicates how often the word is used. It can be observed that *Composites* and *Friction* are high frequency words followed by *Tribology* and *Wear*.

abrasive alloy aluminium aluminum applications
bearing carbon cast coatings
composites dry effect films
flow fluid fretting friction heat hybrid
influence lubricant materials matrix
mechanical metal microstructure model
nanocomposites oil optimization parameters particle process
reinforced response role roughness sliding sprayed
stainless steel stir surface system temperature thermal
transfer tribological wear
welding

Fig. 2 Word Cloud of Single Words in Title Created through Tagcrowd.com

6. DISCUSSION AND CONCLUSION

This paper analyzed the growth of tribology research output, international collaborative share, partner countries, citation profile, and prolific authors and institutes, and identified highly cited papers in India's contribution to world tribology research output during 2001–2012. Indian scientists published 1,293 papers during the period 2001–2012 with a global publication share of 3.83% and with 225 (17.40%) papers produced by international collaborations. Compared to the research fields of dementia (Gupta, Kaur, & Kshitij, 2011) and pheromone biology (Rajagopal et al., 2013), the publication output in this field is in a better position. Indian literature in tribology has grown by 369% between 2001-2006 and 2007-2012, which shows that there is an increasing trend of research activities in tribology research. India was 7th among the top ten most productive countries of the world in tribology research during

2001–2012. Compared to South Korea, Italy, and Russia, the world share of India's publication output is in a better position. However, India produced a small quantity of publications in comparison to China, the USA, and Japan, which produced 10% or more of world publications. 17.4% of the country's papers were contributed with international collaboration and the USA was the most preferred partner. The share of international collaborative papers in India's contribution is greater than for materials science (14.75%) (Kademani, Sagar, & Bhanumurthy, 2011) and medicine (11.87%) (Gupta & Bala, 2011). The internationalization index is 19.8 for Indian tribology research, which is greater than for neuroscience research in India (Shahabuddin, 2013) where it was 16.14. 67% of the country's output received citations in a range between 1 and 552. The citation rate of Indian contribution was 6 which is better than computer science (1.13) (Gupta, Kshitij, & Verma, 2011) and dental science (1.38) (Kaur & Gupta, 2010). Almost 67% of papers received one or more citations (ranges: 1–552) since their time of publication. Prolific institutes produced 53% of the country's output which indicates that the number of institutes engaged in tribology research was limited. Prolific authors produced 22.5% of the country's output which indicates that Indian tribology research is diffused with many authors. Analysis of single words in titles shows that *composites, friction, tribology,* and *wear* are frequently used words by Indian tribologists. The present study concludes that the Indian contribution to world tribology research has increased greatly in the last six years (369%). However, it is noted that world tribology research is presently led by China, the USA, and Japan based on the number of publications.

REFERENCES

Assenova, E., Polzer, G., Tsermaa, Dr., & Kandeva, M. (2013). Selective transfer of materials in the aspect of green tribology. Paper presented at the 13th International Conference on Tribology, Kragujevac, Serbia.

Biswas, S. K. (2007). Research and development in Tribology in India. *Tribology Online, 2*(1), 1–4.

Elango, B., Rajendran, P., & Bornmann, L. (2013).

Global nanotribology research output (1996–2010): A scientometric analysis. *PLOS ONE 8*(12): e81094.

Frame, J. D., & Carpenter, M. P. (1979). International research collaboration. *Social Studies of Science, 9*, 481–497.

Gupta, B. M., & Bala, A. (2011). A scientometric analysis of Indian research output in Medicine during 1999–2008. *Journal of Natural Science, Biology and Medicine, 2*(1), 87–100.

Gupta, B. M., Kaur, H., & Bala, A. (2011). Mapping of Indian diabetes research during 1999–2008: A scientometric analysis of publications output. *DESIDOC Journal of Library and Information Technology, 31*(2), 143–152.

Gupta, B. M., Kaur, H., & Kshitij, A. (2011). Dementia research in India: A scientometric analysis of research output during 2002–11. *Annals of Library and Information Studies, 59*(4), 280–288.

Gupta, B. M., Kshitij, A., & Verma, C. (2011). Mapping of Indian computer science research output, 1999–2008. *Scientometrics, 86*(2), 261–283.

Hirsch, J. E. (2005). An index to quantify an individual's scientific research output. *Proceedings of the National Academy of Sciences, 102*(46), 16569–16572.

Jost, P. (1966). *Lubrication (Tribology) A report on the present position and industry's needs.* Department of Education and Science, H.M. Stationary Office, London.

Kademani, B. S., Sagar, A., & Bhanumurthy, K. (2011). Research and impact of materials science publications in India: 1999–2008. *Malaysian Journal of Library and Information Science, 16*(2), 63–82.

Karpagam, R., Gopalakrishnan, S., Natarajan, M., & Ramesh Babu, B. (2011). Mapping of nanoscience and nanotechnology research in India: A scientometric analysis, 1990–2009. *Scientometrics, 89*(2), 201–522.

Kaur, H., & Gupta, B. M. (2010). Mapping of dental science research in India: a scientometric analysis of India's research output, 1999–2008. *Scientometrics, 85*(1), 361–376.

Ma, H., Ho, Y. S., & Fu, H. Z. (2011). Solid waste

related research in Science Citation Index Expanded. *Archives of Environmental Science, 5*, 89–100.

Malarvizhi, R., Wang, M. H., & Ho, Y. S. (2010). Research trends in adsorption technologies for dye containing wastewaters. *World Applied Sciences Journal, 8*(8), 930–942.

Moya-Anegón, F., Guerrero-Bote, V. P., Bornmann, L., & Moed, H. F. (2013). The research guarantors of research papers and the output counting: A promising new approach. *Scientometrics, 97*(2), 421–434.

Mukhopadhyay, A. (2011). Tribology: A potential source of energy savings in industry. *Propagation – A Journal of Science Communication, 2*(2), 165–168.

Rajagopal, T., Archunan, G., Surulinathi, M., & Ponmanickam, P. (2013). Research output in pheromone biology: a case study of India. *Scientometrics, 94*(2), 711–719.

Rajendran, P., Manickaraj, J., & Elango, B. (2013). Scientometric analysis of India's research output on wireless communication (2001–2012). *Journal of Advances in Library and Information Science, 2*(3), 105–111.

Schubert, A., & Glänzel, W. (2007). A systematic analysis of Hirsch-type indices for journals. *Journal of Informetrics, 1*(2), 179–184.

Shahabuddin, S. M. (2013). Mapping of neuroscience research in India – A bibliometric approach. *Current Science, 104*(12), 1619–1626.

Singh, V., Vimal, J., & Chaturvedi, V. (2012). A study on development of industrial tribology in India with some future prospects. *International Journal of Mechanical and Industrial Engineering, 2*(4), 31–34.

Sinha, B., & Joshi, K., (2012). Analysis of India's solar photovoltaics research output. *Annals of Library and Information Studies, 59*(2), 106–121.

Sun, J., Wang, M. H., & Ho, Y. S. (2012). A historical review and bibliometric analysis of research on estuary pollution. *Marine Pollution Bulletin, 66*(1), 13–21.

Tellez, H., & Vadillo, J. M. (2010). Bibliometric study of journal publications on analytical chemistry 2000–2007: Publication productivity and journal preferences by country. *Analytical and Bioanalytical Chemistry, 397*, 1477–1484.

Varaprasad, S. J. D., & Ramesh, D. B. (2011). Activity and growth of chemical research in India during 1987–2007. *DESIDOC Journal of Library and Information Technology, 31*(5), 387–394.

Zhang, X, C., Huang, D. S., & Li, F. (2011). Cancer nursing research output and topics in the first decade of the 21st century: Results of a bibliometric and co-word cluster analysis. *Asian Pacific Journal of Cancer Prevention, 12*, 2055–2058.

3

TAKES: Two-step Approach for Knowledge Extraction in Biomedical Digital Libraries

Min Song *

Department of Library and Information Science
Yonsei University, Korea
E-mail: min.song@yonsei.ac.kr

ABSTRACT

This paper proposes a novel knowledge extraction system, TAKES (Two-step Approach for Knowledge Extraction System), which integrates advanced techniques from Information Retrieval (IR), Information Extraction (IE), and Natural Language Processing (NLP). In particular, TAKES adopts a novel keyphrase extraction-based query expansion technique to collect promising documents. It also uses a Conditional Random Field-based machine learning technique to extract important biological entities and relations. TAKES is applied to biological knowledge extraction, particularly retrieving promising documents that contain Protein-Protein Interaction (PPI) and extracting PPI pairs. TAKES consists of two major components: DocSpotter, which is used to query and retrieve promising documents for extraction, and a Conditional Random Field (CRF)-based entity extraction component known as FCRF. The present paper investigated research problems addressing the issues with a knowledge extraction system and conducted a series of experiments to test our hypotheses. The findings from the experiments are as follows: First, the author verified, using three different test collections to measure the performance of our query expansion technique, that DocSpotter is robust and highly accurate when compared to Okapi BM25 and SLIPPER. Second, the author verified that our relation extraction algorithm, FCRF, is highly accurate in terms of F-Measure compared to four other competitive extraction algorithms: Support Vector Machine, Maximum Entropy, Single POS HMM, and Rapier.

Keywords: Semantic Query Expansion, Information Extraction, Information Retrieval, Text Mining

*Corresponding Author: Min Song
Associate professor
Department of Library and Information
Science, Yonsei University, Korea
E-mail: min.song@yonsei.ac.kr

1. INTRODUCTION

Knowledge Extraction (KE) is a relatively new research area at the intersection of Data Mining (DM), Information Extraction (IE), and Information Retrieval (IR). The goal of knowledge extraction is to discover knowledge in natural language texts. In terms of knowledge extraction, a variety of types of knowledge can be pulled out from textual data, such as linguistic knowledge and domain-specific lexical and semantic information hidden in unstructured text corpora (Poon & Vanderwende, 2010; Zhou & Zhang, 2007). In light of extracting entities, IE is pertinent to knowledge extraction. It locates specific pieces of data from corpora of natural language texts and populates a relational table from the identified facts. Since the start of the Message Understanding Conferences (MUCs), IE has addressed the issue of transforming unstructured data into structured, relational databases. The transformed text corpus can be mined by various IE techniques such as the application of statistical and machine-learning methods to discover novel relationships in large relational databases.

Developing an IE system is a challenging task. Recently, there has been significant progress in applying data mining methods to help build IE systems (Blaschke, Hirschman, Shatkay, & Valencia, 2010). The major task of these IE systems is entity or relation extraction, such as gene extraction and protein-protein interaction extraction (Airola, Pyysalo, Björne, Pahikkala, Ginter, & Salakoski, 2008; Kim, 2008; Miyao, Sagae, Saetre, Matsuzaki, & Tsujii, 2009). IE techniques typically involve several steps such as named-entity tagging, syntactic parsing, and rule matching. These required steps to transform text are relatively expensive. Processing large text databases creates difficult challenges for IE in leveraging and extracting information from relational databases. IE

techniques proposed so far are not feasible for large databases or for the web, since it is not realistic to tag and parse every available document. In addition, IE requires a dictionary of entities and relational terms or well-defined rules for identifying them. This requirement posed by IE is challenging because unstructured text corpora tend to be 1) non-uniform and incomplete, 2) synonymous and aliased, and 3) polysemous (Carpineto & Romano, 2010). These factors are attributed to low recall of IE systems reported in the literature. Other major problems with current IE techniques are that they are labour intensive in terms of processing text collections and require extensive knowledge on the target domain (Califf & Mooney, 2003). Although it is currently feasible to apply sentence parsers or named entity extraction tools to the entire PubMed database, a portability issue with doing so remains problematic particularly when it is applied to other types of datasets other than PubMed. Due to these issues, IE is not applicable to some domains where human intervention is necessary or when domain experts are not available.

The goal of this paper is to develop an integrated knowledge extraction system, TAKES, that overcomes the aforementioned issues with current IE systems. TAKES stands for Two-step Approach for Knowledge Extraction System. The specific research objectives are 1) whether keyphrase-based query expansion improves retrieval performance and 2) whether Feature-enriched Conditional Random Field (FCRF)-based information extraction enhances the extraction accuracy. By enabling both to retrieve promising documents that contain target biological entities relations and to extract those target entities and relations, TAKES helps curators and biologists discover new entities and relations buried in a large amount of biomedical data. Figure 1 shows the overall diagram of TAKES.

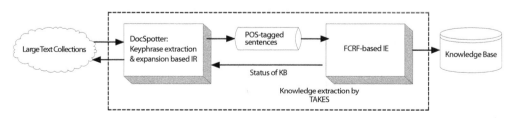

Fig. 1 Overall Diagram of TAKES

Although several papers have suggested the development of a scalable knowledge extraction system (i.e., Textpresso) (Agichtein & Gravano, 2003; Banko & Etzioni, 2007; Hu & Shen, 2009; Shatkay & Feldman, 2003; Muller, Kenny, & Sternberg, 2004), the proposed technique is differentiated and unique from existing knowledge extraction systems in the following ways. First, we introduce a novel query expansion technique based on keyphrases, while others are based on a single term or are combined with a rule-based learning technique like Ripper (Cohen & Singer, 1996). Second, our system is based on unsupervised query training whereas others are based on supervised querying learning. Third, we introduce a FCRF-based extraction technique for knowledge extraction to information extraction tasks. In addition, seamlessly integrating retrieval and extraction into a knowledge extraction system is a major strength of our approach, and it is proven that TAKES is highly effective by the experimental results.

The details of TAKES are provided in Section 3. The experimental results show that two main components of TAKES, DocSpotter and FCRF, outperformed the other compared query expansion and information extraction techniques, respectively. The detailed description is provided in Section 4.

The rest of the paper is organized as follows: Section 2 proposes and describes a novel knowledge extraction technique; Section 3 explains the experimental settings and evaluation methodologies. We report and analyze the experimental results in Section 4. Section 5 concludes the paper and suggests future work.

2. APPROACH AND METHOD

In this section, we describe the architecture of TAKES (Figure 2). Note that the components in blue boxes (DocSpotter) are described in Section 2.1.2, and the components in red boxes (FCRF) are described in Section 2.2.2. TAKES uses a pipelined architecture and extracts target entities with as little human intervention as possible.

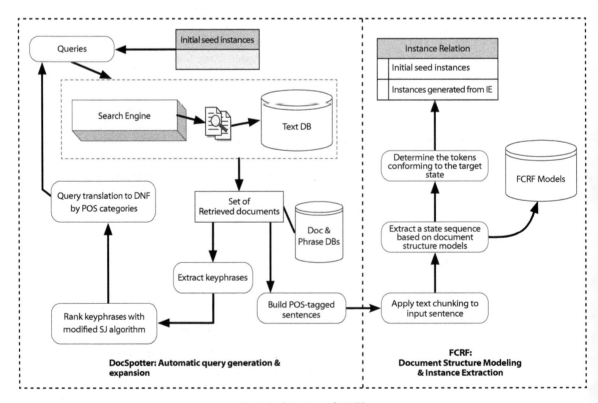

Fig. 2 Architecture of TAKES

The TAKES algorithm works using the following steps:

Step 1: Starting with a set of user-provided seed instances (the seed instance can be quite small), our system retrieves a sample of documents from the text databases. Note, an instance denotes a protein-protein interaction pair. At the initial stage of the overall document retrieval process, we have no information about the documents that might be useful for the goal of extraction. The only information we require about the target relation is a set of user-provided seed instances, including the specification of the relation attributes to be used for document retrieval. We construct some simple queries by using the attribute values of the initial seed instances to extract the document samples of a predefined size using the search engine.

Step 2: The instance set induces a binary partition (a split) on the documents: those that contain instances or those that do not contain any instance from the relation. The documents are labeled automatically as either positive or negative examples, respectively. The positive examples represent the documents that contain at least one instance. The negative examples represent documents that contain no instances.

Step 3: TAKES next applies data mining and IR techniques to derive queries targeted to match—and retrieve— additional documents similar to the positive examples.

Step 4: TAKES then applies a CRF-based state sequence extraction technique over the documents. It models a set of document structures using the training documents. These models are kept in the model base which will serve as an engine for extracting state sequence from the documents.

Step 5: The system queries the text databases using the automatically learned queries from Step 3 to retrieve a set of promising documents from the databases and then returns to Step 2. The whole procedure repeats until no new instances can be added into the relation or we reach the pre-set limit of a maximum number of text files to process.

2.1. DocSpotter

DocSpotter is a novel querying technique to iteratively retrieve promising documents, specifically tuned for information extraction. DocSpotter uses several DM and Natural Language Processing (NLP) techniques. First, DocSpotter adopts a key-phrase-based term selection technique combined with data mining and natural language processing techniques. Second, it proposes a query weighting algorithm combined with the modified Robertson Spark-Jones (RSJ) weight algorithm and the Information Gain algorithm. Third, it translates a query to the Disjunctive Normal Form (DNF) by POS (Part-Of-Speech) term categories.

2.1.1 Data Collections for DocSpotter Evaluation: Subset of MEDLINE and TREC

Two different data collections, TREC and MEDLINE, were used for the evaluation for DocSpotter.

MEDLINE: We collected a subset of MEDLINE data consisting of 264,363 MEDLINE records from PubMed at http://www.ncbi.nlm.nih.gov/pubmed. These records were retrieved in the XML format by PubMed APIs provided in the Entrez E-Utilities package. After we collected the records, we queried BIND PPI DB with PubMed ID to identify what records contain PPI pairs. Out of these 264,363 records, there are 4521 records containing protein-protein interaction pairs (Table 1). Since the collected dataset does not have a sufficient number of records that contain protein-protein interaction pairs, we decide to include the records containing protein-protein pairs from other sources than human expert-curated databases such as OMIM (Online Mendelian Inheritance in Man) and DIP (Database of Interacting Proteins). The reason for this decision is that we are interested in how well DocSpotter can find the records that have not been covered in these two databases. Out of 4521 records, 4100 records were identified by OMID and DIP and the rest of the records, 421, are from other sources (He, Wang, & Li, 2009).

Table 1. Statistics of the MEDLINE Data

No. of Records Indexed	No. of Terms	No. of Unique Terms	Document Length	No. of Records Containing PPI
264363	61515989	303077	232	4521

TREC: To evaluate the performance of DocSpotter on the standard IR evaluation collection, we used TREC data (TREC-5, TREC-6, and TREC-7 ad hoc test set). These TREC ad hoc test sets have been used in many different tracks of TREC including the TREC-5 routing track, the TREC-7 ad hoc track, and the TREC-8 ad hoc track. We purchased these TREC data collections from Linguistic Data Consortium (LDC). The ad hoc task investigates the performance of systems that search a static document collection using new query statements. The document set consists of approximately 628,531 documents distributed on three CD-ROM disks (TREC disks 2, 4, and 5) taken from the following sources: Federal Register (FR), Financial Times (FT), Foreign Broadcast Information Service (FBIS), LA Times (LAT), Wall Street Journal, PA Newswire, and Information from Computer Select disks.

The query sets and document collections used in these tasks are shown in Table 2. Two tasks were conducted for evaluation. The first task is to retrieve results for the query sets from 251 to 400 used in TREC 5, 6, and 7. The second task with MEDLINE data is to retrieve MEDLINE records that contain protein-protein interaction pairs with two IR systems, PubMed and Lemur, to query MEDLINE data.

Table 2. Documents and Queries Used in TREC Ad Hoc Tasks

Task	Documents	Queries
TREC5	TREC disks 2,4	251-300
TREC6	TREC disks 4,5	301-350
TREC7	TREC disks 4,5	351-400

There were 25 initial queries provided for the experiments. These queries consisted of 3 to 5 protein-protein interaction pairs. Figure 3 shows the initial query used to retrieve the documents from PubMed. The initial queries were passed to either PubMed or Lemur to retrieve the initial set of retrieved documents. DocSpotter was applied to extract keyphrases and expand queries based on the top N ranked keyphrases. The performance of DocSpotter and other comparison techniques is measured by average precision, precision at rank n, and F-measure on MEDLINE and

TREC-5, 6, and 7 data. The details of the performance measure are described in Section 3.

```
  <init_query>
<terms protein1="MAP4" protein2=" Mapmodulin"/>
<terms protein1="WIP" protein2="NCK"/>
<terms protein1="GHR" protein2="SHB"/>
<terms protein1="SHIP" protein2="DOK"/>
<terms protein1="LNK" protein2="GRB2"/>
<terms protein1="CRP" protein2="Zyxin"/>
  </init_query>
```

Fig. 3 Initial Query Used for Protein-Protein Interaction Tasks

2.1.2 DocSpotter Description

The keyphrase extraction technique used for DocSpotter consists of two stages: 1) building the extraction model and 2) extracting keyphrases. Input of the "building extraction model" stage is training data whereas input of the "extracting keyphrases" stage is test data. These two stages are fully automated. Both training and test data are processed by the three components: 1) Data Cleaning, 2) Data Tokenizing, and 3) Data Discretizing. Through data cleaning and tokenizing, we generate candidate keyphrases. Three feature sets were chosen and calculated for each candidate phrase: 1) TF*IDF, 2) Distance from First Occurrence, and 3) POS Tagging. Since these features are continuous, we need to convert them into nominal forms to make our machine learning algorithm applicable. Among many discretization algorithms, we chose the equal-depth (frequency) partitioning method which allows for good data scaling. Equal-depth discretization divides the range into N intervals, each containing approximately the same number of samples. During the training process, each feature is discretized. In DocSpotter, the value of each feature is replaced by the range to which the value belongs.

Keyphrase Ranking

Automatic query expansion requires a term-selection stage. The ranked order of terms is of primary importance in that the terms that are most likely to be useful are close to the top of the list. We re-weight candidate keyphrases with an Information Gain measure. Specifically, candidate keyphrases are ranked by an Information Gain, GAIN(P), a measure of expected reduction in entropy based on the "usefulness" of an attribute A. The usefulness of an attribute is determined by the degree of uncertainty reduced when the attribute is chosen. This is one of the most popular measures of association used in data mining. For instance, Quinlan (1993) uses Information Gain for ID3 and its successor C4.5 which are widely-used decision tree techniques. ID3 and C4.5 construct simple trees by choosing at each step the splitting feature that "tells us the most" about the training data. Mathematically, Information Gain is defined as:

$$GAIN(P_i) = I(p,n) - E(P_i) \qquad (1)$$

where P_i is value of candidate phrase that falls into a discrete range. $I(p,n)$ measures the information required to classify an arbitrary tuple.

Each candidate phrase, extracted from a document, is ranked by the probability calculated with GAIN(P). In our approach, $I(p,n)$ is stated such that the class p is where a candidate phrase is "keyphrase" and the class n is where a candidate phrase is "non-keyphrase." Many query re-ranking algorithms are reported in literature (Robertson, Zaragoza, & Taylor, 2004). These algorithms attempt to quantify the value of candidate query expansion terms. Formulae estimate the term value based on qualitative or quantitative criteria. The qualitative arguments are concerned with the value of the particular term in retrieval. On the other hand, the quantitative argument involves some specific criteria such as a proof of performance. One example of the qualitative-based formula is the relevance weighting theory.

While there are many promising alternatives to this weighting scheme in IR literature, we chose the Robertson-Sparck Jones algorithm (Robertson & Sparck, 1976) as our base because it has been demonstrated to perform well, is naturally well suited to our task, and incorporating other term weighting schemes would require changes to our model.

The F4.5 formula proposed by Robertson and Jones has been widely used in IR systems with some modifications (Okapi). Although a few more algorithms were derived from the F4.5 formula by Robertson and Jones, in this paper we modify the original for keyphrases as shown:

$$P(w) = \log \frac{\left(\dfrac{r+0.5}{R-r+0.5} \right)}{\left(\dfrac{n-r+0.5}{N-n-R+r+0.5} \right)} \qquad (2)$$

$$KP(r) = \sqrt{\frac{GAIN(p) * P(w)}{2}} \qquad (3)$$

$P(w)$ is the keyphrase weight, N is the total number of sentences, n is the number of sentences in which that query terms co-occur, R is the total number of relevant sentences, and r is the number of relevant sentences in which the query terms co-occur. We combine Information Gain with the modified F4.5 formula to incorporate keyphrase properties gained (see formula 3). All candidate keyphrases are re-weighted by KP(r) and the top N ranked keyphrases are added to the query for the next pass. The N number is determined by the size of the retrieved documents.

Query Translation into DNF

A major research issue in IR is easing the user's role of query formulation through automating the process of query formulation. There are two essential problems to address when searching with online systems: 1) initial query formulation that expresses the user's information need; and 2) query reformulation that constructs a new query from the results of a prior query (Abdou & Savoy, 2008). The latter effort implements the notion of relevance feedback in IR systems and is the topic of this section. An algorithm for automating Boolean query formulation was first proposed in 1970. It employs a term weighting function first described in Frants and Shapiro (1991) to decide the "importance" of terms which have been identified. The terms were aggregated into "sub-requests" and combined into a Boolean expression in disjunctive normal form (DNF). Other algorithms that have been proposed to translate a query to DNF are based on classification, decision-trees, and thesauri. Mitra, Singhal, and Buckely (1998) proposed a technique for constructing Boolean constraints.

Our POS category-based translation technique differs from others in that ours is unsupervised and is easily integrated into other domains. In our technique, there are four different phrase categories defined: 1) ontology phrase category, 2) non-ontology noun phrase category, 3) non-ontology proper noun phrase category, and 4) verb phrase category. Phrases that have corresponding entities in ontologies such as MESH and WordNet belong to the ontology phrase category. Synonym relations are used for the entity matching between phrases in a query and ontologies entities. We include the verb phrase category as a major category because important verb phrases play a role in improving the retrieval performance. Keyphrases within the category are translated into DNF and categories are then translated into Conjunctive Normal Form. As explained earlier, within the same category the phrases are combined with the OR Boolean operator. Between categories, the terms are combined with the AND Boolean operator. Figure 4 illustrates how the original query (CDC and H1N1 and country) is expanded and translated into the final query with MESH. We index the MESH tree in XML, and the query term is used to look up the MESH index to select the closest match between the term and the MESH entry. Our query translation technique does not currently address the problem of translating ambiguous terms.

2.2. FCRF

In this section, we describe FCRF, a novel extraction technique based on incorporating various features into Conditional Random Fields (CRF). CRF is a discriminative undirected probabilistic

graphical model to help the IE system cope with data sparseness (Lafferty, McCallum, & Pereira, 2001).

2.2.1 Data Collections for FCRF Evaluation

We use OMIM and DIP as references to compare the number of articles needed to be retrieved and extracted by TAKES in order to rebuild the protein-protein interactions or gene-disease interactions for each species. OMIM is a database of human genes and genetic disorders (McKusick, 1998). With OMIM, our task is to extract gene-disease interaction. For our experiment, we used the data set compiled by Ray and Craven (2001). DIP (Xenarios & Eisenberg, 2001) is a knowledge base about the biological relationships of protein-protein interactions and is constructed by human experts manually, a many-year effort. DIP, the manually curated knowledge database, serves as an ideal testbed to verify the performance of our TAKES system. It contains the information of protein names, protein-protein interaction pairs, and the MEDLINE abstracts from which the protein-protein pairs are manually extracted for a few species such as human beings, yeast, fruit flies, house mice, Helicobacter pylori, and Escherichia coli (See Table 3).

The performance of FCRF and other comparison techniques is measured by precision, recall, and F-measure on MEDLINE data combined with OMIM and DIP, The details of the performance measure are described in Section 3.

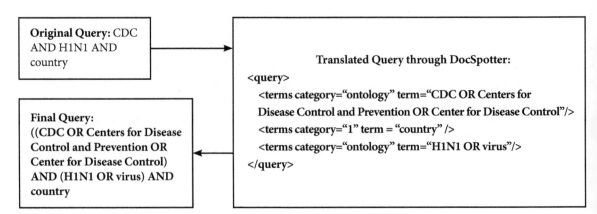

Fig. 4 An Example of Query Translation

Table 3. Protein-Protein Interactions from DIP

Organism	Protein	Protein Interactions	# of relevant abstracts from MedLine
Drosophila melanogaster (fruit fly)	7050	21017	7065
Saccharomyces cerevisiae (yeast)	4726	15364	4740
Helicobacter pylori	710	1425	710
Homo sapiens (Human)	753	1128	848
Escherichia coli	421	516	418
Mus musculus (house mouse)	191	279	298

2.2.2 Feature-Enriched CRF (FCRF) Models

CRF is a probabilistic framework for labeling and segmenting sequential data. The underlying idea of CRF is that of defining a conditional probability distribution over label sequences given a particular observation sequence, rather than a joint distribution over both label and observation sequences. The advantage of CRFs over HMMs is their conditional nature, resulting in the relaxation of the independence assumptions required by HMMs in order to ensure tractable inference (Lafferty, McCallum, & Pereira, 2001). In this paper, we incorporate various features such as context, linguistic, part-of-speech, text chunking, and dictionary features into the extraction decision. Feature selection is critical to the success of machine learning approaches. We will illustrate how to calculate values of feature functions.

Entity extraction can be thought of as a sequence segmentation problem: each word is a token in a sequence to be assigned a label (e.g. PROTEIN, DNA, RNA, CELL-LINE, CELL-TYPE, or OTHER). Let $o = <o_1, o_2, ..., o_n>$ be a sequence of observed words of length n. Let S be a set of states in a finite state machine, each corresponding to a label $l \in L$ (e.g. PROTEIN, DNA, etc.). Let $S = <s_1, s_2, ..., s_n>$ be the sequence of states in S that correspond to the labels assigned to words in the input sequence o. Linear-chain CRFs define the conditional probability of a state sequence given an input sequence to be:

$$P(s \mid o) = \frac{1}{z_o} \exp \left(\sum_{i=1}^{n} \sum_{j=1}^{m} \lambda_j f_j(s_{i-1}, s_i, o, i) \right)$$

where Z_0 is a normalization factor of all state sequences, $f_j(s_{i-1}, s_i, o, i)$ is one of m functions that describes a feature, and λ_j is a learned weight for each such feature function. These weights are set to maximize the conditional log likelihood of labelled sequences in a training set: $D = \left\{ \langle o,l \rangle_{(1)}, ..., \langle o,l \rangle_{(n)} \right\}$

$$LL(D) = \sum_{i=1}^{n} \log \left(P(l_{(i)} \mid o_{(i)}) \right)$$

When the training state sequences are fully labelled and unambiguous, the objective function is convex, thus the model is guaranteed to find the optimal weight settings in terms of $LL(D)$. Once these settings are found, the labelling for the unlabelled sequence can be done using a modified Viterbi algorithm. CRFs are presented in more complete detail by Lafferty et al. (2001).

Text Chunking Feature

Text chunking is defined as dividing text into syntactically correlated parts of words (Kudo & Matsumoto, 2000). Chunking is a two-step process: identifying proper chunks from a sequence of tokens (such as words), and then classifying these chunks into grammatical classes. A major advantage of using text chunking over full parsing techniques is that partial parsing, such as text chunking, is much faster and more robust, yet sufficient for IE. SVM-based text chunking was reported to produce the highest accuracy in the text chunking task (Kudo & Matsumoto, 2000). The SVM-based approaches, such as the inductive-learning approach, take as input a set of training examples (given

as binary valued feature vectors) and find a classification function that maps them to a class. In this paper,
we use Tiny SVM (Kudo & Matsumoto, 2000) in that
Tiny SVM performs well in handling a multi-class
task. Figure 5 illustrates the procedure of converting a
raw sentence from PubMed to the phrase-based units
grouped by the SVM text-chunking technique. The top
box shows a sentence that is part of abstracts retrieved
from PubMed. The middle box illustrates the parsed
sentence by POS taggers. The bottom box shows the final conversion made to the POS tagged sentence by the
SVM-based text chunking technique.

Part-Of-Speech Feature

Part of speech information is quite useful to detect
named entities. Verbs and prepositions usually indicate a named entity's boundaries, whereas nouns not
found in the dictionary are usually good candidates
for named entities. Our experience indicates that five
is also a suitable window size. We used the Brill POS
tagger to provide POS information.

Dictionary Feature

We use a dictionary feature function for every
token in the corpus. This feature, described as "dic-

Example raw sentence retrieved from PubMed:
"For many of these genes, the effect of an isw2 mutation is partially masked by a
functional Sin3-Rpd3 complex"

Example input sentence tagged with POS:
many /JJ/ of /IN/ these /DT/ genes, /NN/ the /DT/ effect/NN/ of /IN/ an /DT/ isw2/
CD/ mutation /NNP/ is /VBZ/ partially/RB/ masked /VBN/ by /IN/ a /DT/
functional /JJ/ Sin3-Rpd3 /CD/ complex /NN/

Example input sentence processed with text chunking technique.
Noun Group [many /JJ/ of /IN/ these /DT/ genes,]
Noun Group [/NN/ the /DT/ effect/NN/ of /IN/ an /DT/ isw2 /CD/ mutation/NNP/]
Verb Group[is /VBZ/ partially/RB/masked /VBN/]
PREP Group [by /IN/]
Target Noun Group [a /DT/ functional /JJ/ Sin3-Rpd3 /CD/ complex /NN/]

Fig. 5 A Procedure of Sentence Parsing. JJ: adjective; IN: preposition; DT: determiner; CD: cardinal number; NN: singular noun; NNP:
proper noun; VBZ and VBN: verb; RB: adverb

Context Feature

Words preceding or following the target word may
be useful for determining its category. It is obvious
that the more context words analyzed the better and
more precise the results gained. However, widening
the context window rapidly increases the number of
possibilities to calculate. In our experience, a suitable
window size is five.

tionary name" plus length of token string, informs us
of whether a token matches a dictionary entry and
whether it is part of a multi-token string that matches
a compound named entity or named entity phrase in
the dictionary.

3. EVALUATION

We evaluate TAKES on two different tasks for Information Retrieval and Information Extraction in a biomedical domain. The performance evaluation of TAKES accounts for effectiveness of each component (retrieval and extraction) to the overall evaluation. The first set of experiments aims at evaluating the performance of DocSpotter. The second set of experiments focuses on evaluating the performance of FCRF. The details of our experimental evaluation are provided in the sub-sections.

3.1. Evaluation of DocSpotter and FCRF

In this section, we explain methodologies and strategies used for evaluation of DocSpotter and FCRF. To evaluate the performance of DocSpotter, we implemented two query expansion algorithms. The first algorithm is SLIPPER which is a rule-based query expansion technique (Cohen & Singer, 1996). The second algorithm is BM25, which is a statistical expansion technique (Robertson, Zaragoza, & Taylor, 2004). These two algorithms are well-accepted query expansion algorithms (Feng, Burns, & Hovy, 2008).

In evaluation of FCRF, we do not attempt to capture every instance of such tuples. Instead, we exploit the fact that these tuples tend to appear multiple times in the types of collections that we consider. As long as we capture one instance of such a tuple, we consider our system to be successful. To evaluate this task, we adapt the recall and precision metrics used by IR to quantify the accuracy and comprehensiveness of our combined table of tuples. Our metrics for evaluating the performance of an extraction system over a collection of documents D include all the tuples that appear in the collection D.

We conduct a series of experiments. We start with a few protein-protein interaction pairs or gene-disease interaction pairs and then let TAKES automatically construct queries, select the relevant articles from MEDLINE, and extract the protein-protein interaction for each species. We repeat the experiments for each species several times with different seed instances and take the average of the articles numbers. Identifying several key algorithms proposed in IE from our literature review, we implement

five IE algorithms that were reported to produce high extraction accuracy. These five algorithms are 1) Dictionary-based (Blaschke, Andrade, Ouzounis, & Valencia, 1999), 2) RAPIER (Cohen & Singer, 1996), 3) Single POS HMM (Ray & Craven, 2001), 4) SVM (Kudo & Matsumoto, 2000), and 5) Maximum Entropy (Manning & Klein, 2003).

3.2. Evaluation Measure for DocSpotter and FCRF

The retrieval effectiveness of DocSpotter was measured by precision at rank n and non-interpolated average precision. Using the precision at rank n for the IR evaluation is based on the assumption that the most relevant hits must be in the top few documents returned for a query. Relevance ranking can be measured by computing precision at different cut-off points. Precision at rank n does not measure recall. A new measure called *average precision* combines precision, relevance ranking, and overall recall. Average precision is the sum of the precision at each relevant hit in the hit list divided by the total number of relevant documents in the collection. The cutoff value for the number of retrieved documents is 1000 in the TREC evaluation. In the evaluation of DocSpotter, we used 200 as the cutoff value in that the collection size in our evaluation is smaller than in the TREC evaluation.

$$AP = \left(\sum_{i=1}^{R} \frac{i}{rank_i} \right) / R \qquad (4)$$

where R = number of relevant docs for that query and i/ranki = 0 if document i was not retrieved.

The extraction effectiveness of FCRF was measured by Recall, Precision, and F-measure. In IE, the evaluation of system performance is done with an answer key that contains annotations and their attributes (also called slots) that the system should find from the input. Precision (P) and recall (R) have been used regularly to measure the performance of IE as well as IR. Recall denotes the ratio of the number of slots the system found correctly to the number of slots in the answer key. In addition, since F-measure provides a useful tool for examining the relative performance of systems when one has better precision and the other better recall, we report this number where it is useful.

4. EXPERIMENTAL RESULTS AND ANALYSIS

In this section, we briefly describe the experimental settings designed to evaluate DocSpotter and FCRF and report the experimental results. The experiments are conducted to investigate two research problems studied in this paper: 1) the effectiveness of DocSpotter, a query expansion technique and 2) the effectiveness of FCRF, an information extraction technique.

4.1. Experimental Results with DocSpotter

As stated in the previous section, DocSpotter, the keyphrase-based query expansion algorithm, was evaluated with two different data sets and search engines. The subsections below report the experimental results with these combinations. We used 25 initial queries for both MEDLINE – PubMed and MEDLINE – Lemur. In order to examine whether query drift (i.e., the presence of aspects or topics not related to the query in top-retrieved documents) exists, we ran ten iterations in each query expansion experiment. Two measures, average precision and precision at top 20 documents, were utilized for performance evaluation of our query expansion algorithm. We limited the number of retrieved documents to 200. The four query expansion algorithms shown below are used for the experiments:

- **BM25:** Okapi BM25 algorithm.
- **SLP:** SLIPPER, a Rule-based AdaBoost algorithm
- **KP:** Keyphrase-based query expansion algorithm
- **KP+C:** In addition to the KP formula, this algorithm employs Boolean constraints by POS type of keyphrases and serves the key algorithm for DocSpotter.

Experimental Results of DocSpotter on TREC Data

Table 4. Results for TREC 5 with our four query expansion algorithms executing the query set 251-300

Algorithm	TREC 5	
	Avg. P	P@20
BM25	0.1623	0.3252
SLP	0.1299	0.2656
KP	0.1938	0.3368
KP+C	0.1985	0.3398

Table 4 shows the overall performance of the four algorithms executing the query set 251-300 on TREC 5 data. The results show that KP has the best performance in average precision as well as in precision at top twenty ranks (P@20) compared to other algorithms. To confirm the differences among the conditions, we conducted an ANOVA for the P@20 TREC 5 results. This showed an overall effect of condition $F(3,196)=17.64$, $p<0.01$. We also conducted individual t-tests essentially as specific comparisons. Our prediction that KP would be better than BM25 was confirmed $t(49)=-7.37$, $p<0.01$ (one-tailed) at n-1 degrees of freedom (50 queries). Similarly, our prediction that KP+C would be better than KP was confirmed $t(49)=-4.72$, $p<0.01$ (one-tailed).

Tables 5 and 6 show similar results to those obtained for TREC 5. The three new algorithms improve the retrieval performance on TREC 6 and 7. As with TREC 5, the KP+C algorithm outperforms BM25 and SLP algorithms in average precision and in P@20.

DocSpotter, the keyphrase-based technique combined with the POS phrase category, produces the highest average precision. One of the best results on

Table 5. Results for TREC 6 with our four query expansion algorithms executing the query set 301-350

Algorithm	TREC 6	
	Avg. P	P@20
BM25	0.1797	0.3160
SLP	0.1358	0.2654
KP	0.2098	0.3390
KP+C	0.2114	0.3424

Table 6. Results for TREC 7 with our four query-expansion algorithms executing the query set 351-400

Algorithm	TREC 7	
	Avg. P	P@20
BM25	0.2229	0.3837
SLP	0.1502	0.3044
KP	0.2343	0.3878
KP+C	0.2458	0.4024

TREC 5 is 19.44 and 32.40 in average precision and P@20 respectively (Mitra, Singhal, & Buckely, 1998). On TREC 6, their best results are 20.34 and 33.50 in average precision and P@20. The algorithm KP+C produces 21% and 48% better than these results on TREC 5 in average precision and P@20. On TREC 6, it is 39% and 22% which are better than the results reported by Mitra et al. (1998).

Experimental Results of DocSpotter on MEDLINE Data

The experimental results for MEDLINE with PubMed are shown in Table 7. Our keyphrase-based technique combined with the POS phrase category produces the highest average precision. Our two algorithms (KP and KP+C) improve the retrieval performance on the tasks of retrieval documents containing protein-protein interaction pairs. The KP+C algorithm gives the best average precision. The worst performance was produced by a rule-based algorithm (SLP) both in average precision and precision at top 20.

The overall performance of the query expansion algorithms is poor in terms of average precision (Figure 6) and precision at top 20. There might be two possible reasons that cause this overall poor performance. First, PubMed is based on an exact match retrieval model which makes the keyphrase-based query expansion less effective. Second, the size of the database, which contains more than 18 million documents, is too big.

We also explored the effect of a sequence of query expansion iterations. Table 8 shows the results for five query expansion iterations. The second column shows the number of retrieved documents from MEDLINE per iteration. The third column displays the number of retrieved documents containing protein-protein pairs. The fourth column is the F-Measure. For F-Measure, we used b=2 because recall is more important than precision in the tasks of retrieving the documents containing protein-protein interaction pairs. Our results show that F-Measure generally increases as the number of iterations increases, and the results indicate that a sequence of query expansion iterations has an impact on the overall retrieval performance.

Table 7. Results for MEDLINE – PubMed with Four Query Expansion Algorithms

Algorithm	MEDLINE	
	Avg. P	P@20
BM25	0.1282	0.2727
SLP	0.1051	0.2366
KP	0.1324	0.2844
KP+C	0.1522	0.2996

Table 8. Query Expansion Iterations for MEDLINE - PubMed

Iteration	No. retrieved docs	No. docs containing protein-protein pairs	F-Measure (%)
1	30	18	47.76
2	609	289	51.65
3	832	352	51.27
4	1549	578	53.69
5	1312	545	53.21

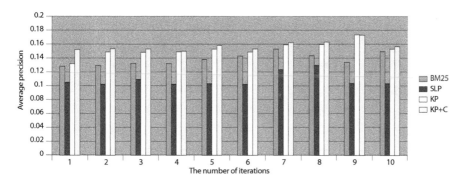

Fig. 6 Experimental Results for MEDLINE –PubMed

In addition, we compared DocSpotter with another query expansion algorithm on MEDLINE – Lemur. For this experiment, approximately 0.26 million MEDLINE records were indexed and searched with Lemur. As indicated in Table 9, the best performance was produced by the keyphrase-based query expansion algorithm with the POS phrase category (KP+C) both in average precision and precision at top 20. The baseline query expansion algorithm was the next highest followed by BM25.

Overall, these results with MEDLINE-Lemur are no different from the previous results. One interesting observation is that MEDLINE-Lemur produces higher scores of average precision and precision at top 20 than other dataset-search engine combinations. The reasons for these higher scores are because 1) the data collection drawn from MEDLINE is homogeneous in terms of the subject matter of the collection and 2) Lemur search engine is the better search engine to work with over PubMed.

4.2. Experimental Results with FCRF

The results of experiments to evaluate the performance of FCRF on the task of protein-protein interaction extraction are shown below. In these experiments, five machine learning algorithms were trained using the abstracts with proteins and their interactions were processed by the text chunking technique. With this set of data, these systems extracted protein-protein interactions from the retrieved documents using DocSpotter. This gave us a measure of how the protein interaction extraction systems perform alone. Performance was evaluated using ten-fold cross validation and measuring recall and precision. Since the task was to extract interact-

ing protein-pairs, we did not consider matching the exact position and every occurrence of interacting protein-pairs within the abstract. To evaluate these systems, we constructed a precision-recall graph. Recall denotes the ratio of the number of slots the system found correctly to the number of slots in the answer key, and precision is the ratio of the number of correctly filled slots to the total number of slots the system filled.

Our experiments show that RAPIER produces relatively high precision but low recall. Similar results are observed in the Single POS HMM method which also gives high precision but low recall. MaxEnt produces the second best results, although recall is relatively lower than precision.

SVM produces better results than RAPIER or Single POS HMM but worse than MaxEnt and FCRF. Among these five systems, FCRF outperforms RAPIER, single POS HMM, SVM, and MaxEnt in terms of precision, recall, and F-measure. As shown in Table 10, F-Measure of FCRF is 59.83% whereas RAPER is 44.13%, SVM is 51.44%, single POS HMM is 50.58%, and MaxEnt is 53.04%.

We conducted another set of tests to investigate whether the results observed above are reproduced. To this end, we used input data that was obtained from DocSpotter as discussed. Since iterative query expansion is able to retrieve multiple sets of documents, we used a set of documents retrieved in each round.

Table 11 shows the experimental results with a new set of incoming data from DocSpotter. The apparent pattern of the results resembles the one reported in the previous run (Table 10). As indicated in Table 11, FCRF produced the best performance: precision

Table 9. Results for MEDLINE-Lemur with Four Query Expansion Algorithms

Algorithm	MEDLINE (0.26million)	
	Avg. P	P@20
BM25	0.2433	0.3798
SLP	0.1975	0.3241
KP	0.2645	0.3912
KP+C	0.2692	0.3933

Table 10. Comparison of Extraction System Performance in First Round

Extraction System	Precision	Recall	F-Measure
RAPIER	60.17%	34.12%	44.13%
SVM	68.98%	48.23%	51.44%
MaxEnt	69.32%	49.03%	53.04%
Single POS HMM	67.40%	47.23%	50.58%
FCRF	71.34%	52.09%	59.83%

Table 11. Comparison of Extraction System Performance in Second Round

Extraction System	Precision	Recall	F-Measure
RAPIER	57.12%	37.53%	44.87%
SVM	70.32%	42.37%	52.51%
MaxEnt	70.89%	43.22%	53.27%
Single POS HMM	66.58%	44.01%	52.80%
FCRF	73.13%	52.35%	60.32%

73.13%, recall 51.91%, and F-measure, 59.36%. The next highest score is produced by MaxEnt. RAPIER produces the lowest precision, recall, and F-Measure.

We repeated the same experimental tests over the 10 different datasets that were sent from DocSpotter. Figure 7 shows the results of the five extraction methods, FCRF, Single POS HMM, RAPIER, SVM, and MaxEnt in F-Measure. FCRF outperforms the other four algorithms. FCRF produces between 56.32% and 61.12% in F-Measure. Single POS HMM produces between 42.84% and 53.32% in F-Measure. RAPIER produces between 42.23% and 45.95% in F-Measure. SVM produces between 50.20% and 57.43% in F-Measure. MaxEnt's performance is in between 51.23% and 58.23% in F-Measure.

5. CONCLUSION AND FUTURE WORK

In this paper, we proposed a hybrid knowledge extraction algorithm drawn from several research fields such as DM, IR, and IE. Specifically, we developed a novel extraction algorithm that consists of 1) keyphrase-based query expansion to spot promising documents and 2) Feature-enriched Conditional Random Field-based information extraction. We also conducted a series of experiments to validate three research hypotheses formed in this paper.

The major contributions of this paper are three-fold. First, this paper introduced a novel automatic query-based technique (DocSpotter) to retrieve articles that are promising for extraction of relations from text. It assumed only a minimal search interface to the text database, which can be adapted to new domains, databases, or target relations with minimal human effort. It automatically discovered characteristics of documents that are useful for extraction of a target relation and refined queries per iteration to select potentially useful articles from the text databases. Second, a statistical generative model, Feature-enriched Conditional Random Field (FCRF), was proposed for automatic pattern generation and instances extraction. Third, we conducted a comprehensive evaluation of TAKES with other state-of-

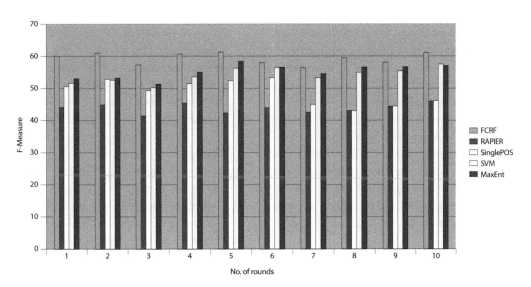

Fig. 7 Overall Extraction Performance of the Five Algorithms over 10 iterations

the art algorithms. We collected 264,363 MEDLINE records from PubMed, and we also used TREC ad hoc track data collections to evaluate DocSpotter. Among MEDLINE records harvested, 4521 records contain protein-protein interaction pairs. With these records as well as OMIM and DIP protein-protein interaction databases, we evaluated the performance of FCRF. As reported in Section 4, both DocSpotter and FCRF achieved the best performance over the other comparison algorithms. As a follow-up study, we will use BioInfer, the unified PPI database, for the PPI database from which protein-protein pairs are extracted (Pyysalo, Ginter, Heimonen, Björne, Boberg, Järvinen, & Salakoski, 2007).

The results of this paper stimulate further research in several directions. First, given that key-phrase-based query expansion is proven to be effective, it is worthwhile to investigate how effective it is to apply the keyphrase-based technique to other research problems such as text summarization and categorization. Text summarization is the process of identifying salient concepts in text narrative, conceptualizing the relationships that exist among them, and generating concise representations of input text that preserve the gist of its content. Keyphrase-based text summarization would be an interesting approach to summarization in that summarizing the collections with top N ranked keyphrases generates semantically cohesive passages. In addition, a keyphrase-based approach could be applied to automatic class modeling. For example, keyphrases can be extracted from text descriptions, such as functional requirements and class model descriptions. With extracted keyphrases, we can identify a set of core classes and its relationship with other classes.

Second, it is interesting to investigate how FCRF performs when it is applied to other types of relation extractions such as subcellular-localization relation extraction. In addition, applying FCRF to other domains such as Web data extraction would be a challenging but interesting research project. In addition to relation extraction, FCRF can be applied to entity extraction such as extracting CEO names from newswires.

Third, we plan to conduct additional evaluations on other data collections such as TREC Genomics and BioCreative data. These are the standard collections that allow us to compare DocSpotter and FCRF with other state-of-the-art algorithms.

6. ACKNOWLEDGEMENTS

This research was supported by the Bio & Medical Technology Development Program of the National Research Foundation (NRF), funded by the Ministry of Science, ICT & Future Planning (Grant No. 2013M3A9C4078138).

REFERENCES

Abdou, S., & Savoy, J. (2008). Searching in Medline: Query expansion and manual indexing evaluation. *Information Processing and Management, 44*(2), 781-789.

Agichtein, E., & Gravano, L. (2003). Querying text databases for efficient information extraction. *Proceedings of the 19th IEEE International Conference on Data Engineering (ICDE)*, 113-124. New York.

Airola, A., Pyysalo, S., Björne, J., Pahikkala, T., Ginter, F., & Salakoski, T. (2008). All-paths graph kernel for protein-protein interaction extraction with evaluation of cross-corpus learning. *BMC Bioinformatics, 9*:S2.

Banko, M., & Etzioni, O. (2007). Strategies for lifelong knowledge extraction from the web. *Proceedings of the 4th International Conference on Knowledge Capture*, 95-102.

Blaschke, C., Andrade, M. A., Ouzounis, C., & Valencia, A. (1999). Automatic extraction of biological information from scientific text: Protein-Protein interactions. *Proceedings of the First International Conference on Intelligent Systems for Molecular Biology*, 60-67. New York.

Blaschke, C., Hirschman, L., Shatkay, H., & Valencia, A. (2010). Overview of the Ninth Annual Meeting of the BioLINK SIG at ISMB: Linking Literature. *Information and Knowledge for Biology, Linking Literature, Information, and Knowledge for Biology, 6004*: 1-7.

Califf, M. E., & Mooney, R. (2003). Bottom-up relational learning of pattern matching rules for information extraction. *Journal of Machine Learning Research, 2*, 177-210.

Carpineto, C., & Romano, G. (2010). Towards more effective techniques for automatic query expansion. *Research and Advanced Technology for Digital Libraries*, 851-852.

Cohen, W., & Singer, Y. (1996). Learning to query the web. *Proceedings of the AAAI Workshop on Internet-Based Information System.*

Feng, D., Burns, G., & Hovy, E. (2008). Adaptive information extraction for complex biomedical tasks. *BioNLP 2008: Current Trends in Biomedical Natural Language Processing*, 120–121. New York.

Frants, V.I., & Shapiro, J. (1991). Algorithm for automatic construction of query formulations in Boolean form. *Journal of the American Society for Information Science, 42*(1), 16-26.

He, M., Wang, Y., & Li, W. (2009). PPI finder: A mining tool for human protein-protein interactions. *PLoS One, 4*(2): e4554. Epub 2009 Feb 23.

Hu, X., & Shen, X. (2009). Mining biomedical literature for identification of potential virus/bacteria. *IEEE Intelligent System, 24*(6), 73-77. New York.

Kim, M. Y. (2008). Detection of protein subcellular localization based on a full syntactic parser and semantic information. *Fifth International Conference on Fuzzy Systems and Knowledge Discovery, 4*, 407-411.

Kudo, T., & Matsumoto, Y. (2000). Use of support vector learning for chunk identification. *Proceedings of CoNLL- 2000 and LLL-2000*, 142-144. Saarbruncken, Germany; New York.

Lafferty, J., McCallum, A., & Pereira, F. (2001). Conditional random fields: Probabilistic models for segmenting and labeling sequence data. *Proceedings of the ICML' 01.*

Manning, C., & Klein, D. (2003). Optimization, maxent models, and conditional estimation without magic. *Tutorial at HLT-NAACL 2003.* New York.

McKusick, V.A. (1998). Mendelian inheritance in man. *A catalog of human genes and genetic disorders,* 12th ed. Johns Hopkins University Press: Baltimore, MD.

Mitra, C.U., Singhal, A., & Buckely, C. (1998). Improving automatic query expansion. *Proceedings of the 21st Annual International ACM SIGIR Conference on Research and Development in Information Retrieval*, 206-214. New York.

Miyao, Y., Sagae, K., Saetre, R., Matsuzaki, T., & Tsujii, J. (2009). Evaluating contributions of natural language parsers to protein-protein interaction extraction. *Bioinformatics, 25*(3), 394-400.

Muller, H.W., Kenny E.E., & Sternberg, P.W. (2004). Textpresso: An ontology-based information retrieval and extraction system for biological literature, *PLoS Biol.* Nov,2(11), e309.

Poon, H., & Vanderwende, L. (2010). Joint inference for knowledge extraction from biomedical literature. *Proceedings of the North American Chapter of the Association for Computational Linguistics.* Stroudsburg, NJ: Human Language Technologies 2010 conference. Los Angeles, CA.

Pyysalo, S., Ginter, F., Heimonen, J., Björne, J., Boberg, J., Järvinen, J., & Salakoski, T. (2007). BioInfer: A corpus for information extraction in the biomedical domain. *BMC Bioinformatics, 8*(50).

Quinlan, J. R. (1993). *Programs for machine learning.* San Mateo, CA: Morgan Kaufmann.

Ray, S., & Craven, M. (2001). Representing sentence structure in hidden markov models for information extraction. *Proceedings of the 17th International Joint Conference on Artificial Intelligence.* Seattle, WA: Morgan Kaufmann.

Robertson, S. E., Zaragoza, H., & Taylor, M. (2004). Simple BM25 extension to multiple weighted fields. *Proceedings of the thirteenth ACM international conference on Information and knowledge management*, 42-49. New York.

Robertson, S.E., & Sparck, J.K. (1976). Relevance weighting of search terms. *Journal of the American Society for Information Science, 27*, 129-146.

Shatkay, H., & Feldman, R. (2003). Mining the biomedical literature in the genomic era: An overview. *Journal of Computational Biology, 10* (6), 821-855.

Xenarios, I., & Eisenberg, D. (2001). Protein interaction databases. *Current Opinion in Biotechnology, 12*(4), 334-339.

Zhou, G., & Zhang, M. (2007). Extracting relation information from text documents by exploring various types of knowledge. *Information Processing and Management, 43*(4), 969-982.

4

Interactive Information Retrieval: An Introduction

Pia Borlund*

Royal School of Library and Information Science
University of Copenhagen, Denmark
E-mail: sjc900@iva.ku.dk

ABSTRACT

The paper introduces the research area of interactive information retrieval (IIR) from a historical point of view. Further, the focus here is on evaluation, because much research in IR deals with IR evaluation methodology due to the core research interest in IR performance, system interaction and satisfaction with retrieved information. In order to position IIR evaluation, the Cranfield model and the series of tests that led to the Cranfield model are outlined. Three iconic user-oriented studies and projects that all have contributed to how IIR is perceived and understood today are presented: The MEDLARS test, the Book House fiction retrieval system, and the OKAPI project. On this basis the call for alternative IIR evaluation approaches motivated by the three revolutions (the cognitive, the relevance, and the interactive revolutions) put forward by Robertson & Hancock-Beaulieu (1992) is presented. As a response to this call the 'IIR evaluation model' by Borlund (e.g., 2003a) is introduced. The objective of the IIR evaluation model is to facilitate IIR evaluation as close as possible to actual information searching and IR processes, though still in a relatively controlled evaluation environment, in which the test instrument of a simulated work task situation plays a central part.

Keywords: interactive information retrieval, IIR, evaluation, human-computer information retrieval, HCIR, IIR evaluation model, user-oriented information retrieval, information retrieval, IR, history

1. INTRODUCTION

Interactive information retrieval (IIR), also known as human-computer information retrieval (HCIR) (Marchionini, 2006), concerns the study and evaluation of users' interaction with IR systems and their sat-

*Corresponding Author: Pia Borlund
Professor
Royal School of Library and Information Science
University of Copenhagen, Denmark
E-mail: sjc900@iva.ku.dk

isfaction with the retrieved information. 'Interactive' implies the involvement of human users in contrast to the notion of information retrieval (IR) only, which points to the system-oriented approach to IR signified with the Cranfield model (Cleverdon & Keen, 1966; Cleverdon, Mills & Keen, 1966). This approach is also referred to as TREC style evaluation (e.g., Belkin, 2008). Cool and Belkin (2011, p. 1) explain how the distinction between IR and IIR is found in the early history of computerized IR systems, especially in regard to their evaluation as carried out by different disciplinary groups. The history of IR evaluation can be traced back to 1953, and constitutes the origin of IR research as an empirical discipline with the series of tests that led to the Cranfield model (e.g., Ellis, 1996; Swanson, 1986). The different disciplinary groups mentioned by Cool and Belkin (2011, p. 1) are those of Computer Science and Library and Information Science addressing IR and IIR, respectively.

A user-oriented approach to IR has always existed in parallel to the system-oriented approach to IR evaluation, but the establishing of the IIR research area is relatively recent and takes its start in the early 1990s. Robertson and Hancock-Beaulieu (1992) explain the change and shift in focus that led to the establishing of the research area of IIR with the presentation of the three revolutions: the cognitive revolution, the relevance revolution, and the interactive revolution. At the same time Ingwersen (1992) published his book *Information Retrieval Interaction*, which points to the same tendency, namely a shift in focus from system-oriented IR towards IIR.

The objective of the present paper is to introduce the research area of IIR. We take an explicit focus on 'evaluation', because much research in IR deals with IR evaluation methodology due to the core research interest in IR performance, system interaction, and satisfaction with retrieved information (Järvelin, 2011, p. 113). Further, we approach the evaluation focus from a historical perspective. The idea is that we better understand IIR when we know where it comes from. For that reason we start out by introducing, in Section 2, the series of tests that led to the Cranfield evaluation model, which IIR is an alternative to. Hereafter Section 3 presents three iconic user-oriented studies and projects that all have had impact on how IIR is perceived and understood today: The MEDLARS test, the Book

House fiction retrieval system, and the OKAPI project. The three revolutions by Robertson and Hancock-Beaulieu (1992) are presented in Section 4, which stipulates the modern and contemporary requirements to IIR evaluation. Section 5 presents current IIR evaluation by introducing the IIR evaluation model that uses simulated work task situations as an instrument of testing. Section 6 holds concluding statements and presents further readings to the research area of IIR.

2. THE CRANFIELD MODEL

As stated in the Introduction section the evaluation tradition of IR systems can be traced back to 1953, when two separate tests were carried out in the USA and UK, respectively. These were the Uniterm-tests of the Armed Services Technical Information Agency (ASTIA, USA) (Gull, 1956), and Cranfield (UK) (Cleverdon, 1960; Thorne, 1955). The research teams were evaluating the performance of the UNITERM system (developed by Mortimer Taube) against more conventional approaches to subject indexing and retrieval. These two tests became the first in a series of pioneering performance tests of indexing systems that led to the development of the Cranfield evaluation model. Central to this development is Cyril Cleverdon, who was the librarian of the College of Aeronautics at Cranfield (later the Cranfield Institute of Technology and Cranfield University). Cleverdon followed closely the USA-based ASTIA-Uniterm test, and he headed the UK tests. The UK test was designed building on the experiences of the ASTIA-Uniterm test. The Cranfield model and the related series of tests have over the years been described and discussed by numerous scholars (e.g., Ellis, 1996; Robertson, 1981; Sanderson, 2010; Sharp, 1964; Sparck Jones, 1981b; Swanson, 1965) in addition to the original publications (Cleverdon, 1960; Cleverdon, 1962; Cleverdon & Keen, 1966; Cleverdon, Mills & Keen, 1966; Gull, 1956; Thorne, 1955).

The two initial tests, the ASTIA-Uniterm team and the Cranfield-Uniterm team, differed from each other with respect to the employed evaluation methodology. In the case of the ASTIA-Uniterm test, two groups of people were involved. One group consisted of the indexing staff of ASTIA, and the second group consisted of staff from Mortimer Taube's company, Documentation Inc. The basic idea of the experiment was to use the *same* document collection–The existing ASTIA collection of 15,000 documents. Then each group indexed the document collection employing their own indexing system. The ASTIA group indexed the documents employing the operational ASTIA alphabetical subject heading list, and the staff from Documentation Inc. used the Uniterm system. Both groups then searched the document collections by the same 98 requests, which had been submitted to ASTIA in the normal course of its activities, and then they compared the relevance of the retrieved documents. The relevance definition employed by the groups was that of relevance to the request. The ASTIA team retrieved 2,220 documents that they considered relevant. The staff of Documentation Inc. retrieved 1,560 documents that they thought relevant. The retrieved document overlap in common to the two groups was only 580 documents. They were able to agree that 1,390 documents were relevant to the 98 requests. Of the total number of 3,780 documents retrieved by the two groups 1,577 documents were considered relevant by one group but irrelevant by the other. The two groups were unable to come to an agreement over which documents were relevant to which requests. Further, no decision procedure was made to help resolve their differences. The breakdown of the tests by the disagreements of the groups on the definition of relevance is to be considered the 'birth' of the relevance discussion to IR. Unfortunately, the relevance discussion within the groups was not given full-hearted attention, probably due to the groups' possible interest in the performance of each of their indexing systems. Ellis (1996, p. 2) comments on this by saying:

> It is unfortunate that the form of the dispute between the two groups is overshadowed by the fact that neither of the two parties could be said to be entirely disinterested in the outcome of the tests. Obviously, the ASTIA indexers would not look kindly on a system such as Uniterm which effectively transforms the, arguably, intellectual task of assigning subject headings to a document into the entirely clerical procedure of extracting keywords from a document's title or abstract. On the other hand, the staff of

Documentation Incorporated were unlikely to favour any result which did not demonstrate the superiority of their product, particularly if the potential for prestigious and lucrative military contracts might depend on that result.

Later that year the Cranfield-Uniterm test was carried out in the UK (Cleverdon, 1960; Thorne, 1955). Basically, the Cranfield-Uniterm experiment had the same objective as that of the ASTIA-Uniterm test, that is, to compare the performance of the Uniterm system against a more conventional indexing system. However, the Cranfield team employed a different evaluation methodology in their experiment. Instead of using the actual document collection, a limited collection of 200 documents on the subject of aeronautics was set up, i.e. the dawn of the 'test collection' concept. From this collection a selection of 'source' documents was chosen. Based on the source documents 40 artificial requests were generated, to which the individual source documents represented the answers. The 40 requests were searched on the sub-collection of the 200 documents. Relevance was defined as the success in retrieving the source documents from which the corresponding requests were generated. In this way the Cranfield team avoided a relevance discussion like the one that ruined the ASTIA-Uniterm test. The main criticisms of the methodology was in regard to the employment of source documents. Ellis (1996, p. 3) summarises the criticisms as follows:

1. Only a single figure performance value was obtained (based on retrieval of the source documents); no corresponding figures were obtained for the retrieval of non-source documents, whether those might be considered 'relevant' or 'irrelevant'.

2. A-term based system might be said to be favoured over a concept-based system if the derivation of the artificial requests was influenced by the terms used in the source documents.

The Cranfield-Uniterm test functioned as a pilot experiment to the succeeding Cranfield I and Cranfield II tests. The Cranfield I test (Cleverdon, 1962) which was concerned with the comparative performance of four different indexing systems and made use of the principle of source documents, was carried out on a much larger scale than the initial Cranfield-Uniterm test (size of collection: 18,000 documents; number of requests: 1,200). In addition to the Cranfield-Uniterm test, the searches which failed to retrieve the source documents were subsequently analysed, in order to locate the failure of the retrieval: the request, the searching, the indexing, or the system.

The Cranfield I test was met with extensive criticism due to the dual role of the employment of source documents. Further, Swanson (1965, p. 6) points out that in an operational situation a source document generally does not exist, and that the relationship between the source document and the query was too close. Sharp (1964) recommends that "the source-document principle should be dropped and future tests carried out on the basis of taking into account *all* relevant documents retrieved" (Sharp, 1964, p. 174).[1]

The principle of source documents was abandoned in the Cranfield II test. The Cranfield II test (Cleverdon & Keen, 1966; Cleverdon, Mills & Keen, 1966), was a test of 33 different types of indexing languages, which varied in terminologies and structures. The test was based on a document collection consisting of 1,400 documents and 211 generated requests. Prior to the search, relevance of the documents to the search requests was determined. This was done in a two-step procedure. First, students of aeronautics searched the document collection and identified the relevant documents. Hereafter the relevant documents were sent to the generators of the given requests for proofing. The retrieval performance was defined as the retrieval of documents which had previously been identified as relevant to the request and measured according to the ratios of recall and precision.[2]

The described series of tests are worthy of consideration for two reasons: partly because the difficulties that were experienced in carrying them out influenced the methodology of subsequent tests, and partly because the features of these tests are embodied in today's main IR evaluation model, the Cranfield model. The Cran-

field model derives directly from Cranfield II and is based on the principle of test collections: that is, a collection of documents; a collection of queries; and a collection of relevance assessments. The Cranfield model includes also the measurement of recall and precision ratios.

The Cranfield model constitutes the empirical research tradition on the development and testing of IR systems employed by the system-oriented approach to IR. The emphasis in this research tradition is on controlled laboratory tests. The objective of the employment of the Cranfield model is to keep all variables controlled and to obtain results which can state conclusions about retrieval systems in general. However, from an IIR point of view the Cranfield model suffers from limitations due to its restricted assumptions on the cognitive and behavioural features of the environment in which interaction with IR systems takes place. But with all respect it should be noted that Cleverdon and his colleagues were not blind to the user-oriented side of IR, which is seen in their comment on how the ideal evaluation of IR systems would be to use "actual questions with a relevance assessment made at the time by the questioner from complete texts" (Cleverdon, Mills & Keen, 1966, p. 15). However, at that time this was not possible. The MEDLARS test by Lancaster (1969), presented in Section 3.1, is an illustrative example of what was possible, but also of how information searching of scientific information took place in the mid-1960s.

3. USER-ORIENTED IR

This section introduces three iconic user-oriented IR studies and projects which reflect the different approaches to user-oriented IR that have formed IIR evaluation as of today: the MEDLARS test, the Book

---

[1] Sharp's recommendation is based on a review of the Cranfield-Western Reserve University test (Aitchison & Cleverdon, 1963) which was carried out at the same time as the Cranfield I test, employing the same evaluation methodology. This test is known also as Cranfield I½.

[2] Recall is the ratio of relevant documents retrieved over the total number of relevant document in the collection. Precision is the ratio of relevant documents retrieved over the total number of documents retrieved (Aitchison & Cleverdon, 1963, p. XII). Precision was originally called relevance, but was renamed from Cranfield II in order to avoid confusion with the general concept of relevance (Cleverdon, Mills & Keen, 1966, pp. 9-18).

House system, and the Okapi project. The MEDLARS test is interesting in that it is contemporary to that of Cranfield II, and as Cool and Belkin (2011, p. 10) put it the test should be well remembered for its attention to the human dimensions of failure analysis in IR systems. The MEDLARS test (Lancaster, 1969) can be viewed as top-down evaluation of an existing system in contrast to the Book House project, which took a bottom-up approach in the development of the Book House fiction retrieval system via a series of user studies, e.g., of user fiction requests (Pejtersen, 1980; Pejtersen & Austin, 1983; 1984), picture associations (Pejtersen, 1991), and search strategies for fiction literature (Pejtersen, 1992; Rasmussen, Pejtersen & Goodstein, 1994). With the introduction of online public access catalogues (OPACs) in the mid-1970s (in effect, an end-user IR system)—this type of research and system development came into focus. OPACS are in reality the first type of end-user IIR systems. The Book House project was about the development of a coherent end-user supporting OPAC. In addition, to be fully comprehensive in its empirical foundation of the system, the Book House system is a relevant innovation because it was ahead of its time and shows how icon-based fiction retrieval and the information needs of ordinary users were addressed. Similar to the Book House research the foci of the Okapi project were concerned with that of OPACs and their use. The research foci of Okapi can at a general level, in line with that of the Book house system, be categorised into three areas: IR functionality, navigation, and search strategy implementation; interface issues; and information searching behaviour and use. But more importantly Okapi is a showcase example of how system-oriented and user-oriented IR systems evaluations complement each other with the Okapi team's involvement in TREC from the very beginning. No doubt the work and experiences from the Okapi research have contributed to the recognition of the three revolutions presented in Section 4.

3.1 The MEDLARS Test

The present MEDLARS review is a description of the evaluation carried out and reported on by Lancaster (1969).[3] The MEDLARS system (now known as Medline[4] and PubMed[5]) has been evaluated by others beside Lancaster (1969), for instance by Salton (1972) in his comparison of the conventional indexing of MEDLARS and automatic indexing by the SMART system.[6] The reader should note that MEDLARS was not an end-user system at the time of testing; instead information search specialists searched on behalf of the user. At this time a question for information was put in writing and mailed to the National Library of Medicine and the questioner would wait for a reply (Robertson & Hancock-Beaulieu, 1992, p. 460). Lancaster (1969, p. 119) describes MEDLARS as "a multi-purpose system, a prime purpose being the production of *Index Medicus* and other recurring bibliographies." The aim of Lancaster's MEDLARS test was to evaluate the existing system and to find out ways in which the performance of the system could be improved.

The planning of the MEDLARS evaluation began in December 1965 and was carried out during 1966 and 1967. Lancaster (1969, p. 120) outlines the principal objectives of the evaluation as: 1) to study the demanded types of search requirements of MEDLARS users; 2) to determine how effectively and efficiently the present MEDLARS service meets these requirements; 3) to recognise factors adversely affecting performance; and 4) to disclose ways in which the requirements of MEDLARS users may be satisfied more efficiently and/or economically.

Lancaster (1969, p. 120) further explains how the users were to relate the prime search requirements to the following factors:

1. The *coverage* of MEDLARS (i.e., the proportion of the useful literature on a particular topic that is indexed into the system, within the time limits imposed).

---

[3] MEDLARS is an acronym for MEDical Literature Analysis and Retrieval System.
[4] Medline URL: http://medline.cos.com/
[5] PubMed URL: http://www.ncbi.nlm.nih.gov/pubmed/
[6] SMART is an acronym for System for the Mechanical Analysis and Retrieval of Text.

2. Its *recall* power (i.e., its ability to retrieve "relevant" documents, which within the context of this evaluation means documents of value in relation to an information need that prompted a request to MEDLARS).

3. Its *precision* power (i.e., its ability to hold back "non-relevant" documents).

4. The *response time* of the system (i.e., the time elapsing between receipt of a request at a MEDLARS centre and delivery to the user of a printed bibliography).

5. The *format* in which search results are presented.

6. The amount of *effort* the user must personally expend in order to achieve a satisfactory response from the system.

The document collection used was the one currently available on the MEDLARS service at the time, which according to Robertson (1981, p. 20) had the size of approximately 700,000 items. 302 real information requests were used to search the database, and the users requesting the information made the relevance assessments. A recall base was generated based on a number of documents judged relevant by the users in response to their own requests, but found by means outside MEDLARS. The sources for these documents were (a) those already known to the user, and (b) documents found by MEDLARS staff through sources other than MEDLARS or *Index Medicus*. Subsequently, each user was asked to assess relevance of a sample of the output from the MEDLARS search, together with selected documents from other sources (Robertson, 1981, p. 20). The relevance assessments were carried out with reference to three categories (degrees) of relevance: major, minor, or no value. In addition, the users explained their relevance judgements by indicating why particular items were of major, minor, or no value to their information need (e.g., see Martyn & Lancaster, 1981, p. 165 for an example of the relevance questionnaire used in the MEDLARS test). Precision and relative recall ratios were calculated and compared to the degree of exhaustivity[7] and specificity[8] of the requests as expressed by use of the controlled entry vocabulary. Analysis of failures was carried out, and a classification of reasons for failure was devised (Lancaster, 1969, p. 125, Table 5).

Variables were built into the test. The primary variable concerned the level of interaction between the user and the system. The interaction could take place at three different levels, which refers to, i.e., the originality or level of influence on the expression of the user's information request (Lancaster, 1969, p. 120). At the first level the interaction takes place as a *personal interaction* that is, the user makes a visit to a MEDLARS centre and negotiates his requirements directly with an information search specialist. The second level of interaction is identified as *local interaction*, which means that the user's information request comes by mail to the centre, but is submitted by a librarian or information specialist on behalf of the requester. The third interaction level concerns *no local interaction*, which implies that no interference by a librarian or information specialist has taken place in the process of interpreting or translating the request into the controlled vocabulary used by MEDLARS. In other words, the request comes directly by mail from the requester. The different levels of interaction enabled a comparison of the results obtained. The main product of the test was a detailed analysis of the reasons for failure. The result is interesting, because "it appears that the best request statements (i.e., those that most closely reflect the actual area of information need) are those written down by the requester in his own natural-language narrative terms" (Lancaster, 1969, p. 138). For the user-oriented approach to IR systems evaluation this result is seen as a strong piece of evidence and motivation for exactly this type of evaluation. That only the user who owns the information need can represent and assess that information need hereby gives insight into how well the system works under real-life operational conditions in a given situation and context at the time the information is requested.

The results, the focus, and the approach of the MED-

---

[7] Exhaustivity and specificity are well-established concepts within indexing. Exhaustivity refers to the comprehensiveness of the indexing in question, which consequently affects retrieval results.

[8] Specificity refers to the accuracy of the indexing. Specificity of indexing makes for high precision and low recall.

LARS test helped contemporary system-driven researchers to understand problems of IR as well as to comprehend how to design future systems and tests. In the following quotation, Sparck Jones (1981a, p. 230) comments on the effect of Lancaster's test by describing the situation prior to the MEDLARS test:

> It was thus not at all obvious how systems should be designed to perform well, modulo a preference for recall or precision, in particular environments, especially outside established frameworks like those represented by the Medlars system, or for situations and needs clearly resembling those of existing systems.

Robertson (1981, pp. 20-21) describes how Cranfield II and MEDLARS are two of the classical tests, with Cranfield II being a highly controlled and artificial experiment, and MEDLARS being an investigation of an operational system, as far as possible under realistic conditions. They both play a significant part in creating the archetypes of tests, by each representing the opposite poles of the system-and user-oriented spectrum.

3.2. The Book House Fiction Retrieval System

The Book House system is a pictogram and icon based system designed for the retrieval of fiction literature. The development of the Book House system started in the 1970s and was headed by Annelise Mark Pejtersen. The initial development of the Book House system, including the work on the Book Automat, started while Pejtersen was employed at the Royal School of Librarianship, Denmark (now the Royal School of Library and Information Science). Later the research and development project of the Book House system followed her to Risø National Laboratory (near Roskilde, Denmark). Pejtersen (1992) describes the Book House system as "an interactive, multimedia, online public access catalogue [OPAC] designed to support casual novice users in information retrieval. It uses icons, text and animation in the display interface in order to enhance the utility of the system" (Pejtersen, 1992, p. 359). Further, the main characteristic of the system is its metaphoric use of the familiar (Danish) public library of which the user is invited into a virtual space version. The Book House metaphor is chosen in support of the user's memory and navigation by locat-

ing information about the functionality and content of the system in a coherent and familiar spatial representation (Rasmussen, Pejtersen & Goodstein, 1994, p. 290). In other words, the Book House system presents a spatial metaphor built around a library that houses fiction (Pejtersen, 1989, p. 40), and is not to resemble a bookshop, as indicated by Wilson (2011, pp. 145-146).

The pictorial interface of the Book House system deserves a brief description for the sake of the reader's visualisation and imagination of it. The interface of the Book House system, which the user meets first, is a picture of a house built of books with people entering it via the open front doors. The user accesses the Book House system by clicking with the computer mouse at the open front doors, and enters the hall of the house. The Book House consists of several rooms. Basically, the user 'walks' through the rooms with different arrangements of books and people (Rasmussen, Pejtersen & Goodstein, 1994, p. 289). The first room of the Book House is the hall. Here the user can choose between different library book collections represented by rooms (in fact different databases). These are the children's collection; the adults' collection; or a merged version of the previous two collections known as the 'family collection.' The type of collection is illustrated with the people in front of the entrances of the collection rooms, and put in writing on top of the entrances. In front of the children's collection children are pictured; similarly adults are positioned in front of the adults' collection; and together a child and a grown-up person are ready to enter the family collection. No matter what collection the user chooses the collection rooms look the same, with the only differences being the people inhabiting them and the size of the furniture. If the children's collection has been selected the user meets only children in that room and so on. Having chosen any of the three collection rooms, the next room contains a choice of search strategies. The choice of search strategy takes the user one step deeper into the Book House. To maintain an overview of where the user is, a horizontal breadcrumb trail is displayed at the top of the screen that shows all the steps taken, and the user can return to any previous step of the trail by clicking that icon.

The development of the Book House system and the evaluation of the concepts underlying the design, as well as the means chosen for implementation, have involved a considerable amount of empirical studies. Initially, a classification system for fiction literature was developed based on an empirical field study of users' information requests. The analysis of the requests revealed that basically fiction requests can be categorised into five so-called 'dimensions.' These are: 1) the subject-matter of the book (e.g., a mystery novel); 2) the frame of the book with reference to time and place (e.g., a historical novel); 3) the author's intention or attitude (e.g., a humorous book); 4) the accessibility of the book (e.g., an easy read book, or a book with big letters); and 5) 'other request formulations' (e.g., something like Emily Brontë) (Pejtersen, 1980, pp. 148-149). This part of the research is reported in, e.g., Pejtersen (1980) and Pejtersen and Austin (1983; 1984).

The research continued with the construction of a thesaurus based on users' word associations relying on the fiction classification system (Pejtersen, Olsen & Zunde, 1987). This further led to research into a picture association thesaurus for implementation into the Book House system (Pejtersen, 1991). Two tests were carried out before an actual implementation of the picture association thesaurus. Pejtersen (1991, p. 119) describes how the focus on the first test was primarily "to determine whether it was feasible for designers to associate pictures from keywords chosen from different dimensions of the classification scheme used in the database of the Book House and draw small pictures to represents these words". The second test was concerned with "whether a sufficient consensus could be achieved between designers' conception of associative relationships between pictures and keywords and that of different groups of potential users of the system" (Pejtersen, 1991, p. 119). With the picture association thesaurus implemented into the Book House the usability and effectiveness were tested in a real work context.

Pejtersen (1992, p. 362) further explains how it was possible, based on an interaction study of user-librarian negotiations, to verify five different search strategies. Of these five strategies four were used to design the navigation and the retrieval functionality of the Book House system. Briefly, the strategies are: 1) *bibliographic strategy*, when searching for a known item; 2) *analytical strategy*, the search for book attributes matching users' need; 3) *analogy strategy*, an associa-

tive type of search based on analogies between known books and unread books building on best-match algorithms; 4) *browsing strategy*, intuitive searching (browsing) of book shelves looking at book contents and book cover pictures for recognition of something of interest; and 5) *empirical strategy*, which is based on feedback and check routines, that is, the users' acceptance and rejection of documents proposed by the system based on a comparison match of books and the user's indication of his or her information need (Pejtersen, 1992, p. 362; Rasmussen, Pejtersen & Goodstein, 1994, pp. 275-76). It is the fifth strategy, the *empirical strategy*, which is not implemented into the Book House. The *empirical strategy* is commonly known and implemented in other systems as relevance feedback mechanisms. As such the research and development of the Book House, based on users' IR and searching behaviour, empirically verifies relevance feedback as an end-user search strategy.

The four implemented search strategies are visualised and illustrated in the room of the Book House where the user chooses the search strategy. The strategies are depicted as metaphors with a functional analogy to users' activities in a library. Four persons are viewed using the library and the strategies of browsing (that is, browsing pictures or browsing book descriptions), analogy search, and the analytical type of search. The bibliographic strategy is available as a sub-search strategy of the analytical strategy.

The Book House system itself was evaluated in an operational setting of the public library of Hjortespring in Denmark over a six-month period in 1988. The test participants were the actual users of the public library, children as well as adults, ranging from the age of seven to 70, and resulting in 2850 search logs and 75 complete user observations (e.g., Goodstein & Pejtersen, 1989, p. 168).

As a development and research project the Book House system is unique. Every single test involved operational conditions and test participants, and even the so-called laboratory tests of the implemented search strategies made use of test participants (librarians were invited to the laboratory). Briefly summarised, the Book House research project counts the following essential contributions: the development of a classification system for fiction literature; the development and construction of a picture association thesaurus; the verification of library end-user search strategies as well as the implementation of these strategies; and the development of a transparent, analogy, and icon based interface (at a time when the use of icons was not an interface tradition). The interface is self-explanatory through the visualisation of the public library environment, including the presentation of library activities, which the users can recognise without problems. The Book House system is also to be seen as a revolutionary new type of OPAC. The problem with the traditional OPACs was that they merely functioned as an electronic version of the traditional card catalogue; secondly, most OPACs reflected primarily the librarians' use and need for a work tool, not the users' need for a tool to direct them to the information objects. In these respects the Book House system made a difference as it was based on observations and field studies of end-users' use of libraries. It provided the users with an OPAC, made for the users, presented in the frame and context of the familiar public library environment. Another important contribution by the Book House development is the gained experience on *cognitive domain analyses*. These experiences have been assembled together in a very extensive and comprehensive framework for work (task) centred evaluation and design (e.g., Pejtersen & Fidel, 1998; Pejtersen & Rasmussen, 1998; Rasmussen, Pejtersen & Goodstein, 1994). The framework model is due to its illustrative representation of the evaluation boundary levels, popularly referred to as the 'onion-model.' The evaluation framework is recently discussed in detail in the very recommendable book by Fidel (2012).

3.3. The OKAPI Project

Okapi is the name of a series of generations of test retrieval systems.[9] Okapi can be viewed as a test bed including an experimental test system (or versions of systems), and can as such be considered the user-oriented IR approach's answer to Salton's SMART project within the system-oriented IR evaluation approach (e.g., Salton, 1981). The foci of the system tests and the

different installations of the systems are reported in a number of publications (e.g., Beaulieu & Jones, 1998; Beaulieu, Robertson & Rasmussen, 1996; Robertson & Hancock-Beaulieu, 1992; Robertson, 1997a; Walker & De Vere, 1990; Walker, 1989). Even an entire issue of the *Journal of Documentation* (Robertson, 1997b) has had the theme of Okapi and IR research. The Okapi systems have had homes at various locations. From 1982-1989 Okapi was based at the Polytechnic of Central London (now the University of Westminster). From 1989 Okapi has been located at City University, London.

Okapi is a test search system designed for end-users who are not expert searchers. Okapi has throughout its history been used as the basis for real services to groups of users. The initial Okapi investigations started out with Okapi functioning as an OPAC that was made available in a number of British libraries to the actual users of those libraries. Since then, various Okapi systems have been made available in similar ways to groups of researchers over a network with a database of scientific abstracts (Robertson, 1997a, p. 5). The operational setup of the Okapi was made specifically with the purpose to create an environment in which ideas could be subject to user trials. The operational setup of the Okapi investigations allowed for end-users to be observed in a large variety of ways, from straight transaction logs to questionnaires, interviews, and direct observation (Robertson, 1997a, p. 5). This means that the Okapi team received additional qualitative-based information on the functionality and performance of, e.g., relevance feedback. Robertson (1997a, p. 5) explains how the quality of user-oriented Okapi investigations supply evidence concerning relevance feedback, not just on its retrieval effectiveness in the usual sense, but also on the ways in which users actually make use of it, and how useful they find it. The Okapi project has contributed to the understanding that users can be given access to sophisticated IR and feedback techniques and that users are capable of using these techniques effectively. At the same time the research shows that there are difficulties involved in

---

[9] Okapi is an acronym for Online Keyword Access to Public Information.

providing these techniques, and that users have to be given guidance in the use of these techniques, as pointed out by Robertson (1997a, p. 6).

Robertson (1997a, pp. 3-4) elegantly describes the typical Okapi system and its underlying probabilistic-based retrieval and relevance feedback mechanisms:

> What the user sees first is an invitation to enter a query in free-text form. This free-text query is then parsed into (generally) a list of single word-stems; each stem is given a weight based on its collection frequency. The system then produces a ranked list of documents according to a best-match function based on the term weights, and shows the user titles of the top few items in the list. The user can scroll the list and select any title for viewing of the full record. Having seen the full record, he or she is asked to make relevance judgement ("Is this the kind of thing you want?") in a yes/no term. Once the user has marked a few items as relevant, he or she has the opportunity to perform relevance feedback search ("More like the ones you have chosen?"). For this purpose, the system extracts terms from the chosen documents and makes up a new query from these terms. This is normally referred to as query expansion, although the new query may not necessarily contain all the original terms entered by the user. The new query is run and produces a ranked list in the usual fashion, and the process can iterate.

The quotation by Robertson regarding a typical Okapi system session reveals the multi-layer nature of the system architecture and use of the system, which is in accordance with the broad system definition in the present user-oriented IR evaluation approach. The broad definition is further reflected in the investigative and experimental division of the focus of Okapi tests on: IR system techniques, information searching behaviour, and interface issues. The inclusion of research on interface issues emphasizes the point of difference between the two main approaches to IR systems evaluation made by Ingwersen (1992, p. 87)

about the question as to where IR systems end and the automatic interface intermediary begins. The interface research of Okapi concerns interaction issues such as the user's perception of system functions in relation to information searching tasks (e.g., Beaulieu, 1997; Beaulieu & Jones, 1998). Via Okapi, research attention is given to the issue of the 'cognitive load' that IR systems put on the users. Cognitive load refers to the intellectual effort required from the user in order to work the system. As such the research areas of IR and human computer interaction (HCI), especially with the introduction of OPACs and IIR systems, become overlapping. Beaulieu and Jones (1998, pp. 246-247) explain that cognitive load "involves not only the requirement to understand conceptual elements of the system [...] but to make meaningful decisions based on that understanding. When searchers have to make decisions without adequate understanding, their efforts can be counter-productive for overall system effectiveness." This they illustrate with an example of how users who do not realize how query expansion operates may avoid the trouble of making relevance judgements if they can, and lose one important advantage of probabilistic retrieval. So the ideal interface for an IIR system is one that meets the (inexperienced) end-user as transparent and self-explanatory so that no extra cognitive burden is put on the user–like the Book House system.

The Okapi project further serves as a very good example of how the two main approaches to IR systems evaluation complement each other. In that, Okapi has taken part in several TREC[10] tracks over the years, e.g., ad hoc, routing, interactive, filtering, and web tracks. TREC is an annual research workshop and provides for large-scale test collections and methodologies, and builds on the Cranfield model (Voorhees & Harman, 2005a). TREC is hosted by the U.S. Government's National Institute of Standards and Technology (NIST). According to Robertson, Walker, and Beaulieu (1997, p. 20) the Okapi team uses TREC to improve some of the automatic techniques used in Okapi, specially the term weighting function and the

---

[10] TREC is an acronym for Text REtrieval Conference. For more information about TREC, the reader is directed to the book *TREC: Experiments and Evaluation in Information Retrieval* by Voorhees and Harman (2005b), as well as to the following URL: http://trec.nist.gov/.

algorithms for term selection for query expansion. Prior to TREC, the Okapi team had worked only with operational systems or with small-scale partially controlled experiments with real collections (Robertson, Walker & Beaulieu, 1997, p. 23). As such TREC is a change of test culture and environment to the Okapi test tradition. The Okapi team maintains an interest in real users and information needs because to them the most critical and most difficult areas of IR system design are in the area of interaction and user interfaces (Robertson, Walker & Beaulieu, 1997, p. 32). The Okapi team sees their participation in the TREC experiments as complementary to the real user studies (Robertson, 1997a, p. 6). Further, Okapi's participation in TREC illustrates how systems, or elements of systems, at some point may be tested according to system-oriented principles, as well as how the interactive functionality of parts or more 'finished' and complete IIR systems are best evaluated and validated by involvement of end-users and potentially dynamic information needs. Okapi's participation in TREC also shows that the boundaries between the two evaluation approaches are not clear-cut.

The Okapi project represents a strong and illustrative case of user-oriented IR systems evaluations (e.g., Beaulieu & Jones, 1998; Beaulieu, Robertson & Rasmussen, 1996; Robertson & Hancock-Beaulieu, 1992; Robertson, 1997a; Walker & De Vere, 1990; Walker, 1989). Further, Okapi demonstrates in relation to TREC the complementary nature of the two main approaches to IR systems evaluation. In addition, Okapi and the series of tests in which probability-based IR techniques such as relevance feedback have been tested emphasise the need for alternative approaches to evaluation of IIR techniques and search facilities, which we focus on in the following section with the presentation of the three revolutions. Though the present introduction of Okapi is made from a historical viewpoint it is appropriate to point out that Okapi is still active and maintained. Okapi has been extended to handle XML documents and element retrieval for INEX[11] (Lu, Robertson & MacFarlane, 2006; Lu,

Robertson & MacFarlane, 2007; Robertson, Lu & MacFarlane, 2006). The Okapi-Pack, which is a complete implementation of the Okapi system, is available from the Centre For Interactive Systems Research (CISR) at City University for a nominal fee when used for research purposes only (URL: http://www.soi.city.ac.uk/~andym/OKAPI-PACK/).

4. THE THREE REVOLUTIONS

In 1992 Robertson and Hancock-Beaulieu (1992) wrote a paper on the current status of the evaluation of IR systems. The paper was a follow-up of Robertson's chapter in the book *Information Retrieval Experiment*, edited by Sparck Jones (1981c) and dedicated to Cyril Cleverdon. For decades this book remained the one substantial book on the evaluation of IR systems. But with their follow-up paper Robertson and Hancock-Beaulieu present a call for alternative approaches to IR systems evaluation: that is, alternative with respect to the Cranfield model. They explain and illustrate the need for alternative approaches to IR systems evaluation with what they refer to as: the *cognitive revolution*; the *relevance revolution*; and the *interactive revolution*.

The *cognitive revolution* concerns the nature of an information need and its formation process. As a result of the *cognitive revolution* the information need is viewed as a reflection of an anomalous state of knowledge (ASK) (Belkin, 1980; Belkin, Oddy & Brooks, 1982) on the part of the requester. This refers to how an information need is understood and acknowledged as a dynamic and individual concept. This means that an information need, from the user's perspective, is a personal and individual perception of a given information requirement (Belkin et al., 1993), and that an information need for the same user can change over time (e.g., Ellis, 1989; Kuhlthau, 1993; Spink, Greisdorf & Bateman, 1998).

The *relevance revolution* points to the increasing acceptance that a stated request put to an IIR system is not the same as an information need, and therefore

---

[11] INEX is an acronym for INitiative for the Evaluation of XML retrieval. For more information about INEX the reader is directed to: URL: http://inex.is.informatik.uni-duisburg.de/

relevance should be judged in relation to the need rather than the request. In addition, there is a growing recognition of the multidimensional *and* dynamic nature of the concept of relevance (e.g., Borlund, 2003b; Schamber, Eisenberg & Nilan, 1990). The multidimensional nature of relevance, the fact that relevance is not an absolute quality, is empirically documented, for instance, by how relevance can be divided into classes and types of relevance, and by how the concept is applied with reference to various criteria and degrees and at different levels. A compiling list by Schamber (1994) of 80 relevance criteria that influence users' relevance judgements imply that the concept of relevance consists of many facets and therefore should not be treated as a binary variable (relevant/not relevant). The dynamic nature of relevance is demonstrated by, e.g., Bruce (1994), and Spink and colleagues (Spink, Greisdorf & Bateman, 1998) who found that users' relevance criteria may change over the course of session time.

The third and final revolution, the *interactive revolution*, points to the fact that IR systems have become interactive and consequently cannot be evaluated without including the interactive seeking and retrieval processes. IIR systems are defined as systems where the user dynamically conducts searching tasks and correspondingly reacts to system responses over session time. Thus, the foci of IIR system evaluation may include all the user's activities of interaction with the retrieval and feedback mechanisms as well as the retrieval outcome itself.

These three revolutions point to requirements that are not fulfilled by the system-driven IR evaluation approach based on the Cranfield model. The Cranfield model does not deal with dynamic information needs but treats information needs as a static concept entirely reflected by the user request and search statement. This implies the assumption that learning and modifications by users are confined to the search statement alone. Furthermore, this model has a strong tradition for using only binary, topical relevance, ignoring the fact that relevance is a multidimensional and dynamic concept (Borlund, 2003b). The conclusion is that the batch-driven mode of the Cranfield model is not suitable for the evaluation of IIR systems which, if carried out as realistically as possible, requires human interac-

tion, potentially dynamic information need interpretations, and the assignment of multidimensional *and* dynamic relevance. In essence this is about, on the one hand, control over experimental variables, observability, and repeatability, and on the other hand, realism (Robertson & Hancock-Beaulieu, 1992, p. 460). The three revolutions summarise the fundamental causes that have led to the current demand for alternative approaches to the evaluation of IIR systems.

5. IIR EVALUATION AS OF TODAY

The call for IIR evaluation approaches as presented by Robertson and Hancock-Beaulieu (1992) is supported by numerous scholars (e.g., Belkin, 2008; Ellis, 1996; Harter, 1996; Järvelin, 2011; Saracevic, 1995). Belkin (2008, p. 52) addresses in his 2008 ECIR Keynote the general need for more user-oriented IR research and in particular the need for alternative evaluation approaches to the Cranfield model. Belkin explicitly highlights *the IIR evaluation model* by Borlund (e.g., Borlund, 2003a), which employs simulated work task situations as the central instrument for testing, as such an attempt.

5.1 The IIR Evaluation Model

The IIR evaluation model meets the requirements of the three revolutions put forward by Robertson and Hancock-Beaulieu (1992) in that the model builds on three basic components: (1) the involvement of potential users as test participants; (2) the application of dynamic and individual information needs (real, and simulated information needs); and (3) the employment of multidimensional and dynamic relevance judgements. The cognitive revolution concerning the individual and dynamic nature of information needs is taken into account by allowing test participants to work with personal and individual information need interpretations of both their own and simulated information needs. The test participants' need interpretations are allowed to develop and mature over session time for the same test participant, a dynamic nature which is proved to be strongly connected to the process of assessing relevance (Borlund & Ingwersen, 1997). The relevance revolution is taken into account by having relevance judged in relation to the need– and in addition, in relation to the underlying situation of the need. Furthermore, the concept of relevance is in a way appropriate to its dynamic and multidimensional nature by being assessed interactively in a non-binary way (e.g., Borlund 2003b). The interactive revolution is incorporated into the IIR evaluation model by having the test participants work with personal information need interpretations which they try to satisfy through information searching and retrieval processes.

The aim of the IIR evaluation model is to facilitate IIR evaluation as close as possible to actual information searching and IR processes, though still in a relatively controlled evaluation environment. The IIR evaluation model builds on the concept of a stable simulated work task situation in order to frame the simulated information need situation, but allowing for its modification and development (by learning processes) during searching and retrieval. Both the information need and the derived request (or 'topic') are thus allowed to shift focus during the process. At the same time, the simulated work task situation acts as the point of reference against which situational relevance is measured. Situational relevance is understood as an assessment which points to the relationship between an information object presented to the user and the cognitive situation underlying the user's information need. As a generic concept, it may refer to the usefulness, usability, or utility of such objects in relation to the fulfilment of goals, interests, work tasks, or problematic situations intrinsic to the user. This understanding is in line with the interpretation proposed by Schamber, Eisenberg, and Nilan (1990). Basically, the IIR evaluation model consists of three parts:

Part 1. A set of components which aims at ensuring a functional, valid, and realistic setting for the evaluation of IIR systems;

Part 2. Empirically based recommendations for the application of the concept of a simulated work task situation; *and*

Part 3. Alternative performance measures capable of managing non-binary based relevance assessments.[12]

Part 1 and 2 concern the collection of data, whereas Part 3 concerns data analysis. As such the IIR evaluation model is comparable to the Cranfield model's two main parts: the principle of test collections and the employment of recall and precision. The first part of the model deals with the experimental setting. This part of the model is identical to the traditional user-oriented approach in that it involves potential users as test participants, applies the test participants' individual and potentially dynamic information need interpretations, and supports assignment of multidimensional relevance assessments (that is, relevance assessment according to various types of relevance, several degrees of relevance, and multiple relevance criteria) and dynamic relevance assessments (allowing that the users' perception of relevance can change over time) (Borlund, 2003b). The IIR evaluation model differs from the traditional user-oriented approach with the introduction of simulated work task situations as a tool for the creation of simulated, but realistic, information need interpretations. Hence, Part 2 outlines recommendations for how to create and use simulated work task situations, presented in detail in Section 5.1.1. No doubt the major challenge is the design of realistic and applicable simulated work task situations.

The set of components combined with the second part of the model, recommendations for the application of simulated work task situations, provides an experimental setting[13] that enables the facilitation of evaluation of IIR systems as realistically as possible with reference to actual information seeking and retrieval processes, though still in a relatively controlled evaluation environment. The third and final part of the model is a call for alternative performance measures that are capable of managing non-binary based relevance assessments, as a result of the application of the Parts 1 and 2 of the model. The dominating

---

[12] With respect to the performance measures of recall and precision traditionally employed.

[13] An experimental setting, in this context, necessarily includes a database of information objects as well as the system(s) under investigation. However, these components are not explicitly dealt with here. It is assumed that the system to be tested, other technical facilities, and the facilities of where to carry out the experiment are already arranged for.

use of the ratios of recall and precision for the measurement of the effectiveness of IR performance, also within the traditional user-oriented approach to IR systems evaluation, has forced researchers to reconsider whether these measures are sufficient in relation to the effectiveness evaluation of IIR systems. Spink and colleagues comment on the situation in the following way: "[t]he current IR evaluation measures are… not designed to assist end-users in evaluation of their information seeking behavior (and an information problem) in relation to their use of an IR system. Thus, these measures have limitations for IR system users and researchers" (Spink, Greisdorf & Bateman, 1998, p. 604). Nevertheless, the reason for the measures' well-established positions is due to the clear and intuitively understandable definitions combined with the fact that they represent important aspects of IR, are easy to use, and the results are comparable (Sparck Jones, 1971, p. 97). However, the measures view relevance as a binary concept and do not allow for the often non-binary approach taken in, e.g., the user-centred approaches. Further, the measures do not distinguish between the different types of relevance involved, but treat them as one and the same type. In order to illustrate the need for alternative performance measures, the measures of Relative Relevance (RR) and Ranked Half-Life (RHL) (Borlund & Ingwersen, 1998) were introduced, followed up by the stronger measures of cumulative gain (CG) with, and without, discount by Järvelin and Kekäläinen (2000). The RR measure is intended to satisfy the need for correlating the various types of relevance applied in the evaluation of IR and specifically IIR systems. The RHL informs about the position of the assessed information objects in regard to how well the system is capable of satisfying a user's need for information at a given level of perceived relevance. In line with RHL, the CG measures are positional measures. The assumptions of the CG measures are that:

· Highly relevant documents are more valuable than marginal ones; *and*
· The lower the ranked position of a retrieved document, the less valuable it is for the user, because the less likely it is that the user will ever examine it.

(Järvelin & Kekäläinen, 2000, p. 42)

The recommendation is to apply these measures in combination with the traditional performance measures of recall and precision. A discussion of the strengths and weaknesses of the RR, RHL, and CG measures can be found in the book by Ingwersen and Järvelin (2005).

5.1.1 The Test Instrument of a Simulated Work Task Situation.

The simulated work task situation is a short textual description that presents a realistic information-requiring situation that motivates the test participant to search the IR system (Borlund, 2003a). A simulated work task situation serves two main functions: 1) it causes a 'simulated information need' by allowing for user interpretations of the simulated work task situation, leading to cognitively individual information need interpretations as in real life; and 2) it is the platform against which situational relevance is judged by the test participant (Borlund & Ingwersen, 1997, pp. 227-228). More specifically it helps to describe to the test participants:

· The source of the information need;
· The environment of the situation;
· The problem which has to be solved; *and* also
· Serves to make the test participants understand the objective of the search.

(Borlund & Ingwersen, 1997, pp. 227-228)

As such the simulated work task situation is a stable concept, i.e., the given purpose and goal of the IR system interaction. Figure 1 depicts a classic example of a simulated work task situation tailored towards university students.

Further, by being the same for all the test participants experimental control is provided, and the search interactions are comparable across the group of test participants for the same simulated work task situation. As such the use of simulated work task situations ensures the IIR study will possess both realism and control.

The issue of realism of the descriptions of the simulated work task situations is very essential in order for the prompted search behaviour and relevance assessments of the test participants to be as genuine as intended. Therefore realism is emphasised in the requirements of how to employ simulated work task situations (Borlund, 2003a). In brief, the requirements are as follows:

1) To tailor the simulated work task situations towards the information environment and the group of test participants;

2) To employ either a combination of simulated work task situations and indicative requests (simulated situations), or simulated work task situations only;

3) To employ both simulated work task situations and real information needs within the same test;

4) To permute the order of search jobs;

5) To pilot test; *and*

6) To display employed simulated work task situation when reporting the IIR study.

A well-designed simulated work task situation should be tailored to fit the type of searching under study and the group of test participants, and is one which:

· The test participants can relate to;

· They can identify themselves with;

· They find topically interesting; *and*

· The simulated work task situation must also provide enough imaginative contexts in order for the test participants to be able to relate to and apply the situation.

If the evaluation takes place by involvement of university students then the simulated work task situation should be to describe a situation they can relate to, which they can identify themselves as being in, and to present a topic of searching they find interesting. The described situation should be authentic, relevant, and realistic to the university students – males and females – so that it leads to realistic interpretations and interactions with the simulated information needs. The requirement to tailor the simulated work task situations entails homogeneity of the group of test participants. They need to have something in common, which can form the foundation for the design, tailoring, and use of the simulated work task situations.

The second requirement concerns evaluation by use of either a combination of simulated work task situations and indicative requests, or only simulated work task situations. This requirement provides for an option to direct the searching or help the test participants with determining what to search for. When testing one can decide to include or exclude the indicative request (see Figure 1). When included, the simulated work task situation is followed up with a suggestion of what to search for in the form of an indicative request. When excluded the simulated work task situation stands alone. Previous research (Borlund 2000a; 2000b) shows that test participants make use of the indicative request in different ways: to some the indicative request made it easier to generate the search formulations as they picked the search terms from the indicative requests. Another test participant revealed that the indicative request helped him understand what was expected from him. Yet another test participant explained that he did not use the indicative request in relation to the query formulation, but had found it useful when scanning for relevant information. This indicates that the use of the indicative requests can be constructively applied in combination with the simulated work task situations.

The third requirement concerns how to employ a combination of simulated work task situations (simulated information needs) and the test participants' gen-

---

Simulated situation:

Simulated work task situation: After your graduation you will be looking for a job in industry. You want information to help you focus your future job seeking. You know it pays to know the market. You would like to find some information about employment patterns in industry and what kind of qualifications employers will be looking for from future employees.

Indicative request: Find, for instance, something about future employment trends in industry, i.e., areas of growth and decline.

Fig. 1 Example of a simulated situation/simulated work task situation (e.g., Borlund, 2003a)

uine information needs–both when pilot testing and when carrying out the actual evaluation. This means that the test participants should prepare real, personal information needs which they search as part of the evaluation. Hence, genuine information needs function as a baseline against the simulated information needs, hereby acting as a control on the search interaction derived from the searching of simulated work task situations. In addition, the genuine information needs provide information about the systems' effect on real information needs. The inclusion of genuine information needs is also useful in the pilot test (requirement no. 5) because personal information needs can inspire 'realistic' and user-adaptable simulated work task situations.

The fourth requirement advises to permute the order of search jobs between the test participants so that no test participants are presented with the same simulated work tasks and their own personal information need in the same order. This is to neutralise any effect on the results in terms of bias of search interaction and relevance assessment behaviour of the test participants as well as the test participants' increasing system knowledge and possible knowledge of domain topicality of the simulated work tasks situations.

The fifth requirement concerns the ever-good test practice of pilot testing prior to actual evaluation. When pilot testing the test setting, the test procedure, the collected data, and the test participants' perceptions of the simulated work task situations are evaluated, and adjusted accordingly if required. As mentioned it is most useful to instruct the pilot-test participants to contribute with real, personal information needs as these needs can inspire simulated work task situations that are ideal for the group of test participants. If that is the case, then subsequent pilot testing is required in order to evaluate the test participants' view of the new simulated work task situation(s).

The sixth and final requirement points out the fact that the employed simulated work task situations must be depicted when the study is reported. Otherwise the reader is not able to assess the realism of the employed tailored simulated work task situation with respect to the target group of test participants, and hence assess the value and strength of the reported results of the study.

Simulated work task situations satisfy the experimental demands illustrated with the relevance and the cognitive revolutions (Robertson & Hancock-Beaulieu, 1992). These demands are that relevance should be judged in relation to the need rather than the request, and that an information need should be acknowledged as individual and dynamic, the process of the need formation being a situation-driven phenomenon. By applying simulated work task situations the test participants can work with personal and individual information need interpretations, which can develop and mature over session time for the same test participant. The dynamic nature of the information need formation is strongly connected to the dynamic nature of assessing relevance. By the application of simulated work task situations, non-binary relevance and the type of the information searching and retrieval processes involved in the use of an IIR system is available for studying. Schamber, Eisenberg and Nilan (1990, p. 774) draw the following conclusions on the nature of relevance and its role in information behaviour:

1. Relevance is a multidimensional cognitive concept whose meaning is largely dependent on users' perceptions of information and their own information need situations;

2. Relevance is a dynamic concept that depends on users' judgements of quality of the relationship between information and information need at a certain point in time; *and*

3. Relevance is a complex but systematic and measurable concept if approached conceptually and operationally from the user's perspective.

The first and second conclusions support both the application of situational relevance and non-binary relevance assessment. In addition, the third conclusion supports the application of simulated work task situations by implying that, while the number of relevant information objects retrieved is still a parameter to be measured, the relevance of an information object is defined not solely by the topic of the user's query, but by how useful the information contained in the retrieved information object is in relation to the information need and the underlying situation–as in real life.

6. CONCLUDING REMARKS AND FURTHER READINGS

The ambition of this paper has been to introduce IIR, and in particular IIR evaluation, because of the large quantity of IR research in IR evaluation and methodological issues (Järvelin, 2011). The point of departure has been historical, starting out with an introduction to the Cranfield model, to which IIR evaluation is the counterpart. The ASTIA and Cranfield tests constitute the empirical tradition of IR, and the experiences earned from these tests explain how IR ended up with the rigid definitions of the nature of the information need and relevance. The co-existing user-oriented IR research is exemplified with The MEDLARS test, and the development of end-user IR systems (OPACs) emphasised the need for alternative approaches to IR evaluation. In this paper illustrated with the Book House system for fiction retrieval and the research project of Okapi. The need for alternative approaches to IR evaluation is nicely summarised by Robertson and Hancock-Beaulieu (1992) in the form of the three revolutions: the cognitive, the relevance, and the interactive revolutions. The three revolutions present the modern and contemporary requirements to IIR evaluation. As an example of current IIR evaluation methodology the IIR evaluation model by Borlund is introduced (e.g., Borlund, 2000a; 2000b; 2003a). The IIR evaluation model meets the requirements of the three revolutions, not the least due to the employment of the test instrument of a simulated work task situation. Despite the qualities of the IIR evaluation model more research is needed. For example, a reoccurring issue is that of generalization of IIR evaluation results. This issue is also addressed by Belkin in his 2008 ECIR Keynote, when he points out how the contradictions between the necessity for realism and the desire for comparability and generalization have not yet been solved (Belkin, 2008, p. 52). Belkin is not the only one to comment on the need for further research on IIR evaluation. Järvelin (2011, p. 137) puts it as follows: "Information retrieval evaluation will not be remembered in history books for solving easy problems. Solving the difficult ones matters. Task-based and user-oriented evaluations offer such problems. Solving them can potentially lead to signifi-

cant progress in the domain."

For further reading on IR systems evaluation from a historical point of view the reader is directed to the book in memory of Cleverdon edited by Spark Jones (1981) titled *Information Retrieval Experiment*. For more concrete guidelines the reader is recommended the hands-on paper by Tague-Sutcliffe (1992) with ten decisions to make when conducting empirical IR research, or the compendium paper by Kelly (2009) on methods for evaluating IIR systems with users. Also the ARIST chapters by Harter and Hert (1997), and Wang (2001) are recommendable when considering approaches, issues, and methods for IR systems evaluation and evaluation of information user behaviour. The book by Ingwersen and Järvelin (2005), which aims at integrating research in information seeking and IR, deserves attention, too. So does the recent book by Fidel (2012) that carefully outlines the framework for cognitive domain analyses deriving from the Book House project. The book by Xie (2008) on IIR in digital environments is also worth mentioning, and so is the excellent ARIST chapter by Ruthven (2008) which introduces IIR from the perspective of searching and retrieval. Finally, attention should be given the book edited by Ruthven and Kelly (2011) about interactive information seeking, behaviour, and retrieval.

ACKNOWLEDGEMENT

In memory of Professor Emeritus F. W. Lancaster, who passed away during the writing of this paper. He showed us the importance of thorough test design for the evaluation and study of systems performance and human interaction with information.

REFERENCES

Aitchison, J. & Cleverdon, C. (1963). *Aslib Cranfield research project: Report on the test of the Index of Metallurgical Literature of Western Reserve University*. Cranfield: The College of Aeronautics.

Beaulieu, M. & Jones, S. (1998). Interactive searching and interface issues in the Okapi Best Match Probabilistic Retrieval System. *Interacting with Computers*, 10, 237-248.

Beaulieu, M. (1997). Experiments on interfaces to support query expansion. *Journal of Documentation*, (53)1, 8-19.

Beaulieu, M., Robertson, S. & Rasmussen, E. (1996). Evaluating interactive systems in TREC. *Journal of the American Society for Information Science*, 47 (1), 85-94.

Belkin, N.J. (1980). Anomalous states of knowledge as a basis for information retrieval. *The Canadian Journal of Information Science*, (5), 133-143.

Belkin, N.J. (2008). Some(what) grand challenges for information retrieval. *ACM SIGIR Forum*, 42 (1), 47-54.

Belkin, N.J., Cool, C., Croft, W.B. & Callan, J.P. (1993). The effect of multiple query representation on information retrieval system performance. In R. Korfhage, E. Rasmussen, & P. Willett (Eds.), *Proceedings of the 16ᵗʰ ACM Sigir Conference on Research and Development of Information Retrieval. Pittsburgh*, 1993. New York: ACM Press, 339-346.

Belkin, N.J., Oddy, R. & Brooks, H. (1982). ASK for information retrieval: Part I. Background and theory. *Journal of Documentation*, 38 (2), 61-71.

Borlund, P. & Ingwersen, P. (1997). The development of a method for the evaluation of interactive information retrieval systems. *Journal of Documentation*, 53 (3), 225-250.

Borlund, P. & Ingwersen, P. (1998). Measures of relative relevance and ranked half-life: Performance indicators for interactive IR. In B.W. Croft, A. Moffat, C.J. van Rijsbergen, R. Wilkinson, & J. Zobel (Eds.), *Proceedings of the 21ˢᵗ ACM Sigir Conference on Research and Development of Information Retrieval*. Melbourne, 1998. Australia: ACM Press/York Press, 324-331.

Borlund, P. (2000a). *Evaluation of interactive information retrieval systems*. Åbo: Åbo Akademi University Press. Doctoral Thesis, Åbo Akademi University.

Borlund, P. (2000b). Experimental components for the evaluation of interactive information retrieval systems. *Journal of Documentation*, 56 (1), 71-90.

Borlund, P. (2003a). The IIR evaluation model: A framework for evaluation of interactive information retrieval systems. *Information Research*, 8 (3). Retrieved from http://informationr.net/ir/8-3/paper152.html

Borlund, P. (2003b). The concept of relevance in IR. *Journal of the American Society for Information Science and Technology*, 54 (10), 913-925.

Bruce, H.W. (1994). A cognitive view of the situational dynamism of user-centered relevance estimation. *Journal of the American Society for Information Science*, 45, 142-148.

Cleverdon, C.W. & Keen, E.M. (1966). *Aslib Cranfield Research Project: Factors determining the performance of indexing systems. Vol. 2: Results*. Cranfield.

Cleverdon, C.W. (1960). *Aslib Cranfield Research Project: Report on the first stage of an investigation into the comparative efficiency of indexing systems*. Cranfield: the College of Aeronautics.

Cleverdon, C.W. (1962). *Aslib Cranfield Research Project: Report on the testing and analysis of an investigation into the comparative efficiency of indexing systems*. Cranfield.

Cleverdon, C.W., Mills, J. & Keen, E.M. (1966). *Aslib Cranfield Research Project: Factors determining the performance of indexing systems. Vol. 1: Design*.

Cool, C. & Belkin, N.J. (2011). Interactive information retrieval: History and background. In I. Rutven & D. Kelly (Eds.), *Interactive information seeking, behaviour and retrieval*. London: Facet Publishing, 1-14.

Ellis, D. (1989). A behavioural approach to information retrieval systems design. *Journal of Documentation*, 45 (3), 171-212.

Ellis, D. (1996). *Progress and problems in information retrieval*. London: Library Association Publishing.

Fidel, R. (2012). *Human information interaction: An ecological approach to information behavior*. Cambridge, MA: MIT.

Goodstein, L.P. & Pejtersen, A.M. (1989). *The Book House: System functionality and evaluation*. Roskilde, Denmark: Risø National Laboratory, (Risø-M-2793).

Gull, C.D. (1956). Seven years of work on the organization of materials in the special library. *American Documentation*, 7, 320-329.

Harter, S.P. & Hert, C.A. (1997). Evaluation of information retrieval systems: Approaches, issues, and methods. In M.E. Williams (Ed.), *Annual Review of Information Science and Technology*, 32, 1997, 3-94.

Harter, S.P. (1996). Variations in Relevance assessments and the measurement of retrieval effectiveness. *Journal of the American Society for Information Science*, 47 (1), 37-49.

Ingwersen, P. & Järvelin, K. (2005). *The turn: Integration of information seeking retrieval in context*. Dordrecht, Netherlands: Springer Verlag.

Ingwersen, P. (1992). *Information retrieval interaction*. London: Taylor Graham.

Järvelin, K. & Kekäläinen, J. (2000). IR evaluation methods for retrieving highly relevant documents. In N.J. Belkin, P. Ingwersen, & M.-K. Leong (Eds.), *Proceedings of the 23rd ACM Sigir Conference on Research and Development of Information Retrieval*. Athens, Greece, 2000. New York, N.Y.: ACM Press, 2000, 41-48.

Järvelin, K. (2011). Evaluation. In I. Rutven & D. Kelly (Eds.), *Interactive information seeking, behaviour and retrieval*. London: Facet Publishing, 113-138.

Kelly, D. (2009). Methods for evaluating interactive information retrieval systems with users. *Foundations and Trends in Information Retrieval*, 3 (1-2), 1-224.

Kuhlthau, C.C. (1993). *Seeking meaning: A process approach to library and information science*. Norwood, NJ: Ablex Publishing.

Lancaster, W.F. (1969). Medlars: Report on the evaluation of its operating efficiency. *American Documentation*, 20, 119-142.

Lu, W., Robertson, S.E. & Macfarlane, A. (2007). CISR at INEX 2006. In N. Fuhr, M. Lalmas, and A. Trotman (Eds.), *Comparative Evaluation of XML Information Retrieval Systems: 5th International Workshop of the Initiative for the Evaluation of XML Retrieva (INEX 2006)*, Dagstuhl, Germany, LNCS 4518, Springer-Verlag, (2007), 57-63.

Lu, W., Robertson, S.E. & Macfarlane, A. (2006). Field-Weighted XML retrieval based on BM25. In N. Fuhr, M. Lalmas, S. Malik, & G. Kazai (Eds.), *Advances in XML Information Retrieval and Evaluation: Fourth Workshop of the INitiative for the Evaluation of XML Retrieval (INEX 2005)*, Dagstuhl, 28-30 November 2005, Lecture Notes in Computer Science, Vol 3977, Springer-Verlag,

Marchionini, G. (2006). Toward human-computer information retrieval bulletin. In June/July 2006 *Bulletin of the American Society for Information Science*. Retrieved from http://www.asis.org/Bulletin/Jun-06/marchionini.html

Martyn, J. & Lancaster, F.W. (1981). *Investigative methods in library and information science: An introduction*. Virginia: Information Resources Press. 1981. (2nd impression September 1991).

Pejtersen, A.M. & Austin, J. (1983). Fiction retrieval: Experimental design and evaluation of a search system based on users' value criteria (Part 1). *Journal of Documentation*, 39 (4), 230-246.

Pejtersen, A.M. & Austin, J. (1984). Fiction retrieval: Experimental design and evaluation of a search system based on users' value criteria (Part 2). *Journal of Documentation*, 40 (1), 25-35.

Pejtersen, A.M. & Fidel, R. (1998). A framework for work centered evaluation and design: A case study of IR on the web. Grenoble, March 1998. [Working paper for MIRA Workshop, Unpublished].

Pejtersen, A.M. & Rasmussen, J. (1998). Effectiveness testing of complex systems. In M. Helander (Ed.), *Handbook of human-computer interaction*. Amsterdam: North-Holland, 1514-1542.

Pejtersen, A.M. (1980). Design of a classification scheme for fiction based on an analysis of actual user-librarian communication and use of the scheme for control of librarians' search strategies. In O. Harbo, & L. Kajberg (Eds.), *Theory and application of information research. Proceedings of the 2nd International Research forum on Information Science*. London: Mansell, 146-159.

Pejtersen, A.M. (1989). A library system for information retrieval based on a cognitive task analysis and supported by an icon-based interface. In *Proceedings of the 12th Annual International ACM SIGR Conference on Research and Development in Information Retrieval* (SIGIR 1989), ACM, 40-47.

Pejtersen, A.M. (1991). *Interfaces based on associative semantics for browsing in information retrieval*. Roskilde, Denmark: Risø National Laboratory, (Risø-M-2883).

Pejtersen, A.M. (1992). New model for multimedia interfaces to online public access catalogues. *The Electronic Library*, 10 (6), 359-366.

Pejtersen, A.M., Olsen, S.E. & Zunde, P. (1987). Development of a term association interface for browsing bibliographic data bases based on end users' word associations. In I. Wormell (Ed.),

Knowledge engineering: expert systems and information retrieval. London: Taylor Graham, 92-112.

Rasmussen, J., Pejtersen, A.M. & Goodstein, L.P. (1994). *Cognitive systems engineering.* N.Y.: John Wiley & Sons.

Robertson, S.E. & Hancock-Beaulieu, M.M. (1992). On the evaluation of IR systems. *Information Processing & Management*, 28 (4), 457-466.

Robertson, S.E. (1981). The methodology of information retrieval experiment. In K. Sparck Jones (Ed.), *Information retrieval experiments.* London: Buttersworths, 9-31.

Robertson, S.E. (1997a). Overview of the Okapi Projects. *Journal of Documentation*, 53 (1), 3-7.

Robertson, S.E. (Ed.). (1997b). Special issue on Okapi. *Journal of Documentation*, 53 (1).

Robertson, S.E., Lu, W. & MacFarlane, A. (2006). XML-structured documents: Retrievable units and inheritance. In H. Legind Larsen, G. Pasi, D. Ortiz-Arroyo, T. Andreasen, & H. Christiansen (Eds.), *Proceedings of Flexible Query Answering Systems 7th International Conference*, FQAS 2006, Milan, Italy, June 7-10, 2006, LNCS, 4027, Springer-Verlag, (2006), 121-132.

Robertson, S.E., Walker, S. & Beaulieu, M. (1997). Laboratory experiments with Okapi: Participation in the TREC programme. *Journal of Documentation*, 53 (1), 20-34.

Ruthven, I. & Kelly, D. (Eds.). (2011). *Interactive information seeking, behaviour and retrieval.* London: Facet Publishing.

Ruthven, I. (2008). Interactive information retrieval. *Annual Review of Information Science and Technology*, 24 (1), 2008, 43-91.

Salton, G. (1972). A New comparison between conventional indexing (MEDLARS) and automatic text processing (SMART). *Journal of the American Society for Information Science*, (March-April), 75-84.

Salton, G. (1981). The smart environment for retrieval system evaluation: Advantages and problem areas. In K. Sparck Jones (Ed.), *Information retrieval experiments.* London: Buttersworths, 316-329.

Sanderson, M. (2010). Test collection based evaluation of information retrieval systems. *Foundations and Trends in Information Retrieval*, 4 (4), 247-375.

Saracevic, T. (1995). Evaluation of evaluation in information retrieval. In E.A Fox, P. Ingwersen, & R. Fidel (Eds.), *Proceedings of the 18th ACM Sigir Conference on Research and Development of Information Retrieval.* Seattle, 1995. N.Y.: ACM Press, 138-146.

Schamber, L. (1994). Relevance and information behavior. In M.E. Williams (Ed.), *Annual Review of Information Science and Technology (ARIST).* Medford, NJ: Learned Information, INC., 29, 3-48.

Schamber, L. Eisenberg, M.B. & Nilan, M.S. (1990). A re-examination of relevance: Toward a dynamic, situational definition. *Information Processing & Management*, (26), 755-775.

Sharp, J. (1964). Review of the Cranfield-WRU test literature. *Journal of Documentation*, 20 (3), 170-174.

Sparck Jones, K. (1971). *Automatic keyword classification for information retrieval.* London: Buttersworths.

Sparck Jones, K. (1981a). Retrieval system tests 1958-1978. In K. Sparck Jones (Ed.), *Information retrieval experiments.* London: Buttersworths, 213-255.

Sparck Jones, K. (1981b). The Cranfield tests. In K. Sparck Jones (Ed.), *Information retrieval experiments.* London: Buttersworths, 256-284.

Sparck Jones, K. (Ed.). (1981c). *Information retrieval experiments.* London: Buttersworths.

Spink, A., Greisdorf, H. & Bateman, J. (1998). From highly relevant to not relevant: Examining different regions of relevance. *Information Processing & Management*, 34 (5), 599-621.

Swanson, D.R. (1965). The evidence underlying the Cranfield results. *Library Quarterly*, 35, 1-20.

Swanson, D.R. (1986). Subjective versus objective relevance in bibliographic retrieval systems. *Library quarterly*, 56, 389-398.

Tague-Sutcliffe, J. (1992). The pragmatics of information retrieval experimentation, revisited. *Information Processing & Management*, 28(4), 467-490.

Thorne, R.G. (1955). The efficiency of subject catalogues and the cost of information searches. *Journal of Documentation*, 11(3), 130-148.

Voorhees, E.M. & Harman, D.K. (2005a). The text retrieval conference. In E.M. Voorhees & D.K. Harman (Eds.). *TREC: Experiment and evaluation in information retrieval.* Cambridge, Massachusetts: The MIT Press. 3-19.

Voorhees, E.M. & Harman, D.K. (Eds.) (2005b). *TREC: Experiment and evaluation in information retrieval*. Cambridge, Massachusetts: The MIT Press.

Walker, S. & De Vere, R. (1990). *Improving subject retrieval in online catalogues: 2. Relevance feedback and query expansion*. London: British Library. (British Library Research Paper 72).

Walker, S. (1989). The Okapi online catalogue research projects. In *The Online catalogue: developments and directions*. London: The Library Association, 84-106.

Wang, P. (2001). Methodologies and methods for user behavioral research. In M.E. Williams (Ed.), *Annual Review of Information Science and Technology*, 34, 1999, 53-99.

Wilson, M. (2011). Interfaces for information retrieval. In I. Rutven, & D. Kelly (Eds.), *Interactive information seeking, behaviour and retrieval*. London: Facet Publishing, 139-170.

Xie, I. (2008). *Interactive information retrieval in digital environments*. IGI Publishing.

5

Growth Analysis of Cancer Biology Research, 2000-2011

Keshava *
Dept. of Studies and Research in
Library and Information Science
Tumkur University, India
keshtut@gmail.com

B. N. Thimmaiah
Dept. of Studies and Research in
Library and Information Science
Tumkur University, India
thimmegowda55@gmail.com

K. B. Agadi
Gujarath Central University
Library, India
kbagadi@gmail.com

ABSTRACT

Methods and Material: The PubMed database was used for retrieving data on 'cancer biology.' Articles were downloaded from the years 2000 to 2011. The articles were classified chronologically and transferred to a spreadsheet application for analysis of the data as per the objectives of the study.

Statistical Method: To investigate the nature of growth of articles via exponential, linear, and logistics tests.

Result: The year wise analysis of the growth of articles output shows that for the years 2000 to 2005 and later there is a sudden increase in output, during the years 2006 to 2007 and 2008 to 2011. The high productivity of articles during these years may be due to their significance in cancer biology literature, having received prominence in research.

Conclusion: There is an obvious need for better compilations of statistics on numbers of publications in the years from 2000 to 2011 on various disciplines on a worldwide scale, for informed critical assessments of the amount of new knowledge contributed by these publications, and for enhancements and refinements of present Scientometric techniques (citation and publication counts), so that valid measures of knowledge growth may be obtained. Only then will Scientometrics be able to provide accurate, useful descriptions and predictions of knowledge growth.

Keywords: Scientometric, Cancer biology, PubMed, Relative growth rate, Exponential trend

*Corresponding Author: Keshava
Associate Professor
Dept. of Studies and Research in
Library and Information Science
Tumkur University, India
keshtut@gmail.com

1. INTRODUCTION

Cancer can be defined as a disease in which a group of abnormal cells grow uncontrollably by disregarding the normal rules of cell division. Normal cells are constantly subject to signals that dictate whether the cell should divide, differentiate into another cell, or die. Cancer cells develop a degree of autonomy from these signals, resulting in uncontrolled growth and proliferation. If this proliferation is allowed to continue and spread, it can be fatal; almost 90% of cancer-related deaths are to tumour spreading. The foundation of modern cancer biology rests on a simple principle that virtually all mammalian cells share similar molecular networks that control proliferation, differentiation, and cell death.

Phenomenal advances in cancer research have given an insight into how cancer cells develop (Hejmadi, 2010). The growth of literature is a key work for all scholars and students of comparative literature (Chadwick, 1986). The changes in the size of literature over a specific period are termed as growth literature. Gilbert (1978) has reviewed the existing literature on the indicators of growth of knowledge in scientific specialties, and has listed many ways of measuring it, noting their strengths and limitations and commenting, at the same time, on their uses. Gupta, Sharma, and Karisiddappa (1977) suggested two approaches that have normally been considered in understanding knowledge growth: (i) Qualitative and (ii) Quantitative. A qualitative approach suggests structural or descriptive models of knowledge growth, while a descriptive model uses social phenomenon to explain diffusion and creation of knowledge. A quantitative approach employs summarization of statistics to describe the observed behaviour, while applying growth and technology diffusion models and bibliometric/Scientometric techniques. Many studies have been made on the growth of literature in the field of science literature but only very few studies have been conducted on cancer biology research. Hence an attempt has been made to analyse the growth of cancer biology research literature. The authors studied only growth indicators as a pilot study for further study, viz. collaborative research trend; cross national analysis; obsolescence; etc.

2. OBJECTIVES

- To study and explore the applicability of selected growth models in the world in cancer biology literature;
- To determine the rate of growth of cancer biology literature by calculating relative growth rates and doubling time for publications;
- To fit both a modified exponential curve and logistic curve for the original publications data, studying actual growth.

3. REVIEW LITERATURE

Literature growth studies have become very common in the field of Bibliometrics, Informatrics, and Scientometrics. Studying growth patterns in the NLM's serials collection and in Index Medicus journals between 1966 and 1985, Leeds (1964) "Law of Exponential Growth" has been further dealt with by Tague, Beheshti, and Rees-Potter (1981), and by Ravichandra Rao and Meera (1992). The exponential growth of the literature is described mathematically by the exponential function YT =a.ebt where YT represents the size at time t, a is the initial size, and b is the continuous growth rate which is related to the annual percentage growth rate r, as: r =100(eb-1). Egghe and Ravichandra Rao (1992) concluded, however, that the power model (with exponent >1) is the best growth model for sciences and technology fields, while the Gompertz S-shaped distribution better fits databases of the social sciences and the humanities.

4. SCOPE AND LIMITATION

The present study is confined to cancer biology literature as reflected in the PubMed database from the years 2000 to 2011. $R_t(P) = \frac{1}{t}\left[\log_e p(t) - \log_e p(0)\right]$

5. METHODOLOGY

The PubMed database was used for retrieving data on 'cancer biology'. Articles were downloaded covering the years 2000 to 2011. The articles were classified chronologically and transferred to a spreadsheet application, and the data is analysed as per the objectives of the study.

6. STATISTICAL METHOD

To investigate the nature of growth of articles via exponential, linear, and logistic tests. The exponential growth is defined as

$$F(t) = a\, e^{bt}$$

Where

a = the initial size of literature, i.e. at time t=o and b, the continuous growth rate is related to the percentage by which the size increases each year.

The logistic has a lower limit and an upper limit or a ceiling beyond which the size cannot grow, and can be represented mathematically as

$$U_t = \frac{K}{1+\mu}$$

Where,

U = expected size of literature

K and μ = constants and t= time.

Similarly, the linear growth is represented as

$$U_e = a + bt$$

Relative Growth Rate (RGR) and Doubling Time (Dt) has been applied. RGR means the increase in the number of articles per unit of time. The mean RGR of articles over the specific period of interval is represented as

$$R_t(P) = \frac{1}{t}\left[\log_e p(t) - \log_e p(0)\right]$$

R_t = Relative Growth Rate of articles over the specific period of time

$\log_e p(0)$= Logarithm of initial number of articles

$\log_e p(t)$= Logarithm of final number of articles

Similarly, RGR of subject articles has increased in number of articles per unit of time. The mean RGR of subject articles R_t(SA) over specific period of time is determined as

$$R_t(SA) = \frac{1}{t}\left[\log_e p(t) - \log_e p(0)\right]$$

R_t(SA) = Relative Growth Rate of articles over the specific period of time

$\log_e p(0)$= Logarithm of initial number of articles

$\log_e p(t)$= Logarithm of final number of articles

D_t (Doubling Time) has been calculated using the following formula:

$$\text{Doubling Time } D_t = 0.693/R$$

D_t (Doubling Time) is directly related to RGR and is defined as the time required for the articles to double in number from the existing amount. If the number of articles in a subject doubles during a given period, then the difference between logarithms of number at the beginning and at the end of this period must be the logarithm of the number 2. We used a Napier logarithm and so the taken value of $\log_e 2$ is 0.693. Hence, as per this (0.693) and an average growth rate we calculated by what time interval does the Napier logarithm of numbers increase by 0.693. So the Doubling Time is calculated as

$$D_t(SA) = \frac{\log_e 2}{R_t(SA)} = \frac{0.693}{R_t(SA)}$$

Here, D_t (SA) = average doubling time of subject articles

7. ANALYSIS AND DISCUSSION

As Table 1 clearly indicates, the value of an average RGR of articles R_t(P) increased gradually from 0.57 to 2.05. Correspondingly, the values of Doubling Time of the publication of articles D_t(P) increased gradually from 2002 (1.84 years) to 2011 (4.10 years). The mean relative growth R_t(P) for the first 6 years (from 2000 to 2005) indicates a growth rate of 1.00, whereas for the latter 6 years (from 2006 to 2011) it increased to 1.92. The linear and exponential growth trend is fitted to number of articles for the years 2000 to 2011. Table 1 and Figs. 2 and 3 reveals that the R^2 value for the exponential trend (0.9427) is more than that of the linear trend (0.9339); this indicates that the exponen-

Table 1. Relative Growth-rate (RGR) and Doubling Time (Dt) of Articles in Cancer Biology from 2000 to 2011

Year	No. of Articles	Cumulative	$\log_e 1^p$	$\log_e 2^p$	$R_t(P)$	Mean $R_t(P)$	$D_t(P)$	Mean $D_t(P)$
2000	341	341	5.83	5.83	0		0	
2001	440	781	6.08	6.66	0.57		1.15	
2002	517	1298	6.24	7.16	0.92		1.84	
2003	450	1748	6.10	7.46	1.36		2.71	
2004	525	2273	6.26	7.72	1.47		2.93	
2005	529	2802	6.27	7.93	1.67	1.00	3.33	1.99
2006	569	3371	6.34	8.12	1.78		3.56	
2007	681	4052	6.52	8.30	1.78		3.57	
2008	728	4780	6.59	8.47	1.88		3.76	
2009	750	5530	6.62	8.61	2.00		4.00	
2010	869	6399	6.76	8.76	2.00		3.99	
2011	944	7343	6.85	8.90	2.05	1.92	4.10	3.83
Total	7343	40718						

R^2 (Linear trend for no. of articles) = **0.9339**
R^2 (Exponential trend for no. of articles) = **0.9427**
R^2 (Exponential trend for cumulative no. of articles) = **0.9138**

tial trend is more suitably fitted as compared to the linear trend. Further, the exponential trend is fitted to cumulative number of articles from 2000 to 2011. The R^2 value for this trend is 0.9138; this shows 91.38% variation observed from the cumulative number of articles.

Furthermore, mean $D_t(P)$ for the first six years was 1.99 and increased to 3.83 in the latter six years, i.e. from 2006 to 2011. It shows that the mean relative growth of cancer biology literature has shown an increasing trend. This may be due to the interdisciplinary and multidisciplinary nature of research and the communication patterns of medical researchers.

The year wise analysis of the growth of articles output shows that growth is poor in the year 2000 to 2005 and then there is a sudden increases in productivity during the years 2006 to 2007 and 2008 to 2011. The high productivity of articles during these years may be due to their significance in cancer biology literature, having received prominence in research. Another

reason is the research area may benefit from good infrastructure facilities in R&D institutions,

8. SUGGESTIONS

a) Since the growth of literature is on an exponential trend, medical libraries may think of resource sharing and networking options in order to avoid financial constraints;
b) Medical libraries may allocate budget for various resources scientifically.

9. CONCLUSION

The many papers have tried to estimate the growth of knowledge in various ways, as many questions have been raised about the validity and reliability of Scientometrics measures for this process. It appears

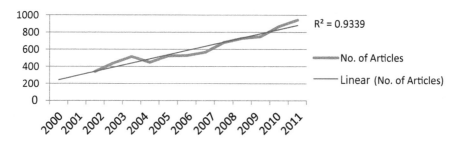

Fig. 1 Linear trend for no. of articles

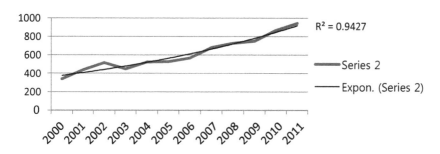

Fig. 2 Exponential trend for no. of articles

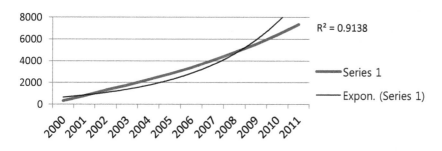

Fig. 3 Exponential trend for cumulative no. of articles

that, for the "growth of knowledge" subfield, the time is not yet ripe for a logarithmic decline in the number of first-rate papers. There is an obvious need for better compilation of statistics on numbers of publications in the years from 2000 to 2011 in various disciplines on a worldwide scale, for informed critical assessments of the amount of new knowledge contributed by these publications, and for enhancement and refinement of the present Scientometrics techniques (citation and publication counts), so that valid measures of knowledge growth may be obtained. Also, studies of literature growth need to become more exact in the description of their models and more rigorous in the application of statistical tests to determine how well these models fit reality. Only then will Scientometrics be able to provide accurate, useful descriptions and predictions of knowledge growth.

REFERENCES

Chadwick, H.M., & Chadwick, N.K. (1986). *Growth of literature*. Cambridge: Cambridge University Press. (Original work published 1932).

Egghe, L., & Ravichandra Rao, I.K. (1992). Classification of growth models based on growth rates and its applications. *Scientometrics, 25*(1), 5-46.

Gilbert, G.N. (1978). Measuring the growth of science: A review of indices. *Scientometrics, 1*(1), 9-34.

Gupta, B.M., Sharma, P., & Karisiddappa, C.R. (1977). Growth of research literature in scientific specialties: A modeling perspective. *Scientometrics, 40*(3), 507-528.

Hejmadi, M. (2010). *Introduction to cancer biology*, 2nd ed. London: Bookboon.

Keshava. (2004). *Scientometric analysis of social science research in India* (Ph.D. thesis). Dept. of Library and Information Science, Karnataka University, Dharwad.

Line, M.B., & Roberts, S. (1976). Growth and composition of social science literature. *International Social Science Journal, 28*(1), 122-159.

Orr, R.H., & Leeds, A.A. (1964). Biomedical literature: Volume, growth, and other characteristics. *Federation Proceedings, 23*(6), 1310-1331.

Ravichandra Rao, I.K., & Meera, B.M. (1991). Growth and obsolescence of literature: An empirical study. In I.K. Ravichandra Rao (Ed.), *INFORMETRICS '91: Selected Papers from the Third International Conference on Informetrics, 9-12 August 1991* (pp. 377-394). Bangalore, 1992.

Roberts, S.A., & Chak, M. (1981). Size growth and characteristics of the serial literature of geography. *Social Science Information Studies, 1*(5), 317-388.

6

Henry Fayol's 14 Principles of Management: Implications for Libraries and Information Centres

C. P. Uzuegbu *
Department of Library and Information Science
Michael Okpara University of Agriculture
Nigeria
E-mail: chimezie.patrick.uzuegbu@gmail.com
        fortenews@yahoo.com

C. O. Nnadozie
Department of Library and Information Science
Michael Okpara University of Agriculture
Nigeria
E-mail: cnnadozie2000@yahoo.com
        chumannadozie2000@gmail.com

ABSTRACT

This paper focuses generally on the 'fourteen principles of management' by Henri Fayol. However, it specifically analyses their application to and implications for libraries and information centres. An extensive review of published works on management generally, and library management in particular, was conducted. This yielded vital insights on the original meaning and later modifications of these principles, as well as their application in the management of various organisations. Consequently, the strengths and weaknesses of these principles were examined to determine their suitability in libraries and information centres. Inferences, illustrations, and examples were drawn from both developed and developing countries which gives the paper a global perspective. Based on available literature, it was concluded that Fayol's principles of management are as relevant to libraries as they are in other organisations. The paper, therefore, recommends that in addition to modifying some aspects to make these principles more responsive to the peculiar needs of libraries, further research should be undertaken to expand the breadth of these principles and ascertain their impacts on the management of information organisations.

Keywords: : Library Management, Management Principles, Library and Information Centres, Henry Fayol

*Corresponding Author: C. P. Uzuegbu
Lecturer
Department of Library and Information Science
Michael Okpara University of Agriculture, Nigeria
E-mail: chimezie.patrick.uzuegbu@gmail.com
        fortenews@yahoo.com

1. INTRODUCTION

An organisation can be defined as a group of people who collectively undertake certain actions such as planning, arranging, coordination, structuring, administration, organizing, management, logistics, and the like, in order to achieve a pre-determined goal. An online business dictionary (www.businessdictionary.com) affirms that the word *organisation* is synonymous with words such as: firm, business, company, institution, establishment, corporation, etc. Hence, an organisation can be a business or a government department. In other words, organisations can be private or public; small, medium or large-scale; profit or non-profit oriented. They can also specialize in different endeavours such as manufacturing, repackaging, sales, services, and so on. Library and information centres, as distinct departments of government and non-government institutions, are prime examples of service providing organisations. They are public-service kind of institutions and are comprised of men and women of defined and related knowledge backgrounds, who collectively pursue a goal of providing information services to particular groups of people at different places and times.

In view of this, library and information centres are not completely different from other organisations. All organisations require management to succeed. Management as defined by several researchers and scholars can be summarized as the judicious use of *means* to accomplish an *end* (Stroh, Northcraft, & Neale, 2002). Right from the late eighteenth century to the early nineteenth century, the importance of management as a factor that determines organisational success has all along been buttressed (Robinson, 2005; Witzel, 2003). Several experiments were conducted by different people such as Frederick Taylor, Henri Fayol, Max Weber, Elton Mayo, Abraham Maslow, Douglas McGregor, among others. These theorists are today regarded as the forerunners of management scholarship. The results of their experiments and/or experiences at the earliest industries and companies in Europe and America led to the postulations of several management principles, also called theories or philosophies. However, popular among the several management principles postulated by the management forerunners is Henri Fayol's '14 principles of management' (Witzel, 2003).

The popularity and wide adoption of Henri Fayol's management principles led to his being nicknamed the *father of modern management* (Witzel, 2003; Wren, Bedeian, & Breeze, 2002). Henri Fayol was a French engineer who lived from 1841-1925. Early in life, at about 19 years of age, he followed after his father's engineering profession. He enrolled and graduated from a mining academy in 1860 and took up a mining engineering job in a French mining company. By 1888, Fayol became the director of the company which he later turned around to become the country's biggest industrial manufacturer for iron and steel with over 10,000 staff in 1900. Fayol directed the affairs of this mining company until 1918 (Fayol, 1930; Pugh & Hickson, 2007). As a sequel to his wealth of experience and series of research endeavours, in 1916 Henri Fayol published the '14 principles of management' which later appeared in his boo *Administration Industrielle et Générale* in 1917 (Faylol, 1917; 1930).

Management researchers over the years opine that the '14 principles of management' propounded by Fayol is what metamorphosed into present-day management and administration, especially after 1949 when his book was translated from French to English, as *General and Industrial Administration* (Rodrigues, 2001; Fayol, 1949; Wren, Bedeian, & Breeze, 2002). It is believed also that every organisation on the globe today is influenced by Fayol's principles of management given their applicability to burgeoning administrative formation without which there will be no organisation - as a group of people pursuing a collective goal. It is on this premise, therefore, that this paper is set to critically analyse the implications of Fayol's 14 principles of management as culled from his 1949 publication (Fayol, 1949) with a view to highlighting their implications to the administration of library and information centres.

2. HENRY FAYOL'S 14 PRINCIPLES

2.1. Principle 1: Division of Work

Henry Fayol's first principle for management states that staff perform better at work when they are assigned jobs according to their specialties. Hence, the division of work into smaller elements then becomes paramount. Therefore, specialisation is important as staff perform specific tasks not only at a single time but as a routine duty also. This is good to an extent. In library and information centres, there are such divisions of work. The Readers' Services Department of the library (variously called User Services, Customer Services, Public Services, etc.) also divides its vast jobs into departments and units. Not only has this point been substantiated by other writers, it has also been proved to be applicable to Technical Services Departments (Aguolu & Aguolu, 2002; Ifidon & Ifidon, 2007). Fayol, no doubt, was accurate in his division of work principle in the sense that all jobs cannot be done together by all staff at the same time. Besides, efficiency and effectiveness of work are better achieved if one staff member is doing one thing at a time and another doing a different thing, but all leading to the same collective goal, at the same time. By this, work output can be increased at the end of a given time, especially in a complex organisation where different kinds of outputs altogether count for the general productivity of the organisation. Similarly, taking the cataloguing room of a library for instance, this principle also mandates that as one or two persons catalogue the books, another puts call numbers on them and another registers the titles as part of putting them together and readying them to move to the circulation wing. Even at that same time, another person at the circulation department may be creating space for their recording, shelving, and so forth. This is division of work and at the end of a day's work, the amount of jobs executed for the day can be more meaningful than when every staff member is clustered for each of the job elements, one after another. By implication therefore, staff are assigned permanent duties and are made to report to that duty every day.

However, as observed in recent library practices, some proactive librarians act contrary to this as they, from time to time, reshuffle staff in a way that takes staff to fresh duties. Critically, the era of staff staying put in a particular office or duty-post is nowadays obsolete given the nature of contemporary society. This points to the fact that current management practices in libraries no longer support that method (Senge, 1990) and the reasons are clear. First, in the library and information science profession, the practice of specialisation in one area or aspect is not clearly defined in the first instance. For instance, this is evident in the professorial titles accorded to professors in the library and information science discipline. Many of them are not tied to any specific library and information science research area by their professorial title compared to what obtains in other science, engineering, and social science disciplines. Likewise, in the classroom, even at the research degree level, scholars' research will often be informative of their possible areas of specialisation. But in practice (working in any library and information centre) it is rarely demonstrated. This is one internal point against the staff of libraries staying put in a specific job element for a long time and, for others, all through their service time. After all, teaching and learning in library and information science is generalized in content and scope and thus tends to produce men and women who can take up any job design in the practice of librarianship. So, library managers who allow staff to remain on a given job schedule on the excuse of specialisation may be dwindling job efficiency.

Secondly, judging from observations of the twenty-first century management style, generalisation of job design is advocated contrary to specialisation. Studies conducted in service rendering organisations show how managers in Western countries design jobs to suit all staff (Rodrigues, 2001). Thus, no single job design in today's organisations requires core specialised staff to execute. Going by the evolution of machines, as we can also see in their introduction in library and information centres in the form of computers, automation, digitalization, and so forth, employment of staff is per their ability to use the machines to execute any job in the organisation. Yet, this does not mean that there is no division of work. There is still a division of work formulas but the modification is that staff are now managed to work in any division at any time because of the generalization of the work design. Take the OPAC system for example: there may not be a need to have staff job-tied to the cataloguing workroom because the OPAC system, as a typical job design platform, will allow any staff from any department to add and/or delete content on the library database. So, library and information centres managers should note the paradigm shift from division of work via specialisation to division of work via generalization.

2.2. Principle 2: Authority

This principle suggests the need for managers to have authority in order to command subordinates to perform jobs while being accountable for their actions. This is both formal and informal and is recommended for managers by Fayol. The formality is in the organisational expectations for the manager (his responsibilities), whereas the informality (the authority) can be linked to the manager's freedom to command, instruct, appoint, direct, and ensure that his or her responsibilities are performed successfully. Again, the two are like checks and balances on the manager: he must not abuse power (authority). He must use it in tandem with the corresponding responsibility. Thus, Fayol believed that since a manager must be responsible for his duties, he should as well have authority backing him up to accomplish his duties. This is correct and quite crucial to organisational success.

In library and information centres, such is the case also. The Librarian-in-Charge is responsible for the affairs of the library and has corresponding authority to oversee it. Likewise, his or her deputies, departmental heads, and unit officers are accorded the same in their respective capacities. This makes the work flow smoothly. But by implication, the respective subordinates such as the assistant librarians, library officers, and library assistants or others, as the case may be, become bottled up in the one-man idea cum direction of the librarian. Unfortunately, most departmental heads become so conceited with their status, responsibility, and authority that they do not find it necessary to sometimes intermingle and relate with their staff. As a result, an icy relationship develops with attendant negative consequences, especially industrial disharmony and unwillingness of parties to share knowledge (Ohadinma & Uwaoma, 2000). This may not be in the interests of the library given the saying that "two ideas are better than one" (http://idioms.thefreedictionary.com/).

More so, it is the junior staff members that interact with the practical jobs daily and are likely to regularly have something new in the field to teach the head. Obviously then, there is need for a managerial amendment on this principle. The emphasis should no longer be on power to command subordinates. Rather, it should be on encouragement of staff participation and motivation to take some initiatives. As the research by Blackburn and Rosen (1993) shows, award-winning organisations in the world apply participatory management and staff empowerment against the authority and responsibility principle. With this style, managers and their deputies act more as coordinators rather than dictators. Hence, library and information centres may not need the control-freak type of headship but preferably an orchestra-kind of leadership. Such leadership style will accommodate ideas, innovativeness, meaningful contributions, and freedom of expression from the junior staff, which research has shown to have positive contributions to the growth and success of an organisation (Blackburn & Rosen, 1993).

2.3. Principle 3: Discipline

This principle advocates for clearly-defined rules and regulations aimed at achieving good employee discipline and obedience. Fayol must have observed the natural human tendencies to lawlessness. He perceived the level of organisational disorder that may erupt if employees are not strictly guided by rules, norms, and regulations from management. This is true and has all along resulted in staff control in organisations. But in recent times, it has not been the best method to achieve long-term organisational order and goals. Management scholars have observed that peer group participation and other kinds of informal unions are now taking the control lead in organisations (Mintzberg, 1973). The individual differences amongst staff feared by Fayol, which no doubt led most organisations to break down because of a lack of formal and binding organisational rules or weak and poorly enforced codes of practice (Cavaleri & Obloj, 1993), are seemingly surmountable now through informal control systems. Workers unions and staff groups are getting stronger and stronger every day and have ethics guiding them. In organisations where they are allowed to thrive, management tends to have little or nothing to do towards staff control. As well, they can create resilient problems for managements who will not build a good working atmosphere with them. Yet, they have come to stay nowadays and become stronger every day rather than being suppressed by managements. Trade unionism by staff is, therefore, an element of the democratisation of industrial organisations and government establishments because it accommodates the opinions and interests of the worker in certain management decisions (Ohadinma & Uwaoma, 2000;

Iwueke & Oparaku, 2011). Thus, the use of staff groups or unions is an informal control system. It can help organisations to maintain discipline. One hidden advantage managements that adopt this system have is that they save cost and time *ab-initio* allotted to managerial discipline.

Likewise, in library and information centres, this informal system of discipline can be adopted. Librarians are to become less formal in discipline rather than trying to enforce institutional rules and regulations at all cost. Proactive librarians can have fewer headaches from staff rumours, gossip, and other forms of attack that usually emanate in the process of enforcing institutional rules and regulations. They can achieve this by trying the system of allowing staff to form group(s) in their libraries. For instance, a vibrant junior staff group or senior staff group in a library can go a long way to infuse cooperation, unity, trust, commitment, and order among its members to the benefit of the library as an organisation. As long as the top library management gives them the free hand to exist, they will set up rules that can unite the library organisation more than it can divide it. Anecdotal observation shows that libraries whose staff members are happy with the level of love shown them via visits, celebrating/mourning with them, and so forth are such that have groups or unions in their library. This point is supported by some reports in some management textbooks which clearly suggest that industrial unions help to sustain discipline among their members and sustain industrial harmony (Imaga, 2001; Iwueke & Oparaku, 2011; Ohadinma & Uwaoma, 2000). So, while some managers quickly conclude erroneously that unions exist to fight management and make unnecessary demands, library and information managers should note that such groups can help the system to achieve order and maintain discipline. This out-weighs or counter-balances the fears of their existence.

2.4. Principle 4: Unity of Command

This principle states that employees should receive orders from and report directly to one boss only. This means that workers are required to be accountable to one immediate boss or superior only. Orders-cum-directives emanate from one source and no two persons give instructions to an employee at the same time to avoid conflict. And, no employee takes instructions from any other except from the one and only direct supervisor. This tends to be somehow vague. Fayol was not explicit to show if it means that only one person can give orders or whether two or more persons can give instructions/directives to employees but not at the same time. If the case is the former, this principle is rigid and needs modification, especially in consonance with current realities in many organisations.

Looking at the prevalent situations in most organisations nowadays where work is done in groups and teams, it simply suggests that each group will have a coordinator or supervisor that gives orders. And, this coordinator is not the sole or overall manager. Likewise, in some complex establishments, staff belonging to a given work team would likely take orders from various coordinators at a time. For instance, the head of a Finance Department can give instructions to staff relating to finance; the Electrical Department head can do the same to the staff also relating to power and vice-versa. Thus, in large and small organisations, it is not unusual for a staff member to receive instructions from superiors outside his/her immediate units/sections or departments (Nwachukwu, 1988). In a library, the officer in-charge of cataloguing can instruct the Porter not to allow visitors into the cataloguing workroom; the circulation head can at the same time tell the Porter to watch out for a particular library user at the exit point of the reading hall. These are two different orders from different departments. The Porter, by this, would not say that he cannot take orders from any of them save the Chief Librarian or that only one of them should instruct him and not the two. The Porter may not effectively watch out for the suspected user and at the same have his eyes on the cataloguing workroom wing. However, tact is required as he/she is not expected to flagrantly flout the directives of superiors. The point being stressed is that in modern libraries and information centres, it has become conventional for staff to take orders from multiple bosses even as the primary job is discharged (Agoulu & Aguolu, 2002; Ifidon, 1979).

2.5. Principle 5: Unity of Command

This principle proposes that there should be only one plan, one objective, and one head for each of the plans. Of course, organisations run on established objectives (Drucker, 1954). But, this should not be misinterpreted with departments and units who seemingly have their specific objectives. What Fayol meant is that an organisation will naturally have central objectives which need to be followed and as well departmental and unit goals which also need to be reached in order to meet the unified objective.

Library and information centres are established to collect and manage the universe of information sources and provide information services to their users. But also, there are other goals from departments and units, sometimes differing from each other. This is in line with the job specifications and peculiar work routines of each of the various sub-systems that make up the library (Edoka, 2000; Nnadozie, 2007). However, the activities of each department or unit are aimed at supporting the library's central objective of providing information services to users. And for each of the departments to attain its goals, they set and implement multiple plans (not one plan). So Henri Fayol's original proposal that one plan should be pursued by one head only is no longer tenable. For example, the Circulation Department of the library has to offer lending services and also register library users. Does it mean that it will have separate heads because of the different assignments involved? No; it is true that plans are different, and in this case, one is set for how to register users and the other strategizes how to lend out library materials to people and ensure that they return them, or be responsible for not returning them on time or at all. Yet, that does not call for a separation in the job in terms of headship. Rather, what library managers should insist on is that department goals and plans should be pursued in an orderly manner so that staff will not have to get a special head for each plan of group activity. This approach to management is already in place in most libraries in Africa where few hands are used to deliver multiple tasks due to shortages of staff (Ifidon, 1979 & 1985).

2.6. Principle 6: Subordination of Individual Interests to Organisation's Interests

The interests of the organisation supersede every other interest of staff, individuals, or groups. Imperatively, employees must sacrifice all their personal interests for the good of the organisation. In other words, organisations should not tolerate any staff that are not committed to the organisation's objectives and

order even if it is to the detriment of personal and family interests. This is one hard way of pursuing organisational or corporate success. It may have worked before now, but it is not ideal any longer due to a series of reasons. First, Mayor (1933) and McGregor (1960) have shown that employees can do better at work when they are valued and shown a reasonable sense of belonging. Second, organisations are compliant to the inconsistency of change. They change their objectives as situations warrant and need their staff to adapt fast to the changes. And, one of the fastest ways to get staff to adapt and comply with organisational changes is to invest in the staff. Thus, staff training and retraining, which is at most times cost-effective for management, is not only an investment in the staff for the organisation to reap but also a commitment to staff personal development. During such training sessions, staff enjoy several benefits such as job security, payment of salaries, full sponsorship, and other allowances that makes staff happy and motivated to put in their best when they return from the training programme.

The application of this principle should not be frustrated in library and information centres. Library managers and administrators must learn to make staff work happily. Happy staff will always put in all their best at work. Ways of keeping staff motivated to work happily include, from time to time, showing a commitment to staff both formally and informally. Formal commitments can come from sponsoring staff to further training, short development courses, seminars, and conferences. Some informal commitments include holiday support packages for staff, open and regular communication, and flexibility to staff personal requests. Library managers and administrators also use these formal and informal incentives to show their staff a sense of belonging, thereby making them more productive (Ifidon & Ifidon, 2007). For instance, a staff member permitted to leave office early to pick up her children from school will be glad and, more often than not, reciprocate by a commitment to work during the periods she will be at work. On the contrary, a member that is not permitted to attend to such personal needs and is regimented to the opening and closing hours of work at the library may sit back in his office all day achieving nothing. If a psychological test is conducted on this case, the result may likely show that the latter staff member achieved nothing in the office, not primarily because he wanted to pay back the manager by not working, but more because he was not able to concentrate at work and even when he tried he could not focus because of where his mind was; this is especially so if the family need for which the excuse is denied is crucial. Productive library administrators ensure that an environment is created for staff to have a sense of appreciation, especially when they have some personal needs. Staff with such a sense of appreciation or recognition tend to put in their best in the discharge of their work and pursuit of the library's corporate goals (Aguolu & Aguolu, 2002). Thus, while it was held before that staff should give up their interests for the organisation, now the reverse is the case. This means that organisations commit itself to the interest of the staff so that they can be more productive and committed to the objectives of the organisation.

2.7. Principle 7: Remuneration

Payment of staff salaries should be as deserved. The salary should be reasonable to both staff and management and neither party should be short-changed. The salary of every staff member must be justifiable. A supervisor should receive more pay than line staff. Thus, whoever management appoints to be supervisor takes more than the subordinates by virtue of his or her responsibilities. It does not really matter whether a subordinate works harder and is more productive than the supervisor. As long as management does not promote the subordinate he continues to receive lesser pay to what his boss gets even as he works more than his boss. The above generally encapsulates Fayol's position on remuneration.

However, this approach to the administration of the reward system is gradually giving way in contemporary library management practice. There is a noticeable modification in the application of this principle as it is arbitrary in nature (Ohadinma & Uwaoma, 2000). It is quite agreed that it will be inappropriate for a subordinate to receive more pay than his boss. So, management researchers have complemented Fayol's notion with a new modifications arguing that this system of remuneration discourages hard work and productivity (Cascio, 1987). As a result, the "performance based pay system" recommended by Wallace and Fay (1988)

is what is used nowadays. This pay system supports the idea that organisations should design a performance scale with which staff should be evaluated. Imperatively, productive staff get promoted and take more salary than non-productive staff. In a way also, this was Taylor's (1911) idea that has just re-surfaced. Taylor's idea supports hard work and extra commitment from the staff. His notion was that the more output from an employee, the more pay he receives. So, with this modification, every staff member receives a salary based on his or her measured output.

In present day library and information centres, this productivity measurement scale is adopted. In fact, the performance-based pay system is almost the norm everywhere. The only problem with some libraries and other information-related organisations is that they do not publish and/or orientate their staff on the measurement scaling or promotion criteria. Staff need to understand the criteria and have free access to the document. More so, library managers should as a matter of morality be just in the productivity measurement. Most librarians discourage their hardworking staff or make them resign for another job as they usually envy some member's speed of productivity and promotion. Some library managers and their deputies are in the habit of comparing the number of years a hardworking and productive staff member has spent on the job with the many years some lazy and unproductive staff have given on the same job as a reason for why the former should not rise faster or even above the latter. This point has been raised in some library science textbooks where non-adherence to the principles of the performance-based reward system has been faulted (Aguolu & Aguolu, 2002; Edoka, 2000). Library managers should, therefore, avoid sentiments and award promotions to whoever has worked for them as many times as their hard work qualifies them. This is crucial if a library must retain the best staff and survive in a highly competitive information environment.

2.8. Principle 8: Centralisation

This principle suggests that decision-making should be centralised. This means that decision-making and dishing-out of orders should come from the top management (central) to the middle management, where the decisions are converted into strategies and are interpreted for the line staff who execute them (decentralisation). This is still working in many organisations. Library and information centres also apply this principle. For instance, it is conventional for the Librarian-in-Charge to hold meetings with deputies and/or departmental heads to initiate broad policy guidelines while the deputies and departmental heads take management decisions to their departments and units where they are finally executed and monitored (Ifidon & Ifidon, 2007). Nonetheless, management researchers have found another system which is working for many western organisations. Blackburn and Rosen (1993) observe that successful organisations in the United States of America (USA) apply a group decision making and implementation system. This means that units and departments make decisions and strategize their implementation based on their task, control focus, and job specifics.

Bringing this to the library may nevertheless not be so clear, especially in the beginning. But if it can be tried, it means that library departments will be empowered to meet weekly or monthly, and to make decisions as relating to their department, design their jobs, and draw their roster and schedule of duty. Later on, the decisions and plans of the department will be forwarded to the Librarian-in-Charge for immediate input and approval. Such a system of decision making allows for innovativeness and broad thinking among staff of all levels and also allows the Librarian to be less burdened with the library's daily complaints. As well, librarians can have time to attend the numerous institutions' meetings which they are statutory members of by reason of their position. However, it should be noted that the group decision making system cannot survive in bureaucracy—a system where mails are delayed for long. The Librarian must be committed to treating mail every day. In his absence, he should appoint someone to deputize him. This is because the work group decision-making system requires management to approve or make input to the group's decision before they can commence work. Take for instance where the Digital Library Department of a library has met and taken a decision to be closed to users for three days to enable them to embed an anti-pornography firewall on their server system in order to save it from unauthorized downloads that may crash the server. The decision mail reached the Librarian's desk and for many days it was yet to be treated. Although oral communication to the Librarian can be faster in this case, in a management system where records are necessary for actions, the Librarian's delay in treating the mail would not do any good to the group's decision. So, while the system is good, it requires promptness on actions from both management and staff. Thus, Fayol's 'principle of centralisation' is like a trickle-down decision flow, routing decisions from top to the bottom. But the work group decision system suggested therein is a bottom-up movement, which allows the staff to initiate ideas and job specific decisions for the organisation.

2.9. Principle 9: Scalar Chain

This principle is a product of the formal system of organisation. It is also known as the hierarchy principle. It asserts that communication in the organisation should be vertical only. It insists that a single uninterrupted chain of authority should exist in organisations. Horizontal communication is only allowed when the need arises and must be permitted by the manager. This vertical organisational and communication arrangement is the conventional practice in most library and information centres where orders and similar directives flow from the Librarian-in- Charge to the Deputy Librarians, to the Departmental Heads, and to the Unit or Sectional Heads, respectively (Edoka, 2000; Nnadozie, 2007). This is a four-layer hierarchy. It is neither twelve nor three layers, as Braham (1989) argues that a three-layer organisational hierarchy does better and faster than a twelve-layer hierarchy. Also, it has been shown in research that US-based organisations that practiced one-layer hierarchy systems recorded far better results than others that operated three-layer systems and above (Hinterhuber & Popp, 1992). Nowadays, a horizontal or flat management hierarchy system is advocated against the vertical order canvassed by Henri Fayol. The argument is that the former helps organisations to take decisions and implement them faster without unnecessary bottlenecks, contrary to what is observed in the later. Should this be applied in library and information centres, the implication is that the relatively vertical hierarchy order in most libraries should be displaced with the flat or horizontal hierarchy system. Figure 1 is a comparative illustration of a typical vertical organisational structure and the horizontal alternative being proposed.

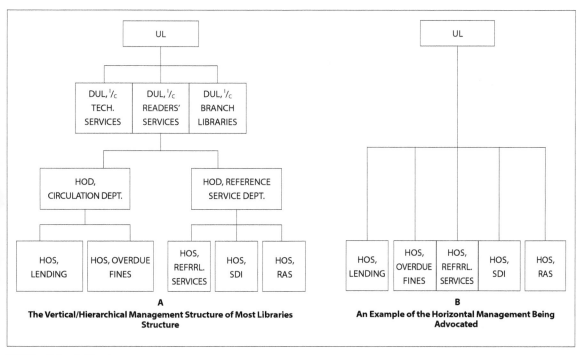

A
The Vertical/Hierarchical Management Structure of Most Libraries Structure

B
An Example of the Horizontal Management Being Advocated

KEY: UL = University Librarian
DUL = Deputy University Librarian
HOD = Head of Department
HOS = Head of Section
SDI = Selective Dissemination of Information
RAS = Readers' Advisory Services

Fig. 1 Scalar chain diagram illustrating Fayol's vertical order and the proposed horizontal order

Based on the above illustration, coupled with the new management findings that a horizontal organisational hierarchy allows for faster decision making and implementation than the vertical order system, library and information centres may have to operate a horizontal hierarchy system (Fig. 1 Diagram B) henceforth. The present system of having divisional heads, departmental heads, and in some cases, unit or sectional heads also (Fig. 1 Diagram A), may have to give way for a flat order where it will only be the Librarian-in-Charge and, most directly, the unit/sectional heads (as per specific job element or focus). However, this may not be welcomed by librarians in some institutions and countries where the deputy and departmental heads positions attract office allowances and other appurtenances. Yet, we must be realistic; such ladders on the management chart may not be helpful for library organisation in the nearest future. But, this one thing can be done also: break down the vertical order (Diagram A) into a flat order (Diagram B), increase the Sections/Units based on job specifics and call them Departments (which is more conventional), and redistribute the office heads in the initial vertical order to head the departments. This way, the fear of losing office/headship allowances and other benefits is averted. The beauty of the horizontal organization being advocated lies in its adaptability to the peculiar needs of both small and large libraries (Ifidon & Ifidon, 2007). Besides, most library staff are at home with its flexibility bearing in mind that positions attained by promotion (such as Senior Librarian or Deputy Librarian positions), are not in any way to be affected in the horizontal system. Hence, Mr. A can be an Assistant Librarian by grade and heads a department while Ms. B can be a Deputy Librarian by grade, also heading a department.

Both of them report directly to the Librarian-in-Chief. Yet, the grade level and rank status of both is not the same and cannot be the same just on the grounds that both of them are departmental heads. Of course, there will be no problem with the remuneration system also as it is based on performance scale (grade level) and not on positional status (the headship privilege). The only thing that may be the same in this case is the headship allowance, if it is across the board for all staff grades. But, the normal annual salary (remuneration) due for each departmental head is purely determined according to grade levels and as such will vary among the heads.

2.10. Principle 10: Order

This is another formal organisational control system which has been interpreted in different ways. Some see it as the rule of giving every material its right position in the organisation and others think that it means assigning the right job to the right employee (Rodrigues, 2001). Whichever is the case, library and information centres must keep every information material in the right place and as well assign staff to jobs that suit them. A Library Assistant is not expected to handle the office and responsibilities of a Senior Librarian. This is because, among other things, their qualifications, job schedule, and remunerations are clearly different (Ifidon, 1985; Ifidon & Ifidon, 2007). However, buttressing more on the first suggested meaning of Henri Fayol's 'principle of order,' it is true that information resources in the library should be kept in the right place. Here, what makes a place right is the ease of access and use it avails the users. Let us take the location of offices for example. In a library complex of two or three floors, the office of Librarian has no convenience in being located at any of the offices at the upper floors. Visitors to the Librarian's office, who have nothing to do with the readings halls and other departments, have no business passing through or across them before they can access the Librarian's office. The Librarian's office should be located on the ground floor where visitors and users can access it easily. Likewise, the porter stand should be accessible to users immediately when they enter the library. This is the prevailing practice in the Nigerian university system in West Africa as most of the library briefs are in line with this proposal (Ifidon, 1985; Ifidon & Ifidon, 2007; Ononogbo, 2008). Users do not have to walk to one point to keep their bags and down to another point before they can enter the library.

In fact, if library and information centres must comply with this principle of order, it must be looked at from a more holistic point of view. For instance, taking a look at the present structure of offices and demarcations of most library buildings in Nigeria, the principle of order is practically compromised. This is in spite of the good suggestions in the available librarians' and architects' briefs for the construction of library buildings (Ifidon, 1985; Ifidon & Ifidon, 2007; Ononogbo, 2008). In a library that wants to infuse order right from the design of its work environment, the transparent partitioning system, as seen in Banks, is ideal for adoption. Nowadays, organisations operate the open office system. An open office is that in which there is little or no privacy as the only partition between offices could be just transparent glass walls. In some cases, dwarf walls or wooden boards are used. The major benefit of this arrangement is that it enhances transparency and ventilation (Idih, Njoku, & Idih, 2011). Staff can see themselves from their offices. The users can see them as well too.

The Readers' Services Departments of the library and their officers are the most likely to adopt this system of office sitting/demarcation. It allows the head of the department to see his staff and users also while they too see them. In this case, there will hardly be room for staff that do unethical things in the library such as sleeping, eating, and gossiping in the office. Likewise, users will be more cautious while in the library because staff from various offices can be watching them. In fact, the transparent partitioning of library staff offices will intuitively drive staff to work and not to relax or chat away during official hours. However, this transparent partitioning system should not be open to users in the case of Technical Departments. But within the technical departments, the offices should be transparent too so that staff can see themselves. These are some important elements of order which could be modified to suit the peculiar needs of libraries.

2.11. Principle 11: Equity

Another word for equity is fairness. Henri Fayol suggested that managers should be fair to their staff. But the fairness required, probably, is such that must make staff to comply with principle No. 6 - subordination of individual interests to organisational interests – which does not lead to desired productivity in organisations nowadays. As suggested earlier under principle No. 6 in this paper, the system of organisation that flourishes in to-day's society is such that accommodates staff and owns them up, as it were. Such organisations make staff feel at home, share a portion of profits with staff, communicate with staff, remain open to staff, share staff feelings, and identify with staff personal/family challenges. This is the type of organisation that succeeds these days. Managers of library and information centres can apply these strategies in their relationships with members of staff. Where they do, they will avoid all forms of partiality, treat all staff equally, deny no staff promotions, and encourage weak staff to shape up. More so, they advise staff regularly on how to grow on the job, mentor staff, avoid favouritism, build up an unbiased attitude, and disallow gossip. Staff of the library are rewarded or punished based strictly on their commitment, faithfulness, and productivity and not on either friendship or filial relationships (Ohadinma & Uwaoma, 2000). This means that openness to all and even- handedness are integral parts of the key to attaining equity in organisations. So, library managers should rather address issues relating to staff before them and not at their backs. In all, impartiality is the kernel of this principle. As a result, it must be upheld by library managers not only in the interests of the library as an organisation, but also for their own good since observation has shown that impartial managers are respected and appreciated by their staff.

2.12. Principle 12: Stability of Personnel Tenure

In this principle, Fayol expresses the need to recruit the right staff and train them on the job with a hope to retain them for long. The basis of this principle is the belief that such staff with a secured tenure will put back into the organisation the knowledge and experience which they may have garnered in the course of working for the organisation. This, however, is considered an old-fashioned way of approaching management. Contemporary management is suggesting the recruitment of staff that are already-made with experience and with the right qualifications. Some organisations have gone further to downsize staff recruited in the old system because of their unwillingness to adapt to new ways of performing jobs in the organisation. As a matter of fact, new generation organisations are not merely keen in re-cruiting men and women whom they will invest much

in from the start in order to get them working for the organisation. However, they are willing to spend on staff members that already have high success profiles and experience so that they can develop the organisation all the more. So, this is the era of recruiting the best qualified staff. The idea is that work can be very productive from the start and afterwards the staff can be trained to improve on what they already know how to do. This is one side of the principle and library and information centres managers should take note of it.

Another angle of Fayol's 'principle of stability of tenure' is that staff should be retained for as long as possible, sometimes up to retirement. But, this is not the order of the day in recent times, as mobility of labour is becoming the culture of many workers. For one, workers believe in having several opportunities—that new jobs can offer such things as better pay, job satisfaction, promotions, job security, societal recognition, and others. But this is not healthy forlibrary and information centres. Brain drain is a factor that should be avoided. In fact, library and information centres should hold firm on Fayol's principle here. Staff should be developed via on the job training, seminars, conferences, mentoring, and further studies. Organisational culture is not always easy to transmit and retain (Shein, 1984) let alone a system to change workers often. The majority of the new workers coming are often from another organisation with a different culture. So, managers of library and information centres should retain Fayol's 'principle of stability of personnel tenure' but must avoid recruiting into the library men and women who will not be productive to the system until they are trained. An element of this is noticeable in the head-hunting and recruitment of subject-specialists by authorities of special libraries. Although this calibre of staff may be new when they report or resume, they have had previous exposure and experience in the public or private sectors (Nnadozie, 2007). When staff are recruited from other establishments, the direct and indirect costs involved in training staff upon employment should therefore be avoided. This, however, does not eliminate the need for on the job mentoring essential for both new and old staff.

2.13. Principle 13: Initiative

A good manager must be one who can be creative to initiate new ideas and also be able to implement them. Fayol was direct to managers at this point. He understood the importance of good ideas to the growth and success of organisations. But, on the contrary, he did not foresee the situation of today where staff are becoming the idea-banks of organisations. This has been observed in Western countries where group problem-solving systems are patronised against dependence on top level management as the problem-solving point (Magjuka, 1991 & 1992). Moreover, Mintzberg's study in his PhD research (Robinson, 2005) confirmed that managers of these days seem not to be very good in initiating and implementing ideas as they are often preoccupied with so many other related and unrelated commitments that, in the end, leave them running after "work current, specific, well-defined and non-routine" activities. So, it is advisable for managers to empower their staff and give them the level playing ground required to initiate and implement new ideas.

In library and information centres, the almost non-existence of new ideas among librarians (especially in developing countries) has made library organisation seem uncreative, stagnant, and old-fashioned. This is the reason why their library customers, especially adolescents and young adults, are resorting to the Internet, since there is nothing new in the library. Whereas the Internet and its accompanying technologies offer a lot of platforms for proactive librarians to work with and retain their customers, a good number of library staff and their managers are rather not systematic and reflective planners. It may be that staff are waiting for the Librarian for initiatives and the Librarians-in-Charge, as managers, are preoccupied with numerous other things. This should not continue if the library organisation hopes to avoid decline and liquidation (Ohadinma & Uwaoma, 2000). Administrators and managers of library and information centres therefore should imbue their subordinates with the confidence to create and develop new ideas, as well as to implement them. Rewards and encouragements should be there for creative and/or innovative staff members so that generation of ideas can become competitive to the glory of the management and for the good of the organisation as a collective body.

2.14. Principle 14: *Esprit de Corps*

This is a French phrase which means enthusiasm and devotion among a group of people. Fayol is of the view that organisations should enforce and also maintain high morale and unity among their staff. This is

imperative as the existence of an organisation is a result of the coming together of men and women under a collective interest. Thus, understanding, love for each other, unity, peace, and common determination is paramount to their success. The saying that *united we stand, divided we fall* is equally applicable in libraries and information centres. In the same manner, managers of library and information centres must ensure that the library organisation is characterized by staff unity and co-operation. This however does not mean that some staff members will not disagree or quarrel. It is natural with some human beings to quarrel once in a while. But library managers must be strategists in such cases to ensure that such misunderstandings amongst staff do not affect common goals of the library organisation.

3. CONCLUSION AND RECOMMENDATIONS

This paper has critically analysed the '14 principles of management' proposed by Henri Fayol (Fayol, 1949). Some of the principles have been redefined and re-interpreted in recent management research to become better and more effective to organisations in their application. Yet a few others have remained as Fayol postulated them and are still widely adopted in the management of today's organisations. Generally, all organisations are similar in some ways in the context of management as a practice. The issue of categorization of organisations, whether profit or non-profit, into manufacturing, marketing, sales, or services as products, does not demean the need for management in all types of organisation. A library and information centre is not different and therefore should also be treated as a business organisation. As a sequel to this, this paper has presented a modification or adaptation of each of Fayol's 14 principles meant to guide managers of library and information centres. The principles are borne out of discourse on Fayol's '14 principles of management.' The new modified principles are comparatively presented in Table 1.

This paper therefore recommends the application of these principles to library administration. More so, research surveys can be conducted on case study bases to show the level of application of Fayol's principles or similar principles in library and information centres. As a matter of fact, research into library management

Table 1. Fayol's 14 Principles and their Implication in Today's Library and Information Centres (LICs)

Principles	Fayol's Proposition	Its Implications for LIC Managers
1	Division of work by specialisation	The job schedule of staff should not be rigid or static. In addition to their core or primary duties, staff should be able to perform other tasks within the organisation.
2	Centralize the organisations of power	Power and authority in any organization should be decentralized without undermining corporate cohesion. This will encourage the creation of new ideas and the harnessing of staff creativity.
3	Formal system of control over staff	The various informal groups within the workplace should be strengthened. For instance, trade unions and other staff groups can be brought on board to exert some influence and control over their members.
4	Staff report to only one head	Staff can report to more than one head and still harmonize directives to work successfully
5	One plan and one head for each plan	Multiple plans from one or more heads at a time is possible in order to advance corporate objectives.
6	Organisation interests first even if at the detriment of staff	The interests and welfare of the staff should not be overlooked. It is only where staff are motivated that they work whole-heartedly for the organisation's interests.
7	Deserving pay system	The pay system should be structured in such a way that the remuneration for workers is strictly performance- based.
8	Top management led decision making system	Creativity should not be stifled. Staff should be emboldened to initiate and implement policies relevant to their areas of specialization.
9	Vertical hierarchy and communication	Horizontal organizational structure and communication should be encouraged to the best interests of the organization
10	Arrangement of staff and things as suitable to management	The overall interests of the customer should be taken into consideration. Arrangement of staff and things as convenient for customers (users)
11	Fairness to staff to make them work more	Fairness to staff to give them a sense of belonging. The resultant feeling of appreciation makes them work harder
12	Recruit, train staff and encourage them to remain	Recruit self-made and experienced staff but sponsor them to on-the-job training on regular basis.
13	Top management conceive and implement new ideas	As much as possible, staff should be empowered to conceive and implement new ideas for the overall benefit of the organization.
14	Ensure high moral and unity among staff	Efforts should be made to ensure high morale and unity of purpose across various cadres of staff

practices and methods should be encouraged. There are several management methods and approaches prevailing in contemporary society and only research can present a reliable picture of what the situation is in library and information centres. So, further research is not only needed to reveal management practices in library and information centres but also to identify contemporary management methods which can be adopted by library managers for the day-to-day administration of library organisation.

REFERENCES

Aguolu, C. C., & Aguolu, I. E. (2002). *Library and information management in Nigeria.* Maiduguri, Nigeria: Ed-Linform Services.

Blackburn, R., & Rosen, B. (1993). Total quality and human resources management: Lessons learned from Baldrige award winning companies. *The Academy of Management Executives, 7* (3), 49-66.

Braham, J. (1989, April). Money talks. *Industry Week, 17,* 23.

Cascio, W. F. (1987). Do good or poor performers leave? A meta-analysis of the relationship between performance and turnover. *The Academy of Management Journal, 30* (4), 744 - 762.

Cavaleri, S., & Obloj, K. (1993). *Management system: A global perspective.* Belmont, CA: Wadsworth.

Drucker, P. (1954). *The practice of management.* New York: Harper & Row.

Edoka, B. E. (2000). *Introduction to library science.* Onitsha, Nigeria: Palma Publishing & Links Coy.

Fayol, H. (1917). *Administration industrielle et générale; prévoyance, organisation, commandement, coordination, controle.* Paris: H. Dunod & E. Pinat.

Fayol, H. (1930). *Industrial and general administration* (J. A. Coubrough, Trans.). London: Sir Isaac Pitman & Sons.

Fayol, H. (1949). *General and industrial management* (C. Storrs, Trans.). London: Sir Isaac Pitman & Sons.

Hinterhuber, H. H., & Popp, W. (1992, January-February). Are you a strategist or just a manager? *Harvard Business Review*, 105-113.

Idih, E., Njoku, J., & Idih, C. (2011). *Business com-munication for office managers.* Owerri, Nigeria: Tropical Publishers.

Ifidon, S. E., & Ifidon, E. (2007). *New directions in African library management.* Ibadan, Nigeria: Spectrum Publishers.

Ifidon, S. E. (1979). Participatory management in libraries. *Bendel Library Journal, 2*(1), 1-10.

Ifidon, S. E. (1985). *Essentials of management for African university libraries.* Lagos, Nigeria: Libriservice.

Imaga, E. U. U. (2001). *Elements of management and culture in organizational behaviour.* Enugu, Nigeria: Rhyee Kerex Publishers.

Iwueke, O. C., & Oparaku, U. D. (2011). *Management.* Owerri: Classic Business Services.

Magjuka, R. F. (1991/1992). Survey: Self-managed teams achieve continuous improvement best. *National Productivity Review* (Spring), 203-211.

Mayo, E. (1933). The human problem of industrial civilization. Cambridge, MA: Harvard University Press.

McGregor, D. (1960). *The human side of enterprise.* New York: McGraw-Hill.

Mintzberg, H. (1973). *The nature of managerial work.* New York: Harper & Row.

Nnadozie, C. O. (2007). *Foundations of library practice.* Owerri, Nigeria: Springfield Publishers.

Nwachukwu, C. C. (1988). *Management: Theory and practice.* Ibadan, Nigeria: Africana-Feb Publishers.

Ohadinma, D. C., & Uwaoma, N. (2000). *Industrial personnel management.* Owerri, Nigeria: Rescue Publishers.

Ononogbo, R. U. (2008). Architect's brief for the design and construction of a university library building: A model draft. *Communicate: Journal of Library and Information Science, 10*(1), 67-77.

Pugh, D.S., & Hickson, D.J. (2007).*Great writers on organisations: The third omnibus edition*, 3rd rev. ed. Farnham, United Kingdom: Ashgate Publishing.

Rodrigues, C. A. (2001). Fayol's 14 principles of management then and now: A framework for managing today's organisations effectively. *Management Decision, 39* (10), 880-889.

Schein, E. H. (1984). Coming to a new awareness of organisational culture. *Sloan Management Re-*

views (Winter), 3-16.

Senge, P. (1990). *The fifth discipline*. New York: Doubleday.

Stroh, L. K., Northcraft, G. B., & Neale, M. A. (2002). *Organisational behavior: A management challenge*. Mahwah, NJ: Lawrence Erlbaum.

Taylor, F. W. (1911). *The principles of scientific management*. New York: Harper & Row.

Witzel, M. (2003). *Fifty key figures in management*. London: Routledge.

Wren, D. A., Bedeian, A. G., & Breeze, J. D. (2002). The foundations of Henri Fayol's administrative theory. *Management Decision, 40* (9), 906-918.

7

Exploratory Study of Developing a Synchronization-Based Approach for Multi-step Discovery of Knowledge Structures

So Young YU *

Department of Library and Information Science
Hannam University, Republic of Korea
E-mail: soyoungyu201@gmail.com

ABSTRACT

As Topic Modeling has been applied in increasingly various domains, the difficulty in naming and characterizing topics also has been recognized more. This study, therefore, explores an approach of combining text mining with network analysis in a multi-step approach. The concept of synchronization was applied to re-assign the top author keywords in more than one topic category, in order to improve the visibility of the topic-author keyword network, and to increase the topical cohesion in each topic. The suggested approach was applied using 16,548 articles with 2,881 unique author keywords in construction and building engineering indexed by KSCI. As a result, it was revealed that the combined approach could improve both the visibility of the topic-author keyword map and topical cohesion in most of the detected topic categories. There should be more cases of applying the approach in various domains for generalization and advancement of the approach. Also, more sophisticated evaluation methods should also be necessary to develop the suggested approach.

Keywords: Synchronization, Ego-centric Network, Topic Modeling, Informetrics

1. INTRODUCTION

The approach of Topic Modeling ("TM") has been applied in various domains, such as tech forecasting, text mining, and informetrics (Griffiths & Steyvers, 2004; Kang et al., 2013; Lu & Zhai, 2008; Park & Song,

*Corresponding Author: So Young YU
Assistant Professor
Department of Library and Information Science
Hannam University, Republic of Korea
E-mail: soyoungyu201@gmail.com

2013; Song et al., 2013; Tang et al., 2012; Titov & Mc-Donald, 2008; Yu, 2013). The foundation and applicability of TM can be described as being fundamental and concrete due to the fact that is based on the Probability Model, which is linked to the Language Model. Development of an advanced method, at the same time, has been an ongoing process in order to enhance the performance of TM and various tools, and its applications have been developed and distributed.

The approach to interpreting the result of TM, however, has been recognized as an area needing growth in resolving the difficulty in characterizing and interpreting topics. Evidential cases of this difficulty have been found in some studies and these studies demonstrate additional efforts, such as inserting topics or eliminating keywords, to reduce the difficulty of interpretation (Hall et al., 2008; Talley et al., 2011). For example, non-informative keywords were eliminated and more informative phrases were added for easier interpretation after executing LDA-based TM analysis on NIH-supported research output in the study of Hall et al. (2008). Similar to the study of Hall et al. (2008), some number of topics were inserted additionally after finding 36 valid topics by applying TM in the research of Talley et al. (2012).

One of the possible reasons for this difficulty could be the de-contextualization of the relation among the top-k keyword in a topic when the output of TM is provided. The most common way of providing the output of TM is a list of top-k keywords of each topic (Chang et al., 2009). The sorted keywords in order of probability, however, would not be enough to deliver the character of a certain topic, which could be inferred from the overall combination of the loaded keywords in the topic (Chuang et al., 2012; Ramage et al., 2009b). And this implies that characterizing the latent topic could be needed in additional works for inferring meaningful contexts from the keyword list.

Another possible reason could be a multi-assigned keyword; that is, a keyword which is assigned to more than two topics at the same time with high probability. This means that the multi-assigned keywords are, probably, frequently occurring keywords in a certain dataset and this could make interpretation vague and lead to several similar names among the topics. Therefore, it could be hard to achieve the distinctiveness of interpretation.

Sophisticated methods of TM and visualization have been suggested to make interpretation easier (Chaney &

Blei, 2012; Chuang et al., 2012). Labeled LDA (Ramage et al., 2009a) and Partially Labeled LDA (Ramage et al., 2011) were developed for enhancing the performance of TM. Several visualization approach and network analysis methods including citation linking have been also applied for the better performance of TM (Mei et al., 2008; Nallapati et al., 2008).

Along with the previous research, this study, therefore, aims to explore an approach to enhance the ease of interpretation by combining social network analysis with topic modeling. In order to contextualize the keywords in a topic and to reduce the number of multi-assigned keywords, co-word analysis, and the concept of a "synchronization network" is applied in refining the result of TM without distracting the topical cohesion in a topic.

Synchronization in a complex network is defined as phase transition when the entire network of nodes begins to emit and receive a signal at the same frequency, and this phenomenon has been detected and researched in various domains (Arenas et al. 2008; Kuramoto & Nishikawa , 1987; Niebur et al., 1991; Pikovsky et al., 2001; Strogatz, 2000; Strogatz, 2001; Strogatz, 2003; Strogatz & Mirollo, 1988). Synchronization can be understood as a dynamic of networks focusing on the change of the property of a node affected by the property of the group of its connected nodes. Various applications of synchronization, such as analysis of genetic networks, systemic analysis on neuronal networks, data mining, opinion dynamics, neuroscience, or social sciences have been developed (Blasius et al. 1999; Buchanan, 2007; Elowitz & Leibler, 2000; Garcia-Ojalvo et al., 2004; Pluchino et al., 2005).

Applications of synchronization in data mining have been proposed for data clustering. The assumption for applying synchronization on data mining is that the dynamics of the data system could be categorized into clusters by detecting synchronization, and most of the previous research focused on dynamic modeling for the detection. Based on statistical methods of data mining, therefore, synchronization has been used in sophisticating the data mining techniques and exploiting the applicability of synchronization in data mining (Jalili, 2013; Jha & Yadava, 2012; Miyano & Tsutsui, 2007a; Miyano & Tsutsui, 2007b; Miyano & Tsutsui, 2008a; Miyano & Tsutsui, 2008b; Miyano & Tsutsui, 2009; Miyano & Tsutsui, 2013; Tilles et al., 2013; Wan et al., 2010).

Along with the previous studies, the application of

synchronization in text mining was explored in this study by applying the concept in deliberating the result of topic modeling. There are operational definitions for the application. It is assumed that a multi-assigned keyword can be re-assigned to a certain topic by synchronizing the topic of the keyword with those of its co-occurring keywords. In this study, therefore, "keywords in co-word network" is matched to "the nodes" in the synchronization network and "re-assignment of one topic to a multi-assigned keyword" is matched for "phase transition." The "entire network" is defined operationally as an ego-centric network of a certain multi-assigned keyword and its connected keywords that were used for determining the topic for the ego.

2. METHODOLOGY

2.1. Research Design

This study suggested the combined approach of text mining and network analysis. The research design of this study is shown in Figure 1. The perplexity from the natural language processing domain was considered in the first step, and topical similarity from text mining was applied in LDA (Latent Dirichlet Allocation, Blei et al., 2003)-based Topic Modeling ("LDATM") and Merging Overlapped Topics ("MOT") steps. The concept of synchronization networks and ego-centric networks from complex networks was applied in the Re-Assigning Multi-Assigned Keyword ("RAMAK") step.

In the subject of Construction & Building Technology, 16,584 bibliographic records of KSCI-indexed articles[1] were collected and pre-processed for topic modeling and co-word analysis. The indexed keywords for the analysis were from an English authors' keyword field, and 2,881 keywords were used in the modeling.

LDATM was performed after 10 times of pre-testing for finding the optimal number of topics, and the top 20 keywords for each topic were selected. After modeling, all pairs of topics with similarity values of 1 by comparing all the probability of the loaded keywords were merged as one topic. The multi-assigned keywords were also identified after merging topics.

For the re-assigning process (RAMAK), a co-word network of 2,486 top 20 keywords was extracted by calculating cosine similarity between keywords from a document-keyword matrix. The Ego-centric network of each multi-assigned keyword was extracted and re-assigned a topic on the ego that was determined by finding the most frequently occurring topic number from its nearest neighbor keywords, with the cosine similarity of their connections in mind.

The details of each process are as follows in 2.2, 2.3, 2.4 and 2.5.

2.2. Data Collection and Pre-Processing

To begin, 16,548 KSCI-indexed articles in the domain of construction and building technology were collected for the analysis. The data fields for articles collected were: publication year, DOI, ISSN, journal name, citation counts, title, author name, affiliation,

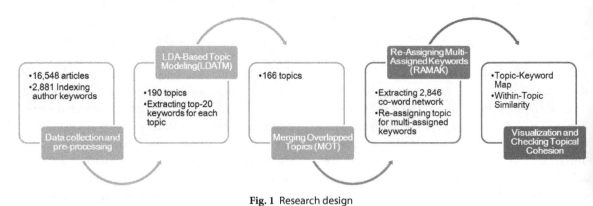

Fig. 1 Research design

---

[1] KSCI (Korea Science Citation Index) is one of the national citation indices of the Republic of Korea and it provides bibliographic records of articles published in 661 national major journals of science and technology. See http://ksci.kisti.re.kr/main/about.ksci.

author keywords, and abstracts. All the text fields, such as title, author keywords, or abstracts were written both in English and Korean. For this study, author keywords were indexed and all syntactic stopwords were eliminated. The total number of indexed terms from author keyword fields is 2,881 as shown in Table 1.

Table 1. Data Collection

KSCI Subject category	No. of indexed journals	No. of indexed articles	No. of citing articles	No. of references	No. of indexed author keywords
Construction & Building Technology	36	16,548	12,425	234,849	2,881

In order to set the number of topics, a perplexity score was calculated with 1,030 times of LDA-Based Topic Modeling. Perplexity score in a corpus means the predictability of a topic model and it is a widely-used metric in topic model evaluation (Asuncion et al., 2009).

Perplexity score is a parameter of how well a probability model predicts a test set (sample) in information theory and measurement of evaluating Language Modelin natural language processing. A lower value means a surer model (Brown et al., 1992).

The modelings were executed with different numbers of topics and 1,000 iterations, and the number of topics in a model has been changed in the range from 10 to 1030 by increasing 10 for each modeling. The number of topics with the lowest perplexity score was estimated as 190.

Stanford Topic Modeling Toolbox 0.4.0 ("TMT," Ramage et al., 2009a) was used in pre-testing. TMT, which has been developed by Stanford National Language Lab, was aimed to support research in social sciences and related fields by applying topic modeling on textual data. It is based on Java and supports LDA, Labeled LDA, and Partially Labeled LDA (Blei et al., 2003; Blei et al., 2006; Ramage et al., 2011).

As a result, the optimal number of topics was estimated as 190 by using perplexity value. The most frequently identified number of topics with a minimum value of perplexity was 190.

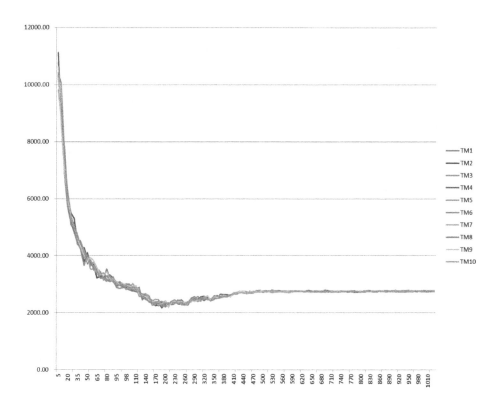

Fig. 2 Changes in perplexity value over the number of topic

Table 2. Perplexity changes in pre-test

# of Topic	LDATM1	LDATM2	LDATM3	LDATM4	LDATM5	LDATM6	LDATM7	LDATM8	LDATM9	LDATM10
10	8975.335	8963.464	8831.376	8649.377	9084.956	9109.842	8783.968	9147.761	8550.985	10055.105
100	2816.215	2792.832	3026.406	2769.778	2824.944	2828.139	2931.039	2904.674	2915.727	2923.103
110	2838.844	2741.301	2868.584	2911.134	2802.437	2768.915	2884.796	2821.816	2957.938	2876.513
120	2899.212	2733.605	2570.985	2759.323	2662.365	2696.362	2616.600	2713.299	2643.197	2733.443
130	2462.717	2606.532	2586.339	2632.329	2637.865	2551.660	2665.585	2666.303	2624.515	2547.768
140	2629.703	2537.296	2529.983	2598.290	2532.595	2481.425	2676.373	2545.855	2584.815	2675.385
150	2543.644	2529.799	2481.421	2493.457	2450.562	2398.660	2526.935	2375.752	2454.982	2613.446
160	2363.844	2378.645	2261.015	2358.277	2424.803	2345.375	2452.961	2334.453	2384.007	2332.292
170	2280.889	2251.022	2281.229	2362.431	2480.557	2386.532	2339.762	2334.752	2392.494	2392.639
180	2254.074	2326.227	2426.930	2339.651	2467.936	2378.713	2280.134	2337.829	2376.632	2401.485
190	2311.001	2366.047	2301.056	2176.891	2236.664	2405.793	2309.904	2417.616	2286.746	2270.426
200	2210.481	2317.458	2313.562	2309.178	2249.580	2323.953	2431.527	2223.865	2408.394	2368.890
210	2296.630	2342.619	2267.309	2291.714	2263.767	2351.669	2257.607	2312.559	2182.767	2286.754
220	2380.728	2321.671	2370.908	2392.573	2414.567	2285.605	2327.877	2415.950	2397.257	2412.482
230	2387.080	2402.662	2362.987	2405.343	2369.918	2324.615	2402.163	2351.932	2400.145	2469.383
240	2452.924	2314.648	2455.086	2425.034	2313.190	2452.122	2403.438	2410.961	2387.761	2333.303
250	2304.188	2315.152	2346.487	2455.857	2445.545	2436.064	2274.259	2351.760	2405.131	2319.241
300	2399.035	2487.912	2414.451	2460.291	2386.524	2578.468	2112.175	2429.788	2457.273	2480.635
400	2583.301	2575.829	2585.134	2603.352	2644.606	2579.357	2561.219	2590.439	2572.175	2634.949
500	2758.263	2769.149	2735.997	2720.636	2761.117	2770.918	2768.335	2758.400	2765.126	2758.162
600	2780.201	2766.005	2745.685	2746.498	2774.380	2755.659	2745.235	2752.476	2756.612	2759.085
700	2736.222	2781.246	2766.452	2761.840	2747.509	2764.499	2773.267	2766.780	2725.437	2741.442
800	2751.469	2733.360	2727.797	2752.880	2743.352	2748.101	2759.525	2756.007	2771.173	2740.718
900	2755.025	2768.088	2762.950	2735.265	2747.222	2777.986	2771.064	2752.937	2749.728	2782.771
1000	2762.954	2776.877	2744.741	2762.338	2780.410	2771.742	2769.924	2751.173	2752.731	2757.215
1010	2760.813	2772.226	2746.074	2743.839	2769.542	2774.740	2756.311	2734.745	2781.271	2765.664
1020	2744.803	2760.696	2772.429	2745.061	2762.559	2774.252	2755.717	2771.226	2782.883	2777.400
1030	2771.209	2757.181	2778.056	2768.634	2745.139	2782.631	2745.651	2765.064	2765.616	2745.922
No_Topic	200	170	160	190	190	220	210	200	210	190

Note: The rest of this table is available upon request.

2.3. Topic Detection and Merging Similar Topics

By setting the number of topics as 190, LDA-based Topic Modeling (LDATM) was performed with 1,000 repetitions. Topic Modeling Toolbox 0.4 was used for the modeling. Each topic was labeled with its topic number, such as 'T1,' and the most dominant topic had a smaller number in the label. The top 20 keywords of each topic were selected to describe the topic and the total number of unique top keywords was 2,846. Stanford TMT 0.4.0 was also used in topic detection.

Merging overlapped Topics (MOT) was executed by calculating similarity between two topics, and the topics are merged at a threshold of 1. The merged topic that 25 topics were merged into was labeled as "T4."

2.4. Extracting Co-Word Network and Re-arranging Multi-Assigned Top-Keywords

The purpose of this step was to re-arrange a multi-assigned top-keyword in LDA-Based TM by assigning the keyword into one topic. There were 609 top-keywords which were assigned to more than two topics at the same time.

In this step, the concept of oscillator in synchronization networks was applied practically to determine and assign one topic to a multi-assigned keyword. In this study, the suggested application is more focused on the result of synchronization itself as a change of the property of a node evoked by its neighbor nodes, rather than modeling the dynamics of synchronization, in order to use the concept of synchronization to assign one topic to a multi-assigned keyword considering the topics which its nearest neighbors were assigned to. That is, the topic of the multi-assigned keyword is determined by the most frequently occurring topic from its nearest neighbors.

The process of applying synchronization is:

a. Extract ego-centric network of a multi-assigned keyword from co-word network.
b. For each neighbor, check the assigned topic numbers.
c. For each topic number pertinent to the neighbor, sum the cosine similarity between ego and its neighbor.
d. Iterate "b-c" for all neighbor nodes.
e. Average the summed cosine similarity for each topic number.
f. Determine the most influential topic number that has the maximum value of averaged cosine similarity.

To extract an ego-centric network, co-occurrence networks among 2,846 top-keywords were extracted by using cosine similarity. For 609 multi-assigned keywords, 609 individual ego-centric networks were extracted. In each network of "EGO," the ego node is a certain multi-assigned keyword. The network consists of the ego and its nearest neighbors, which are directly connected to the ego. The link weight is the cosine similarity between two nodes.

When each keyword is assigned to a certain topic as a result of LDATM and the links are calculated by using cosine similarity, the combination of those LDATM and co-occurrence similarities is used to determine the topic for the "EGO."

For example, assume that there is an ego-centric network for a multi-assigned keyword "EGO" with four nearest neighbor keywords, "N1," "N2," "N3," and "N4." This is a subset of the co-word network consisting of "EGO" and its nearest neighbors as node and links among them. The link weight between two nodes is the cosine similarity score of their co-occurrence in a document. To determine the topic category of the "EGO," the weight score for a certain topic is averaged by using the cosine similarity between the "EGO" and its connected keywords that are assigned in the topic. For instance, N1 and N3 were assigned to Topic [1], while N4 for Topic [3], and N2 for Topic[2] were assigned, respectively, in Figure 3. The topic for "EGO" was re-assigned as Topic[1] because the highest weight was from the combination of N2 and N3 with Topic[1], as shown in Figure 3-(b).

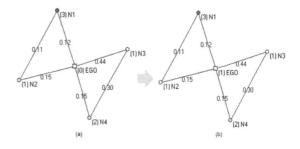

Topic number	Neighbor	Avg. cosine similarity
[1]	N2, N3	(0.15+0.44)/2 = 0.295
[2]	N4	0.15
[3]	N1	0.12

Fig. 3 Example of RAMAK: Re-assigning a topic to a multi-assigned keyword

2.5. Comparison of Maps and Topical Cohesion

To identify the effect of applying RAMAK, comparison of topic-keywords networks was conducted. The topic-keywords maps were made by using PAJEK 3.0 for visual comparison. For seeing a structural difference, the density and average degree of nodes were calculated and compared.

For comparing topical cohesion, "within-topic cosine similarity" was computed. The value of within-topic cosine similarity is an average cosine similarity of all occurring pairs of keywords in a specific topic. For a topic i, cosine similarity (i) for all pairs of keyword$_j$ and keyword$_k$ in the topic i were summed up and divided by the number of the pairs.

Within-topic similarity $(i) = \frac{1}{n}\sum_{i=1}^{n} cosine_i(kwd_j, kwd_k)$

The differences in within topic similarity for all topics were statistically tested by conducting a paired-sample t-test and correlation analysis using SPSS21.

3. RESULTS AND ANALYSIS

3.1. Changes in Major Topics and Related Keywords

Each topic has top 20 keywords after applying LDATM and the number of the top keywords in several topic categories was changed by applying MOT and RAMAK. The number of 20 top keywords in only three topics (T157, T57, and T83) had been kept after reassigning the multi-assigned keywords, and the number of top-keywords in the other 163 topics had been changed. Only three topic categories (T15, T42, and T74) were expanded in terms of size, and another 160 topic categories resulted in fewer top-keywords. This doesn't mean the decrease of the number of top-keywords but the decrease of the number of multi-assigned keywords.

Figure 4 –(a) shows the number of changes in the number of top-keywords for each topic category and Figure 4 –(b) shows the number of topic categories with the size of the topic. The sizes of topics mostly decreased, and only three topics were increased in size. The topics which resulted in less than 10 top keywords are T79 and T612, while the topics with more than 20 top keywords are T15, T42, and T74.

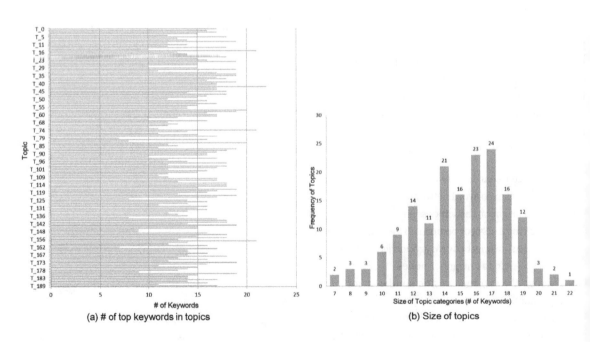

(a) # of top keywords in topics   (b) Size of topics

Fig. 4 Changes in the size of topics

The number of keywords being assigned in more than two topics ("multi-assigned keyword") was 609, which is 21.3% of the total number of unique top keywords (2,864). The number of multi-assigned top-keywords was also decreased to 7, and 602 out of 609 multi-assigned keyword were re-assigned to one topic category by applying RAMAK. The remains of multi-assigned keywords were "Shape memory alloy," "Urban Residential Area," "Design Value Engineering," "Peter Zumthor," "Brittle fracture," "Fatigue crack," and "Housing Satisfaction," which cover several research topics of construction and building technology in general.

The top 10 topics with loaded top keywords were shown in Table 4. As shown in the table, multi-assigned keywords were re-assigned to non-top 10 topics and new top keywords from non-top 10 topics were added to any of the top 10 topics.

For example, the word term of "optimal design" in italics had been loaded to three topics among the top 10 topics; that is, T2, T4, and T8 in LDATM result, and it had been loaded to 33 different topics among the 190 topics. It was re-loaded to T100 after applying MOT and RAMAK. And the word term of "Mixed-Use Development" in T3 and T5 was re-located in T15 by applying MOT and RAMAK.

Adding new top keywords to the top 10 topic categories was made by the application. For example, "global warming" (underlined) in T3 was added to T3 by considering the most prominent topic number among its strongly connected co-words. All newly added top-keywords in the top 10 topics were underlined in Table 4.

Table 3. Major Multi-Assigned Keywords

Keywords	LDATM+MOT	LDATM+MOT+RAMAK	LDATM
Radar rainfall	9	1	33
Optimal design	9	1	33
Forest fire	9	1	33
Conversion	7	1	31
Flexural strength	7	1	7
Sediment transport	6	1	30
Vegetation	6	1	30
Furniture design	6	1	30
Productivity	6	1	6
Composite	6	1	6

Table 4. Comparison of Top 10 Topic Categories and Its Keywords

Topic	20 Top-Keywords (LDATM)	Top-Keywords (LDATM+MOTRAMAK)
T0	Shaking Table Test, Partial Safety Factor, Nuclear Power Plant, Science Museum, Slope Stability, Cold-Formed Steel, Limit State Design, Displacement Ductility, Exhibition Method, Anchor Bolt, EDG(Emergency Diesel Generator), Near-Fault Ground Motion, Flexural Capacity, Reliability-Based Design, Holding Power, Children, Seismic Capacity, RC building, Safety Factor, Sliding	Shaking Table Test, Partial Safety Factor, Nuclear Power Plant, Science Museum, Slope Stability, Cold-Formed Steel, Limit State Design, Exhibition Method, Anchor Bolt, Near-Fault Ground Motion, Reliability-Based Design, Holding Power, Children, RC Building, Safety Factor, Sliding, EDG(Emergency Diesel Generator)

T1	Permeability, Infiltration, Urbanization, Hysteresis, SWMM, Sustainable Design, Soil-Water Characteristic Curve, Construction Project, Unsaturated Soils, Competency, Competency Model, Green Home, City, Sensor, Unsaturated Soil, Natural Elements, Redevelopment, Groundwater Level, Mix Design, Insulation	Permeability, Infiltration, Urbanization, Hysteresis, Sustainable Design, Soil-Water Characteristic Curve, Construction Project, Unsaturated Soils, Competency, Competency Model, Green Home, City, Unsaturated Soil, Natural Elements, Mix Design, _ESP-r_
T2	Small Hydropower, Methanehydrate, Natural gas, Design Parameter, Storage, Specific Output, Rainfall Condition, Equilibrium, Design Flowrate, Load Factor, Trench, Heliostat, Direct Normal Insolation, Capacity, Receiver, Cooling Energy, Flow Duration Curve, Priority, Lighting Energy, _Optimal Design_	Small Hydropower, Methanehydrate, Natural gas, Design Parameter, Storage, Specific Output, Rainfall Condition, Equilibrium, Design Flowrate, Load Factor, Trench, Heliostat, Direct Normal Insolation, Capacity, Receiver, Cooling Energy, _Correlation_
T3	Urban Design, Housing, Urban Landscape, Correlation Analysis, Mixed-Use Development, Urban Spatial Structure, Development, Sea Surface Temperature, Streetscape, Urban, CBD, Integration, Meaning, Residential Environment, Cognitive Map, Design Guidelines, Plan, Architecture, Sense, Circulation System	Urban Design, housing, Urban Landscape, Urban Spatial Structure, Development, Sea Surface Temperature, Urban, CBD, Integration, Meaning, Cognitive Map, Plan, Sense, Circulation System, _Global Warming_
T4	De Stijl, VRS, Optimal Design, Forest Fire, Radar Rainfall, Sediment Transport, Conversion, Kalman Filter, Regional Characteristics, Pan Evaporation, Space-Time, MCDM, Reference Evapotranspiration, Transition, Furniture Design, CORS, Vegetation, Multi Criteria Decision Making, Neo Plasticism, Work Information	De Stijl, VRS, Kalman Filter, Regional Characteristics, Pan Evaporation, Space-Time, MCDM, Reference Evapotranspiration, CORS, Multi Criteria Decision Making, Neo Plasticism, Work Information
T5	Land Use, Model, Thermal Environment, Public Design, Urban Planning, Urban Climate, Shallow-Water Equations, k- Varepsilon, Surface Roughness, RANS, Finite Volume Method, Street Furniture, Landscape, Kappa, Dam-Break, Heat Island, Urban Climate Simulation System, _Mixed-Use Development_, Approximate Riemann Solver, Urban Heat Island	Land Use, Model, Public Design, Urban Planning, Urban Climate, Shallow-Water Equations, k- Varepsilon, Surface Roughness, RANS, Finite Volume Method, Street Furniture, Kappa, Dam-Break, Urban Climate Simulation System, Approximate Riemann Solver, Urban Heat Island, _Method, Vortex_
T6	Drying Shrinkage, Autogenous Shrinkage, Diffusion Coefficient, Chloride Penetration, Bridge Deck, Early Age, Finishing Material, Chloride Ion, Water Content, Architectural Space, Porosity, Diffusion, Cracking, Regression Analysis, Steel Powder, Convection, Fiber, Hydration Heat, Mechanical Behavior, Humidity	Drying Shrinkage, Autogenous Shrinkage, Diffusion Coefficient, Chloride Penetration, Bridge Deck, Early Age, Finishing Material, Chloride Ion, Cracking, Steel Powder, Convection, Hydration Heat, Mechanical Behavior
T7	FEM, Beam-To-Column Connection, Elastic Modulus, Diaphragm, Stress Concentration, Soft Ground, Consolidation, Shear Buckling, Anisotropy, Steel Box-Girder, Stiffener, Parametric Study, Cyclic Loading Test, Strength, Embankment, Steel Box-Girder Bridge, RBDO, Connection, Reliability Based Design Optimization, Added Mass	FEM, Beam-To-Column Connection, Diaphragm, Stress Concentration, Soft Ground, Shear Buckling, Anisotropy, Steel Box-Girder, Stiffener, Steel Box-Girder Bridge, RBDO, Reliability Based Design Optimization, Added Mass, _Fatigue Crack_
T8	De Stijl, VRS, _Optimal Design_, Forest Fire, Radar Rainfall, Sediment Transport, Conversion, Kalman Filter, Regional Characteristics, Pan Evaporation, Space-Time, MCDM, Reference Evapotranspiration, Transition, Furniture Design, CORS, Vegetation, Multi Criteria Decision Making, Neo Plasticism, Work Information	Being merged with T4
T9	Semi-Rigid Connection, Steel Frame, Plastic Hinge, Beam-Column, Structural Optimization, Semi-Rigid, Design Factor, Diagrid, Push-Over, Dynamic Relaxation Method, Shape Optimization, Initial Stiffness, Story Drift, Arc-Length Method, Elasto-Plastic Analysis, Theta, Pushover Analysis, Non-Linearity, Curve, Architectural Planning	Semi-Rigid Connection, Steel Frame, Plastic Hinge, Structural Optimization, Semi-Rigid, Design Factor, Diagrid, Push-Over, Dynamic Relaxation Method, Shape Optimization, Story Drift, Arc-Length Method, Elasto-Plastic Analysis, Theta, Non-Linearity, Curve, _Arrangement, Brittle Fracture_

Note. The rest of this table is available upon request.

3.2. Changes in Knowledge Structure

Both the density and average degree of the topic keyword network were decreased by applying MOT+RAMAK, due to the fact that the links between multiple topics and top keywords were eliminated. Therefore, the network of "LDATM+MOT+RAMAK" was identified as providing a clearer view visually.

The enhancement in visualization could be identified in network structure in terms of density and average degree. The density of the topic-keyword network of LDATM+MOT+RAMAK was decreased to 0.006 from 0.008, so that it could be expected to have less complex link structures. The average number of connected nodes for each node in the network (Avg. Degree) was also decreased to 1.88 from 2.84.

The improvement in visualization was also presented in comparing those maps visually. As shown in Figure 5–(a) and Figure 5 –(b), it can be visually identified that the "LDATM+MOT+RAMAK" network has a more refined and clearer structure between topics and their top keywords. The box indicates a topic category and the eclipse indicates a certain top keyword.

There was only one component in Figure 5-(a), in which all topics and keywords were connected by the multi-assigned keywords. It was obvious that all topics in the analyzed domain were related to each other, but interpretation was difficult because of the visual complexity. The map of Figure 5-(b), which was the result of applying RAMAK, presented a relatively clearer and more easy-to-analyze situation. The number of connected topics and keywords was decreased and most of the topics were differentiated from each other visually.

Table 5. Structure of Topic-Keyword Networks

KSCI Subject category	# of Top-20 Keyword nodes	# of Topic nodes	Density	Avg. Degree
LDATM	2,486	190	0.008	2.84
LDATM+MOT	2,486	166	0.008	2.5
LDATM+MOT+RAMAK	2,486	166	0.006	1.88

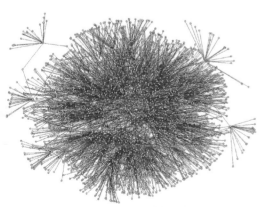

(a) Topic-Keyword map of LDATM+MOT

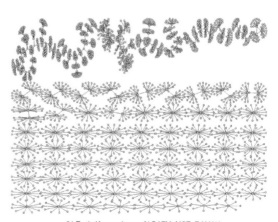

(b) Topic-Keyword map of LDATM+MOT+RAMAK

Fig. 5 Changes in the structure of topic-keyword maps

In addition to the change in overall topic-keywords network structure, a change in the 10 dominant topics and their pertinent keywords was also analyzed. The number of keywords in Figure 6 was 178 and the number of keywords in Figure 7 is 141, because of re-assigning the multi-assigned keywords. As was identified in Table 4, two multi-assigned keywords, that is, "optimal design" and "multi-use development" were re-located

to other topic categories and links between T3 and T5 and between T2 and T4 were eliminated.

It was identified that the changes in dominant topics were not huge, relatively, when comparing the result to Figure 5. It could, therefore, imply that the process of re-assigning multi-assigned keywords could keep the major knowledge structure while refining the relatively peripheral topics.

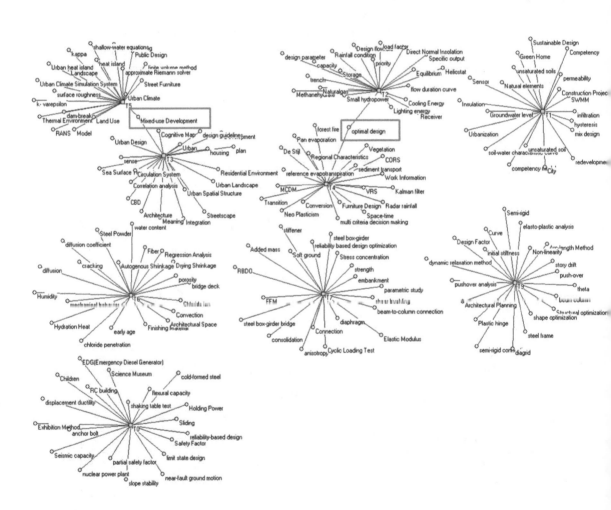

Fig. 6 Dominant topic-keyword map of LDATM+MOT

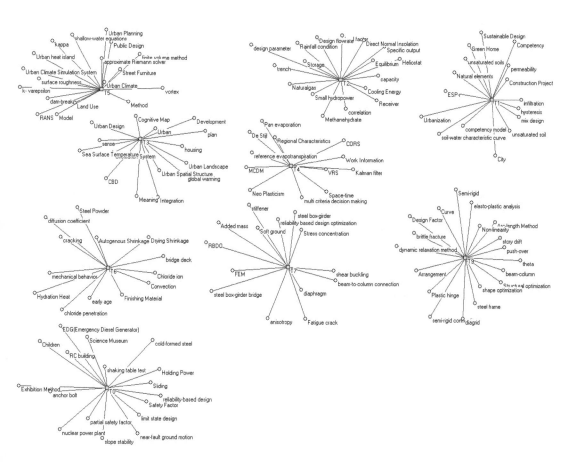

Fig. 7 Dominant topic-keyword map of LDATM+MOT+RAMAK

3.3. Changes in Topical Cohesion

The average value of within-topic cosine similarity over 166 topic categories was increased by 0.029 after re-assigning the multi-assigned keywords, and the difference was statistically significant ($t(166) = -16.27$, $p < .01$). The values of within-topic similarity of 159 topic categories were increased and only seven topic categories had decreased within-topic cosine similarity values.

A paired-samples t-test, therefore, was conducted to evaluate whether the within-topic similarity of LDATM+MOT+RAMAK(B) is higher than that of LDATM+MOT(A). The results shows that the mean of (B) (M= .191, SD =.062) is significantly higher than the mean of (A) (M= .161, SD =.054), $t(166) = -16.27$, $p < .01$.

Table 6 shows the changes of topical cohesion in major topics, and all topics except T2 had an increase in topical cohesion among the keywords in the topic. The value of within-topic similarity of all topics except T2 increased after applying RAMAK.

The 10 topic categories with the highest increase rate and the 10 topic categories with the lowest increase rate are shown in Table 7. The increase rate of within-topic similarity is a ratio of the within-topic similarity of LDATM+MOT+RAMAK based on the within-topic similarity of LDATM. As shown in Table 7, the increase rate below one is only seven topic categories and the values were close to one.

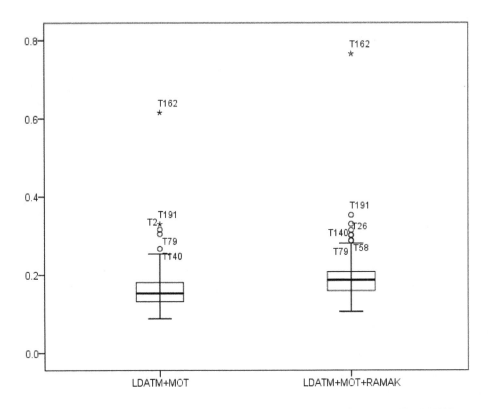

Fig. 8 Difference in within-topic similarity between LDATM+MOT and LDATM+MOT+RAMAK

Table 6. Changes of Topical Cohesion in Major Topics

Topic	Within-Topic Similarity of LDATM+MOT (A)	Within-Topic Similarity of LDATM+MOT+RAMAK (B)	# of Keyword of LDATM+MOT+RAMAK (C)	Increase Rate of Within-Topic Similarity (B/A)
T0	0.200	0.217	16	1.081
T1	0.171	0.200	16	1.167
T2	0.316	0.314	17	0.995
T4	0.330	0.353	12	1.070
T3	0.115	0.139	15	1.205
T5	0.193	0.208	18	1.076
T6	0.122	0.152	13	1.248
T7	0.119	0.152	14	1.283
T9	0.195	0.212	19	1.090

Table 7. Top 10 Topics with the Major Changes in Within-Topic Similarity

Topic	Within-Topic Similarity of LDATM+MOT (A)	Within-Topic Similarity of LDATM+MOT+RAMAK (B)	# of Keyword of LDATM+MOT+RAMAK	Increase Rate of Within-Topic Similarity (B/A)
T179	0.135	0.244	9	1.808
T72	0.098	0.172	10	1.758
T28	0.088	0.145	10	1.650
T148	0.130	0.207	9	1.594
T65	0.141	0.225	10	1.589
T95	0.141	0.221	10	1.565
T14	0.135	0.206	10	1.524
T69	0.132	0.198	13	1.507
T107	0.189	0.280	11	1.486
T86	0.139	0.207	11	1.485
T15	0.206	0.195	21	0.944
T188	0.142	0.135	11	0.957
T143	0.165	0.160	19	0.971
T114	0.112	0.109	18	0.972
T42	0.246	0.240	22	0.977
T79	0.304	0.301	7	0.990
T2	0.316	0.314	17	0.995
T97	0.147	0.148	18	1.002
T189	0.117	0.119	17	1.015
T122	0.131	0.133	19	1.015

Note. The rest of this table is available upon request.

It also implies that a certain topic with fewer top-keywords has a more cohesive structure topically. Spearman's rho was computed between the increase rate of within-topic similarity and the change in the number of keywords. The result of the correlation analysis was statistically significant ($r = -.501$, $p < .01$). The result suggested that if the number of keywords in a topic is smaller, the topic tends to have a more cohesive structure among the keywords topically.

4. CONCLUSIONS

This study combined the approaches of natural language processing, text mining, and network analysis to explore the applicability of the concept of synchronization in the result of topic modeling. As a result of applying the combined approach to the domain analysis of construction and building engineering, visibility not only in the relationships of topic-keyword but also in that of topic-topic was observed as being improved and topical cohesion in a topic was significantly increased overall.

The combined approach of this study could be regarded as being easy to apply with the best of knowledge on the phenomenon of synchronization in a complex network. The approach of re-assigning the multi-assigned keyword after merging similar topics on the result of LDA-based topic modeling is practical and step-wise. Also, the approach suggested in this study could provide more acceptable and interpretable evidence to researchers and experts in a specific domain in order to help them to detect and analyze the overview of the domain based on their knowledge of it, because the approach could reduce complex connections between multi-assigned keywords and topics.

Because the suggested approach of this study is exploratory, there should be more cases of applying the approach in various domains for generalization and advancement of the approach. More sophisticated evaluation, such as performing user evaluation or calculating a ratio of between-topic similarity and within-topic similarity, should also be investigated to develop the advanced methods of the suggested approach.

REFERENCES

Arenas, A., Diaz-Guilera, A., Kurths, J., Moreno, Y., & Zhou, C. (2008). Synchronization in complex networks. *Physics Reports, 469*(3), 93-153.

Asuncion, A., Welling, M., Smyth, P., & Teh, Y. W. (2009, June). On smoothing and inference for topic models. In Proceedings of the Twenty-Fifth Conference on Uncertainty in Artificial Intelligence (pp. 27-34). AUAI Press.

Brown, P. F., Pietra, V. J. D., Mercer, R. L., Pietra, S. A. D., & Lai, J. C. (1992). An estimate of an upper bound for the entropy of English. *Computational Linguistics, 18*(1), 31-40.

Blasius, B., Huppert, A., & Stone, L. (1999). Complex dynamics and phase synchronization in spatially extended ecological systems. *Nature, 399*(6734), 354-359.

Blei, D. M., Ng, A. Y., & Jordan, M. I. (2003). Latent dirichlet allocation. *Journal of Machine Learning Research, 3*, 993-1022.

Blei, D. M., & McAuliffe, J. D. (2010). Supervised topic models. arXiv preprint arXiv:1003.0783.

Chang, J., Gerrish, S., Wang, C., Boyd-Graber, J. L., & Blei, D. M. (2009). Reading tea leaves: How humans interpret topic models. In Advances in neural information processing systems (pp. 288-296).

Chuang, J., Ramage, D., Manning, C., & Heer, J. (2012). Interpretation and trust: Designing model-driven visualizations for text analysis. In Proceedings of the SIGCHI Conference on Human Factors in Computing Systems (pp. 443-452). ACM.

Elowitz, M. B., & Leibler, S. (2000). A synthetic oscillatory network of transcriptional regulators. *Nature, 403*(6767), 335-338.

Garcia-Ojalvo, J., Elowitz, M. B., & Strogatz, S. H. (2004). Modeling a synthetic multicellular clock: Repressilators coupled by quorum sensing. Proceedings of the National Academy of Sciences of the United States of America, *101*(30), 10955-10960.

Jalili, M. (2013). Enhancing synchronizability of diffusively coupled dynamical networks: A survey. *Neural Networks and Learning Systems, IEEE Transactions on, 24*(7), 1009-1022.

Jha, S. S., & Yadava, R. D. S. (2012). Synchronization based saw sensor using delay line coupled dual oscillator phase dynamics. *Sensors & Transducers* (1726-5479), *141*(6), 71-91.

Griffiths, T. L., & Steyvers, M. (2004). Finding scientific topics. Proceedings of the National Academy of Sciences of the United States of America, *101*(Suppl 1), 5228-5235.

Hall, D., Jurafsky, D., & Manning, C. D. (2008). Studying the history of ideas using topic models. In Proceedings of the Conference on Empirical Methods in Natural Language Processing (pp. 363-371). Association for Computational Linguistics.

Kang, B-I., Song, M., Jho, H.S. (2013). A study on opinion mining of newspaper texts based on topic modeling. *Journal of the Korean Library and Information Science Society, 47*(4), 315-334.

Kuramoto, Y., & Nishikawa, I. (1987). Statistical macrodynamics of large dynamical systems. Case of a phase transition in oscillator communities. *Journal of Statistical Physics, 49*(3-4), 569-605.

Lu, Y., & Zhai, C. (2008). Opinion integration through

semi-supervised topic modeling. In Proceedings of the 17th international conference on World Wide Web (pp. 121-130). ACM.

Mirollo, R. E., & Strogatz, S. H. (1990). Synchronization of pulse-coupled biological oscillators. *SIAM Journal on Applied Mathematics, 50*(6), 1645-1662.

Miyano, T., & Tsutsui, T. (2007a). Data synchronization in a network of coupled phase oscillators. *Physical Review Letters, 98*(2), 024102.

Miyano, T., & Tsutsui, T. (2007b). Extracting feature patterns in the health status of elderly people needing nursing care by data synchronization. In Information Technology Applications in Biomedicine, 2007. ITAB 2007. 6th International Special Topic Conference on (pp. 153-156). IEEE.

Miyano, T., & Tsutsui, T. (2008a). Collective synchronization as a method of learning and generalization from sparse data. *Physical Review E, 77*(2), 026112.

Miyano, T., & Tsutsui, T. (2008b). Finding major patterns of aging process by data synchronization. IEICE Transactions on Fundamentals of Electronics, Communications and Computer Sciences, *91*(9), 2514-2519.

Miyano, T., & Tsutsui, T. (2009). Link of data synchronization to self-organizing map algorithm. IEICE Transactions on Fundamentals of Electronics, Communications and Computer Sciences, *92*(1), 263-269.

Miyano, T., & Tatsumi, K. (2012). Determining anomalous dynamic patterns in price indexes of the London Metal Exchange by data synchronization. *Physica A: Statistical Mechanics and its Applications, 391*(22), 5500-5511.

Miyano, T., & Tsutsui, T. (2007). Data synchronization as a method of data mining. In Proceedings of the 2007 International Symposium on Nonlinear Theory and its Applications NOLTA'07 (pp 224-227). Vancouver: NOLTA.

Niebur, E., Schuster, H. G., Kammen, D. M., & Koch, C. (1991). Oscillator-phase coupling for different two-dimensional network connectivities. *Physical Review A, 44*(10), 6895.

Park, J-H. & Song, M. (2013). A study on the research trends in library & information science in Korea using topic modeling. *Journal of Korean Society for Information Management, 30*(1), 7-32.

Pikovsky, A., Rosenblum, M., & Kurths, J. (Eds.). (2003). *Synchronization: A universal concept in nonlinear sciences* (Vol. 12). London: Cambridge University Press.

Pluchino, A., Latora, V., & Rapisarda, A. (2005). Changing opinions in a changing world: A new perspective in sociophysics. *International Journal of Modern Physics C, 16*(04), 515-531.

Ramage, D., Hall, D., Nallapati, R., & Manning, C. D. (2009a). Labeled LDA: A supervised topic model for credit attribution in multi-labeled corpora. In Proceedings of the 2009 Conference on Empirical Methods in Natural Language Processing: Volume 1 (pp. 248-256). Association for Computational Linguistics.

Ramage, D., Rosen, E., Chuang, J., Manning, C. D., & McFarland, D. A. (2009b). Topic modeling for the social sciences. In NIPS 2009 Workshop on Applications for Topic Models: Text and Beyond (Vol. 5).

Ramage, D., Manning, C. D., & Dumais, S. (2011). Partially labeled topic models for interpretable text mining. In Proceedings of the 17th ACM SIGKDD international conference on knowledge discovery and data mining (pp. 457-465). ACM.

Strogatz, S. H., & Mirollo, R. E. (1988). Collective synchronisation in lattices of nonlinear oscillators with randomness. *Journal of Physics A: Mathematical and General, 21*(13), L699.

Strogatz, S. H. (2000). From Kuramoto to Crawford: Exploring the onset of synchronization in populations of coupled oscillators. *Physica D: Nonlinear Phenomena, 143*(1), 1-20.

Strogatz, S. H. (2001). Exploring complex networks. *Nature, 410*(6825), 268-276.

Strogatz, S. (2003). *Sync: The emerging science of spontaneous order*. New York: Hyperion.

Talley, E. M., Newman, D., Mimno, D., Herr II, B. W., Wallach, H. M., Burns, G. A. P. C., Leenders, A. G. M., & McCallum, A. (2011). Database of NIH grants using machine-learned categories and graphical clustering. *Nature Methods, 8*(6), 443-444.

Tang, J., Wang, B., Yang, Y., Hu, P., Zhao, Y., Yan, X., & Usadi, A. K. (2012). Patentminer: Topic-driven patent analysis and mining. In Proceedings of the 18th ACM SIGKDD international conference on knowledge discovery and data mining (pp. 1366-

1374). ACM.

Tilles, P. F., Cerdeira, H. A., & Ferreira, F. F. (2013). Local attractors, degeneracy and analyticity: Symmetry effects on the locally coupled Kuramoto model. *Chaos, Solitons & Fractals, 49*, 32-46.

Titov, I., & McDonald, R. (2008). Modeling online reviews with multi-grain topic models. In Proceedings of the 17th international conference on World Wide Web (pp. 111-120). ACM.

Wan, M., Li, L., Xiao, J., Yang, Y., Wang, C., & Guo, X. (2010). CAS based clustering algorithm for Web users. *Nonlinear Dynamics, 61*(3), 347-361.

Yu, S.Y. (2013). Applying TDP (Topic Descriptor Profile) with article-level citation flow for analyzing research trend, In proceedings of the 2013 Korean Society for Information Management Conference in Autumn (pp. 39-58). Seoul: Korean Society for Information Management.

8

The Impact of Name Ambiguity on Properties of Coauthorship Networks

Jinseok Kim

Graduate School of Library and
Information Science, University of
Illinois at Urbana-Champaign, USA
E-mail: jinseok.kim.uiuc@gmail.com

Heejun Kim

School of Information and Library
Science, University of North Carolina
at Chapel Hill, USA
E-mail: heejunk@email.unc.edu

Jana Diesner *

Graduate School of Library and
Information Science, University of
Illinois at Urbana-Champaign, USA
E-mail: jdiesner@illinois.edu

ABSTRACT

Initial based disambiguation of author names is a common data pre-processing step in bibliometrics. It is widely accepted that this procedure can introduce errors into network data and any subsequent analytical results. What is not sufficiently understood is the precise impact of this step on the data and findings. We present an empirical answer to this question by comparing the impact of two commonly used initial based disambiguation methods against a reasonable proxy for ground truth data. We use DBLP, a database covering major journals and conferences in computer science and information science, as a source. We find that initial based disambiguation induces strong distortions in network metrics on the graph and node level: Authors become embedded in ties for which there is no empirical support, thus increasing their sphere of influence and diversity of involvement. Consequently, networks generated with initial-based disambiguation are more coherent and interconnected than the actual underlying networks, and individual authors appear to be more productive and more strongly embedded than they actually are.

Keywords: bibliometrics, name ambiguity, initial based disambiguation, coauthorship networks, collaboration networks

1. INTRODUCTION

Authorship data are not only used to evaluate individuals for employment, tenure, and funding, but also to understand fundamental principles of scientific collaboration, communication, and productivity. Thus, scholars as well as organizations involved with the progress, promotion, and management of science

*Corresponding Author: Jana Diesner
Assistant Professor
Graduate School of Library and Information Science
University of Illinois at Urbana-Champaign, USA
E-mail: jdiesner@illinois.edu

have a strong interest in gaining a better, actionable understanding of these processes (Torvik, Weeber, Swanson, & Smalheiser, 2005). A known but insufficiently solved problem in this domain is name disambiguation, i.e. identifying whether a set of name strings refers to one or more real-world persons. This task can be very difficult, especially when an author's identity is only represented by a string of characters. For example, when encountering spellings of seemingly similar names, such as 'Smith, Linda' and 'Smith, L.', it is not always clear whether these names represent the same person or not. The given problem can get more complicated, especially when people use different names, e.g. due to marriage, translating their name into another language, or inconsistent use or spelling of names.

One solution to solve name ambiguity is to manually inspect bibliometric data. For example, two name instances that appear in two different citation records can be evaluated for identity by considering additional information, e.g. people's web pages or curricula vitae, as well as meta-data on the publication, including keywords and index terms. The caveat with this approach is its limited scalability and related costs. Consequently, manual verification can hardly be applied to large datasets that contain thousands or millions of name instances.

A more scalable solution is computational approaches that consider attribute data. To achieve high accuracy with this approach, scholars have typically used a two-step process (Treeratpituk & Giles, 2009): First, a pair of names appearing in bibliometrics records are compared to each other based on attributes of the author(s), e.g. the surface form of their name as well as their affiliation, and of the paper, e.g. its title and the title of the journal. These pairwise comparisons produce similarity profiles between any pair of name instances, where distance is determined based on rules as well as metrics such as edit-distance functions. The similarity profiles are then used to make a binary decision per pair ('yes' for matched names or 'no' for unmatched names) or to calculate some (probabilistic) similarity score between 0 and 1. In a second step, the authors' names are clustered based on the decision or score of pairwise comparisons. For more details on this procedure, we refer readers to Smalheiser and Torvik (2009).

Yet another automated approach in this field is a solution based on heuristics that are employed to assign identities to name instances based on one or more parts of a name string. Regular expressions, which identify morphological similarities and different types of congruence on the surface-form level between any pair of name instances, are commonly used for this purpose. For example, if two name instances share the same last name and same first name initials, these two names can be assumed to refer to the same author (e.g., Newman, 2001). In fact, this kind of approach has become a dominant name disambiguation strategy in coauthorship network research (Strotmann & Zhao, 2012). A major reason for the wide adoption of this strategy is that name ambiguity has been supposed to have small to moderate impact on the resulting network data and analysis results (Barabasi et al., 2002; Milojević, 2013; Newman, 2001). This assumption has been insufficiently investigated. We herein fill this gap and complement prior work on this issue by comparing the statistical properties of coauthorship networks constructed from a) a proxy for ground truth data, more specifically from the DBLP Computer Science Bibliography (DBLP hereafter) (Ley, 2002) and b) network data built from the same dataset, but after applying initial based disambiguation to it.

In the following, we first review how errors or biases induced by initial based name disambiguation have been addressed in prior work. Then, we empirically estimate the impact of initial based disambiguation on network data and findings. We conclude with a discussion of research implications.

2. BACKGROUND

The following three approaches to name disambiguation based on initials and last names have been suggested for coauthorship network research (Milojević, 2013). First, one could rely on any given author's first name initial plus their last name. This is also known as the "first initial method." With this approach, matches in the last name and the initial of the first name are regarded as referring to the same person, regardless of the existence of or differences in middle name initials. The second approach considers the initials of the first and the middle name. This is also known as the "all initial method." Here, matches in first and middle name initials and in last names are assumed to represent the same person. The third way is a hybrid method, which uses the first initial method as a baseline. Then, if a name entailing a first name initial and a last name has two or more potential match candidates with names entailing different middle name initials, all potential match candidates are considered as different identities.

Table 1. Illustration of Types of Initial Based Disambiguation

Methods	Examples from Milojević (2013)	Decision
First Initial Method	Jackson, P. Jackson, P. A. Jackson, P. S.	all the same author
All Initial Method	Jackson, P. Jackson, P. A. Jackson, P. S.	three authors
Hybrid Method	If 'Jackson, P.' has TWO or more match candidates with different middle name initials, Jackson, P. Jackson, P. A. Jackson, P. S.	three authors
	If 'Jackson, P.' has only ONE match candidate with a middle name initial, Jackson, P. Jackson, P. A.	all the same author

To gain a better understanding of which of these methods has been used or studied in bibliometrics research, we screened 298 articles that contain the term 'co-author' or 'coauthor' in the title, abstract, or keyword section in eight journals from 1978 to 2013. We considered the following journals: *Information Processing & Management, Journal of Information Science, Journal of Informetrics, Journal of the American Society for Information Science and Technology, Physica A, Physical Review E, Plos One*, and *Scientometrics*. About 70% of the retrieved articles were focused on studying a) the number of authors per paper to analyze trends over time or b) coauthoring across institutions and nations (e.g. Leydesdorff & Sun, 2009). Both applications do not require author name disambiguation in most cases. However, name disambiguation is needed for the remaining 30% of papers, where coauthorship networks are analyzed in which node names consist of last names and first- and/or middle-name initials (e.g., datasets from Web of Science or Scopus). In some of these papers it is clearly indicated that they used the first initial method (9 papers, e.g. Bettencourt, Lobo, & Strumsky, 2007; Liben-Nowell & Kleinberg, 2007) or all initial method (4 papers, e.g. Milojević, 2010; Newman, 2001).

Only one paper disambiguated with the hybrid method (Yoshikane, Nozawa, Shibui, & Suzuki, 2009). Some scholars just indicated that an initial based disambiguation had been performed without details on the strategy (6 papers, e.g. Barabasi et al., 2002; Fiala, 2012; Lee, Goh, Kahng, & Kim, 2010; Rorissa & Yuan, 2012). Several others clearly stated that they did not resolve name ambiguities at all but relied on full surnames and initialized given names to identify authors (e.g. Braun, Glanzel, & Schubert, 2001; Lariviere, Sugimoto, & Cronin, 2012; Wagner & Leydesdorff, 2005).

In general, the majority of scholars using initial-based disambiguation have acknowledged the problem of misidentifying authors (i.e., merging and splitting of identities) when relying on initials for name disambiguation. Some have, however, also argued that disambiguation approaches do not significantly affect research findings. For example, Newman (2001) assumed that the numbers of unique authors identified by first initial and all initial disambiguation correspond to the lower and upper bound of the "true" number of unique authors, respectively. Based on this assumption, he found that most of the statistical properties of coauthorship networks disambiguated by first and all initial methods showed errors or differences of "an order of a few percent." Many scholars cited Newman's approach to justify their use of initial based disambiguation (e.g. Barabasi et al., 2002; Goyal, van der Leij, & Moraga-Gonzalez, 2006; Liben-Nowell & Kleinberg, 2007; Milojević, 2010).

One common problem with initial based disambiguation in coauthorship network studies is that the assumption of the supposedly mild effects of disambiguation errors has not been tested against ground-truth data. An exception here is the work by Milojević (2013), who tested the accuracy of initial based disambiguation on synthetic datasets. However, the accuracy of the simulated data against ground-truth data was not verified. Overall, the identification of biases and errors induced by initial based disambiguation is only possible if ground truth data is available. Since human-disambiguated coauthorship data are extremely rare and only available on a small scale, scholars have been using highly accurate computational solutions as a proxy (Fegley & Torvik, 2013; Strotmann & Zhao, 2012). Even though the most advanced algorithms cannot guarantee perfect disambiguation (Diesner & Carley, 2009), this strategy allows for comparing datasets and results based on initial based disambiguation and computationally disambiguated datasets. For example, Fegley and Torvik (2013) showed that initial based disambiguation can "dramatically" distort identified collaboration patterns. They compared two coauthorship networks that were generated from the same dataset (9 million names in MEDLINE): one network was disambiguated with advanced algorithms (accuracy of up to 99%) and the other by the all initial method. Through this, they found that all initial disambiguation estimated the number of unique authors as about 2.2 million while their algorithmic disambiguation identified almost 3.2 million unique authors from the same dataset. Strotmann and Zhao (2012) disambiguated names in more than 2.2 million papers from MEDLINE and found that, when disambiguated by the first initial method, about fifty of the top 200 most cited scholars are Asian authors (such as Wang, J.) who are actually merged identities. However, except for the field of biomedicine, where Fegley and Torvik (2013) as well as Strotmann and Zhao (2012) conducted such studies, we have no understanding of the impact of disambiguation strategies and their errors rates on the data and any results computed over the data, nor on any policy implications made based on these results.

The herein presented study is in line with the work by Fegley and Torvik (2013) and Strotmann and Zhao (2012) in that it attempts to estimate the effect of errors that are due to initial based disambiguation by comparing coauthorship networks generated from the same dataset by using different disambiguation methods. Our study differs from prior work in that we consider different domains, namely computer science and information science. There is a rich body of prior work on coauthorship network studies in these fields, and many of the papers used the initial based disambiguation method (e.g. Fiala, 2012; He, Ding, & Ni, 2011; Rorissa & Yuan, 2012). In the following section, we outline the characteristics of the dataset and metrics for measuring network properties used herein.

3. METHODOLOGY

3.1. Data

We used data from DBLP. The DBLP database is a service developed by Dr. Michael Ley at Trier University, Germany (Ley, 2002). Each publication record in DBLP includes at least the author's names as well as title and year of publication. DBLP mainly covers the field of computer science in a broad sense. This includes various key journals from library and information science, such as *Journal of the American Society for Information Science and Technology, Journal of Information Science, Journal of Informetrics, Information Society, Library Trends*, and *Scientometrics*.

DBLP is well known for its high quality citation data. This is partially due to the fact that the DBLP team has dedicated database management efforts to name disambiguation (Ley, 2002, 2009). DBLP uses full names as much as possible, which is believed to alleviate errors with splitting and merging identities. Also, it exploits diverse string matching algorithms as well as coauthorship information to assign names to the presumably correct author identities. For some suspicious cases of split or merged identities, manual inspection is employed. Thus, although DBLP inevitably contains errors, it is internationally respected by computer scientists and information scientists for its accuracy (Franceschet, 2011). Hence, DBLP has been used as a data source for more than 400 scientific studies of name disambiguation, collaboration patterns, and data management (Ley, 2009).

As of March 2014, DBLP contained almost 2.5 million records for journals, proceedings, books and reviews. From these, we selected records of journal papers because the majority of coauthorship studies have focused on journal articles. We retrieved a total of 1,076,577 records of papers published in 1,409 journals, containing 2,812,236 name instances and spanning a period from 1936 to the beginning of 2014. Here, the number of name instances refers to the count of all names in the data regardless of duplicates. This means that, for example, 'Linda Smith' may appear three times in the dataset since she has published three papers, while the count of the unique name is just one. From this dataset, we excluded papers with no author name or authored by a single author. We made this decision since most of the previous coauthorship network studies excluded single authored papers from analysis. This reduction process resulted in 816,643 papers (2,557,898 name instances). Our selected subset contains 75.9 % of all the papers we retrieved and 91.0 % of all name instances included in all the papers we retrieved. This not only indicates that coauthoring is the norm in these fields, but also further substantiates the need for a precise understanding of the impact of disambiguation on coauthorship networks.

3.2. Generating Coauthorship Networks

In a social network, two agents (nodes) are connected by a line (edge) if they interact with each other, exchange resources, or share an affiliation or activity (Knoke & Yang, 2008). In a coauthorship network, which is a special type of social network, two authors get linked if they coauthor a publication. To test the performance of initial based disambiguation in terms of accuracy, we generated three coauthorship networks from the same dataset. First, by using the raw dataset of 816,643 papers, we constructed a proxy of the ground-truth network. Next, we disambiguated names in the same dataset by using the first and all initial disambiguation methods, and generated a network from each dataset. We excluded the hybrid method from our analysis because it has not been frequently used except in one empirical study by Yoshikane et al. (2009). For the first and all initial disambiguation methods, some preprocessing is required. Name instances in DBLP are represented as given name plus last name (e.g. Linda Smith). This is in contrast to other bibliometrics datasets where an author's name is provided as a last name followed by a given name (e.g. Smith, Linda or Smith, L.). To apply name initial disambiguation, the last name and given name of a name instance should be distinguished from each other. This can mostly be done by locating the last name part in a name string (e.g., Chang in 'Alan Chin-Chen Chang'). The problem is that it is sometimes unclear which name part is a last name or a given name. For example, in some Spanish-speaking countries, the norm is to have two given names and two last names, e.g. "Juan Antonio Holgado Terriza," where the last names are "Holgado Terriza." Again, in most cases, this can be dealt with by locating the last name part that is indicated by a hyphen (e.g., Sangiovanni-Vicentelli in 'Alberto L. Sangiovanni-Vicentelli'). However, some name instances contain no such clue. To deal with such cases, we downloaded records of 57,099 papers published in 99 top journals in computer science (including some journals also categorized into infor-

mation science) between 2009 and 2013 using the *Journal Citation Report 2013* from the Web of Science (Thompson Reuters). From 185,518 name instances in the last name plus given name format, we extracted 3,892 unique cases of a last names with two or more name parts (e.g., Hernandez del Olmo) and 140 single last name prefixes (e.g., 'das' or 'van de'), and applied this information to detect last names of about 120,000 name instances in our dataset.

3.3. Measurements

We selected the following six metrics since they are commonly used in coauthorship network studies. We used the social network analysis package *Pajek* (de Nooy, Mrvar, & Batagelj, 2011) to compute these metrics on our data.

Productivity: This is measured as the total number of papers per unique author. Merged and split identities directly impact this metric as they can inflate or deflate the number of publications per person.

Number of Coauthors (Degree Centrality): Two scholars are connected if they appear as coauthors on a paper. The degree centrality (short *degree*) of an actor (node) refers to the number of direct connections that he or she has. Here, only the existence of collaboration ties between authors is considered (binary ties), while the number of co-authored papers (ties weighted by frequency) is disregarded. We made this decision to resemble common procedure in coauthorship studies (Barabasi et al., 2002; Moody, 2004; Newman, 2001). In short, the degree of an author represents the number of her unique collaborators.

Density: Density measures the proportion of the number of actual ties over the number of possible ties (excluding self-loops). Network scholars have considered this measure as an indicator of network cohesion (Wasserman & Faust, 1994), although this is controversial (Friedkin, 1981).

Components: A component is a maximal subgraph where any node can reach any other node in one or more steps. Scholars typically look at the size of the largest component and the number of components, which together inform us about the coherence or fragmentation of a network (Newman, 2001).

Shortest Path: The shortest path, also known as the geodesics, between two authors is the minimum number of steps between them. In this study, the average shortest paths of all authors in each dataset (Brandes, 2008) are reported. Only the lengths of existing paths were averaged.

Clustering Coefficient: The clustering coefficient measures the average fraction of a person's coauthors who have also published together (Newman, 2001). This type of closure can result from three or more people being involved in the same paper or in different papers. We calculate the clustering coefficient as the ratio of the number of triangles over the number of triples (Fegley & Torvik, 2013). Here, a triangle is a set of three authors who are connected to one another (i.e. via three ties), while a triple is a set of three authors who are held together by exactly two ties.

Assortativity: This measures the extent to which authors collaborate with others who are similar to them in terms of degree. In this study, assortativity is calculated as "the Pearson correlation coefficient of the degrees at either ends of an edge" between any two authors (Newman, 2002).

4. RESULTS

4.1. Number of Unique Authors

The number of identified unique authors from DBLP is shown in Table 2. The last column in this table shows the reduction in the number of individuals – i.e., the effect of collapsing multiple truly distinct authors into clusters of people who happen to share the same name – compared against the DBLP data. Here, DBLP serves as a proxy for ground truth. Overall, the two considered initial based disambiguation methods underestimate the number of unique authors by 30% (all initial method) to 43% (first initial method). This indicates that initial based disambiguation will suggest smaller scholarly communities in computer and information science than there really are.

Table 2. Number of Unique Authors per Method

	Number of Unique Authors	Change (%)
DBLP	775,854	-
All-Initial Method	545,072	-29.75
First-Initial Method	440,981	-43.16

Moreover, our results suggest that the number of unique individuals is greater than the upper bound for unique authors when the upper bound is computed as the largest number of unique authors estimated by the all initial method. This finding contradicts prior work by some researchers, e.g. Newman (2001), but confirms results by others, e.g. Fegley and Torvik (2013). The latter reported that the total number of unique authors as identified by their algorithmic disambiguation (3.17×10^6) exceeded the upper bound generated by the all initial method (2.18×10^6, -31.23%). Also, the ratio of decrease identified by Fegley and Torvik (2013) (-31.23%) is similar to the ratio we found (-29.75%).

4.2. Distributions of Productivity and Number of Coauthors

The underestimation in the number of unique authors indicates that initial based disambiguation merges author identities that should actually be split apart. To illustrate the effect of merged (or split) author identities on statistical properties, the distributions of productivity and number of coauthors (i.e. degree) are shown in Figures 1 and 2. For each cumulative log-log plot, we show the distributions from all three datasets we used: DBLP (red triangles), all initial method (black crosses), and first initial method (blue circles).

The curves of the original DBLP dataset show more downwards curvature compared to those disambiguated by initials. This finding means that, for a given value (x) of productivity or degree, the proportion of authors who have the given value (X = x) or a value above the given value (X > x) increases by initial based disambiguation for the majority of x values. In other words, the blue circle and black cross curves positioned above the red triangle curves indicate that the productivity and degree distributions are distorted: initial based disambiguation methods create merged identities, which leads to an inflation of values for productivity and degree. This pushes the curves both upwards and to the right. Moreover, the curves from both initial based disambiguation methods seem to have a lower, straighter slope than those from the DBLP data, which might be fit by a power-law distribution or Lotka's Law (Barabasi et al., 2002; Huber, 2002; Newman, 2001). Fegley and Torvik (2013, Figure 8) came to the same conclusion: degree distribution from the algorithmic disambiguation shows much more curvature than the one based on all initial based disambiguation. Overall, these findings indicate that the average productivity and number of collaborators can be distorted by initial based disambiguation such that scholars in a target dataset are portrayed as more productive and collaborative than they really are.

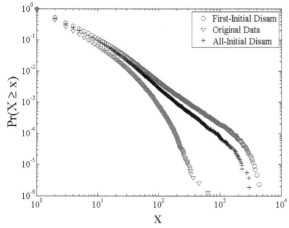

Fig. 1 Cumulative log-log plot of productivity distribution

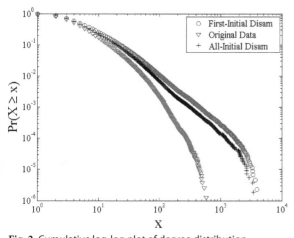

Fig. 2 Cumulative log-log plot of degree distribution

4.3. Statistical Properties from Network Metrics

We report additional statistical properties of the three coauthorship networks in Table 3. First, disambiguation has a much smaller impact on the number of ties than the number of nodes. More precisely, the first initial method reduced the number of ties by

6.03%, and the all initial method by 2.90%. This suggests that merged author nodes typically have distinct sets of coauthors. If two merged author identities have coauthors that are also merged due to name ambiguity, then the ties between each author and coauthor would also be merged, leading to the decrease of ties.

Using initial based disambiguation leads to method-induced increases in network density, average productivity, degree, and the size of the largest component. These increases are expected as they are logical consequences of merging actually distinct people into collective persona. This procedure causes a higher number of publications and collaborators per node and a reduction in the total number of unique authors. When using the all initial method and first initial method, respectively, density doubled and tripled, degree increased by over a third to two thirds, and productivity went up by 43% to 75% – all due to data pre-processing decisions instead of any change in underlying social behavior.

At the same time, we observe inaccurate decreases in the average shortest path length, clustering coefficients (a.k.a. transitivity), assortativity, and the number of components due to using initial based disambiguation. The clustering coefficient is measured as the fraction of triangles (3 nodes with 3 ties between them) over the number of triples connected with exactly two ties. When using initial based disambiguation, the merging of author identities leads to a stronger increase in the number of connected triples (denominator) than the number of triangles (numerator), which again is an expected mathematical consequence. Overall, networks generated with initial based disambiguation are more coherent and interconnected than the underlying true network is, and individual authors appear to be more productive and more strongly embedded than they actually are.

Our findings are consistent with those of Fegley and Torvik (2013) and Velden, Haque, and Lagoze (2011). We also find that the numerical differences between the coauthorship network generated from a reasonable proxy for ground truth versus the networks generated from the same data after pre-processing it with initial based disambiguation methods exceed "the order of a few percent" (Newman 2001).

Table 3. Overview of Statistical Properties of Networks per Method

	DBLP	All-Initial Method	First-Initial Method
No. of Ties	2,660,700	2,583,615	2,500,186
Density	8.84E-06	1.73E-05	2.57E-05
Avg. Productivity (SD)	3.30 (7.33)	4.69 (21.23)	5.80 (34.55)
Avg. Degree (SD)	6.86 (11.53)	9.48 (30.33)	11.34 (41.22)
No. of Components (Ratio of Largest Component Size)	38,008 (84.66%)	16,206 (91.82%)	9,012 (94.68%)
Avg. Shortest Path (Path of Most Distant Nodes)	6.56 (25)	5.18 (18)	4.74 (15)
Clustering Coefficient	0.274	0.105	0.096
Assortativity	0.170	0.106	0.094

5. CONCLUSION AND DISCUSSION

This paper attempts to estimate the impact of initial based disambiguation on coauthorship networks. We disambiguated the DBLP dataset of 0.8 million journal papers by first and all initial methods and compared typically used statistical properties of the resulting networks against each other and to a proxy for ground truth data. We conclude that initial based disambiguation can lead to distorted findings and inaccurate representations of scientific collaborations. When using initial based disambiguation, authors become embedded in ties for which there is no empirical support, which leads to increases in people's spheres of influence and diversity of involvement. As more authors get integrated into larger components, some of them seem to serve as bridges connecting previously disjoint (groups of) authors and to provide shortcuts for connecting people. Overall, initial based disambiguation suggests more cohesive networks and more prolific and integrated authors than actually exist. These are wrongfully induced consequences of data pre-processing choices with potentially strong implications for our understanding and modeling of the patterns and dynamics of scientific collation.

For a selected set of network properties, we showed an overall decrease in network analytical values due to initial based disambiguation. More specifically, this applies to the number of unique authors and collab-

oration ties, average shortest path length, clustering coefficient, assortativity, and the number of components. Other measures increased: network density, author's productivity and degree, and the size of the largest component. In summary, these effects imply that initial based disambiguation produces coauthorship networks that are smaller and less fragmented than the true underlying network is, and represents those networks as ones where people can reach each other more efficiently, are more productive, and have a larger and more diverse set of collaborators.

This study is not without limitations. The findings involve some domain-specificity as our data originate mainly from a specific dataset from computer science and information science. Additional studies on other fields are needed to generalize these conclusions. Second, it is unknown how the distortive effects of initial based disambiguation impact smaller datasets. As name ambiguity increases with the size of the dataset (Fegley & Torvik, 2013), one may expect that in a small scale coauthorship network initial based disambiguation is less detrimental than when applied to larger datasets. As far as we know, our study used the second largest coauthorship network for measuring the impact of initial based disambiguation following Fegley and Torvik (2013). Third, this study lacks detailed explanation of what factors affect the errors of authorship identification by initial based disambiguation. For example, scholars have suggested that

Asian names, especially Chinese, Japanese, and Korean names, contribute more to name ambiguity in authorship identification as they are known to share common last names (Strotmann & Zhao, 2012; Torvik & Smalheiser, 2009). In our study, the majority of the top 100 names that appear frequently when initial based disambiguation applied were Asian names such as Kim, Lee, Zhang, and Wang. The extent to which these ambiguous names cause authorship misidentification may provide a deeper understanding of disambiguation issues. The outlined limitations are topics of our future research.

The main takeaway from this study is that initial based disambiguation can underestimate the number of authors and connections mainly through merging, and, therefore, can distort macroscopic views of the patterns and evolution of collaboration. This implies that coauthorship network research, especially when done based on large scale data, should pay more attention to name ambiguity, and any findings should be treated with caution when names are not properly disambiguated.

ACKNOWLEDGEMENTS

This work is supported by KISTI (Korea Institute of Science and Technology Information), grant P14033, and the FORD Foundation, grant 0145-0558. We would like to thank Vetle Torvik and Andrew Higgins for their comments on this manuscript.

REFERENCES

Barabasi, A. L., Jeong, H., Neda, Z., Ravasz, E., Schubert, A., & Vicsek, T. (2002). Evolution of the social network of scientific collaborations. *Physica a-Statistical Mechanics and Its Applications, 311*(3-4), 590-614. doi: 10.1016/s0378-4371(02)00736-7

Bettencourt, L. M. A., Lobo, J., & Strumsky, D. (2007). Invention in the city: Increasing returns to patenting as a scaling function of metropolitan size. *Research Policy, 36*(1), 107-120. doi: 10.1016/j.respol.2006.09.026

Brandes, U. (2008). On variants of shortest-path betweenness centrality and their generic computation. *Social Networks, 30*(2), 136-145. doi: http://dx.doi.org/10.1016/j.socnet.2007.11.001

Braun, T., Glanzel, W., & Schubert, A. (2001). Publication and cooperation patterns of the authors of neuroscience journals. *Scientometrics, 51*(3), 499-510. doi: 10.1023/a:1019643002560

de Nooy, W., Mrvar, A., & Batagelj, V. (2011). *Exploratory social network analysis with Pajek: Cambridge University Press.*

Diesner, J., & Carley, K. M. (2009). He says, she says, pat says, Tricia says: how much reference resolution matters for entity extraction, relation extraction, and social network analysis. Paper presented at *the Proceedings of the Second IEEE international conference on Computational intelligence for security and defense applications*, Ottawa, Ontario, Canada.

Fegley, B. D., & Torvik, V. I. (2013). Has Large-Scale Named-Entity Network Analysis Been Resting on a Flawed Assumption? *Plos One, 8*(7). doi: 10.1371/journal.pone.0070299

Fiala, D. (2012). Time-aware PageRank for bibliographic networks. *Journal of Informetrics, 6*(3), 370-388. doi: 10.1016/j.joi.2012.02.002

Franceschet, M. (2011). Collaboration in Computer Science: A Network Science Approach. *Journal of the American Society for Information Science and Technology, 62*(10), 1992-2012. doi: 10.1002/asi.21614

Friedkin, N. E. (1981). The Development of Structure in Random Networks: An Analysis of the Effects of Increasing Network Density on Five Measures of Structure. *Social Networks, 3*(1), 41-52.

Goyal, S., van der Leij, M. J., & Moraga-Gonzalez, J. L. (2006). Economics: An emerging small world. *Journal of Political Economy, 114*(2), 403-412. doi: 10.1086/500990

He, B., Ding, Y., & Ni, C. (2011). Mining Enriched Contextual Information of Scientific Collaboration: A Meso Perspective. *Journal of the American Society for Information Science and Technology, 62*(5), 831-845. doi: 10.1002/asi.21510

Huber, J. C. (2002). A new model that generates Lotka's Law. *Journal of the American Society for Information Science and Technology, 53*(3), 209-219. doi: 10.1002/asi.10025

Knoke, D., & Yang, S. (2008). *Social network analysis.* Los Angeles, CA: Sage Publications.

Lariviere, V., Sugimoto, C. R., & Cronin, B. (2012). A

bibliometric chronicling of library and information science's first hundred years. *Journal of the American Society for Information Science and Technology, 63*(5), 997-1016. doi: 10.1002/asi.22645

Lee, D., Goh, K. I., Kahng, B., & Kim, D. (2010). Complete trails of coauthorship network evolution. *Physical Review E, 82*(2). doi: 10.1103/PhysRevE.82.026112

Ley, M. (2002). The DBLP Computer Science Bibliography: Evolution, Research Issues, Perspectives. In A. F. Laender & A. Oliveira (Eds.), *String Processing and Information Retrieval* (Vol. 2476, pp. 1-10): Springer Berlin Heidelberg.

Ley, M. (2009). DBLP: some lessons learned. *Proc. VLDB Endow., 2*(2), 1493-1500.

Leydesdorff, L., & Sun, Y. (2009). National and International Dimensions of the Triple Helix in Japan: University-Industry-Government Versus International Coauthorship Relations. *Journal of the American Society for Information Science and Technology, 60*(4), 778-788. doi: 10.1002/asi.20997

Liben-Nowell, D., & Kleinberg, J. (2007). The link-prediction problem for social networks. *Journal of the American Society for Information Science and Technology, 58*(7), 1019-1031. doi: 10.1002/asi.20591

Milojević, S. (2010). Modes of Collaboration in Modern Science: Beyond Power Laws and Preferential Attachment. *Journal of the American Society for Information Science and Technology, 61*(7), 1410-1423. doi: 10.1002/asi.21331

Milojević, S. (2013). Accuracy of simple, initials-based methods for author name disambiguation. *Journal of Informetrics, 7*(4), 767-773. doi: http://dx.doi.org/10.1016/j.joi.2013.06.006

Moody, J. (2004). The structure of a social science collaboration network: Disciplinary cohesion from 1963 to 1999. *American Sociological Review, 69*(2), 213-238.

Newman, M. E. J. (2001). The structure of scientific collaboration networks. *Proceedings of the National Academy of Sciences of the United States of America, 98*(2), 404-409. doi: 10.1073/pnas.021544898

Newman, M. E. J. (2002). Assortative mixing in networks. *Physical Review Letters, 89*(20), 208701.

Rorissa, A., & Yuan, X. J. (2012). Visualizing and mapping the intellectual structure of information retrieval. *Information Processing & Management,*

48(1), 120-135. doi: 10.1016/j.ipm.2011.03.004

Smalheiser, N. R., & Torvik, V. I. (2009). Author Name Disambiguation. *Annual Review of Information Science and Technology, 43*, 287-313.

Strotmann, A., & Zhao, D. Z. (2012). Author name disambiguation: What difference does it make in author-based citation analysis? *Journal of the American Society for Information Science and Technology, 63*(9), 1820-1833. doi: Doi 10.1002/Asi.22695

Torvik, V. I., & Smalheiser, N. R. (2009). Author Name Disambiguation in MEDLINE. *Acm Transactions on Knowledge Discovery from Data, 3*(3). doi: Doi 10.1145/1552303.1552304

Torvik, V. I., Weeber, M., Swanson, D. R., & Smalheiser, N. R. (2005). A probabilistic similarity metric for Medline records: A model for author name disambiguation. *Journal of the American Society for Information Science and Technology, 56*(2), 140-158. doi: Doi 10.1002/Asi/20105

Treeratpituk, P., & Giles, C. L. (2009). Disambiguating Authors in Academic Publications using Random Forests. *Paper presented at the Jcdl 09: Proceedings of the 2009 Acm/Ieee Joint Conference on Digital Libraries.*

Velden, Haque, A., & Lagoze, C. (2011). Resolving author name homonymy to improve resolution of structures in co-author networks. *Paper presented at the Proceedings of the 11th annual international ACM/IEEE joint conference on Digital libraries.*

Wagner, C. S., & Leydesdorff, L. (2005). Network structure, self-organization, and the growth of international collaboration in science. *Research Policy, 34*(10), 1608-1618. doi: http://dx.doi.org/10.1016/j.respol.2005.08.002

Wasserman, S., & Faust, K. (1994). *Social network analysis: Methods and applications.* New York, NY: Cambridge University Press.

Yoshikane, F., Nozawa, T., Shibui, S., & Suzuki, T. (2009). An analysis of the connection between researchers' productivity and their co-authors' past attributions, including the importance in collaboration networks. *Scientometrics, 79*(2), 435-449. doi: 10.1007/s11192-008-0429-8

9

Information Worlds and Interpretive Practices: Toward an Integration of Domains

Gary Burnett *

School of Information
Florida State University
Tallahassee, USA
E-mail: gburnett@fsu.edu

ABSTRACT

This article proposes an interwoven three-part framework for conceptualizing and analyzing the role of information in human activities, melding the cognitive and affective domain of the individual, the collective domain of the social, and the domain of signification and communication practices, focusing on the ways in which individual characteristics, social context and interaction, and signification and representation work together to form information behavior. The article presents an overview of each of these three domains and discusses the ways in which they are intertwined. It argues that considering the three domains in relation to each other offers a holistic framework within which to consider the ways in which information – needs, behavior, creation, and use – depends simultaneously on all three. It concludes by offering a brief discussion of the implications of the framework for information services, including (but not limited to) libraries.

Keywords: Information Behavior, Information Seeking in Context, Semiotics, Hermeneutics

1. INTRODUCTION

The field of Library and Information Studies has long focused on an evolving range of issues integral to the practice of librarianship *per se*, including not only practical and procedural matters that form part and parcel of daily activities within libraries, but also more abstract concerns related to the organization and pack-

*Corresponding Author: Gary Burnett
Professor
School of Information,
Florida State University
Tallahassee, USA
E-mail: gburnett@fsu.edu

aging of information (e.g. cataloguing, indexing, etc.) and political and policy matters intended to bolster the role of libraries as organizations within broader cultural contexts. In more recent years, the field's focus has extended, with increasing attention paid to non library-centric issues, with information more broadly conceptualized as one of the fundamental building blocks of a culture, something not limited to materials collected and housed within library walls, but central to day-to-day activity in all settings, inextricably interwoven with human interaction.

Part of this broadening of focus from the singular *institution of the library* to information as a part of the very fabric of life has been theoretical, with conceptualizations of *information behavior* similarly expanded from narrow models of information seeking activities within formalized settings to encompass more robust frameworks including a wide variety of factors ranging from affective aspects to contextual and social factors influencing information use. This article falls into this category of work, arguing that multiple factors are necessary for understanding the place of information in our lives, and for conceptualizing the role it plays and the value it has in the construction of human meaning. I attempt to construct an interconnected three-part framework within which to situate information and information-related activities:

1. The cognitive and affective domain of the individual,
2. The collective domain of the social, and
3. The domain of signification and communication practices.

Much of this work draws upon my previous work in theory (e.g. Burnett, Besant, & Chatman, 2001; Burnett & Jaeger, 2008; Burnett, Jaeger, & Thompson, 2008; Jaeger & Burnett, 2010) as well as cultural and philosophical hermeneutics (e.g. Burnett, 2002; Dickey, Burnett, Chudoba, & Kazmer, 2007; Burnett, 2010; Burnett, Whetstone, & Jaeger, 2013), drawing together previously disparate strands of that work and extending it into a – hopefully – more carefully integrated whole.

2. THE DOMAIN OF THE INDIVIDUAL

One of the dominant strands of LIS research has em-

phasized the interaction between an information system of some sort – a database or a library catalog, for instance – and an individual with an information need. As Case (2007) and others have pointed out, attention began to shift in the 1970s away from a prevailing focus on the design and functional characteristics of systems to considering the activities and needs of the individual user. Indeed, much of the history of the field since that shift could be described as being largely concentrated on individuals. Fundamental to this focus is the concept of an information need as defined by Taylor (2015); such a need, as it is transformed (with the help of a librarian acting as an intermediary) from unexpressed visceral need to a finally articulated "compromised need" (p. 251) in the form of a query presented to an information system, structures the basic information seeking process.

While work in this domain has defined the concept of information need in a variety of ways – including, for instance, Belkin's (see, e.g., 1980) "Anomalous States of Knowledge" (ASK) and Dervin's "Cognitive Gap" (see, e.g., 1992) – and has examined a variety of individual characteristics including both the cognitive (Dervin's emphasis on individual sense-making, for instance) and the affective (Carol Kuhlthau's (1991) Information Search Process model), its emphasis has consistently centered on the individual as the primary unit of analysis. Information need, in such an approach, is of necessity defined in terms of the individual: a user comes to seek information because of his or her own unique perception – whether well- or ill-defined – of their own particular interests and needs.

Individuals, however, do not exist in isolation, nor do information systems; rather, they interact within a specific context. However, even context is most often defined with the individual at the center; as Case put it (2007, p. 13) it is "the particular combination of person and situation" that gives meaning to the process of finding, making sense of, and using information. In other words, while the user is never an isolated entity independent of external influences, he or she is, as an active and autonomous agent, the locus at which "need" coalesces into active information seeking and, thus, considered to be the appropriate focus for research on information behavior. As Yu (2012, p. 5) puts it, "the informational properties of individuals ... cannot be replaced by context-denoting concepts .... [A] n individual's information world is a sphere of his/her lifeworld which the person experiences in the role of information agent ... rather than social, economic or any other agent."

Typically, the types of external influence considered to be pertinent influences on the actions of the individual have been defined rather narrowly, with work-related roles typically receiving the most attention (see, e.g., Case 2007 for an overview of such research). Over the past couple of decades, however, this narrow focus on formalized work-related activities has loosened somewhat, perhaps most notably in Savolainen's (1995) conception of Everyday Life Information Seeking, which acknowledges that people do not limit their information activities to only those issues related to their employment, but actively pursue a wide variety of other interests as well. There is, as well, an increasing amount of work examining information in relation to individuals' leisure activities (see, for instance, Hartel, 2003, 2010 and Fulton, 2009).

3. THE DOMAIN OF THE SOCIAL

Often seen as being in opposition to work that focuses on individual agency (but actually complementing it, as I will argue below), another strand of work has concerned itself more expansively with questions of context and the social dimension of information use. In one sense, this move away from attention to an (often decontextualized) individual is necessary: as noted above, individuals do not exist in isolation, but undertake their actions in locations defined by time, space, and a myriad of other external factors. On the other hand, the fact that "context" (because of that myriad of factors) can seem to expand infinitely, as even the fluttering of a butterfly somewhere in the world can demonstrably be considered to be part of "context" writ large (as in Chaos Theory; see Gleick, 1987, for the image of the impact of the butterfly); as Dervin (1996, p. 15) notes, "there is an inexhaustible list of factors that are contextual."

However, as Dervin (1996, p. 15) further notes, "there is a mandate to build conceptual systems which would provide guidance" for considering the role of context in information activities. A wide variety of work takes steps in this direction, including Wiegand's (2003, 2005) arguments for conceptualizations of "Library as

Place" and "Library in the life of the user," as well as studies building on Wiegand's work that investigate the role played by libraries in specific geographic and social settings (see, for instance, Most, 2008). Similarly, Fisher and her colleagues (Fisher, Durrance, & Hinton, 2004; Counts & Fisher, 2010) explore how specific locations function as "Information Grounds" in which the exchange of information is not only wholly situated within a precise place but is also inextricably rooted in the social particulars of that place and its denizens.

In particular, the work of Chatman (e.g. 1991, 1992, 1999, 2000; Burnett, Besant, & Chatman, 2001) turns strongly away from a conceptualization of the individual (and his/her cognitive state) as the defining locus of information-related phenomena. Instead, Chatman considered social factors and influences (rather than individual information needs) as the primary movers shaping how information is conceptualized and used (or avoided) within what she called "Small Worlds." Although a number of details changed in how she deployed her core concepts over time (and although she moved from a focus on information poverty to questions of information use more broadly conceived), Chatman argued for a specific set of factors linked to information use within a Small World (Burnett, Besant, & Chatman, 2001):

- Social Norms, a shared understanding of the acceptability of different kinds of observable behaviors within a world;
- Social Types, or the particular social roles played by individuals – and, particularly, how they are perceived or "typed" by others – within a world;
- Worldview, an agreed-upon perception of what kinds of information are of value within a world and what kinds are not; and
- Information Behavior, the normative activities and practices related to information gathering, use, avoidance, etc.

Although it remains useful for thinking about how social factors and settings exert influence on the information-related activities within a world, Chatman's work relies on an extremely constrained conceptualization of the boundaries defining the limits of a "world," essentially arguing that, while individuals' behaviors are contextualized within their localized Small social World, such worlds are themselves isolated entities allowing few, if any influences from external forces into their settings (Burnett, Besant, & Chatman, 2001).

Clearly, however, just as individuals exist within the social settings of which they are a part (but only a part), those settings – Chatman's Small Worlds – also exist within and are demonstrably shaped by larger social groupings. The lives and behaviors of participants within even the most constrained worlds (such as, for example, the inmates in a women's prison who were the focus of Chatman's 1999 study) are influenced and shaped not only by their immediate surroundings but by a number of other external factors including not only the social worlds of prison guards and administrators, but also the relationships between the prison as an entity and the remote worlds of the legal establishment and the political and economic forces of the outside world. That is, worlds are contiguous to as well as embedded and situated within other worlds; within these worlds information is not meaningful only at the level of the individual, but is a critical – and even defining – part of the structure and interaction of social worlds across levels.

Building on Chatman's work and melding it with Habermas' notion of the "Lifeworld" – a culture-wide sum of all available information resources, pathways, and channels within which both individuals and smaller social worlds are situated – the Theory of Information Worlds (Jaeger & Burnett, 2010) attempts to address three important points:

1. That Chatman's narrow focus on only the smallest of Small Worlds, together with her suggestion that such worlds must be considered in isolation from the larger worlds surrounding them, limited the power of her analysis of the interaction between information and social factors.

2. That human information use – indeed, that all information-related activities – are socially situated and are shaped, at least in part, by social forces in addition to individual information needs and cognitive factors.

3. That "information worlds" as social groupings overlap with and interact with each other, that these worlds may or may not perceive the meaning and value of information in the same ways, and that these differences in perception may lead to conflict between the worlds.

The Theory of Information Worlds thus adds a concept of "Boundaries" – the places at which different worlds come into contact with each other in one way or another – to Chatman's core concepts and renames the concept of "Worldview" as "Information Value," to suggest not only that each world has its own agreed-upon (if often implicit) scale for assessing the importance of different kinds of information but also that the kind of value attached to information (and the appropriate metrics for weighing that value) may differ from world to world. Finally, it should be noted that, although it focuses on social worlds rather than on individual users as the locus of information-related activities, the theory denies neither the importance of individuals nor the relevance of individual preferences, cognitive and affective states, or decisions; rather, it sees those individual characteristics and choices as being embedded within – not isolated from – the social world. Individuals are never fully free agents, but act within a set of norms, constraints, values, and possibilities that are social in nature.

4. THE DOMAIN OF SIGNIFICATION

Human users of information, whether conceptualized as individuals or as social groups, do not interact with information as an abstraction, but always as something encoded and communicated in some way via a material system of representation, whether writing, visualization, or some other medium for recording and storing – in a very literal sense, Buckland's "Information as Thing" (1991). Even purely verbal information exchange via personal interaction and word of mouth relies on linguistic encoding, and differs from other mechanisms for representation primarily in being evanescent rather than persistent in some way. Whether language structure is universal, innate, and a precondition of thought – and whether information can or cannot exist without it – or whether it is merely a social channel for communicating things that exist purely cognitively without encoding (see, for one among many overviews of a closely related debate surrounding Chomsy's linguistics, Colapinto, 2007), for the purposes of the field of LIS, information cannot be usefully conceptualized, sought, retrieved, or used without the mediation of representational practices of some sort; to paraphrase the poet William Carlos Williams (who was talking about poems), information, when packaged and stored for future use, can be seen as "a small (or large) machine made out of words" or some other encoding scheme (Williams, 1969, p. 256).

Although it has not always been informed by linguistic or philosophical approaches, a substantial component of work in the field has, in one way or another, examined the relationship between language (as a form of representation or signification) and information. And, indeed, much of the initial focus on retrieval and other information systems mentioned above directly engaged questions related to language, whether in the use of controlled vocabularies to represent "aboutness" to support user searches of systems (see, for only one recent example among thousands, Gross, Taylor, & Joudrey, 2015) or the different ways in which an information need could be expressed by a user during a search interaction (Taylor, 2015). Other work has brought new ways of addressing the gap between natural language and the more formalized vocabularies found in thesauri through the use of the more rigorously designed but also more flexible and "smarter" language structures found in ontologies (see, for two examples, Compton, 2014; Willis & Losee, 2013), with methods sometimes borrowed from linguistics (see, for instance, Faith, 2013). In addition, some work attempts to use automated approaches either to approximate human language use (e.g. Workman & Stoddart, 2012) or to develop systems to automatically interpret and modify users' system queries (e.g. Symonds et. al, 2014). Still other work has taken a less system-oriented and formalized approach, trusting in the "wisdom of the crowd" through approaches such as user tagging and folksonomies (e.g. Lin, Trattner, Brusilovsky, & He, 2015; Spiteri, 2007).

Although theoretically-oriented approaches have not been as common as such practice-oriented work, a number of researchers have pursued more conceptual concerns, often related to language use as one of the primary ways in which people interact and create shared meaning. For instance, Thellefsen et al. (2014) have used Peircean semiotics to criticize Belkin's individually-oriented cognitive ASK model for lacking a social component in which meaning is created as an interactive process between multiple agents and, ultimately, for being unable to explain how information is understood and turned into knowledge. Semiotics (based often, though not always, on Peirce rather than on Saussure) and its formulation of the relationship between signs,

objects, and interpretants has also been proposed as a framework for understanding the sense-making process (see Liu, 2013) and as a way forward in improving indexing practices (de Almeida et al., 2013) and knowledge organization (Friedman & Smiraglia, 2013).

Given that information, no matter how it is encoded and communicated, relies entirely on a system of signs and that such signs are part of an extended process that includes not only information seekers (that is, individual users) but also information creators and material objects such as books that mediate between creators and consumers, such a focus on the role of language in the creation of meaning seems fully appropriate. As Raber and Budd (2003) have suggested, "information" is a complex and often fuzzy concept, encompassing objects, individual cognitive processes, and social influences; considering it as a system of signs requires that we focus on all aspects of the process rather than solely on either individual cognition or on social context; people, whether considered individually or in groups, interact with information via such a system of signs.

Semiotics offers one path for analyzing those aspects of information related to signification and communication practices. Another approach, drawing upon Iser's reader-response theory, focuses primarily on how individuals, as consumers of texts, construct meaning – or information – through reading, conceived as an active performance (e.g. Mathson, 2011; Finlay, Ni, & Sugimoto, 2012). However, reader-response approaches tend often to minimize factors other than the role of individual cognition in the act of reading; Budd and Raber (1996) and Budd (2006) have proposed discourse analysis as a broader framework not only for understanding reading and interpretation, but also for analyzing how librarians function as mediators between information and users and for exploring how socially-rooted discursive practices shape and influence our perceptions and understanding of information in the first place. Both semiotics and discourse analysis, to varying degrees, emphasize the rootedness of information within two different systems outside of the individual: the semiotic system of language and representation, and the system of social discursive practices. An essential contribution of the more cognitively-oriented approaches to information, as outlined above, however, is that the individual cannot be removed from the equation; information, while it unquestionably relies upon some kind of system of representation (whether linguistic, visual, auditory, or other) for its transmission, and while it (equally unquestionably) is imbued with meaning and value because of the ways in which it is embedded within social practices and contexts, is also sought and used by individuals for their own individual purposes.

Another approach to the domain of signification, drawing upon cultural and philosophical hermeneutics, more fully acknowledges this interconnectedness. Hermeneutics emerged out of Talmudic and Christian traditions as a set of practices for deriving valid interpretations (or readings) of sacred texts (Thompson, 1981). More recent versions of hermeneutics, however, take up a more broadly defined challenge: to theorize about how semiotically-encoded objects (texts, for instance) that are created in one time and place still communicate to readers who find themselves in often radically different contexts – or, to put it in the terms of the Theory of Information Worlds, how texts can communicate across multiple information worlds which may (or may not) share norms and values either with each other or with the texts. As Hans-Georg Gadamer puts it, practices of representation and signification – written language foremost among them – function as "the fundamental mode of operation of our being-in-the-world and the all-embracing form of the constitution of the world" (1976, p. 3). To put this in terms of the field of LIS, the creation, dissemination, seeking, and use of information forms the heart of our engagement with – and understanding of – the world in which we live. In this sense, hermeneutics provides an ideal framework for conceptualizing the entire life-cycle of information.

Like reader-response theory, hermeneutics, in Paul Ricoeur's (1974) formulation, emphasizes the interpretation of texts as an act undertaken at the end of the cycle by a reader; however, it also importantly situates this act as part of the chain that includes the other necessary elements of the process of creating meaning: the writer (or creator of the text), the text itself, and the social contexts within which texts are created and read. While Ricoeur deals specifically with texts, his version of hermeneutics works well when the concept of information is substituted for that of the text – after all, as noted above, information must be encoded or packaged in some way in order to be either stored or used. Indeed, his definition of a text as "a discourse told by somebody, said by somebody to someone else about something"

(1974, p. 30) applies as well to information and its place within discursive practices. Information is created (and packaged) by someone with a particular intention and a vision of a potential audience, it is about something, and it is a "social phenomenon" (1974, p. 31) involving a producer, a set of mediating factors (both objects and actions), and a receiver; it is our way of understanding – and, thus, constructing – the world: "For me, the world is the ensemble of references opened up by every kind of text, descriptive or poetic, that I have read, understood, and loved" (1974, p. 37).

As a guiding framework for research on information behavior, Ricoeur's hermeneutics has the disadvantage of being explicitly uncommitted to any particular methodology. Still, hermeneutic approaches have been proposed for LIS research since at least 1989 (see Benediktsson, 1989), and have been used for studies of a variety of information-related phenomena, including the implications of design decisions for the ability of online personal health records to support patients' ability to understand and conceptualize information related to their own health (Burnett, Whetstone, & Jaeger, 2013); the degree to which both virtual communities (Burnett, 2002) and reference interviews can be seen as hermeneutic processes (Cohen, 1993; Murphy, 2005); the development of ontologies within information systems (Fonesca & Martin, 2005); the evaluation of databases (Boydens & van Hooland, 2011); classification (Paling, 2004); as well as more theoretically-oriented work related to literacy (Suominen & Tuomi, 2015), the creation of knowledge (Suorsa, 2015), and general information theory (Gnoli & Ridi, 2014). As Hansson (2005) has suggested, hermeneutics, in part because of its focus on the mediation of systems of signs in information activities and in part because of how it sees the individual and the social as intertwined factors, can provide a way forward in LIS research.

5. ENTWINED DOMAINS

As the above overviews suggest, the three domains – the individual, the social, and signification – are inextricably intertwined with one another. Individuals occupy the domain of the social and interact with one another through the mediation of signs. Or, to put it another way, the domain of the social is the broad context within which identifiable beings with unique cognitive and affective characteristics (i.e., individuals) live, exchange information, and engage with each other using a wide variety of signification and representational practices. Indeed, the domain of the social can arguably be seen as a complex system in which language and a wide variety of cultural artifacts and objects – as well as cultural institutions – play a semiotic role, carrying – and, perhaps, communicating – meaning (or, in LIS terms, information). Attempts to understand and use that meaning take place at both the level of the individual and as part of an ongoing and interactive social process.

Using Ricoeur's hermeneutics (1974) as a guide suggests that, although information objects (i.e., information that has been encoded and packaged as a "thing" in Buckland's (1991) sense) are necessary, information itself is neither static nor disengaged, but is, rather, one component of a complex process involving all three domains. Information transfer requires several interlocking stages:

1. Production of information, including an intent to communicate or demonstrate something to some kind of audience on the part of an agent, whether an individual or a social collective.

2. A medium by means of which that intent – or something approximating it – is encoded and turned into a "thing." This encompasses not only obvious media such as texts of various kinds, but also mediating information systems such as databases and institutions such as libraries dedicated to the storage and retrieval of information.

3. Some kind of process through which information is sought, obtained, encountered, acquired, or otherwise engaged with. This can include, obviously, traditionally-conceptualized information seeking activities such as those described above, but it also includes a wide range of other activities both individual and social.

4. An interpreting agent (again, whether an individual or a social group of some kind), who may or may not be the audience envisioned by the creating agent, and who may or may not understand the information encoded in the object in the way the creating agent intended. And

5. Some kind of acknowledgement, response, or impact. That is, as Bateson's famous formulation (1972) puts it, information is something that makes a

"difference" in some way, which is one of the things that gives it value.

Activities related to all of these stages can be construed to be information behavior of some kind or another. That is, conceptualizations of information behavior should not be limited only to those parts of the process related to needing, finding, or using information, but should also take into account production and the ways in which information is deemed to be worth creating as well as how it is encoded and packaged.

This process is neither seamless nor unproblematic. It is clear that what could be called "slippage" occurs between each stage. The creators of information may or may not, for instance, make decisions that allow them to accurately or clearly express their intentions; the encoding of information using some kind of communicating medium (such as language) is limited by things like usage and discursive norms, community practices, formal characteristics of particular genres, etc.; the audience may be quite different from that anticipated by the creators; and the ways in which the audience interprets, understands, or uses the information may (as both reader-response theory and hermeneutics suggest) bear little resemblance to the creator's intention.

Acknowledgement of such "slippage" echoes the insights of some post-structuralist theory, and in particular Jacques Derrida's (e.g. 1998) argument that communication practices always contain the seeds of their own dissolution or deconstruction. However, whereas Derrida's formulation of this "slippage" has, with some justification, been criticized as either radically relativist or even a form of nihilism (e.g. Wolin, 1993), hermeneutics accepts it as a given part of the complexities of communicating across the distances of space and time. Ricoeur (1974, p. 43) addresses this issue through his concept of "distanciation" as an inescapable characteristic of communicating via signs; he suggests that the difficulty of grappling with and trying to understand a text transforms the reader's distance from the writer into a new kind of closeness in which fruitful understanding can occur:

Distanciation is … the dynamic counterpart of our need, our interest, and our effort to overcome cultural estrangement. Writing and reading take place in this cultural struggle. Reading is the *pharmakon*, the "remedy," by which the meaning of a text [or information] is "rescued" from the estrangement of distanciation and put in a new proximity, a proximity which suppresses and preserves the cultural distance and includes the otherness within the ownness.

Ricoeur (1974) calls this process of turning distance into closeness the "mode of 'as if' ('as if you were there')." Ricoeur applies the "mode of 'as if'" explicitly to the world of printed texts and literary genres, but it can be extended to the concept of information as well. Information produced according to the norms and discursive standards of existing genres – that is, information that has been encoded for distribution, storage, and use according to existing practices – becomes a primary way of interacting with the world in which we live; despite the slippage and "distanciation" inherent in the process, it is "as if" information could be transferred seamlessly through the "ensemble of references" provided by texts (Ricoeur, 1974, p. 37).

It is important to emphasize, once again, that this process entwines – and, indeed, requires – all three of the domains outlined above. It is, as Ricoeur makes clear through his use of the first person pronoun, the individual, with his or her own cognitive and affective makeup, who engages with information. And yet this individual engagement is inherently part of an ongoing social process, as the individual is situated within a social context and is, of necessity, engaging with information created by others for purposes other than his or her own; further, the practices involved in information production, distribution, and archiving – publication, libraries, the media, etc. – are social practices. And, finally, the domain of signification – language, discursive practices, modes of representation – provides the set of tools that make the entire process possible in the first place. It is, in a very real sense, the locus of interaction between individuals and other individuals, between individuals and social collectives, and across different social groupings; signification practices form the glue that holds information worlds together and makes them work.

6. IMPLICTIONS FOR LIS RESEARCH AND PRACTICE

This article argues for a holistic framework within which to consider the ways in which information – needs, behavior, creation, and use – depends simultaneously on three different but intertwined domains:

the individual, the social, and signification. Although it began with an observation that the concerns of the field of LIS have shifted from a focus on libraries and librarianship to a broader conceptualization of information as a fundamental part of life and social interaction, it should be clear that libraries still play a central role in the world of information. Thus, the framework outlined here has some important implications not only for understanding information as a phenomenon both within and outside of libraries, but also for library practices and the field of librarianship.

The three domains, considered independently, offer a number of important points for information provision in any setting, including libraries. Consideration of the domain of the individual makes it clear that, while there are inescapable important external influences (including both of the other two domains), people also make decisions and have interests and needs rooted in their own individuality; "one size fits all" approaches to information provision run the risk of missing this point. The domain of the social, on the other hand, foregrounds the fact that individuals and their actions are always situated in specific times and places and within identifiable information worlds that help to shape users' activities. Further, because information systems – including libraries – are also created within specific social contexts to meet goals and provide services that are clearly social in nature, analysis of such systems requires attention to those social factors that guide developers' decisions about design and functionality. As I have argued elsewhere (Burnett, Whetstone, & Jaeger, 2013), the concepts outlined in the Theory of Information Worlds provide a powerful analytic tool for thinking about how systems, through their design, "project" a set of sometimes opaque assumptions about things like social norms and information values that both enable and constrain information seeking and use. Similarly, the domain of signification makes it clear that information systems and practices – as well as individuals and social groupings – are always built out of and, of necessity, use signification practices (including, but not limited to, language practices) to facilitate information access and use; understanding of these signification practices not only can help us understand how signification structures shape and influence information, but can also can suggest ways in which information services and systems can be improved and made more transparent.

One important implication of the three domains is that, while it is often assumed that the concept of information behavior is somehow only relevant at the user end of information work, system design and development can – and should – also be thought of as a type of information behavior. Decisions made during the development process both "project" a vision about the intended purpose, function, and meaning of information tools, and make material a set of assumptions about which user behaviors are to be supported and which are not. Users, that is, can only engage with systems in ways that have been built into those systems. Research about systems and research about users should, then, inform each other rather than being thought of as radically independent of each other; and both are inextricably intertwined with all three domains.

Good information practice can benefit from attention to each of the three domains, but can perhaps benefit even more powerfully from attention to the ways in which the three interact with one another. This is not to suggest that all LIS researchers should suddenly embrace holistic methods that draw upon individual, social, and signification models and approaches. Rather, it is important to remember that research within any of the three domains can offer something of value to research within the other domains. Individuals do not exist apart from either social groups or signification practices, just as groups are made up of individuals who use signification practices to interact. Information is the point at which the three intersect, and research into information phenomena – even when it is not "holistic" – should help illuminate that intersection.

REFERENCES

Bateson, G. (1972). *Steps to an ecology of mind: Collected essays in anthropology, psychiatry, evolution, and epistemology*. San Francisco: Chandler Publishing.

Belkin, N.J. (1980). Anomalous states of knowledge as a basis for information retrieval. *The Canadian Journal of Information Science, 5*, 133-143.

Boydens, I., & van Hooland, S. (2011). Hermeneutics applied to the quality of empirical databases. *Journal of Documentation, 67*(2), 279-289.

Buckland, M.K. (1991). Information as thing. *Journal of the American Society for Information Science, 42*, 351-360.

Budd, J.M. (2006). Discourse analysis and the study of communication in LIS. *Library Trends, 55*(1), 65-82.

Budd, J., & Raber, D. (1996). Discourse analysis: Method and application in the study of information. *Information Processing & Management, 32*, 217-226.

Burnett, G. (2002). The scattered members of an invisible republic: Virtual communities and Paul Ricoeur's Hermeneutics. *Library Quarterly, 72*(2), 155-178.

Burnett, G. (2010). Improvising community: A hermeneutic analysis of deadheads and virtual communities. In J. Tuedio, & S. Spector (Eds.), *The Grateful Dead in concert: Essays on live interpretation* (pp. 251-266). Jefferson, NC: McFarland.

Burnett, G., Besant, M., & Chatman, E.A. (2001). Small worlds: Normative behavior in virtual communities and feminist bookselling. *Journal of the American Society for Information Science & Technology, 52*(7), 536-547.

Burnett, G., Dickey, M., Kazmer, M., & Chudoba, K. (2003). Inscription and interpretation of text: A cultural hermeneutic examination of virtual community. *Information Research, 9*(1), n.p. Retrieved August 12, 2015, from http://informationr.net/ir/9-1/paper162.html

Burnett, G., & Jaeger, P. T. (2008). Small worlds, life-worlds, and information: The ramifications of the information behaviors of social groups in public policy and the public sphere. *Information Research, 13*(2), n.p. Retrieved August 12, 2015, from http://informationr.net/ir/13-2/paper346.html

Burnett, G., Jaeger, P. T., & Thompson, K. M. (2008). Normative behavior and information: The social aspects of information access. *Library & Information Science Research (07408188), 30*(1), 56-66.

Burnett, G., Whetstone, M., & Jaeger, P. T. (2013). Personal health record interfaces: A hermeneutic analysis. *First Monday, 18*(8), n.p. Retrieved August 12, 2015, from http://firstmonday.org/ojs/index.php/fm/article/view/4748

Case, D.O. (2007). Looking for information: A survey of research on information seeking, needs, and behavior. 2nd ed. Amsterdam, Elsevier.

Chatman, E. A. (1991). Life in a small world: Applicability of gratification theory to information-seeking behavior. *Journal of the American Society for Infor-*

mation Science, 42, 438-449.

Chatman, E. A. (1992). *The information world of retired women*. Westport, CT: Greenwood Press.

Chatman, E. A. (1999). A theory of life in the round. *Journal of the American Society for Information Science, 50*, 207-217.

Chatman, E. A. (2000). Framing social life in theory and research. *The New Review of Information Behaviour Research, 1*, 3-17.

Cohen, J. (1993). The hermeneutics of the reference question. *Australian Library Journal, 42*, 182-189.

Colapinto, J. (2007). The interpreter: Has a remote Amazonian tribe upended our understanding of language? *The New Yorker, 83*(3). Retrieved August 12, 2015, from http://www.newyorker.com/magazine/2007/04/16/the-interpreter-2.

Counts, S., & Fisher, K.E. (2010). Mobile social networking as information ground: A case study. *Library & Information Science Research, 32*(2), 98-115.

Compton, B.W. (2014). Ontology in information studies: Without, within, and withal knowledge management. *Journal of Documentation, 70*(3), 425-442.

De Almeida, C.C., Spotti, Lopes Fujita, M., dos Reis, D.M. (2013). Peircean semiotics and subject indexing: Contributions of speculative grammar and pure logic. *Knowledge Organization, 40*(4), 225-241.

Derrida, J. (1998). Of Grammatology (G. C. Spivak, Trans.). Baltimore: Johns Hopkins Press.

Dervin, B. (1992). From the mind's eye of the user: The sense-making qualitative-quantitative methodology. In J. Glazier & R.R. Powell (Eds.), *Qualitative research in information management* (pp. 61-84). Englewood, CA: Libraries Unlimited.

Dervin, B. (1997). Given a context by any other name: Methodological tools for taming the unruly beast. In *Information Seeking in Context: Proceedings of an International Conference on Information Seeking in Context, Tampere, Finland, 1996*. London: Taylor Graham Publishing, pp. 13-38.

Dickey, M. H., Burnett, G., Chudoba, K. M., & Kazmer, M. M. (2007). Do you read me? Perspective making and perspective taking in call center chat communications. *Journal of the Association of Information Systems, 8*(1), 547-70.

Faith, A. (2013). Linguistic analysis of taxonomy creation and validation. *Key Words, 21*(1), 11-15.

Finlay, S.C., Ni, C., & Sugimoto, C.R. (2012). New methods for an old debate: Utilizing reader response to investigate the relationship between collaboration and quality in academic journal articles. *Library & Information Science Research, 34*(2), 131-137.

Fisher, K.E., Durrance, J.C., & Hinton, M.B. (2004). Information grounds and the use of need-based services by immigrants in Queens, New York: A context based, outcome evaluation approach. *Journal of the American Society for Information Science & Technology, 55*(8), 754-766.

Fonesca, F.T., & Martin, J.E. (2005). Toward an alternative notion of information systems ontologies: Information engineering as a hermeneutic enterprise. *Journal of the American Society for Information Science & Technology, 56*(1), 46-57.

Friedman, A., & Smiraglia, R.P. (2013). Nodes and arcs: Concept map, semiotics, and knowledge organization. *Journal of Documentation, 69*(1), 27-48.

Fulton, C. (2009). Quid pro quo: Information sharing in leisure activities. *Library Trends, 57*(4), 753-768.

Gadamer, H. (1976). *Philosophical hermeneutics* (D.E. Linge, Trans.). Berkeley, CA: University of California Press.

Gleick, J. (1987). *Chaos: Making a new science*. New York: Viking.

Gnoli, C., & Ridi, R. (2014). Unified theory of information, hypertextuality, and levels of reality. *Journal of Documentation, 70*(3), 443-460.

Gross, T., Taylor, A.G., & Joudrey, D.N. (2015). Still a lot to lose: The role of controlled vocabulary in keyword searching. *Cataloging & Classification Quarterly, 53*(1), 1-39.

Hansson, J. (2005). Hermeneutics as a bridge between the modern and the postmodern in library and information science. *Journal of Documentation, 61*(1), 102-113.

Hartel, J. (2003). The serious leisure frontier in library and information science: Hobby domains. *Knowledge Organization, 30*(3/4), 228-238.

Hartel, J. (2010). Managing documents at home for serious leisure: A case study of the hobby of gourmet cooking. *Journal of Documentation, 66*(6), 847-874.

Jaeger, P. T., & Burnett, G. (2010). *Information Worlds: Social context, technology, & information behavior in the age of the Internet*. New York: Routledge.

Kuhlthau, C. (1991). Inside the search process: Information seeking from the user's perspective. *Journal of the American Society for Information Science, 42*(5), 361-71.

Lin, Y., Trattner, C., Brusilovsky, P., & He, D. (2015). The impact of image descriptions on user tagging behavior: A study of the nature and functionality of crowdsourced tags. *Journal of the Association for Information Science & Technology, 66*(9), 1785-1798.

Liu, Z. (2013). A semiotic interpretation of sense-making in information seeking. *Library Philosophy & Practice*, 1-5.

Mathson, S.M. (2011). Engaging readers, engaging texts: An exploration of how librarians can use reader response theory to better serve our patrons. *Library Philosophy & Practice*, 88-99.

Most, L. (2008). The library as place in rural North Florida: A study of the Gadsden County Public Library System (Unpublished doctoral dissertation). Florida State University, Tallahassee, FL.

Murphy, S. A.. (2005). The reference narrative. *Reference & User Services Quarterly, 44*(3), 247-252.

Paling, Stephen. (2004). Classification, rhetoric, and the classificatory horizon. *Library Trends, 52*(3), 588-603.

Raber, D. & Budd, J.M. (2003). Information as sign: Semiotics and information science. *Journal of Documentation, 59*(5), 507-522.

Ricoeur, P. (1974). *Interpretation Theory: Discourse and the surplus of meaning.* Fort Worth, TX: Christian University Press.

Savolainen, R. (1995). Everyday life information seeking: Approaching information seeking in the context of "Way of Life." *Library & Information Science Research, 17*, 259-294.

Spiteri, L.F. (2007). The structure and form of folksonomy tags: The road to the public library catalog. *Information Technology & Libraries, 26*(3), 13-25.

Suominen, V., & Tuomi, P. (2015). Literacies, hermeneutics, and literature. *Library Trends, 63*(3), 615-628.

Suorsa, A.R. (2015). Knowledge creation and play – A phenomenological approach. *Journal of Documentation, 71*(3), 503-525.

Symonds, M., Bruza, P., Zuccon, G., Koopman, B., Sitbon, L., & Turner, I., (2014). Automatic query expansion: A structural linguistic perspective. *Journal of the Association for Information Science & Technology, 65*(8), 1577-1596.

Taylor, R. (2015). Question negotiation and information seeking in libraries. *College & Research Libraries, 75*(3), 251-267.

Thellsefsen, T., Sorensen, B., & Thellefsen, M. (2014). The information concept of Nicholas Belkin revisited: Some semiotic comments. *Journal of Documentation, 70*(1), 74-92.

Thompson, J.B. (1981). *Critical hermeneutics: A study in the thought of Paul Ricoeur.* Cambridge: Cambridge University Press.

Wiegand, W.A. (2003). To reposition a research agenda: What American studies can teach the LIS community about the library in the life of a user. *Library Quarterly, 73*(4), 369-382.

Wiegand, W.A. (2005). Library as place. *North Carolina Libraries, 63*(3/4). Retrieved August 12, 2015, from http://www.ncl.ecu.edu/index.php/NCL/article/viewFile/70/88.

Williams, W.C. (1969). Author's introduction to The Wedge. In *Selected essays* (pp. 255-257). New York: New Directions.

Willis, C. & Losee, R.M. (2013). A random walk on an ontology: Using thesaurus structure for automatic subject indexing. *Journal of the American Society for Information Science & Technology, 64*(7), 1330-1344.

Wolin, R. (1993). *The Heidegger controversy: A critical reader.* Cambridge, MA: MIT Press.

Workman, T.E. & Stoddart, J.M. (2012). Rethinking information delivery: Using a natural language processing application for point-of-care data discovery. *Journal of the Medical Library Association, 100*(2), 113-120.

Yu, L. (2012). Towards a reconceptualization of the "information worlds of individuals." *Journal of Librarianship and Information Science, 44*(1), 3-18.

10

Impact of Self-Citations on Impact Factor: A Study Across Disciplines, Countries and Continents

Ramesh Pandita *

BGSB University
Rajouri, Jammu & Kashmir, India
E-mail: rameshpandita90@gmail.com

Shivendra Singh

University College of Nursing
Baba Farid University of Health Sciences
(BFUHS), Punjab, India
E-mail: shiv.mail@gmail.com

ABSTRACT

Purpose. The present study is an attempt to find out the impact of self-citations on Impact Factor (IF) across disciplines. The study examines the number of research articles published across 27 major subject fields covered by SCImago, encompassing as many as 310 sub-disciplines. The study evaluates aspects like percentage of self-citations across each discipline, leading self-citing countries and continents, and the impact of self-citation on their IF.
Scope. The study is global in nature, as it evaluates the trend of self-citation and its impact on IF of all the major subject disciplines of the world, along with countries and continents. IF has been calculated for the year 2012 by analyzing the articles published during the years 2010 and 2011.
Methodology/Approach. The study is empirical in nature; as such, statistical and mathematical tools and techniques have been employed to work out the distribution across disciplines. The evaluation has been purely undertaken on the secondary data, retrieved from SCImago Journal and Country Ranking.
Findings. Self-citations play a very significant part in inflating IF. All the subject fields under study are influenced by the practice of self-citation, ranging from 33.14% to 52.38%. Compared to the social sciences and the humanities, subject fields falling under the purview of pure and applied sciences have a higher number of self-citations, but a far lesser percentage than the social sciences and humanities. Upon excluding self-citations, a substantial amount of change was observed in the IF of subject fields under study, as 18 (66.66%) out of 27 subjects fields faced shuffle in their rankings. Variation in rankings based on IF with and without self-citation was observed at subject level, country level, and continental level.

Keywords: Citation Analysis, Self-citations, Author self-citations, Journal self-citations, Impact Factor

*Corresponding Author: Ramesh Pandita
Assistant Librarian
BGSB University
Rajouri, Jammu & Kashmir, India
E-mail: rameshpandita90@gmail.com

1. INTRODUCTION

Citation analysis is a subject of significant interest among the research scholars across the globe, factually for being one of the oldest methods to gauge the impact of a research article. Impact Factor (IF) and Hirsch Index (h-index) are two quality parameters employed to judge the quality of research articles and both the parameters are computed on the basis of number of citations received by an article, applied to compute the IF or h-index of a journal or an author. Researchers across the globe mostly prefer to publish their research results in those journals, which have higher IF. The higher the Impact Factor of a journal, higher is the rate of rejection of articles submitted to such journals and thus better supposed is the quality of articles published in high IF journals.

Metric studies like IF and h-index computed for authors, journals, and so on are purely based on the citation analysis, received by research publications. Given the fact, it becomes imperative to know how far the self-citations play a part in inflating the IF or h-index of journals, or for that matter of authors or countries. In the present study, an attempt has been made to work out the impact of self-citation on IF across disciplines, countries, and continents. The focus has been laid on assessment of IF and to examine the overall percentage difference in IF, both with and without self-citation.

1.1 Impact Factor

IF is calculated on the basis of citations received by a research publication. The concept was first suggested by Gross and Gross in 1927, who said that counting references can be used to rank scientific journals, but it was Eugene Garfield who in 1955 was instrumental in devising the formula to compute the impact of scientific journals of repute by undertaking computations on the basis of citations received by scientific publications published by these journals. Garfield suggested that Impact Factor can be calculated for any given period of time, but to evaluate the current impact of publications, he suggested computing IF by undertaking the publications of the preceding two years for which the Impact Factor is to be calculated. As per the Web of Knowledge, Journal Impact Factor (JIF) is "the average number of times articles

from the journal published in the past two years have been cited in the Journal Citation Report (JCR) year." Garfield was also of the view that generally the role in research is played by current awareness service (CAS); as such, within a span of two years these research publications catch the attention of potential researchers. Over a period of time the concept of Impact Factor has been extended to various other fields, and in computing the IF of authors, countries and subject disciplines, or even for that matter as of late, web-IF has started gaining popularity in the research circles.

1.2 Self-Citation

As per the Thomson and Reuters journal citation report (JCR), "A self-citation is a reference to an article from the same journal. Self-citations can make up a significant portion of the citations a journal gives and receives each year." In simpler terms, we can say a journal self-citation is a practice whereby a research work published in a particular journal includes references from the research works published in the same journal previously. Farrara and Romero (2013) in their study defined self-citation as such: "A self-citation $C_P{}^S \rightarrow Q$ is any citation appearing in a paper P pointing to paper Q, whose set of authors are respectively $A[P]$ and $A[Q]$, for which it holds true: $A\ P \cap A\ Q \neq \varnothing$, i.e., the intersection of the sets of authors is not empty."

2. OBJECTIVES OF THE STUDY

- To understand and examine the trend of self-citation across disciplines and its impact on Impact Factor across disciplines, countries, and continents.
- To reflect on the self-citations of the world's top thirty cited countries of the subjects under study and to determine the variation in their Impact Factor by excluding self-citations.

3. LITERATURE REVIEW

Some of the earlier studies undertaken in the field of self-citations relevant to the present study have been reviewed hereunder.

Tagliacozzo (1977) in his study concerning the practice of self-citation in scientific literature undertook an analysis of 180 research articles and observed that nearly 17% of citations in Plant Physiology and Neurobiology are self-citations. Similarly, **Bonzi and Snyder (1990)** in a similar kind of study analyzed 120 publications and found an average of 11% self-citations across disciplines, which varied from 16% to 3% among physical and social sciences. These studies indicate the fact that there is nothing new about the practice of self-citation and it has been there for quite long now. Besides, the trend of self-citation varies considerably from subject to subject and as of late the practice has assumed a much larger shape.

Nederh et al. (1993), Moed and Velde (1993) and **Leeuwen, Rinia, and Van Raan (1996)**, in their respective studies concerning the trend of self-citation, found that during the period 1985 to 1994, 29% self-citations were recorded in physics and chemistry each and this percentage was higher during the first year of publications. **Van Raan (1998)** in his study upheld the practice of self-citations by saying that they cannot be neglected for the fact that such practices allow us to perform corrections. Factually, self-citing an earlier work in a new work eliminates the chances of any missing link in the research work.

White (2001) suggested that there is no need to get carried away by the practice of self-citations as these can be easily identified and can be easily excluded while computing the JIF, as they have a potential effect on the JIF. Accordingly, editors have grown conscious of the growing awareness among authors towards publishing their research results in high IF journals and as such have begun to manipulate the IF of their journals (**Jennings, 2001**). These studies are a clear indication of the fact that self-citations play a very important role in inflating the IF of journals, or for that matter of individuals.

Hyland (2003) in his study has opined that self-citation accentuates the expertise of a researcher in any given field of activity and perpetuates one's credibility and interpretation of such specific research findings. Surely, the importance of self-citations by no means can be undermined as these citations redirect us to earlier sources over which the present work has been built up to a larger extent, along with authors' or individuals' earlier understandings and contributions in the given field. **Neuberger and Couinsell (2002)** and **Sevinc (2004)**, in their respective studies, have reported on instances whereby manuscripts submitted for publication in journals were returned to authors with remarks by the editors to add some references from that very particular journal of some relevant previously published articles. All this clearly reflects that the trend of journal self-citation is going around quite intentionally, where editors and publishers are manipulating the JIF as per their connivance and to their suitability. **Gami et al. (2004)** raised concerns and criticized the IF as a metric for the fact that it is influenced by the practice of self-citation.

Kaltenborn and Kuhn (2004) are of the view that there is a growing consciousness among publishers and editors of journals about the importance of Journal Impact Factor (JIF), whereby researchers prefer to publish their research results in those journals which have higher IF. There is no denial of the fact that editors want their journals to have a high Impact Factor, firstly to attract the authors and also to present their publication as superior and qualitative to that of others. **Anseel, Duyck, and Baene (2004)** while assessing the impact of self-citations over psychology journals, found that upon adjusting the self-citations, the Impact Factor of journals with higher IF decreased by around 15%, while as, in the case of mid and low IF psychology journals the IF declined between 35% and 45%, respectively.

Frandsen (2007) in his study of journal self-citations and JIF mechanisms undertook an analysis of the impact of self-citations by studying 32 economics journals, and observed that with the increase in the self-citation, the JIF increases. Frandsen is also of the view that the self-citing rate and self-cited rate are positively related. **Campanario (2011)** undertook a study on the impact of citations in general and self-citations in particular on the Impact Factor of journals on a yearly basis. Campanario chose to analyze 40 different journals on a yearly basis during the period 1998 to 2007 and found that self-citations on the whole resulted into increase of 54% increase and 42% decrease in the journal Impact Factor.

King et al. (2013) in their study based on gender self-citation analyzed over 1.6 million articles of JSTOR published after the 1950's and found that, compared to women, men self-cite their own earlier research work at a higher rate and 10% of cited articles are self-cited. The authors also observed that the gender gap of self-citation over the past 50 years has increased, despite a fair amount of women joining academics. Of the total references studied, the authors found that 9.4% are self-citations and molecular biology has the highest rate of self-citation and classical studies the lowest.

Farrara and Romero (2013) in their study worked on the discounted h-index (dh-index) to present a method whereby we can mitigate the impact of self-citations while computing the impact evaluation of journals and authors. The authors in their experiment observed a decrease of 3% to 23% in author h-index and a decrease of 2.5% to 22% in the journal h-index. Since both the IF and the h-index are computed on the basis of citations received by a research article, accordingly we can work out the discounted IF for both the authors and the journals, and so the result has been actually computed in the analysis part of this particular study.

Most of the research studies reviewed concerning the field of self-citations and their impact on IF have revealed that self-citations play a very significant role in inflating IF.

4. METHODOLOGY

This study has been undertaken on secondary data retrieved from SCImago Journal and Country Rankings on June 21, 2014, accessible at http://www.scimagojr.com/index.php. The data upon retrieval was in semi-struc-tured form; as such, it was first structured in the desired form given the objectives of the study. Structuration of data was done after retrieving it on a yearly basis for each individual subject, for each individual country, and for each individual continent. To analyze the data for a continent, affiliation of each contributing country was sought with the respective continent by using the world atlas. Also, to perform some basic expressions like drawing percentage, division, subtraction, and so on, mathematical tools and techniques were employed.

Impact Factor has been calculated by adopting the method devised by Garfield, and accordingly the rankings undertaken in each table referenced below are based on the Impact Factor. The higher the Impact Factor of a subject discipline, country, or continent, the higher is its ranking. Accordingly, (R_1) is the ranking calculated with self-citations and (R_2) is the revised ranking, calculated without self-citations. The difference computed in the IF with and without self-citation gets reflected in R_2, which as a result will give insights about the impact of self-citations on the Impact Factor.

4.1 Analysis Approach & Tool

The Impact Factor for each individual subject field, country, and the continent has been computed for articles published during the year 2010 and 2011 and the citations received during the year 2012.

Tool							
Subject Discipline /Country /Continent	Articles Published (2010+2011) & (% Share)	Total citations received in 2012 & (% Share)	Impact Factor (2012)	Total Self-citations received in 2012 & (% SC)	Impact Factor without Self-Citations & (% Decrease)	Ranking based on IF with self-citations	Ranking based on IF without Self-citations
	A_P	T_C	T_C/A_P	S_C	$(T_C-S_C)/A_P$	R_1	R_2

- A_P — Articles published during (2010+2011)
- T_C — Total citations received by A_P during 2012
- $IF_{(2012)}$ — Impact Factor (2012)
- $IF=T_C/A_P$ — Impact Factor with Self-citations
- S_C — Self-citations
- (IF_{-SC}) — Impact Factor without Self-citations
- $(IF_{-SC})=(T_C-S_C)/A_P$ — Impact Factor without Self-citations
- $S_C\%=S_C/T_C\times100$ — Self-citation Percentage
- R_1 — Rank with Self-citations
- R_2 — Rank without Self-citations

The tool has been applied in all the three tables as per the scheme of things worked out.

5. RESULTS

The computations of the present study are based on Impact Factor, involving no complex mathematical calculations. The expressions drawn for a percentage have not been rounded off, hence may reflect slight variation while computing figures for 100%.

Table 1. Variation in Rankings Across Disciplines Based on Impact Factor (IF) With and Without Self-Citations

Subject Discipline	Articles Published (2010+2011) & (% Share)	Total citations received in 2012 & (% Share)	Impact Factor (2012)	Total Self-citations received in 2012 & (% S_C)	Impact Factor without Self-Citations & (% Decrease)	Ranking based on IF with Self-citations	Ranking based on IF without Self-citations
	A_P	T_C	T_C/A_P	S_C	$(T_C - S_C)/A_P$	R_1	R_2
Multidisciplinary	79066 (1.27)	64402 (3.40)	0.814	21431 (33.27)	0.543 (33.29)	1	1
Physics and Astronomy	451185 (7.29)	219376 (11.61)	0.486	72718 (33.14)	0.325 (33.12)	2	2
Biochemistry, Genetics, & Molecular Biology	546453 (8.82)	256761 (13.58)	0.469	92836 (36.15)	0.299 (36.24)	3	3
Neuroscience	93456 (1.51)	43494 (2.30)	0.465	16873 (38.79)	0.284 (38.92)	4	5
Immunology and Microbiology	161158 (2.60)	72560 (3.84)	0.450	26305 (36.25)	0.287 (36.22)	5	4
Earth and Planetary Sciences	230862 (3.73)	91288 (4.83)	0.395	42838 (46.92)	0.209 (47.08)	6	8
Chemistry	352240 (5.69)	135936 (7.19)	0.385	61345 (45.12)	0.211 (45.19)	7	7
Medicine	1158228 (18.71)	392829 (20.79)	0.339	131147 (33.38)	0.225 (33.62)	8	6
Environmental Science	213184 (3.44)	62820 (3.32)	0.294	29257 (46.57)	0.157 (46.59)	9	10
Pharmacology, Toxicology, & Pharmaceutics	129597 (2.09)	37600 (1.98)	0.290	15885 (42.24)	0.167 (42.41)	10	9
Energy	74229 (1.19)	19310 (1.02)	0.260	8082 (41.85)	0.151 (41.92)	11	11
Agricultural and Biological Sciences	398288 (6.43)	102176 (5.40)	0.256	45094 (44.13)	0.143 (44.14)	12	12
Mathematics	246185 (3.97)	55447 (2.93)	0.225	22493 (40.56)	0.133 (40.88)	13	13
Materials Science	339346 (5.48)	74813 (3.95)	0.220	35388 (47.30)	0.116 (47.27)	14	14
Chemical Engineering	165493 (2.67)	35599 (1.88)	0.215	17638 (49.54)	0.108 (49.76)	15	17
Health Professions	34922 (0.56)	7208 (0.38)	0.206	3225 (44.74)	0.114 (44.66)	16	15
Psychology	79470 (1.28)	16090 (0.85)	0.202	8261 (51.34)	0.098 (51.48)	17	20
Nursing	50446 (0.81)	9601 (0.50)	0.190	4029 (41.96)	0.110 (42.10)	18	16

Decision Sciences	28343 (0.45)	5211 (0.27)	0.183	2365 (45.38)	0.100 (45.35)	19	18
Computer Science	282577 (4.56)	49154 (0.026)	0.173	24427 (49.69)	0.087 (49.71)	20	22
Dentistry	19202 (0.31)	2978 (0.15)	0.155	1053 (35.35)	0.100 (35.48)	21	19
Economics, Econometrics, & Finance	59585 (0.96)	9199 (0.48)	0.154	3861 (41.97)	0.089 (42.20)	22	21
Engineering	565551 (9.13)	79015 (4.18)	0.139	40251 (50.94)	0.068 (51.07)	23	25
Veterinary	40863 (0.66)	5582 (0.29)	0.136	2449 (43.87)	0.076 (44.11)	24	23
Social Sciences	230693 (3.72)	27353 (1.44)	0.118	13761 (50.30)	0.058 (50.84)	25	26
Business, Mgt., and Accounting	79510 (1.28)	9418 (0.49)	0.118	3890 (41.30)	0.069 (41.52)	26	24
Arts and Humanities	78641 (1.27)	4263 (0.22)	0.054	2233 (52.38)	0.025 (53.70)	27	27
Total	6188773	1889483	0.305	749135 (39.64)	0.184 (39.67)		

T_C-Total Citations, S_C-Self-citations, IF-Impact Factor, R_1-Ranking with Self-citations and R_2-Ranking without Self-citations

In the above tabulations, the IF of the subject fields under study has been computed with and without self-citations to draw their R_1 & R_2 ranking based on IF, as per the proposed research tool. At the global level, a total of 1,889,483 citations were received by all the 27 major subject disciplines under study, of which 749,135, (39.64%) are self citations, constituting more than one third of total citations received. The multidisciplinary subject field emerged as the major subject field with the highest 0.814 Impact Factor, followed by Physics & Astronomy and then Biochemistry, Genetics, & Molecular Biology with 0.486 and 0.469 IF, respectively. The Arts & Humanities subject field stands at the bottom of the table with a minimum 0.054 IF, and the percentage of self-citations of each individual subject field varies considerably.

Arts and Humanities have a maximum 52.38% self-citations, followed by Psychology and Engineering with 51.34% and 50.94%, respectively. Physics and Astronomy is the subject field having a minimum 33.14% self-citations, followed by multidisciplinary subjects and medicine with self-citations percentages of 33.27% and 33.38%, respectively. The percentage of self-citation is drawn in proportion to the total citations received.

The interesting fact is that Medicine, despite being the third lowest self-citation percentage subject field, has the maximum number of self-citations to its credit with an overall self-citations share percentage of 17.5% (131,147). Medicine is followed by Biochemistry, Genetics, & Molecular Biology and then Physics & Astronomy, with an overall self-citation share percentage of 12.39% (92,836) and 9.70% (72,718), respectively.

There is a need to understand the fact that having a greater number of self-citations may not necessarily result in a greater percentage of self-citation and vice-versa. But if a subject field has received a greater number of self-citations, the number has a greater impact on its IF. The Impact Factor of a subject field with and without self-citations shows a considerable change, as at gross global level, 39.67% decline was recorded in Impact Factor for all the subject fields when taken together.

Of the total citations received by all the subject fields under study, Medicine receives the maximum (392,829, 20.79%) number and percentage of citations, followed by Biochemistry, Genetics, & Molecular Biology (256,761, 13.58%) and Physics & Astronomy (219,376, 11.61%). 14 subject fields have citations share percentages between 1.02% and 7.19%, while as, 10 subject fields each have received less than a 1% share of total citations, with Dentistry at a minimum (2,978, 0.15%) citations share percentage.

In terms of overall publications share percentage, it

is again Medicine which has the maximum (1,158,228, 18.71%) publications to its credit, followed by Engineering and then Biochemistry, Genetics, & Molecular Biology with a share percentage of 9.13% (565,551) and 8.82% (546,453), respectively. Dentistry is the subject field which stands at the bottom of the table with the minimum (19,202, 0.31%) publications share percentage.

The variation in IF is around the same percentage as that of self-citations. The Arts and Humanities have shown the maximum (53.70%) decrease in IF followed by Psychology and Engineering with 51.48% and 51.07%, respectively.

The ranking of each subject field has shown a considerable variation, as out of 27 subject disciplines 18 faced variation, either to the next lower or earliest higher, which also means 66.66% of subject fields faced changes in their rankings.

The subject fields which slumped in their ranking include: Neuroscience, Earth & Planetary Sciences, Environmental Sciences, Chemical Engineering, Psychology, Computer Sciences, Engineering and Social Sciences;

while the subject fields which improved in their ranking include Immunology & Microbiology, Medicine, Pharmacology, Toxicology & Pharmacy, Health Professions, Nursing, Decision Sciences, Dentistry, Economics, Econometrics & Finance, Veterinary Sciences, and Business Management and Accounting. However, in the remaining 9 (33.33%) subject fields no change was observed in their rankings.

The Impact Factor of the world's thirty leading cited countries during the year 2012 has been worked out accordingly. Upon computing the Impact Factor of countries, Switzerland, Denmark, and the Netherlands emerged as the countries with the maximum Impact Factor of 0.529, 0.429, and 0.471, respectively, while Russia stands at the bottom of the table with 0.275 IF.

Of the total citations received by countries at the individual level, China has received the maximum 59.15% self-citations, followed by the U.S 56.92%, Iran 50.72%, India 46.03%, and Brazil 38.10%. Israel stands at the bottom of the table with a minimum of 20.68% self-citations.

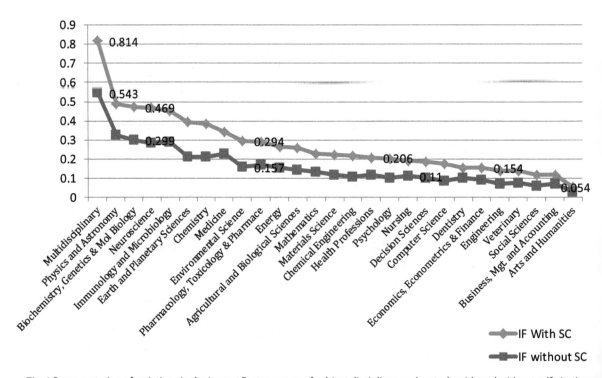

Fig. 1 Representation of variations in the Impact Factor curves of subject disciplines under study with and without self-citations

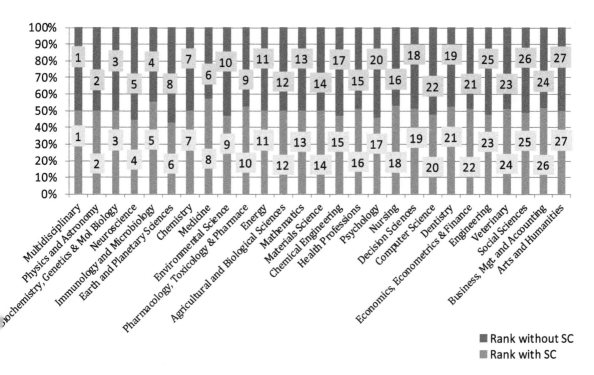

Fig. 2 Representation of change in ranking based on IF of the subject disciplines with and without self-citations

Table 2. Variation in Impact Factor (IF) and Ranking Thereof, With and Without Self-Citation, Across World's Thirty Leading Cited Countries

Country	Articles Published (2010+2011) & (% Share)	Total citations received in 2012 & (% Share)	Impact Factor (2012)	Total Self-citations received in 2012 & (% S_C)	Impact Factor without Self-Citations & (% Decrease)	Ranking based on IF with Self-citations	Ranking based on IF without Self-citations
	A_P	T_C	T_C/A_P	S_C	$(T_C-S_C)/A_P$	R_1	R_2
Switzerland	81847 (1.32)	43328 (2.29)	0.529	10624 (24.51)	0.399 (24.57)	1	1
Denmark	43352 (0.70)	21366 (1.13)	0.492	5146 (24.08)	0.374 (23.98)	2	2
Netherlands Antilles	113019 (1.82)	53264 (2.81)	0.471	13707 (25.73)	0.350 (25.69)	3	3
Sweden	69519 (1.12)	29928 (1.58)	0.430	7073 (23.63)	0.328 (23.72)	4	4
Belgium	63244 (1.02)	26314 (1.39)	0.416	6347 (24.12)	0.315 (24.27)	5	6
Austria	44217 (0.71)	18434 (0.97)	0.416	4014 (21.77)	0.326 (21.63)	6	5

Singapore	34499 (0.55)	14283 (0.75)	0.414	3871 (27.10)	0.301 (27.29)	7	7
Finland	36134 (0.58)	13936 (0.73)	0.385	3331 (23.90)	0.293 (23.89)	8	9
Norway	36837 (0.59)	13994 (0.74)	0.379	3717 (26.56)	0.278 (26.64)	9	10
United Kingdom	361457 (5.84)	135967 (7.19)	0.376	46896 (34.49)	0.246 (34.57)	10	11
Israel	40815 (0.65)	15324 (0.81)	0.375	3170 (20.68)	0.297 (20.80)	11	8
Germany	333359 (5.38)	124040 (6.56)	0.372	46558 (37.53)	0.232 (37.63)	12	17
Australia	153820 (2.48)	56333 (2.98)	0.366	18925 (33.59)	0.243 (33.60)	13	14
Italy	191644 (3.09)	69795 (3.69)	0.364	24455 (35.03)	0.236 (35.16)	14	15
Canada	200822 (3.24)	70470 (3.72)	0.350	20980 (29.77)	0.246 (29.71)	15	12
United States	1289360 (20.83)	445165 (23.56)	0.345	253416 (56.92)	0.148 (57.10)	16	23
Portugal	38266 (0.61)	12887 (0.68)	0.336	3523 (27.33)	0.244 (27.38)	17	13
France	243582 (3.93)	80280 (4.24)	0.329	26268 (32.72)	0.221 (32.82)	18	18
Spain	177298 (2.86)	57773 (3.05)	0.325	18857 (32.63)	0.219 (32.61)	19	19
Greece	40325 (0.65)	12419 (0.65)	0.307	2987 (24.05)	0.233 (24.10)	20	16
South Korea	151378 (2.44)	37033 (1.95)	0.244	11758 (31.75)	0.166 (31.96)	21	20
Poland	73557 (1.18)	17708 (0.93)	0.240	6298 (35.56)	0.155 (35.41)	22	22
Japan	281829 (4.55)	66286 (3.50)	0.235	24467 (36.91)	0.148 (37.02)	23	24
Taiwan	91417 (1.47)	21548 (1.14)	0.235	6909 (32.06)	0.160 (31.91)	24	21
China	744309 (12.02)	144051 (7.62)	0.193	85215 (59.15)	0.079 (59.06)	25	30
Brazil	122374 (1.97)	23077 (1.22)	0.188	8793 (38.10)	0.116 (38.29)	26	25
Iran	79843 (1.29)	13846 (0.73)	0.173	7024 (50.72)	0.085 (50.86)	27	29
Turkey	78432 (1.26)	13584 (0.71)	0.173	4582 (33.73)	0.114 (34.10)	28	26
India	202306 (3.26)	34573 (1.82)	0.170	15914 (46.03)	0.092 (45.88)	29	28
Russian Federation	93470 (1.51)	15939 (0.84)	0.170	5855 (36.73)	0.107 (37.05)	30	27
Rest of world	676442 (10.93)	186538 (9.87)	0.275	48455 (25.97)	0.204 (25.81)		
Total	6188773	1889483	0.305	749135 (39.64)	0.184 (39.67)		

T_C-Total Citations, S_C-Self-citations, IF-Impact Factor, R_1-Ranking with Self-citations and R_2-Ranking without Self-citations

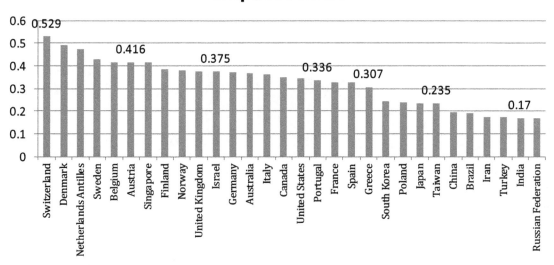

Fig. 3 Impact Factor representation of countries

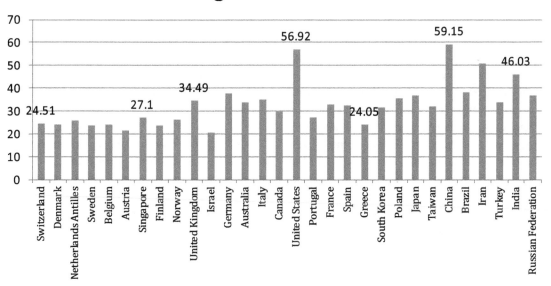

Fig. 4 Self-citations percentage representation

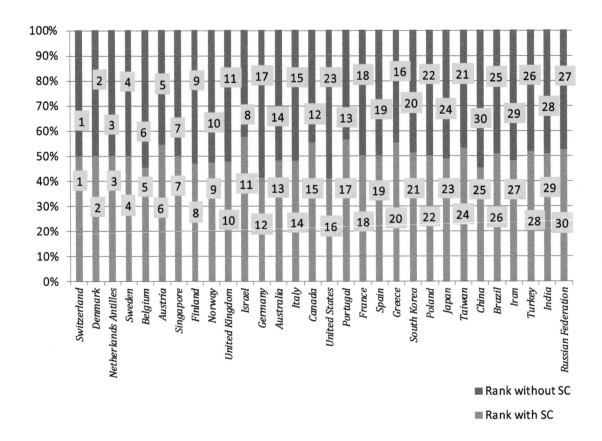

Fig. 5 Representation of change in the rankings of countries based on IF of the subject disciplines with and without self-citations

There is almost a linear but substantial decline in the IF of countries after computing IF without self-citations in the world's thirty leading cited countries. The trend gets equally reflected in Fig. 5, reflecting changes in rankings, based on the IF of countries with and without self-citations. On the whole, 22 (73.33%) countries faced variation in their rankings, while as, no change was observed in the ranking of 8 (26.67%) countries. Countries which slipped in their rankings include Belgium, Finland, Norway, the United Kingdom, Germany, Australia, Italy, the United States, Japan, China, and Iran; and the countries whose ranking improved include Austria, Israel, Canada, Portugal, Greece, South Korea, Taiwan, Brazil, Turkey, India, and the Russian Federation.

The United States is the leading country in the world to receive the maximum (445,265, 23.56%) citations share percentage at a global level, followed by China with 144,051 (7.62%) and the United Kingdom (135,967, 7.19%) citations share percentages. Of the total 30 tabulated countries, 16 countries have received citations from 1.13% to 6.56% and 11 countries have received less than 1% of citations each.

The United States leads the table with the maximum (1,289,380, 20.83%) global publications share percentage, followed by China and United Kingdom with a share percentage of 12.02% (744,309) and 5.84% (361,457), respectively. Singapore figures at the bottom of the table in terms of its publications share percentage of 0.55% (34,499).

Table 3. Variation in Impact Factor Across Continents With and Without Self-Citations

Continent	Articles Published (2010+2011) & (% Share)	Total citations received in 2012 & (% Share)	Impact Factor (2012)	Total Self-citations received in 2012 & (% S_C)	Impact Factor without Self-Citations & (% Decrease)	Ranking based on IF with Self-citations	Ranking based on IF without Self-citations
	A_P	T_C	T_C/A_P	S_C	$(T_C-S_C)/A_P$	R_1	R_2
Europe	2264069 (36.58)	818897 (43.33)	0.361	252583 (30.84)	0.250 (30.74)	1	1
Oceania	183635 (2.96)	66161 (3.50)	0.360	21572 (32.60)	0.242 (32.77)	2	2
North America	1541506 (24.90)	527696 (27.92)	0.342	277043 (52.50)	0.162 (52.63)	3	4
South America	190265 (3.07)	44086 (2.33)	0.231	13502 (30.62)	0.160 (30.73)	4	5
Africa	122200 (1.97)	27918 (1.47)	0.228	7656 (27.42)	0.165 (27.63)	5	3
Asia	1887098 (30.49)	404725 (21.41)	0.214	176779 (43.67)	0.120 (43.92)	6	6
Total	6188773	1889483	0.305	749135 (39.64)	0.184 (39.67)		

T_C-Total Citations, S_C-Self-citations, IF-Impact Factor, R_1-Ranking with Self-citations and R_2-Ranking without Self-citations

The scenario of continents is altogether different and has been computed by taking together the publications and citations of different countries falling under a particular continent. Accordingly, Europe leads in the table of continents with an IF of 0.361, followed by Oceania and North America with their individual IF scores of 0.360 and 0.342, respectively. Asia stands at the bottom of the table with an IF of 0.214. In terms of overall publications share percentage, Europe again leads the table with a share of 36.58% (2,264,069), followed by Asia and North America with their individual publications share percentage of 30.49% (1,887,098) and 24.90% (1,541,506), respectively. Africa stands at the bottom of the table with its lowest publications share percentage of 1.97% (122,200).

The IF curves of the continents with and without self-citations, show a considerable difference. 91.97% of the total global publications have come from the Europe, Asia, and the North America, while as, the remaining 8.03% have come from the Oceania, South America, and the Africa. In terms of variation in IF at continental level, North America showed the maximum 52.63% decline in the Impact Factor, followed by Asia with 43.92%. The IF of Oceania and Europe declined by 32.77% and 30.74%, respectively, while as, the Africa showed the minimum decline of 27.63% in its IF.

In terms of citations share percentage at global level, Europe has received the maximum 43.33% (818,897), followed by North America and Asia with their share percentages of 27.92% (527,696) and 21.41% (404,725), respectively. However, of the total citations received by Africa 27.42% are self-citations, followed by South America with 30.62%, and Europe with 30.84%. North America is the largest continent which has the highest 52.50% self-citations.

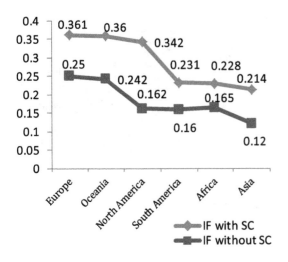

Fig. 6 IF variation representation of continents

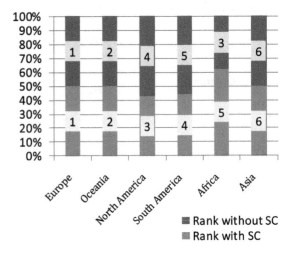

Fig. 7 Ranking variation representation of continents

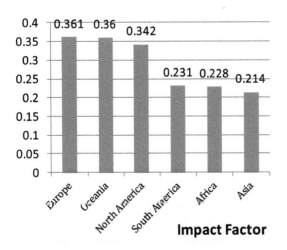

Fig. 8 IF representation of continents

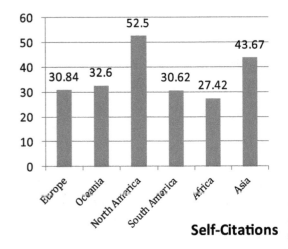

Fig. 9 Self-citation %age representation of continents

6. SUMMARY OF FINDINGS AND DISCUSSION

The practice of self-citation is advocated, so long as the authors carry forward their earlier work or continue their studies from earlier stages. The practice of this kind of self-citation is purely regarded as ethical, as it is more purposive and justified; whereas, at the same time, if the practice of self-citation is carried out with an aim to inflate individuals' or journals' IF,

then surely the practice cannot be regarded as ethical. As highlighted in the introductory section that IF or h-index has somewhat become the parameter to gauge the impact of a research article, as such the practice of manipulation of citations by self-citing one's own articles helps one to inflate both the IF and the h-index. It is evident from the findings that 39.64% self-citations helped to inflate the IF of all the 27 subjects under study from 0.184 to 0.305, an inflation of 65.76%, and more than 66.66% of subject fields felt the impact, as 18 out of 27 subject fields faced variation in their rankings, which varied from 33.12% to 53.70%, hence reflecting the impact on their ranking.

The self-citations received by the subject fields are almost in proportion of the total number of citations received by each individual subject field. Compared to Arts & Humanities, which recorded the highest 52.38% self-citations during the period of study, Physics & Astronomy received the lowest 33.14% self-citations. Psychology and Engineering are the other two leading self-citing subject fields having 51.34% and 50.94% self-citations, respectively. There are subject fields which have received a far greater number of self-citations, but still enjoy a lesser percentage of self-citations, include Multidisciplinary subjects (33.27%), Medicine (33.38%), Dentistry (35.35%), Biochemistry, Genetics, & Molecular Biology (36.15%), Immunology and Microbiology (36.25%), and Neuroscience (38.79%).

There is a considerable variation in the self-citations percentage and numbers of citations which various subject fields have received, this variation in self-citations leaves enough scope for some more advanced studies in direction, as what makes professionals from a particular science to self-cite more than the professionals from other sciences who self-cite far less. But apparently the reason can be owed to the following:

- As is apparent from Table 1 above, the amount of research undertaken in the field of Social Sciences and Arts & Humanities is far less than the research work undertaken in the fields of natural and pure sciences and so is the proportion of citations received by the articles published in respective sciences. The larger the proportion of research publications available for review, the lesser will be the proportion of self-citations, and vice-versa.
- The amount of research undertaken in continents like Africa, Australia, and South America is far less than those of Asia, Europe, and North America. For obvious reasons, the lesser the rate of research carried out by a country or continent the lesser will be the percentage of self-citation from these continents. Accordingly, the higher the rate of research undertaken, the greater are the chances of having the highest percentage of self-citations.

Aksnes (2003), while studying over 45,000 scientific publications published between the period 1981-1996 in Norway and found that of the total citations, 36% are self-citations, having a direct bearing with the number of co-authors of publications. Research work undertaken on the co-authorship pattern may reflect a greater percentage of self-citations for the reason that each co-author of a particular publication may self-cite a particular work in his/her next work, thereby increasing the chances of receiving a higher number of self-citations by a particular publication; while as, for obvious reasons, research work undertaken as a single author permits far fewer chances to receive a significant number of self-citations. Aksnes also observed that poorly cited papers have a far greater percentage of self-citations than those of highly cited papers. Aksnes further observed that there was no uniformity in self-citation practice across scientific disciplines.

The practice of regional or national self-citation by and large appears unintentional, but it is quite interesting to see that the countries which have generally recorded a higher number and percentage of self-citations are either developed countries or are the fastest-developing countries, so this somewhat leaves sufficient scope for advanced study to see and assess the reasons for greater self-citations in such countries, which generally is seen because of better research done and the quality of literature available in these countries. This gets better corroborated by the fact that China has recorded 59.15% self-citations in their research publications during the period of study, followed by the U.S 56.92%, Iran 50.72%, India 46.03%, Brazil 38.10%, Germany 37.53%, Japan 36.91%, Russia 36.73%, Poland 35.56%, Italy 35.03%, the United Kingdom 34.49%, Australia 33.59%, Spain 32.63%, Taiwan 32.06%, South Korea 31.75%, France 26.54%, and many more.

Arguments are also being made about the practice of journal self-citation, as to whether the practice is intentional or unintentional so as to be rated as ethical or unethical. There is no denial of the fact that IF metrics for both authors and journals can be easily manipulated with the practice of self-citation, hence an unethical practice. The practice of self-citation is somewhat acceptable in academic circles and is termed as ethical if the same is undertaken for justified reasons. Researchers are of the view that journal impact is always a consideration among editors and self-citation can prove a very handy tool.

6.1 Limitations

It was practically impossible to work out the citations received in 2012 of the articles published in 2010 and 2011; hence a uniform pattern was followed for all the subject disciplines under study by calculating the total publications for the year 2010 and 2011 and the total citations received by these subjects in the year 2012, and not specifically of the articles of the period under study, which otherwise should have been the case to calculate Impact Factor. Besides, how exhaustive our citation count is can be termed as a limiting factor. The moment indexing services add new journals in their database the figures reflect variation, which nevertheless has been taken care of by reflecting the date of data retrieval.

7. CONCLUSION

It is quite evident from analysis that self-citations play a very significant role in inflating the IF of subject disciplines, the countries, or the continents, and so holds it true about inflating IF scores of authors and journals. As reflected in the rankings with and without self-citations, there is a considerable decline in the Impact Factor of each individual subject field.

The practice of self-citation reflects a mix of both the positives and the negatives, whereby if on one hand, the importance of self-citations cannot be undermined for being purposive, on the other hand, if the same is undertaken only for inflating one's IF or any other impact parameter, then there is surely a need to regulate such unethical practices. Given the evidence of manipulation of parameters set to judge the impact of a research publication as per one's suitability, this somewhat warrants change, either by setting new parameters which may not be easily influenced or by doing away with those aspects which influence such manipulations.

However, researchers all across the globe are of the view that editors of journals and reviewers can play a commendable part in doing away with the practice of unnecessary and unwarranted self-citations by suggesting authors to do away with those journal and author self-citations which are least required or have no relevance at all with the study. And to this effect, Garfield and **Welljams-Dorof (1992)** opined that ex-

cessive self-citations are well apparent and that these should be done away with during the review process of articles.

REFERENCES

Adair, J. G., & Vohra, N. (2003). The explosion of knowledge, references, and citations: Psychology's unique response to a crisis. *American Psychologist, 58* (1), 15-23.

Aksnes, D. W. (2003). A macro study of self-citation. *Scientometrics, 56* (2), 235-246.

Anseel, F., Duyck, W., De Baene, W., & Brysbaert, M. (2004). Journal Impact Factors and self-citations: implications for psychology journals. *American Psychologist, 59* (1), 49-51.

Bonzi, S., & Snyder, H. W. (1990, January). Patterns of self-citation across fields of inquiry. *Proceedings of the ASIS Annual Meeting 27,* 204-207.

Campanario, J. M. (2011). Large increases and decreases in journal Impact Factors in only one year: The effect of journal self-citations. *Journal of the American Society for Information Science and Technology, 62*(2), 230-235.

Ferrara, E., & Romero, A. E. (2013). Scientific impact evaluation and the effect of self-citations: Mitigating the bias by discounting the h-index. *Journal of the American Society for Information Science and Technology, 64*(11), 2332-2339.

Frandsen, T. F. (2007). Journal self-citations analyzing the JIF mechanism. *Journal of Informetrics, 1*(1), 47-58.

Gami, A. S., Montori, V. M., Wilczynski, N. L., & Haynes, R. B. (2004). Author self-citation in the diabetes literature. *Canadian Medical Association Journal, 170* (13), 1925-1927.

Garfield, E. (1955). Citation indexes to science: a new dimension in documentation through association of ideas. *Science, 122*(3159), 108-11. Retrieved from http://garfield.library.upenn.edu/essays/v6p468y1983.pdf

Garfield, E., & Welljams-Dorof, A. (1992). Citation data: their use as quantitative indicators for science and technology evaluation and policy-making. *Science and Public Policy, 19* (5), 321-327.

Gross, P. L. K., & Gross, E. M. (1927). College libraries

and chemical education. *Science, 66*, 385-9.

Hirsch, J. E. (2005). An index to quantify an individual's scientific research output. *Proceedings of the National academy of Sciences of the United States of America, 102* (46), 16569-16572.

Hyland, K. (2003). Self-citation and self-reference: Credibility and promotion in academic publication. *Journal of the American Society for Information Science and Technology, 54*, 251-9.

Journal citation reports: Impact factor (2015). *Web of Knowledge*. Retrieved from http://admin-apps.webofknowledge.com/JCR/help/h_impfact.htm

Kaltenborn, K. F., & Kuhn, K. (2004). The journal Impact Factor as a parameter for the evaluation of researchers and research. *Revista Espanola de Enfermedades Digestivas, 96* (7), 460-476.

King, M. M., Correll, S. J., Jacquet, J., Bergstrom, C. T., & West, J. D. (2015). Men set their own cites high: Gender and self-citation across fields and over time. Working paper. Retrieved from http://www.eigenfactor.org/gender/self-citation/SelfCitation.pdf

Moed, H. F., & Van der Velde, J. G. M. (1993). Bibliometric profiles of academic chemistry research in the Netherlands. *Report submitted to Netherlands Foundation for Chemical Research, Netherlands.*

Nederhof, A. J., Meijer, R. F., Moed, H. F., & Van Raan, A. F. (1993). Research performance indicators for university departments: A study of an agricultural university. *Scientometrics, 27* (2), 157-178.

Neuberger, J., & Counsell, C. (2002). Impact Factors: Uses and abuses. *European Journal of Gastroenterology & Hepatology, 14* (3), 209-211.

SCImago (2007). SJR - SCImago Journal & Country Rank. Retrieved from http://www.scimagojr.com

Sevinc, A. (2004). Manipulating Impact Factor. An unethical issue or an editor's choice. *Swiss Medical Weekly, 134*, 410.

Tagliacozzo, R. (1977). Self-citations in scientific literature. *Journal of Documentation, 33* (4), 251-265.

Van Leeuwen, T. N., Rinia, E. J., & Van Raan, A. F. J. (1996). Bibliometric profiles of academic physics research in the Netherlands. *Research Report to the Netherlands Organization for Scientific Research (NWO), Physics Division (FOM), Utrecht. Report CWTS*, 96-09.

Van Raan, A. F. J. (1998). The impact of international collaboration on the impact of research results. *Scientometrics, 42* (3), 423-428.

White, H. (2001). Authors as citers over time. *Journal of the American Society for Information Science and Technology, 52* (2), 87-108.

11

Sino-South Korean Scientific Collaboration Based On Co-Authored SCI Papers

Junwei Sun

WISE Lab
Dalian University of Technology, China
E-mail: sjw1002@126.com

Chunlin Jiang*

Institute of Science of Science and S&T Management
Dalian University of Technology, China
E-mail: chunlinj7873@163.com

ABSTRACT

Using statistic and bibliometric methods to characterize scientific cooperation between China (excluding Hong Kong, Macao, and Taiwan) and South Korea through their bilateral co-authored papers covered by the Science Citation Index CD-ROM, 1991-2010, in our paper we exploit the feature of their cooperation in four levels: time sequence, academic community, key fields, and institution distribution. From the time sequence we know that collaboration between China and Korea starts in 1991, reaching the first peak during 2004-2007. As for the academic community, the number of Chinese corresponding authors (2414) is slightly lower than that of Korea (2700). Regarding the 27 high yield authors, there are only 4 coming from China. Korea has a higher active level than Chinese authors. China and Korea tend to cooperate with each other on strong disciplines such as physics, chemistry, material science, engineering, mathematics, pharmaceutical, computer science and biology. Furthermore, they also attach great importance to basic research and high-tech cooperation. Besides, Chinese Academy of Sciences ranks at the top 1 among the distribution of institutions. As a majority of the collaborative institutions are universities, the participation of non university institutions is relatively low. There are 7 Korean universities among the top ten institutions, while Yanbian University and Tsinghua University in China rank respectively as third and fourth. Seoul National University, accompanied by Korea University and Yonsei University as the three top Korean universities, is also among the top among the cooperating institutions.

Keywords: Bibliometric Methods, Sino-South Korean, Scientific Collaboration, SCI paper

*Corresponding Author: Chunlin Jiang
Deputy Director
Institute of Science of Science and S&T Management
Dalian University of Technology, China
E-mail: chunlinj7873@163.com

1. INTRODUCTION

Since China and South Korea (hereafter "Korea") established diplomatic relations in politics on August 24, 1992, the two countries have kept intensive contact with each other in economic, scientific, educational, and cultural fields. The signing of the "scientific cooperation between China and Korea protocol" in September 1992 witnessed the beginning of scientific cooperation between the two countries. Since then the leaders of the two countries positively promote deep and wide scientific collaboration through various policy supports. Besides, both China and Korea are devoted to strengthening private activities among enterprises, universities, and research institutions. To raise the high quality of international scientific research personnel and to improve educational levels, the two countries continually promote cooperation by running research projects. Chongqing University of Posts and Telecommunications, accompanying Korea universities such as Inha University, Sun Moon University, and Konkuk University, has carried out scientific cooperation for 14 years (Lee, 2009). All of the universities have not only yielded substantial achievements, but also accumulated valuable experiences about international scientific cooperation. Research institutions' collaboration was various in forms, such as establishing joint research centers, participating in joint research projects, and exchanging scientific tours. As of March 25, 2012, China has published 929,220 SCI papers during 1991-2010, with Korea publishing 382,243. The USA accounts for the highest proportion, followed by Japan, Germany, Britain, Canada, Australia, France, Singapore, and South Korea. Korea ranks in the top 9 from the Chinese international scientific collaborative view. The USA accounts for 13.58% in Korean scientific collaboration, higher than the proportion of USA-China cooperation, followed by Japan, China, Germany, Canada, Britain, India, Russia, and France. China ranks in the top 3 from the Korean international scientific collaborative view. China has become an important scientific collaboration partner of Korea.

In an earlier study on international scientific collaboration, Frame and Carpenter(1979) found that the size of a national scientific effort, and a number of extra-science factors such as history, geography, politics and language, all play a strong role in determining how much international collaboration occurs and who collaborates with whom in the international scientific community. That is, scientific collaboration easily takes place between countries which are geographically close and share historical and linguistic backgrounds (Choi, 2012). China and South Korea are neighbors, facing each other across the sea with a friendly traditional relationship. What is more, the two countries are not only regionally close, but are both influenced by Confucian culture which makes them having similar values and cultural identities. Therefore the two countries have a good foundation to collaborate with each other.

There is growing interest in researching international scientific collaboration between China and other countries, such as the United States (Suttmeier, 2008; Tang & Shapira, 2011), and Russia, France, Japan, Europe, and South Korea. As for Sino-South Korean scientific collaboration, Kim (1999) characterized international scientific cooperation in Korea through the numbers of internationally co-authored papers covered by the SCI CD-ROM, 1994-1996. During this period, the country with the highest rate of cooperation with Korea is the USA (42%), followed by Japan, Italy, Germany, the UK, and France. Kim (2005) has also investigated Korean science and international collaboration during 1995 to 2000 through an analysis of journal publications. From the paper we know that among the top-ten collaborating countries, only the Chinese and the Canadians' share of collaborative publications with Korea increased between the two periods under consideration. China ranked number four in the distribution of Korea's international partners, followed by the USA, Japan, and Germany. Kim H.-N. et al (2012) investigated the agricultural innovation systems of Korea and China from the perspective of triple helix innovation. Kim (2007) has analyzed the effectiveness of Korea's Biotechnology Stimulation Plans, with a comparison with four other Asian nations, referring to China. Haustein et al (2011) focused on eleven countries in the Asia-Pacific region including Australia, China, Indonesia, Japan, Malaysia, New Zealand, Singapore, South Korea, Taiwan, Thailand and Vietnam by evaluating their national research output with the help of biblio-metric indicators in particular.From the literature review, we can see that there are not enough papers to study the scientific cooperation between China and Korea compared to the necessity of research in-cluding region adjacency, trade frequency, and cul-tural similarity. Furthermore, the papers studied the collaboration condition mainly from qualitative as-pects which limit our specific and objective under-standing. In our paper, we exploit the key area and characteristic of their collaboration in four levels: time sequence, academic community, key fields, and institution distribution for the better presentation of new characteristics between China and South Ko-rea, 1991-2010.

2. DATA AND METHOD

Data were collected from the Web of Science during the period 1991-2010 through the numbers of their bilateral co-authored papers. The 'bilateral cooperation papers' are defined as all of the authors with an address in Korea or China so that it can re-flect the interests and trends between the two coun-tries precisely.

Co-authorship of scientific publications is easy to compute and obviously linked to collaboration (Gi-uliani et al, 2010). Scientific cooperation between countries is a kind of abstract relation, essentially, which requires an effective method to measure. Under this circumstance, the co-authored scientific publications are a way to measure the collaboration between countries to some extent. Therefore we re-trieved the bilateral co-authored papers covered by the Science Citation Index CD-ROM to characterize scientific cooperation between China and Korea using statistic and bibliometric methods for 1991-2010.

3. RESULTS AND DISCUSSION

From the time sequence of the co-authored SCI papers, we can see that collaboration between Chi-na and Korea starts in 1991. The relatively small share of Korean international collaboration with China can be partially explained by the isolation of Chinese science from the international community (Kim, 2005). Mainly thanks to government policy support, the collaboration between the two coun-tries attained a high growth rate during 2006-2007.

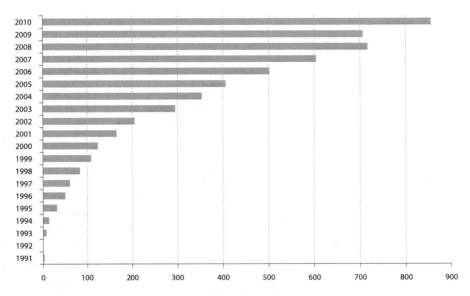

Fig. 1 Time Sequence of Co-Authored Papers

From the Chinese side, the "national long-term plan for science and technology (2006-2020)" and the "eleventh five-year plan" put forward the national independent innovation strategy which plays a very important role in the number of Chinese SCI papers. In 2006, the "eleventh five-year plan" promulgated by the Ministry of Science and Technology makes it clear that it is of great need to further bilateral cooperation with Europe, America, Japan, Korea and other countries aiming at achieving substantial achievements in basic research, scientific frontiers, high technology, related industries, and so on etc.

papers account for Chinese SCI papers. In the same way, C/B means the proportion that co-authored SCI papers account for Korean SCI papers. The number of Chinese SCI papers adds up to 929,140, while Korea is 382,210, the co-authored is 5,290, and the percentage of co-authored papers accounts for 0.57% and 1.38% separately. It suggests that the proportion of Korea in China's scientific collaboration is much smaller comparing China in Korea. That means China is becoming a more important scientific partner in Korean scientific collaboration territory. Actually, there are great potentials for their further cooperation. From the table below

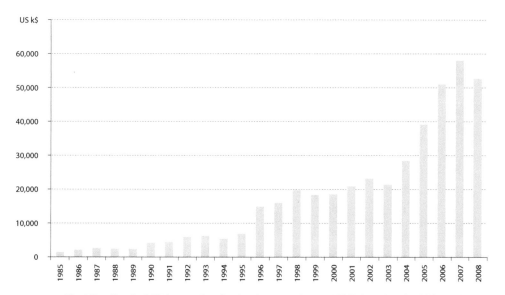

Fig. 2 Funding for R&D Internationalization Program. *Source*: MOST (2003) and KICOS (2008)

From the Korean side, just as the figure above show, the Korea government has increased fund support of international project since 1996, reaching a peak during 2004-2007. The flow of government funds played a guiding part in Korea international scientific collaboration. To some extent, it contributes to the increase of the scientific cooperation between China and Korea.

In order to see the yearly distribution of their SCI papers from a more intuitive perspective, we make statistics for the number of Chinese, Korean, and co-authored papers respectively, named A, B, C. We define C/A as the proportion that co-authored SCI

we know that the number of co-authored papers in Korean SCI papers exceeded 1% since 2002 for the first time, reaching 1.91% in 2010. It suggests that China has increasingly become an important scientific cooperation partner of Korea. In 2006, the number of Chinese SCI papers exceeded Korean for the first time and maintained a high growth rate until 2010. The co-authored SCI papers maintained the same growth rate with each of the two countries over time, 2006 in particular, indicating the development of their cooperation. In addition, we could not ignore that Chinese SCI papers are superior in number compared to Korea during this time.

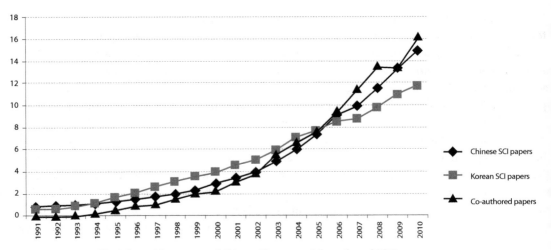

Fig. 3 Annual Percentage of Chinese, Korean, and Co-authored SCI Papers

Table 1. Annual Percentage of Chinese, Korean, and Co-authored SCI Papers

Year	Chinese SCI Paper A		Korean SCI Paper B		Co-authored SCI Paper C			
	NO.	%	NO.	%	NO.	%	C/A	C/B
1991	7838	0.84%	2197	0.58%	3	0.06%	0.04%	0.14%
1992	8864	0.95%	2526	0.66%	0	0	0.00%	0.00%
1993	9380	1.01%	3373	0.88%	6	0.11%	0.06%	0.18%
1994	10156	1.09%	4316	1.13%	13	0.25%	0.13%	0.30%
1995	12499	1.35%	6383	1.67%	32	0.61%	0.26%	0.50%
1996	14162	1.52%	7831	2.05%	51	0.96%	0.36%	0.65%
1997	16186	1.74%	9931	2.60%	61	1.15%	0.38%	0.61%
1998	18647	2.01%	11670	3.05%	83	1.57%	0.45%	0.71%
1999	21166	2.28%	13561	3.55%	108	2.04%	0.51%	0.80%
2000	27255	2.93%	14979	3.92%	123	2.33%	0.45%	0.82%
2001	31833	3.43%	17384	4.55%	165	3.12%	0.52%	0.95%
2002	36547	3.93%	19256	5.04%	204	3.86%	0.56%	1.06%
2003	45565	4.90%	22625	5.92%	294	5.56%	0.65%	1.30%
2004	56050	6.03%	27004	7.07%	353	6.67%	0.63%	1.31%
2005	68076	7.33%	29351	7.68%	406	7.68%	0.60%	1.38%
2006	84198	9.06%	32500	8.50%	502	9.49%	0.60%	1.54%
2007	91922	9.89%	33413	8.74%	605	11.44%	0.66%	1.81%
2008	106551	11.47%	37338	9.77%	717	13.55%	0.67%	1.92%
2009	123824	13.33%	41755	10.93%	707	13.37%	0.57%	1.69%
2010	138421	14.90%	44817	11.73%	856	16.18%	0.62%	1.91%
Total	929140		382210		5290			

4. THE ACADEMIC COMMUNITY OF CO-AUTHORED SCI PAPERS

As we all know, the number of papers is not the only indicator to measure scientific contribution. The number of corresponding authors is also important for reflecting the status of each country in scientific cooperation. Thus we put forward the bilateral cooperation dominant-subordinate rate, which means the number of the country identification of the first author accounting for the total amount of the co-authored papers. If the ratio is more than 50%, it indicates that the country is in a dominant position in scientific cooperation. If the ratio is less than 50%, it indicates that the country in a subordinate status. In view of the example of English literature, we take the corresponding author as our target according to English author arrangement practice. Therefore, in the ratio above, corresponding author equals to the first author. Results show that the number of Chinese corresponding authors (2,414) is slightly lower than that of Korea's (2,700), with the dominant-subordinate rate 45.63% and 51.04%, respectively. Korea has a slight advantage over China in their scientific collaboration. Through the corresponding author's annual distribution, we can find that in the period 1991-2000, corresponding authors are few in number, and the coincidence curve almost shows that the two countries are in the same position. In the period 2002-2006, the curve shows that both countries are dominant. After 2006, Korea is gradually in the leading position, while China has narrowed the gap considerably since 2009.

In addition to the corresponding authors, we also take the highly productive authors as our statistical object. Of our data, authors who published 50 papers or above in the data set are analyzed. Among the 27 high yield authors, there are only 4 coming from China. The unbalanced distribution demonstrates different activity levels of the two countries in scientific co-operation. The high activity level of Korea indicates that it is inclined to choose Chinese authors as research partners. Besides, most of the highly productive authors come from university settings. A partial explanation for the markedly high research output from academic institutions may be that university researchers aim to publish much of their work in prestigious international journals (Kim, 2005).

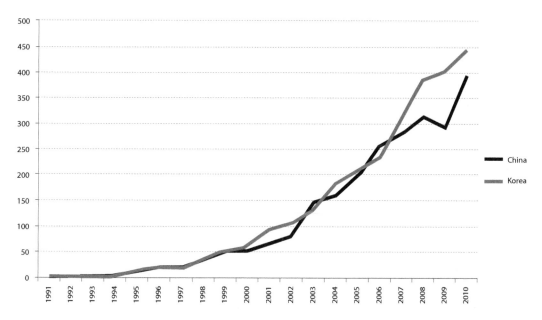

Fig. 4 Corresponding Author Distribution of Co-authored SCI Papers

Table 2. Distribution of Highly Productive Authors

No.	High Yield Authors	Papers	Nation	Institution
1	CHO YJ	106	Korea	UNIV ULSAN
2	KIM SH	105	Korea	KYUNGPOOK NATL UNIV
3	LEE KY	105	Korea	YONSEI UNIV
4	KANG SM	92	Korea	GYEONGSANG NATL UNIV
5	LEE JH	92	Korea	DONG A UNIV
6	KIM JK	77	Korea	HALLYM UNIV
7	KIM J	76	Korea	AJOU UNVI
8	LEE SH	76	Korea	KOREA ATOM ENERGY RES INST
9	ZHANG S	69	China	YAN BIAN UNIVERSITY
10	KIM JH	68	Korea	SEOUL NATL UNIV
11	KIM H	66	Korea	KYUNG HEE UNVI
12	KIM K	65	Korea	GWANGJU INST SCI & TECHNOL
13	LEE J	63	Korea	YONSEI UNVI
14	LI Y	63	China\Korea	YANTAI UNIVERSITY\YONSEI UNVI
15	KANG SB	61	Korea	KOREA MATERIAL RES INST
16	KIM HJ	57	Korea	KOREA INST SCI TECHNOL
17	LEE S	56	Korea	GYEONGSANG NATL UNVI
18	YEON KH	56	Korea	CHUNGBUK NATL UNIV
19	HUANG YL	55	Korea	PUKYONG NATL UNVI
20	SEO HJ	55	Korea	PUKYONG NATL UNVI
21	KIM SJ	54	Korea	DONG A UNIV
22	PARK SJ	54	Korea	INHA UNVI
23	KIM DH	53	Korea	YONSEI UNVI
24	KIM JS	52	Korea	KOREAUNIVERSITY
25	LEE MH	51	Korea	CHONBUK NATL UNVI
26	LI C	51	China	YAN BIAN UNIVERSITY
27	LIU ZQ	50	China	LIAONING NORMAL UNIVERSITY

5. KEY FIELDS OF SCIENTIFIC COOPERATION

In this section, we use the subject category of the co-authored papers to search for their key fields. We choose the WoS (Web of Science) subject category mainly because of the data source. In the meantime, we take the Essential Science Indicators (ESI) which can evaluate the subject influence through the ranking from the Papers, Citations, and Citations per paper level as our accessory appliances. The ESI has been updated as of November 1, 2012 to cover a 10-year plus 8-month period, January 1, 2002-August 31, 2012. Therefore, we have retrieved the data spanning 2002.01.01 to 2010.12.31 for the sake of subject ranking. Due to the subject category differences between Web of Science and ESI, we have to integrate the two methods. This distinction has been presented specifically in Table 3. The left part shows the top 10 subjects which are based on WoS, while the right part ranking is based on the ESI.

According to the statistics of SCI subject classification, we find that the discipline of scientific cooperation mainly focuses on material science, physics, chemistry, mathematics, pharmaceutical, and metallurgical engineering. The physical field can also be divided into applied physics, physical chemistry, and multidisciplinary physics. In the field of mathematics, both basic mathematics and applied mathematics are included.

Studies show that scientific cooperation between countries mainly concentrates on their own strong fields, followed by a country's strong discipline, and rarely in their weak research fields (Z.Michel et al, 2000). Through ESI subject evaluation, we can see that the discipline which China and Korea cooper-

ate with each other in has a high world rank as well. It is in keeping with the previous studies that the scientific cooperation of the two countries is mainly in strong research fields for both. In addition, the citations per paper of Korea are higher than that of China in physics, materials science, and chemistry.

Generally, basic subjects (mathematics, logic, astronomy and astrophysics, earth science and space science, physics, chemistry, life science) are more inclined to cooperation than applied subjects (Kim, 2005). The rule gets perfect interpretation in Chinese and Korean scientific cooperation. Mathematics, physics, chemistry, and biology, etc. account for a large proportion in scientific cooperation. The two countries both attach great importance to the basic research field, so as to lay a solid foundation to build an innovative country system. The Korean government spares no effort to strengthen basic innovation research investment for keeping up with the pace of developed countries. Basic research investment in 2009 accounted for 29.3% among the government R&D budget, reaching 31.3% in 2010, and was expected to rise to 35.0% by 2012 (Yindong Song, 2011). Apart from government investment support, Korea also makes full use of international science and technology resources, conducting extensive international cooperation in basic research

Table 3. Discipline Distribution of Co-authored SCI Papers

Subject Categories (Web of Science)			Papers Ranking		Citations Ranking		Citations per Paper Ranking	
	NO.	%	C	S	C	S	C	S
MATERIALS SCIENCE MULTIDISCIPLINARY	601	12.93	1	5	2	7	44	34
PHYSICS APPLIED	405	8.71	2	9	4	12	59	49
CHEMISTRY MULTIDISCIPLINARY	297	6.34	2	11	2	11	45	29
MATHEMATICS APPLIED	287	6.18	2	12	2	13	40	57
ENGINEERING ELECTRICAL ELECTRONIC	262	5.64	2	5	4	12	52	72
CHEMISTRY PHYSICAL	251	5.40	--	--	--	--	--	--
PHARMACOLOGY PHARMACY	244	5.25	3	8	6	9	65	46
PHYSICS MULTIDISCIPLINARY	212	4.56	--	--	--	--	--	--
METALLURGY METALLURGICAL ENGINEERING	206	4.43	--	--	--	--	--	--

Note. C is short for China; S is short for Korea; '--' means no data.

fields. The comparative advantage in Chinese basic research fields makes it possible for basic research cooperation. A Chinese and Korean joint commission held a meeting in Dalian in 2012, researching an agreement on project cooperation and holding academic seminars.

In addition, China and Korea also attach great importance to high-tech cooperation, nanotechnology being a good symbol. In order to adapt to the revolution of science and technology and to meet its challenges, many countries are looking for a way out. Science and technology, especially the development of high tech is beginning to be the first choice. On this condition, Korea launched a "national long-term development prospect." China also compiles for its country a "high technology research and development program," the "863" plan. Thanks to the government's substantial support, Korea's wireless communications, semiconductors, computer, biological engineering, artificial intelligence, nuclear power generation, and so on, are already at or near the world's advanced levels. China and Korea not only have common demand in developing high tech, but have a strong complementary aspect to each other, which lays a foundation in scientific cooperation. More than that, both China and Korea need to strengthen bilateral and even multilateral cooperation in solving global issues such as the energy crisis, environmental pollution, climate warming, infectious diseases, and so on.

Table 4. WoS Specific Subject Categories

Subject categories	Number of co-authored papers	percentage
MATERIALS SCIENCE MULTIDISCIPLINARY	760	14.36%
PHYSICS APPLIED	484	9.15%
MATHEMATICS APPLIED	346	6.54%
CHEMISTRY MULTIDISCIPLINARY	317	5.99%
MATHEMATICS	311	5.88%
ENGINEERING ELECTRICAL ELECTRONIC	286	5.40%
CHEMISTRY PHYSICAL	266	5.03%
PHARMACOLOGY PHARMACY	265	5.01%
PHYSICS MULTIDISCIPLINARY	256	4.84%
PHYSICS CONDENSED MATTER	244	4.61%
METALLURGY METALLURGICAL ENGINEERING	217	4.10%
ENGINEERING CHEMICAL	191	3.61%
BIOCHEMISTRY MOLECULAR BIOLOGY	183	3.46%
CHEMISTRY MEDICINAL	182	3.44%
POLYMER SCIENCE	181	3.42%
BIOTECHNOLOGY APPLIED MICROBIOLOGY	169	3.19%
NANOSCIENCE NANOTECHNOLOGY	151	2.85%
MECHANICS	139	2.63%
ENGINEERING MECHANICAL	137	2.59%
OPTICS	125	2.36%

6. INSTITUTIONAL DISTRIBUTION OF CO-AUTHORED SCI PAPERS

Because of the globally networked research environment, national institutions can no longer be considered as isolated components of an international system of research, technology, and innovation. The exchange of knowledge across national (regional) borders has become increasingly common in recent decades (Kwon et al, 2012). This can be clearly shown in the scientific collaboration between China and South Korea, which rank among the top 100 co-authored institutions. Results show that universities play an important role in the scientific cooperation between China and Korea. The university, as the most active body, holds the obvious talent advantage during international scientific cooperation. The Chinese government has clearly stated that "Constructing a group of high level universities, especially a number of world famous research universities, is urgent to receive our goals to accelerate the construction of a science and technology innovation system." From the table we find that the Chinese Academy of Sciences ranks as the top 1. It is the highest academic institution of the People's Republic, the national natural science and high technology research and development center, focusing on the substantive cooperation among international matters. There are 7 Korean universities among the top ten institutions, while Yanbian University and Tsinghua University of China rank

Table 5. Distribution of Top 20 Institutions

No.	Country	Institution	Papers	Percent
1	China	CHINESE ACAD SCI	619	11.70%
2	Korea	SEOUL NATL UNIV	480	9.07%
3	China	YANBIAN UNIV	387	7.31%
4	Korea	YONSEI UNIV	347	6.56%
5	Korea	GYEONGSANG NATL UNIV	316	5.97%
6	Korea	KOREA ADV INST SCI TECHNOL	253	4.78%
7	Korea	INHA UNIV	235	4.44%
8	Korea	PUSAN NATL UNIV	217	4.10%
9	China	TSING HUA UNVI	210	3.97%
10	Korea	POHANG UNIV SCI TECHNOL	210	3.97%
11	Korea	CHONBUK NATL UNIV	196	3.70%
12	Korea	KOREA UNIV	191	3.61%
13	Korea	CHUNGNAM NATL UNIV	189	3.57%
14	Korea	CHUNGBUK NATL UNIV	180	3.40%
15	Korea	KYUNGPOOK NATL UNIV	171	3.23%
16	Korea	CHANGWON NATL UNIV	157	2.97%
17	China	HARBIN INST TECHNOL	153	2.89%
18	Korea	HANYANG UNIV	150	2.83%
19	Korea	PUKYONG NATL UNIV	148	2.80%
20	China	PEKING UNIV	142	2.68%

respectively at third and fourth. Yanbian University is a comprehensive university located in Jilin province. The national identity and physical proximity lay a solid foundation for the scientific collaboration between them. Seoul National University, accompanied by Korea University and Yonsei University, as the three top universities are among the top in cooperation among institutions.

The cooperating Chinese universities mainly distribute in the three northeastern provinces and eastern coastal area, relatively less in the central and western areas. There are 8 universities in the three northeastern provinces, with 4 in Liaoning province. The distribution is related not only to the regional closeness, but inseparably to the rich resources and solid foundation for heavy industry in the northeast-

ern provinces. As for the eastern coastal area, Qingdao, Shanghai, Suzhou, Hefei, Nanjing, Hangzhou and other coastal cities are included. This distribution is closely related to the broad market in the eastern coastal area.

Moreover, the collaborative cities are mainly developed or provincial capital cities and rarely small and medium-sized cities, with 12 universities in Beijing and Shanghai alone. Most of the collaborative universities are key universities directly under the ministry of education, with key state laboratories, solid scientific research strengths, and strong research teams. Furthermore, the types of most universities are science, engineering, and comprehensive, which is consistent with their key cooperative fields.

Table 6. Geographical Distribution of Top 20 Institutions

No.	Province	University
1	Heilongjiang Province	Harbin Institute of Technology
2	Jilin province	Yanbian University Jilin University Jilin Institute of Chemical Technology
3	Liaoning province	Dalian University of Technology Liaoning Normal University Shenyang Pharmaceutical University Northeastern University
4	Beijing	Tsinghua University Peking University
5	Peking University	Shandong University Ocean University of China
6	Jiangsu province	Suzhou University Nanjing University
7	Shanghai	Shanghai Jiaotong University Fudan University Shanghai University Tongji University
8	Zhejiang Province	Zhejiang University
9	Hubei Province	Wuhan University Wuhan University of Technology
10	Hunan province	Central South University
11	Anhui Province	University of Science and Technology of China
12	Sichuan province	Sichuan University
13	Shaanxi Province	Shaanxi Province

7. RELATIVE POSITIONS OF INTERNATIONAL COOPERATION OF CHINA AND KOREA

International scientific cooperation is increasingly changing from bilateral to multilateral. Both China and Korea are playing their role in international scientific collaboration. Not only partner selection but also regional preferences have different tendencies. Therefore, through the proportion of China or Korea in mutual international cooperation prospects, we can see their relative position of each other from the outside.

The USA accounts for the highest proportion, followed by Japan, Germany, Britain, Canada, Australia, France, Singapore, and South Korea. Korea ranks in the top 9 from the Chinese international scientific collaborative view. China tends to choose developed countries as its scientific cooperation partners. The cooperation field mainly focuses on chemical, physical, material science, engineering, mathematics, biochemistry and molecular biology, computer science, optical, pharmacology, and other disciplines, which agrees with the bilateral cooperation between China and South Korea. The USA accounts for 13.580% in Korean scientific collaboration, higher than the proportion of USA-China cooperation, followed by Japan, China, Germany, Canada, Britain, India, Russia, and France. China ranks in the top 3 from the Korean international scientific collaborative view. China

has become an important scientific collaboration partner of Korea. Although most of Korea's scientific partners are developed countries, unlike China, it also takes some developing countries such as India and Russia into consideration. Korea's international cooperation field focuses on physics, engineering, chemistry, material science, biochemistry and molecular biology, computer science, pharmacology, neuroscience, biological technology, and applied microbiology.

8. CONCLUSIONS

As of March 25, 2012, China has published 929,220 SCI papers during 1991-2010, with Korea 382,243.We have a general understanding of Chinese and Korean scientific cooperation conditions through their bilateral co-authored SCI papers by means of quantitative analysis through time sequence, academic groups, hot fields, and institution distribution during the period 1991-2010. China and Korea have established diplomatic relations for 20 years by 2012, and during the time the two countries have launched all-round, multi-level, and wide-area scientific cooperation. From the time sequence we know that the collaboration between China and Korea started in 1991. As for academic groups, the number of Chinese corresponding authors (2,414)

Table 7. Distribution of Countries with Multilateral Cooperation

China			Korea		
Country	Papers	Percentage	Country	Papers	Percentage
USA	91042	9.978%	USA	51907	13.580%
Japan	30852	3.320%	Japan	17504	4.579%
Germany	20368	2.192%	China	9472	2.478%
England	19038	2.049%	Germany	6114	1.600%
Canada	16820	1.810%	Canada	5122	1.340%
Australia	15454	1.663%	England	4978	1.302%
France	11708	1.260%	India	4432	1.159%
Singapore	9711	1.045%	Russia	4197	1.098%
Korea	9472	1.019%	France	3978	1.041%

was slightly lower than that of Koreans (2,700). China has narrowed the gap considerably since 2009. Among the 27 high yield authors, there were only 4 coming from China. Korea has a higher activity level than Chinese authors. Through the WoS discipline classification, we find that China and Korea tend to cooperate with each other on both strong disciplines such as physics, chemistry, material science, engineering, mathematics, pharmaceutical, computer science, and biology. Furthermore, they also attach great importance to basic research and high-tech cooperation.

Moreover, among the institution distribution, Chinese Academy of Sciences ranks at the top 1. There are 7 Korean universities among the top ten institutions, while Yanbian University and Tsinghua University of China rank respectively at third and fourth. Seoul National University accompanied by Korea University and Yonsei University as the three top universities are among the top in the cooperating institutions. From the institution statistics, we can see that a majority of collaborative institutions are universities and the participation of non-university institutions is not very high. Therefore, the two countries need to further strengthen university-industry collaboration. Korea ranks in the top 9 from the Chinese international scientific collaborative view, while China ranks in the top 3. Both China and Korea have become important international scientific partners for each other as time goes on. They can, and they need to, further their scientific cooperation.

REFERENCES

Choi, S.-J. (2012). Core-periphery, new clusters, or rising stars? International scientific collaboration among "advanced" countries in the era of globalization. *Scientometrics, 90*, 25-41.

Guiliani, F., de Petris, M.P., & Nico, G. (2010). Assessing scientific collaboration through coauthorship and content sharing. *Scientometrics, 85*, 13-28.

Haustein, S., Tunger, D., Heinrichs, G., & Baelz, G. (2011). Reasons for and developments in international scientific collaboration: Does an Asia-Pacific research area exist from a biblio-

metric point of view. *Scientometrics, 86*, 727-746.

KICOS (2008). *Statistics on International R&D Program*. Seoul: Korea Foundation for International Cooperation of Science and Technology.

Kim, H.-N., Huang, M.-H., Jin, F., Bodoff, D., Moon, J.-H., & Choe, Y.-C. (2012). Triple helix in the agricultural sector of Northeast Asian countries: a comparative study between Korea and China. *Scientometrics, 90*, 101-120.

Kim, M.-J. (1999). Korean international co-authorship in science 1994-1996. *Journal of Information Science, 25*(5), 403-412.

Kim, M.-J. (2005). Korean science and international collaboration, 1995-2000. *Scientometrics, 63*(2), 321-339.

Kim, M.-J. (2007). A bibliometric analysis of the effectiveness of Korea's Biotechnology Stimulation Plans, with a comparison with four other Asian nations. *Scientometrics, 72*(3), 371-388.

Kwon, K.-S., Park, H.-W., So, M.-H., & Leydesdorff, L. (2012). Has globalization strengthened South Korea's national research system? National and international dynamics of the Triple Helix of scientific co-authorship relationships in South Korea. *Scientometrics, 90*, 163 - 176.

Lee, Y.-Y. (2009). The discussion of international university scientific cooperation between China and Korea universities,——taking the Chongqing university of posts and telecommunications as an example. *Learn To, 4*, 42-46.

MOST (2003). *The 20 years of HAN Project*. Seoul: Ministry of Science and Technology.

Suttmeier, R.P. (2008). State, self-organization, and identity in the building of Sino-U.S. cooperation in science and technology. *Scientometrics, 32*(1), 5-31.

Tang, L. & Shapira, P. (2011). China-US Scientific Collaboration in Nanotechnology: Patterns and Dynamics. *Scientometrics, 88*, 1-16.

Michel, Z., Elise, B., & Yoshiko, O. (2000), Shadows of the past in international cooperation: Collaboration profiles of the top five producers of science, *Scientometrics, 47*, 627-657.

Song, Y. (2011). A comparative study of science and

technology policy to China and South Korea, *Journal of Qingdao University of science and technology, 27*(3), 67-73.

Frame, J.D. & CarpenterARPENTER, M.P. (1979), International research collaboration. *Social Studies of Science, 9*, 481-497.

12

An Assessment of Records Management Practice in Selected Local Government Councils in Ogun State, Nigeria

Abdullahi A. Bakare

Department of Library and Information Science, College of Information and Communication Technology, Kwara State University, Malete, Ilorin
E-mail: tobayan1@yahoo.com

Abiola A. Abioye

Department of Library, Archival and Information Studies, Faculty of Education, University of Ibadan, Ibadan
E-mail: biolaabioye@yahoo.com

Abdulwahab Olanrewaju Issa *

Department of Library and Information Science, Faculty of Communication and Information Sciences, University of Ilorin, Ilorin
E-mail: lanrewajuwahab@gmail.com

ABSTRACT

What government does/fails to do is conveyed to the public largely by records and information of various types in the public service, without which there will be no government. When records are poorly managed, much time is involved in sorting and locating needed information from large volumes of records. The rate of records misplaced or lost from which useful information for decision making is usually obtained makes it difficult to provide concise and up-to-date records of both past and present operations, raising the challenge of effective record-keeping. Thus this study examined records management practices in selected local government councils in Ogun State, Nigeria, adopting the descriptive survey research method using questionnaires for data collection. Its population comprised 415 records of personnel in the selected councils, of which 208 were sampled using simple random technique. From the 208 copies of the questionnaire administered on the registry personnel, 150 copies were useable, with a 72.12% response rate. Descriptive statistics were used for the analysis. The results indicated a prevalence of paper as the dominant medium for recording/conveying information in the councils with most of those being either in active state, semi-active, and vital and were kept and maintained in the registry, while in-active records were kept in the records store. Storage facilities for record-keeping were insufficient. Security measures against unauthorized access to records were by restrictions and subject users to managerial clearance. The study concluded that council records were in chaos and recommended the formulation of coherent records management policy, adequate budgetary provision, and adequate finance.

Keywords: Records, Records management, Local government council, Registry personnel, Ogun State

*Corresponding Author: Abdulwahab Olanrewaju Issa
Associate Professor
Department of Library and Information Science
Faculty of Communication and Information Sciences
University of Ilorin, Ilorin
E-mail: lanrewajuwahab@gmail.com

1. INTRODUCTION

Information has been regarded as an indispensable asset of any organization, whether public or private. It is presently a parameter for classifying the countries of the world into two main classes, namely information poor and information rich countries. Evidently, information availability, accessibility, and utilization have a strong relationship with the national development of any country. Hence, information is a national resource that can be used to produce value added goods and services (Popoola, 2000). Records and information are inseparable, since they contain information needed for planning, decision making, and control in any organization such as public service institutions. The International Foundation for Information Technology (2010) defines a record as something that represents proof of existence and that can be used to recreate or prove state of existence, regardless of medium or characteristics. A record is either created or received by an organization in pursuance of, or compliance with legal obligations, or in the transaction of business. Records can be either tangible objects, such as paper documents like birth certificates, drivers' licenses, and physical medical x-rays, or digital information, such as electronic office documents, data in application databases, web site content, and electronic mail.

Robek (1995) defines records management as the application of systematic and scientific controls to recorded information required in the operation of an organization's business. The International Standards Organization (2001) defines records management as "the field of management responsible for the efficient and systematic control of the creation, receipt, maintenance, use and disposition of records, including the processes for capturing and maintaining evidence of and information about business activities and transactions in the form of records." It states that records management includes activities such as: setting policies and standards; assigning responsibilities and authorities; establishing and promulgating procedures and guidelines; providing a range of services relating to the management and use of records; designing, implementing and administering specialized systems for managing records; and integrating records management into business systems and processes. Similarly, Wallace, Lee, and Schubert (1992) see records management as the systematic control placed over the life cycle of recorded information from creation to its ultimate disposition or permanent storage. The life cycle of a record includes its conception, creation, distribution, usage, maintenance, storage, disposition, and the archival preservation stage. Dawha and Biu (1993) opine that records management can play an important role in charting the course of policy and determining program priorities. It can also introduce a sense of unity of purpose into the whole administration. Thus, it seeks to create records necessary for the efficient and successful running of an organization; to produce the records when they are needed; to conserve records relevant to the continued operation of the organization; and to create only those records which are necessary.

Local government is the closest tier of government to the people and is also known as grassroots government recognized by law. Maddick (1963) defines local government as a sub-unit of government controlled by a local council, which is authorized by the central government to pass ordinances having a local application, levy taxes or exact labor, and within limits specified by the central government, vary centrally decided policy in applying it locally. The present local government system in Nigeria started with the 1976 local government reforms, which aimed at restructuring the local government administration in conformity with modern society, and at best to make Nigeria's local government administration an ideal in Africa. A typical local government unit should have a population range of 150,000 to 800,000 (Olanipekun, 1988). The reform focuses on the administration of the public at the grassroots level, where the majority of the population in Nigeria resides. Atulomah (2011) observed that improving records management in public institutions will help to eliminate various observed administrative/managerial problems and weaknesses that cause inefficiency and ineffectiveness in the institutions. Therefore, proper care of records could translate into quality service delivery by the government to the populace. No government can function effectively without proper management of records. Governments go and come but the records of their activities remain. Therefore, poor management of records can lead to cost increases in the administration of government. Thus the place of proper records management practices in entrenching good governance, especially at the local government level, cannot be over-emphasized if the local councils are to make significant impact on grassroots governance in Nigeria.

2. STATEMENT OF THE PROBLEM

What government does or fails to do is conveyed to the public, largely, by records and information of various types in the public service. Research findings have shown that adequate management of records provides good information for the provision of welfare and infrastructure to the citizenry. Akor and Udensi (2013) stress that proper records management could help public institutions to manage their information efficiently, fulfill their mandate, protect them from litigation, preserve their corporate memory, and foster accountability and good governance. This can lead to improved healthcare delivery and education, among other benefits. This is to the extent that poor records management inhibits good planning and management of scarce resources.

Observations have shown that there is an alarming rate of records misplacement and loss, from which useful information for decision making is usually derived, in most public institutions. This makes it difficult to provide concise and up-to-date records of all their past and present operations, thereby raising the challenge of effective record keeping. Therefore, the local government that has been observed to have many inter-linking departments in which records are generated on a daily basis also seemed to be experiencing the absence of proper records management. This may lead to low productivity in the local council, thereby obstructing the realization of the Council's prime mandate of affecting the lives of the people at the grassroots level positively, through an unfettered development. Such a condition has a great potential of hampering the success of developmental programs and policies at the local council levels in Nigeria, with the possibility of slowing down national development. Against this backdrop, this study investigated the records management practices in selected local government councils in Ogun State, Nigeria.

3. OBJECTIVES OF THE STUDY

The main objective of this study is to examine the records management practices in selected local government councils in Ogun State, Nigeria. The specific objectives are to:

i.   ascertain the classes of records created, maintained, and used by the selected local government councils, as well as their formats;
ii. determine what storage facilities and level of security are provided for these records;
iii. examine the retrieval tools used in locating records and records retrieval rate; and
iv. identify the barriers to effective records management in the local government councils.

4. REVIEW OF RELATED LITERATURE

4.1. Importance of Records in Organizations

Records are important, without which an organization simply cannot function. The day-to-day operations of any successful organization depend entirely on its records. Many organizations will not survive without keeping, maintaining, and using their records. Akor and Udensi (2013) define a record as any document or other source of information compiled, recorded, or stored in written form or on film, by electronic process, or in any other manner or by any other means. They further state that "State record" refers to any record made and kept, or received and kept, by any person in the course of the exercise of official functions in a public office, or for any purpose of a public office, or for the use of a public office, whether before or after the commencement of this section. Penn (1983) asserts that the records life cycle consists of creation, maintenance, and use, and its disposition. He stresses that if a record is not necessary, do not create it, stressing further the need for the maintenance of records that are created. Therefore, all the stages involved in the records life-cycle must be considered before any record is created. Ogunrombi, Abareh, and Adamu (1998) are of the opinion that an organization cannot but develop a culture of maintaining a record in whatever form which will serve as a reference tool in helping the organization fulfill its obligation for effective management of the problems of that organization.

Popoola (2000) posits that records constitute an

essential instrument of administration without which operational processes and functions cannot be executed in organizations. To Popoola records are barometers for measuring the performance of an organization. In addition, records are the by-products of managerial and administrative activities, and they mirror the overall quality of the organization's business performance. If records are barometers for measuring the performance of any organization, according to Popoola (2000), it then means that without records, no organization can function. Dollar (2000) also sees records as recorded information in any form created or received and maintained by an organization, person, or system in the transaction of a business or the conduct of affairs and kept in a widely accessible form as evidence of such activity. This definition, however, must be recognized as only the starting points for a complete and useful definition. To be meaningful, it must be accompanied by a detailed set of definitions that identify when a record is created and what type of evidence is required to create reliable and authentic records.

4.2. Records Management

Records management is a field of management responsible for the systematic control of the creation, maintenance, use, reproduction, and disposition of records. According to Ette (1984), records management relates to three stages through which records pass, namely the current, semi-current, and non-current stages. At the current stage, records are created and used frequently. In the semi-current stage, which is the intermediate stage, records are referred to occasionally. At the non-current stage, they are no longer referred to but are sent to the archives after appraising them. Alegbeleye (1983) defines records and information management as an all-embracing activity which include form control, correspondence control, reports management and control, active files management, records inventory and appraisal, records retention and disposition, archives management and control, and copy reproduction (reprography). In conventional paper based organizations, such as the local government councils, paper continues to be viewed as the material for records in administrative documentations (Igwoku, 2008). Indeed, Unuigbe (1990) posits that records management deals with the full range of paper work from the creation of a new record to the moment when a decision is made

either to destroy it or keep it for all time. It is the application of systematic analysis and scientific control of business records from their creation through processing, maintenance, protection, and final disposition.

In records management, policies, procedures, and standards cover the creation, receipt, distribution, use, retention, storage, retrieval, protection, preservation, and final disposition of all types of recorded information throughout the organization (Mark, 2001). Ugwunze (1992) asserts that records management involves planning, implementing, and review of the functions for the administration of the records of an organization. Ugwunze stresses that records management helps to control the quantity and quality of information that is created. Thus, the information can be maintained in a manner that effectively serves the needs of the organization. Unighe (2000), quoted by Abioye and Habila (2004), sees records management as quality, quantity, and cost of records, and encompassing the procedures, systems, operations, space, equipment, and staff required to administer the records. It is therefore the responsibility of records management functions to develop and operate systems and procedures for creating, maintaining, and disposing of records necessary for the successful operation of an organization (Abioye & Habila, 2004).

4.3. Records Management Practices in Organizations

Records management practices are vital to every organization aiding in the achievement of certain goals set by the founders of that organization from the conceptualization of that business. Records management occupies a strategic position in the efficient and effective management of public institutions. In fact, the practice is central in the administration of the institutions because it documents the planning and implementation of appropriate courses of services allowing proper monitoring of work (Egwunyenga, 2009). As stated by Robeck, Brown, and Stephens (2002), the reasons why organizations practice records management are to control the creation and growth of records, reduce operating costs, improve efficiency and productivity, assimilate new records management technologies, ensure regulatory compliance, minimize litigation risk, safeguard vital information, support better management decision making, preserve the corporate memory, and foster professionalism in running the business. The need for records preservation is, therefore, paramount to the cultural heritage of the past and for future generations obtainable in any organization (Abdulkareem, Isah, & Issa, 2013).

Akor and Udensi (2013) assert that decision making in an organization is an administrative function and invariably requires information in the form of records. They assert that administration is ordinarily discussed as the art of "getting things done," while emphasizing the processes and methods for insuring incisive action. Principles are set forth for securing concerted action from groups of people. Decisions are made at different levels in the organization—the lower, the middle, and the higher. Irrespective of the level, however, information will be required one way or another. In all spheres of activity, decisions are being made about the allocation of budgetary resources, the prioritization of programs, the granting of social benefits, the commissioning of new projects, the closure of unproductive ventures, the information to release to the public, or the level of classification that certain information requires. Records and archives provide the information that is required by those who make the decisions. The main question therefore is whether or not these records are available to these decision makers and whether or not the decision makers are aware of their existence and thus make use of them for decision making.

Thus efficient and effective management of records helps the critical stakeholders of an organization or institution as well as its administrators who require records to facilitate accurate, timely decisions (Nwankwo, 2001). Decision making is the backbone of administrative actions and administrators execute plans through actions (Akor & Udensi, 2013). Information is every organization's most basic and essential asset, and in common with any other business asset, recorded information requires effective management. Records management ensures that information can be accessed easily and destroyed routinely when no longer needed, and enables organizations not only to function on a day to day basis, but also to fulfill legal and financial requirements. The preservation of the records of government, for example, ensures it can be held accountable for its actions, that society can trace the evolution of policy in historical terms, and allows access to an important resource for future decision making (National Archives of Scotland, 2013).

All organizations create records to support and provide evidence of their transactions. Consequently, records, regardless of their formats, are important sources of information and knowledge. They ensure effective transparency and accountability in decision-making and contribute to national development (International Records Management Trust, 2003; Kemoni, 2007). Therefore, sound management of records, whether electronic or paper, has become a topical issue not only in Nigeria but globally. The World Bank (2006) and the International Records Management Trust (2003) concur that records are essential for the effective and productive functioning of private and public organizations. They assert that records register the decisions and activities of governments and other organizations, and serve as benchmarks against which they can measure their future activities and decisions. Without records, there can be no rule of law and accountability (World Bank, 2006). Consequently, without good records, organizations make ad hoc decisions without the benefit of institutional memories.

Kalusopa (2011) observes that, for organizations to participate meaningfully in the national development process, they must develop the capacity to manage records and information. The reason is that the challenges of conceiving, initiating, implementing, monitoring, and evaluating activities will always require reliable, pertinent, and timely records as well as information. Therefore, every organization has the role to monitor and measure progress with inclusive participatory national economic processes and good corporate ethics that the principles of openness, integrity, and accountability underpin with regards to its records management (Kanyenze, Kondo, & Martens, 2006).

4.4. Records Management in Local Government Councils in Nigeria

The concept of "local government" has been given different meanings by different scholars. Hicky (1966) referred to local government as "the management of services and regulatory functions by locally elected councils and officials responsible to them, under statutory and inspectorial supervision of central legislature and executive, but with enough financial and other independence to admit of a fair degree of local initiative and policy making." The United Nations Office for Public Administration (1961) defines local government as "a political subdivision of a nation or (in a federal system) state, which is constituted by law and has substantial control of local affairs, including the powers to impose taxes or to exact labor for prescribed purposes. The governing body of such an entity can be elected or locally selected." This definition has been widely accepted as reasonably embracing.

Finally, Yakubu (2003), quoting Chief Obafemi Awolowo, referred to local government as "a system of government where local councils make, accept responsibility for, and implement their own decisions subject only to such control as may be exercised by the people through their own regional government." Accordingly, the local government councils under the fourth Schedule of section 7 of the 1999 Nigerian Constitution have numerous functions listed for them. Hence, from the myriad activities with which they are saddled, considerable amounts of records are bound to be generated. It is therefore imperative to have records management programs in place to manage the large volume of records being generated both internally and externally by the local government councils.

Several factors have been identified to have contributed to the absence of good records management practices in local government councils in Nigeria. Alegbeleye (1988), Evborokhai (1990), and Unuigbe (1990) all report the absence of an enforcement of a records management program as contained in the law. Assante (1989) laments the poor management of records in Africa and posits that the major contributing factor to the gross inefficiency and a lack of continuity in policies, procedures, and measures of most African governments and business establishments is not frequent changes in government, as is commonly supposed, but bad management of records. Similarly, Mnjama (1993) remarks that the problems of records management in Africa include lack of resources, poor management, and inappropriate staff and training. These problems are also peculiar to local governments in Nigeria as a subset of African states. Dawha and Biu (1993) examined the archive and records management of the Biu Municipal Council in Nigeria and found that the council has no law governing the implementation of records management, no records center, and lacked in-house manuals or guides for the creation and control of records. From the foregoing review of the literature, it is obvious that of the few studies on records management in Nigeria even fewer are those concerned with the local government councils. Hence, the justification for a study to examine the practices in selected local government areas of Ogun State, Nigeria.

5. METHODOLOGY

The research design adopted for this study is the descriptive survey method using simple random sampling. This research setting is Ogun State, located in the southwest geopolitical zone of Nigeria, and one of the six states in the zone. Its choice for this study arose from the fact that it is one of the earliest exposed states in the federation to western education even as it is rapidly developing in both commerce and industry; this is perhaps owing to its proximity and affinity to Lagos State, the country's commercial capital. As a fast growing state, it is expected to serve as a role model in best practices generally, and in particular, local government administration; hence its choice for this study. The study population comprises the 415 personnel in the registry of the three selected local government councils in Ogun State, namely Sagamu (155), Ikenne (148), and Remo North (112). They are both in the senior and junior categories responsible for handling records in the Registry. From the study population of 415, a sample of 208 was drawn, representing 50.12%. Out of the 208 copies of the questionnaire administered, 150 copies were completed by the respondents and found useable for the purpose of analysis, giving a very high return rate of 72.12%. This is as presented in Table 1.

Apart from the questionnaire, which formed the major instrument for collecting the needed data, the other instrument was the interview, which was conducted with the three (3) heads of Registry in the three local government areas, which had only five questions serving as a follow-up to confirm those contained in the questionnaire. The questionnaire, validated by two experts in archives and records management in the Department of Library, Archival and Information Studies, University of Ibadan, was pilot-tested on thirty (30) staff of the Ilorin East local government area of Kwara, since they would not be a part of the final respondent group. Adopting the Split-half method, the results of their responses yielded a Cronbach's Alpha reliability co-efficient of r=071. The questionnaire was administered and collected back by the researchers personally while the interview was conducted immediately on the completing of the questionnaire. A descriptive data analysis method was employed through tabular presentation and simple percentage.

6. RESULTS

The return rate of the respondents in the three selected local councils is as shown in Table 2.

The result in Table 2 shows that, out of a total of 208 copies of the questionnaire that were administered to the registry personnel in the three selected local government councils, namely the Sagamu, Ikenne, and Remo North local councils respectively, in Ogun State, 150 copies were duly filled and returned giving a return rate of 72.12%. The high return rate recorded here could be attributed to the fact that the researchers were personally involved in both the administration and collection of the questionnaire, a situation that also afforded the researchers the opportunity to conduct

the interview with heads of the Registries in the three Councils immediately.

6.1. Objective 1: Classes of Records Managed and their Formats

Analysis of the classes of records created and their formats is as shown in Table 3.

The table shows that the classes of records managed by the three selected local government councils include: active records, which shows very high response in Sagamu (58.73%), followed by Ikenne (55.32%) and Remo North (50.00%); and vital records, with the same pattern of response but in reverse order with Remo North (47.50%), Ikenne (44.68%), and Sagamu (38.10%), while a few semi-active and in-active records were also kept in the registry. The breakdown of this indicates 3.17% of semi-active records for Sagamu with no response in Ikenne and Remo North, and 2.50% of in-active records for Remo North with no response in Sagamu and Ikenne. That the results showed that all the three Councils studied have records in their registries ranging from active and semi-active to inactive records provided a clear picture of the classification of records

Table 1. Study Population and Sample

LGA	Population	Sample	Percentage
Sagamu	155	78	50.32
Ikenne	148	74	50
Remo North	112	56	50
Total	415	208	50.12

Table 2. Return Rate of the Respondents

Local government	Total administered	Total returned	Percentage
Sagamu	78	63	30.29
Ikenne	74	47	22.60
Remo North	56	40	19.23
Total	208	150	72.12

Table 3. Classes of Records and their Formats

Classes of records	Sagamu No. %	Ikenne No. %	Remo North No. %	Total No. %
Active records	37 (58.73)	26 (55.32)	20 (50.00)	83 (55.33)
Vital records	24 (38.10)	21 (44.68)	19 (47.50)	64 (42.67)
Semi-active records	2 (3.17)	--	--	2 (1.33)
Inactive records	--	--	1 (2.50)	1 (0.67)
Total	**63 (100)**	**47 (100)**	**40 (100)**	**150 (100)**
Records format				
Paper-based records	55 (87.30)	36 (76.59)	40 (100.00)	131 (87.33)
Electronic records	6 (9.52%)	7 (14.89)	--	13 (8.67)
Film-based records	2 (3.18%)	2 (4.26)	--	4 (2.67)
Tape	--	--	--	--
No response	--	2 (4.26)	--	2 (1.33)
Total	**63 (100)**	**47 (100)**	**40 (100)**	**150 (100)**

expected of a typical Records Centre, hence taking no exception to the rule.

The table also revealed that most of these records were in paper format with an overwhelming response coming from Remo North (100.00%), followed by Sagamu (87.30%) and Ikenne (76.59%). A very low percentage in the local government councils indicated that fewer electronic records were maintained, with the highest response in Ikenne (14.89%), followed by Sagamu (9.52%) and no response in Remo North; while the film-based format appeared for Ikenne (4.26%), Sagamu (3.18%), and Remo North without response. That most of the records in these Councils were in paper format suggested that most of their records were not digitally born or created. Given the present overwhelming influence of ICT application to nearly all facets of human endeavor this finding was most unexpected, especially in a highly developed State like the one studied. This makes for an interesting finding indeed, because the natural expectation was that the ICT trend and fashion would be clearly evident in the records management practices in these Councils.

6.2. Objective 2: Records Storage Facilities Available for Records Security

The analysis of the records storage facilities available and the level of records security in the selected local government councils is presented in Table 4.

Table 4 shows that a majority (52.50%) from Remo North, 38.10% from Sagamu, and 12.77% from Ikenne indicated that steel file cabinets constituted their main storage facility. This is closely followed by the computer (28.67%), where the 31.91% of the respondents who indicated this were from Ikenne, 31.75% from Sagamu, and 20.00% from Remo North. This is followed by the use of wooden shelves (17.33%) with 34.04% in Ikenne, 12.50% in Remo North, and 7.94% in Sagamu, as a medium of storage. Only a few respondents indicated that metal shelves, CD-ROMs, and flash drives were used in their respective local government councils with 12.70% from Sagamu, 10.64% from Ikenne, and 5.00% from Remo North for metal shelves; 8.51% from Ikenne, 7.50% from Remo North, and 4.76% from Ikenne for CD-ROMs; while 2.50% from Remo North, 3.17% from Sagamu, and 2.13% from Ikenne indicated flash

Table 4. Records Storage Facilities and Security Measures

Storage medium	Sagamu No. %	Ikenne No. %	Remo North No. %	Total No. %
Computer	20 (31.75)	15 (31.91)	8 (20.00)	43 (28.67)
Metal shelves	8 (12.70)	5 (10.64)	2 (5.00)	15 (10.00)
Wooden shelves	5 (7.94)	16 (34.04)	5 (12.50)	26 (17.33)
Steel file cabinet	24 (38.10)	6 (12.77)	21 (52.50)	51 (34.00)
CD Rom	3 (4.76)	4 (8.51)	3 (7.50)	10 (6.67)
Flash drive	2 (3.17)	1 (2.13)	1 (2.50)	4 (2.67)
Off-site storage facility	--	--	--	--
No response	1 (1.58)	--	--	1 (0.66)
Total	**63 (100)**	**47 (100)**	**40 (100)**	**150 (100)**
Security measures				
Managerial clearance	45 (71.43)	31 (65.96)	30 (75.00)	106 (70.67)
Personal coding	7 (11.11)	4 (8.51)	5 (12.50)	16 (10.67)
Password	3 (4.76)	7 (14.89)	1 (2.50)	11 (7.33)
Locked cabinet	8 (12.70)	5 (10.64)	4 (10.00)	17 (11.33)
Backup to external system	--	--	--	--
Total	**63 (100)**	**47 (100)**	**40 (100)**	**150 (100)**

drives. In all, no respondent indicated that an off-site storage facility is used as a storage medium for the councils' records.

Concerning security measures taken by each of the councils to prevent unauthorized access, mutilation, and stealing of their records, a majority (70.67%) indicated that managerial clearance was often employed, with 75.00% from Remo North, 71.43% from Sagamu, and 65.96% from Ikenne, respectively. Other methods include personal coding, with 12.50% in Remo North, 11.11% in Sagamu, and 8.51% in Ikenne. The use of passwords to complement managerial clearance was not as significant as the responses showed only 14.89% for Ikenne, 4.76% for Sagamu, and 2.50% for Remo North. Also, the use of locked cabinets, 12.70% in Sagamu, 10.64% in Ikenne, and 10.00% in Remo North,

respectively, is considered as essential to safeguard records of the councils. None of the respondents indicated that backups to external systems were considered a significant security measure by the councils. These security and safety measures were completely manual, devoid of taking on all the advantages offered by modern-day information and communication technology facilities. This situation does not show that the Councils were proactive in their records management practices, thus exposing their records to disasters without preparedness and plans, contrary to standard practice in a typical Records Centre. This is as undesirable as it is unacceptable, particularly for a State that is as advanced as Ogun State, expected to have entrenched good practices in all its activities, including their records management practice.

6.3. Objective 3: Retrieval Tools for Locating Records and Records Retrieval Rate

The analysis of retrieval tools as well as the retrieval rate used in locating records in the selected local government councils is as indicated in Table 5.

Table 5 indicates that registers constituted the most common type of finding aid by the councils, where Sagamu had 71.43%, followed by Ikenne (59.57%) and Remo North (55.00%). This pattern is followed by indexes, in a reversed order where Remo North had 20.00%, Ikenne (12.77%), and Sagamu (12.70%). Other types of finding aids included simple lists in Ikenne (12.77%), Sagamu (11.11%), as well as simple lists and functional codes (10.00% and 7.50%, respectively), for Remo North. This finding is an extension of an earlier one, which revealed that the records in these Councils were largely created manually as opposed to digitally, given that the origin of records goes a long way to determining their mode of storage and retrieval, generally. However, in contrast to the non-digital creation of records in the Councils, findings here revealed that the majority of them employed the use of such records storage media as the computer, CD-ROM, and flash drive aside metal shelves. This showed the Councils taking recourse to the trend after all, even though this practice needs to be further entrenched especially at the records creation stage, where it is presently nearly non-existent.

As for the records retrieval rate, the table shows that a majority of the respondents, 46.81% in Ikenne, 42.86% in Sagamu, and 35.00% in Remo North, indicated that it took them an average of 5-10 minutes to retrieve the needed records. Next were the respondents from Remo North (32.50%), Ikenne (25.53%), and Sagamu (25.40%) who indicated an average of 1-5 minutes as their record retrieval rate. Others indicated 10-15

Table 5. Retrieval Tools and Record Retrieval Rate

Types of Finding Aids	Sagamu No. %	Ikenne No. %	Remo North No. %	Total No. %
Simple list	7 (11.11)	6 (12.77)	4 (10.00)	17 (11.33)
Register	45 (71.43)	28 (59.57)	22 (55.00)	95 (63.33)
Calendar	--	--	2 (5.00)	2 (1.33)
Color code	1 (1.59)	3 (6.38)	1 (2.50)	5 (3.33)
Index	8 (12.70)	6 (12.77)	8 (20.00)	22 (14.68)
Functional code	--	--	3 (7.50)	3 (2.00)
No response	2 (3.17)	4 (8.51)	--	6 (4.00)
Total	**63 (100)**	**47 (100)**	**40 (100)**	**150 (100)**
Record Retrieval Rate				
1-5 minutes	16 (25.40)	12 (25.53)	13 (32.50)	41 (27.33)
5-10 minutes	27 (42.86)	22 (46.81)	14 (35.00)	63 (42.00)
10-15 minutes	13 (20.63)	8 (17.02)	8 (20.00)	29 (19.33)
15-20 minutes	5 (7.94)	3 (6.38)	3 (7.50)	11 (7.34)
No response	2 (3.17)	2 (4.26)	2 (5.00)	6 (4.00)
Total	**63 (100)**	**47 (100)**	**40 (100)**	**150 (100)**

minutes, including 20.63% from Sagamu, 20.00% from Remo North, and 17.02% from Ikenne, while only a few indicated 15-20 minutes, with 7.94% for Sagamu, 7.50% for Remo North, and 6.38% for Ikenne. Very few respondents in Remo North (5.00%), Ikenne (4.26%), and Sagamu (3.17%) gave no response to this effect. Given the rather good retrieval time rate as found above, especially since this is a largely manual records environment, the situation will definitely be improved upon when the Councils adopt electronic records management practices. Of great concern, however, is the problem of disorganized records resulting from the retrieval of needed records. Embracing the digital approach will help not only to improve even better the retrieval time rate but also to address perfectly the residual problem of record scattering effects, usually arising from each retrieval exercise, leaving the records situation worse than it was before the search and retrieval.

6.4. Objective 4: Barriers to Effective Records Management in the Councils

Table 6 presents results on barriers against records management.

The table 6 indicates that the problem of inadequate finance was most pronounced in Sagamu (38.09%), followed by Ikenne (21.27%) and then Remo North (25.00%), respectively. As for the lack of equipment and materials, responses from Ikenne (42.55%), Remo North (37.50%), and Sagamu (23.81%) were instructive, while poor maintenance culture has the highest response of 20.00% in Remo North, followed with a huge margin by Ikenne (4.26%) and the lowest in Sagamu (1.59%). Unfavorable climatic conditions recorded low responses in the three local Councils generally with the lowest from Sagamu (1.59%), followed by Ikenne (2.12%) and Remo North (2.50%). Erratic power supply constituted a major barrier in Sagamu (15.87%), then in Ikenne (4.26%) and Remo North (2.50%). The response on the lack of skilled personnel was high for Ikenne (4.26%), followed by Remo North (2.50%), but less for Sagamu (1.59%). Inadequate storage facilities, as a barrier, received high response in Ikenne (8.51%) and Sagamu (7.94%), but was low in Remo North (2.50%). A similar pattern of response was received with respect to lack of management planning as a barrier: Ikenne has 12.77%, Sagamu 9.52%, and Remo North 7.50%, respectively. Noteworthy from these findings is the fact that of all the barriers identified, the absence of a management plan remained the most central because such

Table 6. Barriers to Effective Records Management in the Councils

Barriers	Sagamu No. %	Ikenne No. %	Remo North No. %	Total No. %
Inadequate finance	24 (38.09)	10 (21.27)	10 (25.00)	44 (29.33)
Lack of equipment and materials	15 (23.81)	20 (42.55)	15 (37.50)	50 (33.33)
Poor maintenance culture	1 (1.59)	2 (4.26)	8 (20.00)	11 (7.33)
Unfavorable climatic conditions	1 (1.59)	1 (2.12)	1 (2.50)	3 (2.00)
Erratic power supply	10 (15.87)	2 (4.26)	1 (2.50)	13 (8.67)
Lack of skilled personnel	1 (1.59)	2 (4.26)	1 (2.50)	4 (2.67)
Inadequate storage facilities	5 (7.94)	4 (8.51)	1 (2.50)	10 (6.67)
Lack of management plan	6 (9.52)	6 (12.77)	3 (7.50)	15 (10.00)
Total	**63 (100)**	**47 (100)**	**40 (100)**	**150 (100)**

a plan will naturally incorporate all the needs required for a good records management practice, thereby eliminating most, if not all, of the barriers mentioned here. Furthermore, the absence of such a management plan was a strong indicator of the fact that none of the Councils studied has anything close to a standard records management practice in operation. This situation is undesirable, to say the least.

7. DISCUSSION OF THE FINDINGS AND THEIR IMPLICATIONS

This study is on records management in selected local government councils in Ogun State, Nigeria. The study established the prevalence of paper as the medium for recording and conveying information in the selected local government councils. However, with modern technologies, multiple copies of a record can be created, which may lead to unnecessary large volume of records. Popoola (2003), in Nakpodia (2011), noted that when the creation of records is not properly managed, attainment of goals and objectives becomes a problem. These problems often manifest in the difficulty in locating papers/information, bulky files, wrong filing, wrong titles of files, and having offices cluttered with papers and files. It is therefore important to observe the rule of thumb in records management, which Penn (1983) gave as the necessity of not creating a record when it is not needed. However, the findings showed that most of these paper-based records were active, semi-active, or vital, and maintained by the councils in the registry, while in-active records were kept in the records store.

The study also found that all the steel cabinets mostly used by the local government councils were grossly inadequate and as a result some records were either placed on top of the cabinets or kept on the floor. This act, apart from making information retrieval a difficult task, also endangers the safety of any classified information contained in them. Ajewole (2001) opines that the hallmark of any effective records management is a storage device that facilitates, rather than hampers, a quick retrieval process for prompt usability of the records. Findings of this study further revealed that computers, rather than being used as a medium of storage, were used for records creation.

On the security measures in place to prevent unau-

thorized access to the records, the study revealed that strong restrictions were placed on the use of records. Access to records is usually subjected to managerial clearance. In fact, observations showed that users have to fulfill bureaucratic procedures before being allowed access to records for inspection and needed information for official and public use. Hopler (1976), in Abioye and Habila (2004), notes that records are the life blood of any organization and to treat the matter of storage and protection of these records lightly would be undesirable. He further argues that records which are not properly stored will be at the mercy of agents of records destruction such as rats and termites, and even human destructive tendencies like theft and vandalism, and concludes that if a record is worth keeping, then such records must be adequately stored and protected. Further to this, the preservation of records of government ensures it can be held accountable for its actions, that society can trace the evolution of policy in historical terms, and allows access to an important resource for future decision making (National Archive of Scotland, 2013).

Furthermore, findings of this study indicated that registers were the commonest type of finding aid used in the selected local government councils. This was not surprising, since all records, especially those received, are usually registered as they are filed and their registers can be useful in locating the needed records from their stores. Next to this were index and simple list devices as other types of finding aids employed by these local government councils. This result is similar to the result of a previous study carried out by Abioye (2006). However, the use of color coding as a modern record finding tool was not given adequate attention, especially from an economic point of view. Popoola (2000) submits that the use of color coding can reduce record handling costs significantly in the records office (registry).

The findings also showed that the rate at which records were retrieved took an average of 5-10 minutes in the selected local governments. This is a better record retrieval rate considering the chaotic situation of records management in the local government councils, given the observation that some of the records were scattered over the shelves. However, this assertion only applied to the retrieval of active and vital records, which are kept in the registry. The same cannot be said of non-current and inactive records, which were just carelessly dumped in a records store. Interview responses also revealed that it took an average of 1-2 hours and even at times one or two days to retrieve the needed records from their stores. Each attempt to search for required records in the store further compounded the situation as the records were left more disorganized than before the searcher met them. Abioye (2006) opines that easy retrieval guarantees timely availability of records for decision making. Delay in records retrieval processes is a manifestation of poor records management practices, which breeds inefficiency.

The findings also revealed that a number of barriers were confronting effective management of records in the studied local government councils. These problems range from lack of equipment and materials, inadequate finance, and poor maintenance culture, to inadequate storage facilities. Other problems included erratic power supply, lack of management planning, and lack of skilled personnel. Most of these finding were supported by Popoola (2000).

The implication of these findings is that there is no institutionalized framework for the proper harnessing of public records and information in the studied local government councils. This, in turn, will almost certainly affect the efficient and effective administration of these councils. Considering the strategic position of Ogun State, as one of the foremost parts of Nigeria to be exposed to Western education and development, its Councils' administration should serve as a worthy practice to be emulated by others across the country in terms of institutionalization and standardization. The findings of this study did not reveal this, a situation that is to say the least, undesirable. Therefore, allocation of adequate space and supply of modern and adequate equipment and facilities are necessary for the enhancement of proper storage and easy retrieval of records. Adequate budgetary provisions will ensure that proper funding is available to support records management programs. An adequate management plan provides the basis for systematic procedures for records management. Exhibition of good maintenance culture ensures longevity for those records of permanent value. Adequate power supply will not only support electronic records programs but also ensure their accessibility. A team of skilled personnel will represent the heart and the life-blood of an effective records management program and providing a conducive environment for

records ensures that records are in stable condition. It is therefore imperative that proper attention be paid to all these measures to achieve successful and functional records management practices.

8. CONCLUSIONS AND RECOMMENDATIONS

Records created, used, kept, and maintained by the selected local government councils examined are in four categories, namely active, vital, semi-active, and inactive, most of which were predominantly in paper based format. However, some records were stored in electronic formats such as disc, tape, and film. It must be noted that some of the selected local government councils still make use of archaic wooden shelves as a media of storage where available steel file cabinets were in short supply. The public service institutions' approach to records security are through personal coding, passwords, and seeking managerial clearance before records are used as well as employing trained staff in records security and control, while modern security measures such as locked cabinets and backups to external systems, among other solutions, are not in place.

Records of the selected local government councils were in a chaotic situation. Most of the semi-active and inactive records were usually dumped in the records store. This has the tendency to hamper information retrieval from the records stores when required. The local government councils are faced with a myriad of barriers from lack of equipment and materials, inadequate finance, and poor maintenance culture, to unreliable power supply, lack of skilled personnel, and lack of management plans. It is therefore significant to deal with these factors in a bid to move the local government councils in particular and Nigeria in general into a world where records management strategies exist and impact positively on their governments, their staff, and their people.

On the basis of these conclusions reached, the following recommendations were made:

1. A coherent records management policy should be formulated and provision made for all phases of records' life cycles, namely the records' creation, use and maintenance, and disposition. This policy should be strictly adhered to by the councils' registry staff.

2. Old and archaic storage facilities such as wooden shelves should be discarded while steel file cabinets, presently in short supply, should be provided in sufficient quantities. From an economic point of view and for space management, steel file cabinets with aisle features should be procured and used for filing records. Off-site storage facilities should also be considered, especially where vital records are concerned.

3. Integrated records management programs should be adopted without downplaying any of the components of records management. The councils should adopt a holistic and realistic approach in the establishment, implementation, and administration of a comprehensive records management program.

4. Adequate budgetary provisions should be provided for records management programs in these councils. Adequate finance should be provided to procure modern and adequate storage equipment and facilities.

REFERENCES

Abioye, A. A. (2006). *Records management practices of the Court of Appeal and the Supreme Court in the administration of justice in Nigeria.* (Unpublished thesis, Department of Library, Archival and Information Studies, Faculty of Education, University of Ibadan), 80, 86.

Abioye A. A., & Habila, J. R. (2004). Records management practices in colleges of education in Nigeria: A study of Federal College of Education, Yola and College of Education, Jalingo. *Gateway Library Journal, 7*(2), 68-79.

Ajewole, B. (2001). *Records and information resource management in public service: A theoretical and practical framework.* Lagos: Administrative Staff College of Nigeria (ASCON).

Akor, P. U., & Udensi, J. (2013). An assessment of record management system in establishment division of two universities in Nigeria. *Mediterranean Journal of Social Sciences, 4*(12).

Alegbeleye, G. O. (1983). Towards an integrated records and information management for Nigeria. *Paper presented at the Second General Assembly of West African Regional Branch of International Council on Archives (WARBICA) and Seminar on Archives and Records Management, Jos.*

Alegbeleye, G. O. (1988). Archives administration and records management in Nigeria: Up the decade from amalgamation. *ARMA Records Management Quarterly,* July, 26-30.

Assante, K. B. (1989). *Closing address at the Second West Africa Regional Workshop on Management of Semi-current Records, Accra, Ghana,* 23 July 23 - 19 August.

Atulomah, B. C. (2011). Perceived records management practice and decision making among university administrators in Nigeria. *Library Philosophy and Practice.* Retrieved from http://unllib.uni.edu/LPP/

Dawha, M. K., & Biu, A. B. (1993). Archive and records management in a typical municipal council in Nigeria. *New Library World, 94*(4), 1108.

Dollar, C. M. (2000). *Authentic electronic records strategies for long-term access.* Chicago, IL: Cohasset Associates, 23, 47-50.

Egwunyenga, E. J. (2009). Records keeping in universities: Associated problems and management options in south west geo-political zone of Nigeria. *International Journal of Education Science,* Kamla-Raj, 1(2), 109-113.

Emmerson, P. (1989). *How to manage your records.* Cambridge, UK: TCSA Publishing.

Ette, E. M. (1984). *The Organisation and utilization of the Ibadan archives.* (Unpublished Master's thesis, University of Ibadan, Ibadan).

Evborokhai, A. O. (1990). Records management system. *Lecture delivered at the Principles of Records Management and Archives Administration Course, National Archives Zonal Office, Ibadan,* 23 October - 16 November, 10.

Helen, S., & Tim, M. (1996). Records and information resource management in public service: A theoretical and practical framework. Lagos: Administrative Staff College of Nigeria (ASCON).

Hicky, T. J. D. (1966). Enemies within and enemies without the gates. *Political Quarterly, 37*(2), 159-168.

Hopler, F. B. (1976). Records management practices in Colleges of Education in Nigeria: A study of Federal College of Education, Yola and College of Education, Jalingo. *Gateway Library Journal, 7*(2),

68-79.

Igwoku, I. F. (2008). *An analysis of record management strategies in western Nigeria.* (Unpublished M.Ed. dissertation, Delta State University, Abraka).

International Foundation for Information Technology (2010). Definition of records. Retrieved from http://www.if4it.com.

International Organisation for Standardisation (ISO) (2001). *ISO 15489-1 Information and documentation-records management: Part 1 general.* Geneva: ISO.

International Records Management Trust (IRMT) (2003). *Evidence-based government in the electronic age: Case summaries.* Retrieved from http://ww.irmt.org/evidence/index.html

Kalusopa, T. (2011). *Developing an e-records readiness framework for labour organisations in Botswana.* (Ph.D. thesis, University of South Africa, Pretoria).

Kanyenze, G., Kondo, K., & Martens, J. (2006). *The search for sustainable human development in Southern Africa.* Harare: ANSA.

Kemoni, H. N. (2007). *Records management practices and public service delivery in Kenya.* (Ph.D. thesis, University of KwaZulu-Natal, Pietermaritzburg, South Africa).

Maddick, H. (1963). Introduction. In *Democracy, decentralisation and development.* Bombay: Asia Publishing House.

Mark, C. (2001). *Records and information resource management in public service: A theoretical and practical framework.* Lagos: Administrative Staff College of Nigeria (ASCON).

Mnjama, N. M. (1993). Archives and records management in Africa. *Information Development, 9*(1/2), 83-86.

Abdulkareem, M. Y., Isah, A., & Issa, A. O. (2013). Challenges of digital preservation of manuscripts to the Nigerian education and information systems. *Library & Archival Security, 25*(2), 119-131.

Nakpodia, E. D. (2011). Student's records: Challenges in the management of student personnel in Nigerian tertiary institutions. *Prime Research on Education (PRE), 1*(3), 44-49.

National Archive of Scotland (2013). Records Management. Retrieved from http://www.nas.gov.uk/recordKeeping/recordsManagement.asp

Nwankwo, J. I. (2001). *Fundamentals of management information systems.* Ibadan: Spectrum Books.

Ogunrombi, S. A., Abare, H. M., & Adamu, D. B. (1998). Problem records book: A tool for effective library management in Nigeria university libraries. *Library Bulletin: Nigerian University Library System, 3*(1&2), 101-109.

Olanipekun, J. M. (1988). *Local government in Nigeria.* An address by the chairman, Ibarapa local government area of Oyo State, Nigeria, Africa Leadership Forum, 27 October.

Penn, I. A. (1983). Understanding the life cycle concept of records management. *Records Management Quarterly, 17*(3), 5-8.

Popoola, S. O. (2000). Records management system in the civil service of Oyo State, Nigeria: A cost model approach. (Ph.D. thesis, University of Ibadan, Ibadan).

Popoola, S. O. (2000). Records survey and security of public records. *Paper presented at National Training Workshop on Records Management organized by the Office of Civil Service of the Federation, Establishment and Pensions Office for Desk/Schedule Officers on (GL. 12-14) in Nigerian Public Service, Ijaiye-Ogba, Ikeja, Lagos,* 25-30 September.

Robek, M. F. (1995). *Records and information resource management in public service: A theoretical and practical framework.* Lagos: Administrative Staff College of Nigeria (ASCON).

Robek, M. F., Brown, G. F., & Stephens, D. O. (2002). Information and records management: Document-based information systems (4th ed.). New York: McGraw-Hill, 5-6.

Ugwunze, V. I. (1992). An examination of records management in the University of Lagos Registry. *African Journal of Library. Archival and Information Science, 2*(1), 39-46.

Unuigbe, E. O. (1990). The future of records management in Nigeria. *Nigerian Archives, 2*(3), 26-33.

United Nations Office for Public Administration Conference (1961). *Administrative aspects of decentralisation.* Hague.

Wallace, P., Lee, J. A., & Schubert, D. (1992). Records management: Integrated information system (3rd ed.). Englewood Cliffs, NJ: Prentice Hall.

World Bank (2006). *Why records management? Records management as a key support for development effectiveness.* Retrieved from http://web.worldbank.org/

WBSITE/ EXTERNAL/ EXTABOUTUS/EXTAR-CHIVES/

Yakubu, J. A. (2003). Socio legal essays in local government administration in Nigeria. Ibadan: Demyas Law Books.

13

Features, Functions and Components of a Library Classification System in the LIS tradition for the e-Environment

M P Satija
Guru Nanak Dev University
Amritsar—143005 India
Email: satija_mp@yahoo.com

Daniel Martínez-Ávila *
São Paulo State University
Hygino Muzzi Filho 737 17525-900 Marilia, Brazil
Email: dmartinezavila@marlia.unesp.br

ABSTRACT

This paper describes qualities of a library classification system that are commonly discussed in the LIS tradition and literature, and explains such a system's three main functions, namely knowledge mapping, information retrieval, and shelf arrangement. In this vein, the paper states the functional requirements of bibliographic classifications, which broadly are subject collocation and facilitation of browsing the collection. It explains with details the components of a library classification system and their functions. The major components are schedules, notations, and index. It also states their distinguished features, such as generalia class, form divisions, book numbers, and devices for number synthesis which are not required in a knowledge classification. It illustrates with examples from the WebDewey good examples of added features of an online library classification system. It emphasizes that institutional backup and a revision machinery are essential for a classification to survive and remain relevant in the print and e-environment.

Keywords: Book numbers, Classification, Classification policy, Knowledge classification, Library classification, Online classification, WebDewey

*Corresponding Author: Daniel Martínez-Ávila
Assistant Professor
São Paulo State University
Hygino Muzzi Filho 737 17525-900 Marilia, Brazil
Email: dmartinezavila@marlia.unesp.br

1. PREFACE

Categorization and classification are methods used by humans to organize entities, thoughts, objects, and phenomena. These processes are related to the organization of knowledge and the way people learn, remember, and know about the world. There is a basic human drive to categorize as it allows people to make useful assumptions about new things by making comparisons with well-known things. In common language, the terms classification and categorization are not clearly distinguished, as for instance, dictionaries use both terms indistinctly. However, in Library and Information Science (LIS) some make the distinction (e.g. Taylor & Joudrey, 2009, p. 376): "Categorization can be seen as amorphous or less well-defined grouping; whereas classification can be viewed as a comprehensive hierarchical structure for organizing information resources on linear shelves." In this context, classifications or modern bibliographic classifications emerged in the late 1800s and early 1900s to handle early stages of the print revolution, i.e., to organize, store, and retrieve bibliographic materials. In light of the proliferation and use of simple categorization systems and classifications in physical and electronic environments, such as the use of BISAC (Book Industry Standards and Communications) and other verbal categories in libraries and websites such as Amazon and Google Books, we are reviewing and systematizing the features, functions, and components of library classification systems, according to the LIS literature and tradition of authors such as Ranganathan, that should be considered or at least known in the design and choice of classifications for these new environments.

2. LIBRARY CLASSIFICATION SYSTEMS

A classification is a tool for the organization of the phenomena of the universe or any of its parts or constituents. It groups objects into categories/classes based on shared properties with the purpose of bringing like items together. A modern library classification is a classification of knowledge as it is contained in documents of all sorts. It came into being for the purpose of arranging and retrieving information resources. In libraries, later, it was used for arranging classified catalogs and other information retrieval tools such as bibliographies. A modern library classification is more than knowledge classification, and beyond grouping it has many intellectual and mechanical functions to perform. Since their modern origin in the 1870s, many library classification systems have been designed to organize and access knowledge in libraries.

2.1. General and Special Classifications

A library classification may be general or special in coverage of subject areas. A general classification covers all subjects in the universe of knowledge. A special classification concentrates on a narrower range of topics, or the goods manufactured or services provided by the organization for which the classification has been developed. A special classification also refers to a classification of documents by form such as government reports, fiction, maps, or music. Such a classification is for micro-documents and in-depth subjects.

The taxonomy of the different types of classification has been expanded and systematized by Koch et al. (1997) as follows: universal schemes, national general schemes, subject specific schemes, and home-grown schemes. Universal schemes are intended to classify the entire universe of human knowledge for use by anyone, anywhere. Examples are the Universal Decimal Classification (UDC), the Colon Classification (CC), the Bliss bibliographic classification (BC), the Dewey Decimal Classification (DDC), and the Library of Congress Classification (LCC). National general schemes are universal in subject coverage, but intended for use in a single country. Examples are the Nederlandse Basisclassificatie (BC), the Sveriges Allmáma Biblioteksfórening (SAB), and the Nippon Dewey. This category may also include translated versions of the DDC in various languages incorporating provisions for the classification of local material. Subject specific schemes are designed for use by a particular subject community or domain. Examples are the National Library of Medicine (NLM) scheme for medicine, Iconclass for art resources, Moy's Law Classification, and the London Education Classification, among many others. Home-grown schemes are those devised for use in a particular service or retrieval system or in a library. Examples are Yahoo!'s categories and reader-interest classifications. There is an abundance of homemade library classifications, but these do not survive long in the era of standardized systems.

On the other hand, although the idea of special or subject specific classifications presupposes a greater level of detail, some general classifications, notably the UDC, LCC, and BC-2 (Bliss bibliographic classification, second edition) have been developed in sufficient depth of details to enable them to be adapted to moderately special collections. Thus, the debate between special and general classification is inconclusive. Ranganathan visualized his Colon Classification as a trunk of an elephant: nimble enough to pick up a small twig and strong enough to carry a heavy log of wood (Ranganathan, 1964). The Library of Congress Classification, with its 21 main classes in 29 parts bound in 50 volumes, is *de facto* a confederate of special classifications. The UDC, in its (now ceased) full edition, was issued in series of fascicules suitable for information centers and special collections.

Some of the main general classification systems are:
- Dewey Decimal Classification (1876+) / by Melvil Dewey
- Universal Decimal Classification (1905+) / FID (International Federation for Information and Documentation), now UDCC (Universal Decimal Classification Consortium)
- Expansive Classification (EC, 1892) / by C.A. Cutter
- Library of Congress Classification (1904-)
- Subject Classification (SC, 1906-1939) / by J.D. Drown
- Bibliographic Classification (BC, 1940-1953) / by H.E. Bliss
- Colon Classification (1933-1987) / by S.R. Ranganathan
- Bibliothecal Bibliographical Klassification (BBK, 1960-1970) / by VINITI (All-Russian Institute for Scientific and Technical Information), Russia
- Rider's International Classification (RIC, 1961) / by Fremont A. Rider
- Information Coding Classification (ICC, 1970) / by I. Dahlberg
- Bibliographic Classification second edition (BC-2, 1977-) / by J. Mills and V. Broughton
- Broad System of Ordering (BSO, 1978) / by Eric Coates

Of these, the DDC, UDC, and LCC are considered the big three systems. The CC and BC-2 are ideal and

scientifically sound systems, arguably more complex and grounded than the previous three (see for instance Ranganathan, 1967). However, they have not been implemented and used as widely as the DDC and UDC due to lack of editorial support or a more aggressive marketing of institutions such as OCLC (Online Computer Library Center). The BSO and ICC are not shelf classifications, whereas the fate of the Russian BBK is not known. The rest, namely EC, SC, BC, and RIC, are now only of historical interest.

Over the years, the features of these classifications have evolved and with experience been standardized. A library classification is a system having mutually related components or subsystems with the objective of organizing knowledge in libraries. It has its anatomy (hardware) showing its visible and invisible components, each of which has its supporting functions (physiology).

2.2. Functional Requirements of Bibliographic Classifications

It has been claimed that modern bibliographical work demands a standard classification which:
1. brings together related classes and subjects;
2. is sufficiently subdivided to index everything of its class under the sun, though the level of specificity varies;
3. is capable of further extension and subdivision, as our knowledge grows;
4. is recognized widely so that the users may easily find their way in it and with it;
5. has an extensive index of its classes in alphabetical sequence in order to navigate schedules;
6. has moderately mixed notation which shows hierarchy, is easy for arranging and finding the classified arrangement, is hospitable to new subjects, and allows interdisciplinary combinations;
7. is not subjected to too frequent revision or any drastic reorganization, and is not under experimentation;
8. has a body to market and maintain it with adequate resources and expertise; and
9. is available as a web based online database.

Practically, a library classification performs three functions:
1. Linking an information item on the shelves with its catalog entry. An item's class number forms

part of its call number, and the latter is unique for every item in the library. The library classification thus enables items in a library catalogue to be located from the shelves.

2. It is a tool for information retrieval; hierarchy easily allows the broadening and narrowing of search by truncating a class number from the right; all the alphabetical subject access tools such as subject headings lists, thesauri, and ontologies inherently involve classification of one kind or the other. A thesauro- facet is more than a classification. Use of classification for retrieving information on the web is increasing (Satija & Martínez-Ávila, 2014). Ranganathan's chain indexing is an eminent example of the use of classification for information retrieval (Vickery, 1972). The Classification Research Group (CRG, London) established in 1952 in its manifesto has declared facet classification as the basis of all information retrieval both in manual and machine environments (Maltby, 1978, p. 225).

3. Facilitates browsing the collection, which results in serendipitous discoveries. This is called unknown item approach. In addition, by browsing, users can expect to find related subjects nearby. However, due to the limitations of linear order and division by discipline, not all related subjects can be collocated. The mode of classification is to group together by discipline the topics that the library users are most likely to see together (both on library shelves and in digital collections). This is done by arranging documents in a filiatory sequence, or helpful order. Arrangement of documents or their surrogates is an attempt to suit as many of the users as possible as much of the time as possible (Curwen, 1978).

2.3. Ideal Functions of Library Classification Systems

An ideal library classification system is supposed to have the following broader functions in the order of their generic importance:

1. Cognitive function (Mapping of knowledge)
2. Bibliographic function (Information retrieval)
3. Shelf arrangement function (Locating and browsing documents)

A classification system which performs an upper function also performs lower functions equally well. This means that a cognitively sound classification is equally good at information retrieval and shelf arrangement of documents. A bibliographic classification will also be good at shelf arrangement, but may not be good as a cognitive system. The systematic arrangement of knowledge or of the documents in a collection translates into the following functions:

1. Gives us an overview of the structure of the subject field covered;
2. Helps in the locating of documents, either directly or through the catalog. In this age, the document is no more the unit; one can retrieve a chapter or a paragraph on the one hand, and a group of documents on the other; and
3. Allows meaningful browsing of documents in stacks or their surrogates in a bibliographic database.

The features that a bibliographic classification requires in order to achieve these ends are: a helpful order of subjects at all levels, a brief memorable notation, and a host of techniques and devices for number synthesis.

2.4. What is Necessary for a Library Classification System?

A library classification system should be:

- explicit, recorded, and unambiguous with clear notes and instructions with examples
- available to both classifiers and users
- designed to comprehensively mirror the cognitive structure of subjects to potential users
- designed to cover the literature, information, or knowledge base which it is supposed to organize. In other words, it should be based on literary warrant
- preferably made available in varied but interoperable versions of details to suit libraries of different sizes

2.5. Print and Machine-Readable Formats of Classification Systems

Since the last decade of the previous century, most of the living classification systems have converted their print format into machine readable databases. The DDC, UDC, and the LCC are available both in print and machine readable format. Now the machine readable database is the main source file while the other versions, including the print edition, are its byproducts. In the beginning, the electronic version was used only to help the editors in the editing and publishing of the system. But now the electronic versions have been made available to the users mostly on the web and have many additional valued features apart from being easily kept updated by the publishers. Classification systems in a machine readable database, which these days are in MARC-21 Concise Format for Classification Data, have the following functions (Slavic, 2008):

- searching and browsing of classification by notation; the hierarchy allows to broaden or deepen the search to any point from the right end
- searching notation through an associated verbal expression, that is index and synonymous terms
- sorting and displaying of schedules in various layouts
- automatic tracing of hierarchical and associative linking
- tracing of system rules to the area of their application
- navigation between tables, facets, and subject areas
- tracing historical data through a scheme's lifespan ('replaces/replaced by')
- various outputs and exports
- identification of classes independently of notation

On the other hand, an online classification system does not logically or intellectually differ from its print version, though it has many add-on functions.

2.5.1. Electronic Dewey

The Electronic Dewey, which is a highly value added online version of the DDC, can be searched by words or phrases, numbers, index terms, and Boolean operations. Captions can be browsed and hierarchies can be displayed. An entry also shows frequently used LC subject headings associated with a Dewey number, along with a sample bibliographic record. The Electronic Dewey enables users to classify materials quickly and efficiently. Its latest manifestation is called WebDewey 2.0.

Unlike the print editions, the WebDewey is not constrained by physical size and space. The database includes all built numbers from the relative index of the print version and thousands more added to the electronic version. It also includes the segmentation

(prime) marks used by the Library of Congress to show either the end of an abridged number or the beginning of a standard subdivision. A convenient work area displays and stores the parts of the Dewey number being built as one moves among the schedules and tables for instructions (Satija, 2013, pp. 21-23).

LC subject headings and BISAC headings have been added to each class number by statistical matching. These headings provide additional terms for searching. In WebDewey movement of upward and downward hierarchies is possible by highlighting and clicking. If a number or term is dragged and dropped into a search window, the search for number or the term will begin. Dragging and dropping a Dewey number will show the full record display of the number including caption notes, relative index entries, and associated Library of Congress Subject Headings (LCSH). If the term is dragged and dropped into an index window then the relevant part of the Relative index will be displayed, looking like that of the printed relative index.

There are standard as well as customizable on screen views for the user to set. The standard views are:

a) Search view—search window and DDC number window
b) Browse view—search window, DDC pages window, and DDC number window
c) Scan view—Index window, Search window, and DDC number window
d) Summary view—DDC summary window, Search window, DDC pages window, and DDC number window

In any view users can:

- maximize any window to see a larger display
- choose display to see appropriate LCSH
- choose bibliographic record to see a sample record using the number selected
- change LCSH to review the frequency of headings used with the number
- print contents of a window may by choosing Print; choose Notes to make a permanent record of a DDC number and its specific use
- choose Past to review the searches made during the current session
- use Help to understand a term or procedure

WebDewey has an augmented index with natural language terms from other thesauri to provide an enhanced access. Some of the important advantages of

WebDewey over the traditional print version are:

a) Keyword access to the entire print DDC-23
b) Additional terms and subject headings for search
c) Hierarchic display
d) Standard and formulable view
e) Dragging and dropping of numbers and terms
f) Automatic cuttering for book numbers with two options for constructing four-figure or three figure cutter numbers

However, the basic principles and number building techniques are the same. Future electronic versions may provide some built-in expert system for automatic synthesis of numbers wherever required. Many more surprising features may be in store in the near future, including the one Dewey without notation.

2.5.2. Other online classifications

Other important online classifications are the LC (Classification Plus) and the UDC (UDC-MRF, Master Reference File). During an International Federation of Library Associations and Institutions (IFLA) sponsored international seminar on UDC in June 2007 (www.ulec.org/seminar2007.htm) at the UDCC headquarters, a Dutch software company Magnaview (www.magnaview.nl) presented an innovative visual application of the UDC. It makes possible viewing the UDC MRF in twenty novel ways and interacting with it visually. The software is commercially available from the company for MRF license holders.

3. PARTS OF A LIBRARY CLASSIFICATION SYSTEM

A classification, in essence, is simply a systematically arranged list of subjects and their subdivisions in the universe of knowledge. To be of practical use in libraries, a classification needs additional features, and these are what make it into a system. A library classification scheme has three broader components (Rowley & Hartley, 2008, pp. 171-192):

1. The schedules: in which subjects are listed systematically in arrays and chains showing their inter and intra relationships. The order of subjects in these schedules is not self-evident, and therefore requires:
2. Notation, which is a sort of a code using numbers

and/or letters that have a readily understood order, and which guides the arrangement of subjects in the schedules and documents on shelves; and

3. An alphabetical index to locate terms within lengthy and mazy schedules.

It is often stated that a classification requires a fourth component: a governing body to keep it innovative, current, and for its marketing. Finally, the introduction of the system, usually including instructions and editorial information reflecting the views of the author or the governing body, can constitute another essential part of the system.

3.1. Schedules

A schedule is a systematic list of classes and their subdivisions arranged in a logical way. It is the core or the *terra firma* of the system. Classification schedules comprise the following elements:

- Main classes
- The division and subdivisions of main classes hierarchically or in faceted mode
- Facets, generated by facet analysis
- Sub-facets (arrays), formed by the subdivision of the facets by a single characteristic at a time
- Above all, in the beginning, a summary of main classes and their further division is given, serving as a broader map of the knowledge covered. For example: the DDC and UDC have three summaries called Main classes, Divisions, and Sections, respectively. Apart from providing an overview of the subject, summaries save the time of the classifiers in locating the desired subdivision.

3.1.1. Example

Aida Slavic (2008, p. 5) explains an entry from the online UDC schedules having the following components:

"004.421.2 **Basic mathematical algorithms**

For mathematical theory of algorithms in general use 510.5. Specify mathematical process by colon combination with class 51.

Examples of combination(s):

004.421.2:517.443 Fast Fourier transform
004.421.2:517.535 Algorithms for rational expression
004.421.2:519.17 Graph algorithms
=>519.16
=>519.178

When stored in a database, information implicit in the class information showed above will have to be made explicit using following 7 blocks of data elements:

1. Notation (classification number):

   tables from which notation is taken

   type of notation (simple or composed)

   notation structural elements/components

   relationships between elements: span, phase relationships

2. Broader class

3. Caption

4. Notes:

   Scope note

   Application (instruction) note

   Notation building notes and rules

   Rules for parallel division (derived from; divide)

   Rules for combination and expansion (add, specify by)

   Examples of combination

   Notation history note (replaces, replaced by)

   General content note

   Editorial note

5. References (See also)

6. Class ID (unique identifier of a class)

7. Index (search) terms (keywords)

We can think of these blocks of data as a standard container that we have available to record more detailed information from a specific system."

3.2. Division of Classes

The division of classes must be step by step, that is, by one characteristic at a time. There are two approaches to the division of classes, namely enumerative and faceted. Historically bibliographic classifications have followed enumerative systems in which classes and subclasses have been deduced top down, moving hierarchically from general to specific; this may be called gradation by specialty. This gradual division takes the shape of a funnel. Today, faceted approach prevails.

3.2.1. Enumerative Approach

Enumerative classifications typically start out with a hierarchical structure and list or enumerate concepts within it. Enumerative classifications list or enumerate all possible topics of interest (subclasses) of a particular class in top-down manner. The enumerative method has the following problems (Buchannan, 1979, pp. 105-118):

1. Successive divisions can only properly cover one type of relationship, i.e., hierarchical.

2. Successive subdivisions of classes may be carried unnecessarily, ignoring the literary warrant. Some topics may get repeated under different arrays. That may lead to cross classification.

Enumerative systems today are almost out of fashion, giving way to the faceted approach. It has been said that enumerative systems such as the LCC are not culturally hospitable, since their main goal is to find a place, rather a pigeonhole, for each subject, rather than to build a coherent structure (Kwasnik & Rubin, 2010, p. 42).

On the other hand, the faceted approach may not be clear in representing the structure of knowledge in a specific area. Rather, the enumerative structure might be better in representing the structure of knowledge (e.g., DDC and LCC).

Rowley and Farrow (2000) summarize some of the advantages of enumerative classifications as follow:

- "[Although] there is a temptation to dismiss enumerative classification as antiquated and inflexible, [...] Dewey Decimal Classification and LCC go back a long way and have solid institutional support" (pp. 199-200).

- "Perhaps the strongest inherent advantage of enumerative classification is that it is constructed and displayed in a way that can be intuitively understood" (p. 200).

Indeed, enumerative systems are easy to operate, and for a static universe of knowledge these are the best choice. Alas, there is no such universe of knowledge which is static.

3.2.2. Faceted Approach

However, the impossibility of enumerating all compound and complex subjects and the awareness of the inefficiently enumerative nature of the DDC led Ranganathan to invent the faceted approach for his Colon Classification (Ranganathan, 1989, p. 3). As Vickery put it (1966): "A faceted classification differs from the traditional in that the facets so distinguished are not locked into rigid, enumerative schedules, but are left to combine with each other in the fullest freedom, so that every type of relation between terms and between subjects may be expressed" (p. 13). Faceted classifications are constructed in what can be considered an inductive, bottom-up manner in which the basic concepts are assigned to a few preordained categories or facets (although we also acknowledge that Ranganathan's facet-analytic approach has been argued to be rationalist, e.g., Hjørland, 2014, and thus deductive). In a faceted approach:

- Only isolated concepts assigned to a few ordained categories are listed in arrays and chains.
- Compound and complex classes are formed by synthesis only.
- Classification is easily hospitable to new subjects. This hospitality is multidimensional.
- Class numbers are customized to be co-extensive with the subject of the document.
- Structure of subject is transparent.
- Schedules of subjects are short and slim, but their class number turning capacity is almost infinite.

According to Broughton (2006) some of the advantages of faceted classifications over enumerative classifications include:

- If the structure has a specified order of combination, or citation order, it can be populated with combinations of attributes to generate a more complex structure very similar to an enumerative classification, but with a more rigorous and logical pattern to it (p. 52).
- With an accurate analysis, the members of an array in a faceted classification are all mutually exclusive classes, while enumerative systems on the other hand often produce groupings of classes that are not mutually exclusive (p. 54).
- Where a faceted classification differs most significantly from an enumerative classification is in its potential to combine terms from different facets: the relationships between facets, and between terms from different facets – the inter-facet relationships (pp. 54-55).
- Faceted classification provides a source of vocabulary for the thesaurus; the very structure of the classification helps the identification of the relationships between terms that is essential to the thesaurus. On the other hand, the enumerative classification and its "top-down" [approach] might not be ideal for clearly identifying relationships (pp.

59-60).

As for the Web, it is said that the logical and predictable structure of the faceted system undoubtedly makes it compatible with the requirements of mechanization in a way that enumerative and pre-coordinated systems are not (p. 61). In the Web environment classification is passing through its second golden age.

3.3. Relations in Library Classification

Classification is all about relations. The classification process is essentially correlating or discovering relations between two entities. There are two types of relations, both displayed or inherent, in the classification schedules.

3.3.1. Semantic Relations

Semantic relations are hierarchical, cognate, collocative, and filial. The arrangement of the main classes and their subdivisions into arrays and chains are semantic relations which are deemed helpful to the users. For the arrangement of subclasses in an array, Ranganathan prescribes eight principles of helpful sequence such as chronological arrangement, geographical arrangement, evolutionary arrangement, conventional arrangement, and so on. Hierarchy arranges entities from general to specific, or from whole to parts.

3.3.2. Syntactic Relations

These are grammatical relations among the components/facets of a compound subject. In other words, these relations are governed by citation order. Ranganathan postulated a grand but broader formula in the form of PMEST (Personality, Matter, Energy, Space, Time) in which the facets are arranged in the order of their decreasing concreteness. To arrange facets within Rounds and Levels, Ranganathan formulated an over-arching Wall-Picture principle, which is an analogical name for a dependency principle. Other such picturesque principles that he formulated are the Cow-Calf, and the Whole-Organ principles to arrange facets in a logical order (Ranganathan & Gopinath, 1989, pp. 97-102). The BC-2/CRG also formulated a detailed itemized citation formula which is comprehensive of possible facets in abstract and is free of the confusing concept of Rounds and Levels. This is: Thing-Kind-Part-Property-Material-Process-Operation-Patient-Product-Byproduct-Agent-Space-Time

(Hunter, 2009, pp. 89-93). This formula bypasses the mazy and confusing act of arrangement of entities in Rounds and Levels and it is much simpler. In the 1960s S. R. Ranganathan (1967, pp. 579-582) tried in vain to establish an Absolute Syntax of facets.

3.3.3. Principle of Inversion

The citation order prescribes an arrangement of facets from specific to general, or concrete to abstract. But the arrangement of documents on the shelves or entries in a catalog is in a pedagogical order of general to specific, i.e., in the reverse order of the citation of facets. This general to special order on the shelves is achieved by manipulating the ordinal value of notational digits and indicator digits. In the UDC, the auxiliary facets are arranged in tables 1c-1k, which are in general to specific order, but these are applied in the 1k-1c order. So is the case with the PMEST order of Colon Classification, and hence the inversion (Mills, 1962, pp. 54-64). The inversion principle is embedded in the retroactive notation of the BC-2. Within the overall general to specific order there are four sub-orders:

General treated generally
General treated specially
Special treated generally
Special treated specially

3.4. Main Classes

In both systems the first division is by broad classes called main classes. All current classifications base their main classes on divisions by discipline. Barbara Kyle experimented in vain to design a classification system for social sciences without the notion of main classes. Although arbitrary, there seems no alternative to them. A discipline is a broader division of the universe of knowledge which gives context to the phenomena. Main classes form the first order array of the division of universe of knowledge. These, being conventional, are postulated a bit arbitrarily by the designer of the system (Palmer, 1962, pp. 25-35). The number of main classes and boundaries vary from system to system and from time to time. There are ten main classes in the DDC, 21 in the LCC, and more than 700 in the CC-7.

3.4.1. Generalia Class

As its name implies, this is the general works class

provided to accommodate such books as general encyclopedias, newspapers, magazines, and other poly-topical books, or form classes such as serials, manuscripts, museums, anthologies which cover knowledge in general, or such a portion of it that is impossible to place under any other main class in the schedules. This hold-all class is an essential feature of book classifications. Its place precedes the disciplinary divided subjects.

In providing places for works which on account of their form do not specifically belong to any other main class, the Generalia class may be considered a form class. In its practical form, however, those subjects dealing with varied knowledge cannot be considered as a rigid form class. Thus a Generalia class is more than a form class.

The outline of the Generalia class in the Dewey Decimal Classification is:

000 Knowledge & Systems
010 Bibliographies
020 Library & Information Science
030 Encyclopedias and Books of Facts
050 Magazines, Journals, & Serials
060 Associations, Organizations, & Museums
070 Newspapers, Journalism, & Publishing
080 Quotations, Anthologies
090 Manuscripts and Rare Books

3.4.2. Form Divisions

A book on any particular subject may deal with that subject in various ways, from different viewpoints or in different forms. This may be an encyclopedia, a dictionary, a periodical, an advanced or elementary treatise, or it may be written as history, philosophy, in essay, or another literary form of the subject covered. Books on almost every subject frequently fall into one of these categories. Many schemes recognize their generality of application by converting them into common subdivisions, i.e., a constant set (by name and notation) of divisions which can be used to qualify any subject listed in the schedules. All bibliographical classifications make provisions for such aspects of books by the addition of the so-called (auxiliary) form divisions, or common divisions. In the DDC, such form divisions are now termed as standard subdivisions as given in Table 1 of Volume 1, e.g.,

-01 Theory & Philosophy
-02 Handbooks, etc.

-03 Alphabetical Reference Works
-05 Serial Publications
-06 Conference Proceedings
-07 Study, Teaching, & Research
-08 Anthologies
-09 History, Biography, etc.

These divisions can be added to specify any class number in the schedules. Similar provisions exist in all other library classifications.

3.4.3. Form vs. Subject

Many of the terms representing these forms also correspond to terms used in the main schedules for specific subjects. There is, however, a distinct difference in their meaning and implication. In the main schedules, the terms are used to represent recognized subjects from the field of knowledge, e.g., the Encyclopedia Britannica has the class number 032 in DDC. Similar terms used in the form divisions represent either a special way in which a book is written and produced, or an aspect from which the subject is viewed. In other words, it is not the subject but a subject qualifier. Hence these cannot be used alone. Form divisions are exclusive to a library classification; they form the generalia divisions of a specific class. In practice, these divisions enable a further, more detailed, and convenient grouping of books by format or form to be made on the shelves (Philips, 1961, p. 38). All the dictionaries of science will come together, as do all the histories of science.

3.5. Devices for Synthesis and Phase Relations

A schedule, always equipped with many notes, instructions, devices, and techniques, is more than a systematic list of subjects. These notes and such are for the uniformity of application of these entries, for what is called inter-indexer consistency. These instructions and devices make the system a mint for forging new class numbers for unforeseen subjects of the future. To a classifier, it is a joy and a feeling of accomplishment to synthesize numbers. In a system like the DDC or the UDC, the minted or synthesized numbers may be much more than the explicitly listed numbers. The UDC uses + / : : [ ] : for combination of subjects, e.g.,

3+5   Social Sciences and Natural Sciences
5/6   Science and Technology

2:5   Religion and Science (Relation)
[5+6](05) Journal of Science and Technology

These are devices for classifying interdisciplinary or composite subjects which are in *ad hoc* relations. This type of synthesis is much more sophisticated and detailed in CC and BC-2.

4. NOTATION

A classification notation is a series of codes or symbols which denotes the names of a class or any division or subdivision of a class. Notation forms a convenient means of reference to the arrangement of a classification. Although notation is an important addition to a classification schedule, in no way does it determine its logic, its scope, or its sequence of development. It just furnishes a convenient reference to the arrangement of a classification. The notation is not assigned until the schedule has been worked out in the idea and verbal planes. Ranganathan harshly terms notation as a servant of the Idea Plane to implement the decision taken by the latter. In fact, it is the executive authority of the Idea Plane. Notation is the engine of library classification, far from being any menial servant. Notation itself is not the classification but an essential adjunct for a library classification. Without notation it would be impossible to apply classification to documents. As classification is the "foundation of librarianship," it can be said that notation is the visible structure of practical classification.

Summarizing its usefulness, a notation:

1. is a guide to the sequence of subjects. It places a term in the hierarchy of the schedules. A notation serves to denote the classes, their subdivisions, and the order in which these are arranged without in any way naming or defining them explicitly. It mechanizes the shelf arrangement when documents are replaced at their proper shelves after their use.

2. makes the mapping of knowledge quite visible.

3. helps to construct class numbers for compound and complex classes.

4. makes possible the use of the index. The symbol attached to an index entry is the only means of quick reference to the place of the topic in the schedules.

5. is used as a short sign to be written in various parts of the book—on the spine, back of title-page, ownership label, charging cards, etc.—to facilitate the arrangement of books on the shelves, the recording of issues, and other statistical information.

6. is the basis of chain indexing to derive standardized subject headings for the subject catalog.

The notation is that piece of apparatus without which a book classification cannot function.

4.1. The Qualities of an Ideal Notation

Some are essential and some only desirable. A notational system:

1. should convey order clearly and automatically;

2. should desirably be as brief, simple, and mnemonic as possible without compromising its efficacy; and

3. should be hospitable to new subjects, i.e., allowing insertions at any point without dislocating the existing subjects, and allowing a class to expand its boundaries without drastic reorganization. This is particularly true for the schedules of a book classification, which must be of a semi-permanent nature. Knowledge is growing turbulently since the mid-20th century. In the information and communications technology era, its speed of growth has become tremendous. All this knowledge must be assimilated, mapped, organized, and even reorganized. It is here that the hospitality of the notation is of paramount importance. Notation is the most essential quality for survival of a classification system. Among existing general classification the notation of BC-2 is an ideal.

4.2. Types of Notation

There are two types of notation by pedigree: pure and mixed. Pure notation is comprised of single species of digits, usually either numerals or alphabets. The DDC, which uses Indo-Arabic numerals, is the best example of a pure notation. RIC, which uses only A/Z, is another example of a pure notation. Pure notations, in the face of the growing knowledge and complexity of subjects, are no more possible to employ; their time is long gone by. Mixed notation is obviously comprised of two or more species of digits. Mixed notations can again be divided into two categories, of moderately or highly mixed. The LCC and BC-2, which use only

alphabets and numerals together, are considered ideal models of a library classification notation. The CC and UDC use highly mixed notations which are comprised of alphabets, numerals, punctuation marks, and so on. Moderately mixed notations are elegant and work effectively. The Library of Congress uses an alphabetical notation A-Z for the main classes; the subdivisions are denoted by a second sequence A-Z, and within these divisions a numerical span from 1 to 9999 is used. Gaps are left in between for expansion, e.g.,

U	Military Science
UB	Administration
200	Commanders. Generals
210	Command of Troops. Leadership
220-225	Staffs of Armies
230-235	Headquarters, Aides, etc.
240-245	Inspection. Inspectors
250	Intelligence
260	Attaches
270	Spies

Choice of a notational system can benefit or be detrimental to a classification. The DDC has thrived mostly due to its simple notation, while the CC is smarting under the weight of its highly mixed notation. In the present time, the alphanumeric notation of the BC-2 with all its synthetic devices is the most theoretically advanced system (Hjørland, 2013, p. 546).

4.3. Book Numbers

In a library classification, the class number alone is not able to provide a unique place to a document on the shelves (Satija, 2008, p. 1). For example, there may be many books on the History of Mughal India bearing exactly the same class number. If not further subdivided, there would be pockets of chaos on the shelves within the same group of subjects. For a proper and effective organization and location, those books having the same class number must be further divided granularly. The device to do this is called book number or author number. In the LCC and to some extent in the CC, the book number is a part of the class number. Book numbers usually employ two opposing techniques for sub arrangements: alphabetical by author/ title or chronological by the year of publication. The Library of Congress uses simplified Cutter author numbers as an integral part of the notation to provide a complete call number. DDC classified libraries usually use the Cutter-Sanborn author table to sub arrange books having the same class number by author. The CC further sub-arranges books having the same specific class numbers chronologically by the year of publication. There are numerous locally or home devised book numbering systems.

5. ALPHABETICAL INDEX

The index is an alphabetical list of the terms that are mentioned in the schedules and tables referring to their notations. The index usually includes, as far as possible, all the synonyms of these terms, together with some synthesized subjects even when they are not included in the schedules. The index is a labor-saving device assisting in the navigation across topics in the lengthy and mazy schedules. The index should be used only as an aid to, and not as a means of, classification. The principal virtue of the index is that it ensures that a subject will always be classified in the same place in the schedules. The index to the classification schedules has two purposes:
- to locate topics within the classification
- to bring together related aspects of a subject that appear in more than one place in the schedules, that is to collocate the distributed relatives of a subject. The index brings together what the schedules scatter.

There are two types of indexes:
1. Specific, which gives one entry only for each topic mentioned in the schedules in an alphabetically linear way.
2. Relative, which enumerates mentioned topics, all synonyms, and, to a great extent, shows the relation of each subject to other subjects. Perhaps the best example of a full relative index is that appended to the *Encyclopedia Britannica*, and to the DDC. The relative index of the DDC shows relations between subjects. The index of the Web-Dewey is even much more augmented. In fact, the relative index is a supplementary approach to knowledge organization by discipline. In the present era, all classifications divide knowledge by discipline.

The index of the DDC also includes a selection of synthesized subjects and provides their ready-made

full class numbers. This tempts some classifiers to classify by the index alone –which is something that every classification teacher advises against in the classroom. In the LCC, each class has its own separate index. Faceted classifications only need to index the simple concepts that appear in the schedules.

6. REVISION MACHINERY

Bibliographic classifications are born already out of date. Earlier, it took almost two years between the final editing and publication of a classification. Now, the use of computers has considerably reduced this turn-about time, yet lag is there. Classification systems are necessarily closed rather than open systems. Inserting a new topic at its proper place is not automatic, as it is with a list of subject headings: only a controlling body with technical expertise can determine the correct place of a new topic within the schedules and tables. This revision, update, and maintenance committee is a part of a larger governing body of the system. It has been experienced that classification systems such as Ranganathan's Colon Classification, J.D. Brown's Subject Classification, and C.A. Cutter's Expansive Classification have not survived mostly due to the absence of a body to keep the system current and relevant. There cannot be a self-perpetuating classification as Ranganathan (1949) vaunted of his CC. Most of the credit for the popularity of not-so scientific schemes such as the LCC and the DDC goes to their respective institutional support. These systems are revised regularly and have an assured backing of big institutions. Psychologically, it is also taken by the users as an assurance for the lifelong sustainability of the system. Patronizing libraries have a feeling that there is at least somebody to count on in case of need. It is a sort of after-sale service which every customer needs. This is what the editors of the DDC do under the guidance of the DC Editorial Policy Committee (DCEPC) and OCLC. The DDC/OCLC has gone on further to establish the European Dewey Users Group (EDUG), which discusses the problems of European Dewey users, especially for translation. The DDC has a world-class revision and promotion machinery. That is one of the open secrets of the ever increasing popularity of the DDC. The LCC has a similar assurance, although its revision body is domestic. The value of such an active body can be clearly known from the history of the UDC. The revision of the system was slow paced in the 1960s and 1970s as its parent body, the erstwhile FID, did not have sufficient resources for its progress and promotion. Since the 1980s, the establishment of the UDC Consortium (UDCC) and the appointment of the first full time editor in the person of Professor Ia C. McIlwaine gave it an impetus to the path of progress by leaps and bounds. With many new innovations, products, and services from a somewhat dormant entity, it has become a vibrant system in many ways. Hence, revision machinery is vital to the survival of a classification system (Curwen, 1978). Indeed the institutions are lengthening shadows of strong individuals.

An appurtenance to such bodies is the need of communicating with the users. The UDC had P-notes and the DDC had its irregularly regular DC&, that is, DDC Additions, Notes, and Decisions (AND). These devices communicated changes, conveyed news, and took questions from users. Now, this print media has been replaced by websites and the use of social media. The DDC has its regular blog. Regular communication with users is now easy and a must for its popularity.

7. INTRODUCTION

Though peripheral, the 'introduction' to the system is an integral part of it. It combines the preface, editorial, and instructions to operate the system. Of course it is written last of all like the preface to a book. The introduction outlines in brief the history of the system, its objectives, and purpose. Essentially, it is an operational manual of the system explaining its intricacies and giving tips on how-to-use. It should be simple, clear, and sufficiently illustrated. The DDC introduction has also a glossary of used terms and its separate index to refer back to the terms and concepts used therein and throughout. However, the introduction and notes given under the entries may not be sufficient to interpret and make the intended use of the system. It is not uncommon to see different classifiers interpreting a schedule entry in different ways –many notes appended to an entry notwithstanding. This affects the uniform use of the system, termed as inter-indexer inconsistency. This problem cannot be eliminated alto-

gether but can be minimized with an additional manual for the system. The DDC published such a manual (Comaromi, 1982) which is considered a landmark for a consistent application of the DDC in practice. Since the 20th edition of the DDC (1989), this manual has been included in the introduction, though in a separate section. Today, the introduction to the latest edition of the DDC can be consulted and downloaded at the OCLC website for free (https://www.oclc.org/content/dam/oclc/dewey/versions/print/intro.pdf). In the Colon Classification, the rules portion covers half of the core of the CC. This introduction is also well-illustrated with typical and exceptional rules. The introduction to the UDC that accompanies the tables in the first volume is also a key part of the system. It includes the complete auxiliary tables, instructions, and a summary of the classification. The introduction to the LCC also includes a preface and an outline of the different tables, or texts, that are grouped together. This information is available at the Library of Congress website.

8. SUMMING UP: FEATURES OF A LIBRARY CLASSIFICATION

1. A library classification should be comprehensive, covering the whole field of knowledge as represented in the books.
2. A library classification should be formulated with due regard to the literary warrant, aiming to provide a place for every type of subject and document.
3. A library classification should be systematic, proceeding from the general to the specific.
4. The arrangement of the classes and subdivisions should be made with constant regard for the main purpose of the library classification—the securing of a helpful order convenient to the majority of users.
5. The terms used must be clear and currently accompanied, where necessary, by full definitions. They must refer to the scope of the headings and be equipped with notes and instructions for the guidance of the classifier.
6. The notation of the library classification should be equitably apportioned and capable of allowing alternative locations for certain subjects or classes.

It should make a genuine provision for local variations.

7. The library classification should be equipped with:

a) generalia and form classes.

b) form and geographical common subdivisions.

c) an effective notation. The notation should fit the scheme (not the scheme to the notation) and may include mnemonic, and also synthetic and combinatory devices.

d) a detailed alphabetical index.

1. A library classification should be structurally expansive both in breadth and depth.

2. A library classification should be displayed in a form that is easy to handle and consult, so it can assist users grasping the hierarchy and the layout of the classes.

3. A library classification may have its own system of book numbers.

4. A library classification should be revised regularly, but not too frequently, by an editorial committee working under a governing body.

5. A library classification should have an introduction which explains the aim and purpose of the system, and also works as a concise manual for using the system.

6. A library classification should be maintained (and also made web accessible) as a machine readable database.

7. A library classification must have its website, a newsletter, and someone to answer the problems and questions of its users.

The components of a library classification are summarized in Fig. 1, including those that are external to the system and mainly related to its development, maintenance, and marketing (such as a governing body, an editorial committee, a Research & Development unit, the website and blog of the system, newsletters, and a directory of users); and the components that form the system itself (such as the schedules, auxiliary tables, notation, index, introduction to the system including a manual with example, devices for synthesis and phase relations, and so on).

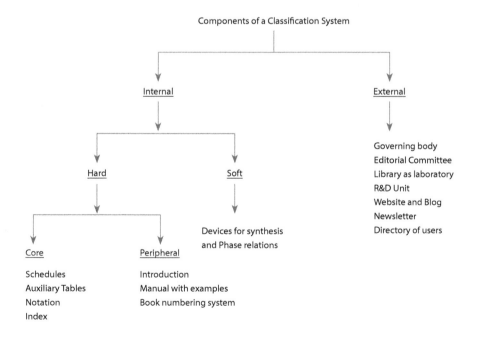

Fig. 1 Components of a classification system

9. CONCLUSION

In this paper, we have presented and systematized some features, functions, and components of a library classification system that are commonly discussed in the LIS traditional practices and published literature. However, these are not always considered for the new e-environments. Although we acknowledge the possibility of other competing approaches to classification (that by the way are also rarely considered in the e-environment), we have based our study on the description of those practices and features that have been commonly used and discussed in the most widely used library classification systems, such as the DDC, UDC, CC, BC-2, etc. Additional questions and possibilities for future studies might include the analysis of possible and practical scenarios in which different features might be applied to classifications such as the DDC and UDC, and the conditions of the practical viability of classifications such as CC and BC-2 to survive and adapt to the new environments.

ACKNOWLEDGMENTS

Thanks are due to Dr. Mrs. Ingetraut Dahlberg for her comments on the first draft of the paper. Dr. Dahlberg founded the International Society for Knowledge Organization in 1989 and remained its president till 1996. She is also the founding editor of the Journal *Knowledge Organization*, then named *International Classification*. We also profoundly thank the anonymous referees who gave valuable suggestions on the first two drafts of this paper.

REFERENCES

Broughton, V. (2006). The need for a faceted classification as the basis of all methods of information retrieval. *Aslib Proceedings: New Information Perspectives, 58* (1/2), 49-72.

Buchanan, B. (1979). *Theory of library classification.* London: Bingley.

Comaromi, J.P. (1982). *Manual on the use of the Dewey Decimal Classification, Edition 19.* Albany, NY: Forest Press.

Curwen, A.G. (1978). Revision of classification schemes: Policies and practices. *Journal of Librarianship, 10*(1), 19-38.

Hjørland, B. (2013). Facet analysis: The logical approach to knowledge organization. *Information Processing and Management, 40,* 545-557.

Hjørland, B. (2014). Is facet analysis based on rationalism? A discussion of Satija (1992), Tennis (2008), Herre (2013), Mazzocchi (2013b), and Dousa & Ibekwe-SanJuan (2014). *Knowledge Organization, 41,* 369-376.

Hunter, E.J. (2009). *Classification made simple* (3rd ed.). Burlington, VT: Ashgate Publishing.

Koch, T., Brümmer, A., Hiom, D., Peereboom, M., Poulter, A., & Worsfold, E. (1997). DESIRE: Project Deliverable. Retrieved from http://cordis.europa.eu/cybercafe/frames/25.htm

Kwaśnik, B.H. & Rubin, V.L. (2004). Stretching conceptual structures in classifications across languages and cultures. *Cataloging & Classification Quarterly, 37*(1), 33-47.

Maltby, A. (1978). *Sayers manual of classification for librarians* (5th ed.). London: Andre Deutsch.

Mills, J. (1962). *A modern outline of library classification.* Bombay: Asia.

Palmer, B. I. (1962). *Itself an education: Six lectures on classification.* London: The Library Association.

Philips, H.W. (1961). *A primer of book classification* (5th ed.). London: AAL.

Ranganathan, S.R. (1949). Self-perpetuating scheme of classification. *Journal of Documentation, 4,* 223-244.

Ranganathan, S.R. (1964). General and special classification: Papers presented to the second International Study Conference on Classification Research Elsinore, 1964. In P. A. Atherton (Ed.), *Classification research: Proceedings of the second International Study Conference, Elsinore, 14-18 Sept, 1965* (pp. 81-93). Copenhagen: Munksgaard, 1965.

Ranganathan, S.R. (1967). *Prolegomena to library classification* (3rd ed.). Mumbai: Asia.

Ranganathan, S.R. (1968). Choice of a scheme for classification. *Library Science Documentation, 5*(1), 1-69.

Ranganathan, S.R. (1989). *Elements of library classification.* New Delhi: UBSPD.

Ranganathan, S.R., & Gopinath, M.A. (1989). *Colon Classification* (Ed. 7, basic and depth version). Bangalore: Sarada Ranganathan Endowment for

Library Science.

Rowley, J., & Farrow, J. (2000). *Organizing knowledge: An introduction to managing access to information* (3rd ed.). Burlington, VT: Ashgate.

Rowley, J., & Hartley, R. (2008). *Organizing knowledge* (4th ed.). Burlington, VT: Ashgate.

Satija, M.P. (2008). *Book numbers: Indian and Cutter*. New Delhi: Viva Books.

Satija, M.P. (2013). *The theory and practice of the Dewey Decimal Classification* (2nd ed.). Oxford: Chandos.

Satija, M.P., & Martínez-Ávila, D. (2014). Use of classification in organizing and searching the web. *Annals of Library and Information Studies, 61*(4), 294-306.

Slavic, Aida. (2008). Faceted classification: Management and use. *Axiomathes, 18*(2), DOI: 10.1007/s10516-007-9030-z

Taylor, A.G., & Joudrey, D.N. (2009). *The organization of information* (3rd ed.). Westport, CT: Libraries Unlimited.

Vickery, B. C. (1966). *Faceted classification schemes*. New Brunswick, NJ: Graduate School of Library Service, Rutgers University.

Vickery, B.C. (1972). Classification principles in natural language indexing systems. In A. Maltby (Ed.), *Classification in the 1970's* (pp. 167-191). London: Clive Bingley.

FURTHER READINGS

Broughton, V. (2015). *Essential classification, 2nd. ed.* London: Facet.

Chan, L.M. (2007). *Cataloguing and classification: An introduction* (3rd ed.). Lanham, MD: Scarecrow Press, pp. 309-318.

Foskett, A.C. (1996). *The subject approach to information* (5th ed.). London LA Publishing, pp. 253-255.

Kumar, K. (2004). *The theory of classification*. New Delhi: Vikas, pp. 388-408.

Kumbhar. R. (2011). *Library classification trends in the 21st Century*. Oxford: Chandos.

Palmer, B.I., & Wells, A.J. (1951). *The fundamentals of library classification*. London: George Allen, pp. 60-75.

Satija, M.P. (2000). Classification: An essay in terminology. *Knowledge Organization, 27*(4), 221-229.

Satija, M.P. (2004). *A dictionary of knowledge organization*. Amritsar: Guru Nanak Dev University.

14

Modeling the Growth of Neurology Literature

Gururaj S. Hadagali *
Department of Library and Information Science
Karnataka University, Dharwad, Karnataka, India
E-mail: gururajhadagali123@gmail.com

Gavisiddappa Anandhalli
Department of Library and Information Science
Karnataka State Women's University, Bijapur, Karnataka, India
E-mail: gavi.vijju@gmail.com

ABSTRACT

The word 'growth' represents an increase in actual size, implying a change of state. In science and technology, growth may imply an increase in number of institutions, scientists, or publications, etc. The present study demonstrates the growth of neurology literature for the period 1961-2010. A total of 291,702 records were extracted from the Science Direct Database for fifty years. The Relative Growth Rate (RGR) and Doubling Time (Dt.) of neurology literature have been calculated, supplementing with different growth patterns to check whether neurology literature fits exponential, linear, or logistic models. The results of the study indicate that the growth of literature in neurology does not follow the linear, or logistic growth model. However, it follows closely the exponential growth model. The study concludes that there has been a consistent trend towards increased growth of literature in the field of neurology.

Keywords: Exponential Model, Growth Models, Linear Model, Logistic Model, Modeling, Neurology, Relative Growth Rate, Scientometrics

1. INTRODUCTION

One of the features of modern research in recent years has been the spectacular development of scientif- ic discoveries and growth of knowledge, say Gupta et al. (2002). This has caused an unprecedented accumu- lation of information and has become a major concern for scientists and researchers (Meera & Sangam, 2010).

*Corresponding Author: Gururaj S. Hadagali
Assistant Professor
Department of Library and Information Science
Karnataka University, India
E-mail: gururajhadagali123@gmail.com

Hence, there is a need to study the growth of scientific knowledge and its dynamics in every field of activity.

The word 'growth' represents an increase in actual size, implying a change of state. In science and technology, growth may imply an increase in number of institutions, scientists, or publications, etc. Ravichandra Rao (1998) says that a change in the size of literature over a specific period of time is termed as 'growth of literature.' One of the features of modern research in the twenty-first century has been the unprecedented and spectacular development in scientific inventions, discoveries, and the growth of knowledge. This has caused an unexpected accumulation of information (Gupta et al., 2002). Hence, there is a need to study this growth of knowledge and its dynamics. Price (1966 & 1975) was one of the pioneering researchers who studied the growth of science and found that the exponential model holds well with high accuracy in the majority of growth data of publications. The fitting of growth models, distributions, and curves to the data on exponentially growing literature and identifying the best fitting one to explain the growth of literature is an important aspect of growth study. The present study is aimed to study the growth of neurology literature published in the Science Direct database.

2. REVIEW OF LITERATURE

The understanding of the process of growth of knowledge in research specialties and its modeling has challenged bibliometricians and sociologists for a long time, say Gupta et al. (1997). Gilberts' (1978) work reveals the existing literature on the indicators of growth of knowledge in scientific specialties and lists many ways of measuring it. The analysis of Gupta et al. (1999) suggests that the growth of Indian physics literature follows a logistic model, while the growth of world physics literature is explained by the combination of logistic and power models.

Seetharam and Ravichandra Rao (1999) in their work compare trends in the growth of Food Science and Technology (FST) literature produced by CFTRI scientists, by food scientists in India, and by food scientists of the world, covering a period between 1950 and 1990. Further, the authors identify the best fitting growth models for actual and cumulative growth of

data through various growth models. Different approaches are introduced by Gupta and Karisiddappa (2000) in their paper for studying the growth of scientific knowledge as reflected through publications and authors. The selected growth models are applied to the cumulative growth of publications and authors in theoretical population genetics from 1907-1980. It is concluded that the power model is observed to be the only model among the models studied which best explains the cumulative growth of publication and author counts in theoretical population genetics.

Karki et al. (2000) investigate Indian Organic Chemistry research activity during 1971-1989 using Chemical Abstracts. The authors conclude that the growth trends for India and world for organic chemistry follow the same patterns and the output in the three sub-fields is not going to saturate in the near future. Gupta et al. (2002) apply selected growth models to the growth of publications in six sub-disciplines of social sciences, namely economics, history, political science, psychology, and sociology in the world. The results show that the power model ($\alpha>0$, $\gamma>1$) followed by logistic models are best describing the cumulative growth of publications in all sub-disciplines. Both power and logistic models are applicable: the power model (as reflected in trend values of $\alpha1$) and logistic model (as reflected in trend values of $\alpha2$) in the case of cumulative growth of publications in history, political sciences, and psychology.

Tsay (2008) explores the characteristics of hydrogen energy literature from 1965-2005 based on the database of Science Citation Index Expanded (SCIE). The study reveals that the cumulative literature on hydrogen energy may be fitted relatively well by an exponential fit. Szydlowski and Krawiec (2009) present a description of knowledge more realistic than simple exponential growth. The study also reveals that the data on symbolic logic exhibit an exponential trend with some periodic oscillation. Ramakrishna (2009) examines the growth of references over the past fifteen years (1994-2008). The results show that the linear growth model provides better fits to the observed data, whereas the exponential model provided the poorest fit.

Sangam et al. (2010) study the growth and dynamics of Indian and Chinese publications in the field of liquid crystals research (1997-2006) by applying growth models as suggested by Egghe and Ravichandra Rao (1992). The authors conclude that these power and growth models are likely to be fully applicable in the growth of Indian, and linear, power, and growth models applicable in the growth of Chinese liquid crystals literature. Bouabid (2011) proposes a model which is proved to be suitable to represent observed citation distribution over time and to interestingly identify with accuracy when the major loss of citations happens. The model fits the observed data from Science Citation Index (SCI) according to R^2 which is greater than 98.9 %. Zhao and Guan (2012) assess the dynamic associations between scientific activity and technological output. The authors use the simultaneous equations model to analyze the reciprocal dependence between science and technology. The result shows that there is no significant connection between R&D expenditures and actual practices of research in terms of publications.

3. OBJECTIVES OF THE STUDY

The specific objectives of the study are

1. to study the growth of neurology literature (RGR) and also compare the growth rate as reflected in the Science Direct database among the world, China, and India.
2. to examine the Doubling Time (Dt.) of the neurology literature.
3. to analyze the fit of neurology literature for cumulative numbers of publications in terms of different models.

4. DATA AND METHODOLOGY

The dataset was collected from the Science Direct database for the period 1961-2010. A total of 291,702 records were received for fifty years. Science Direct is one of the most comprehensive database covering all subjects. Most of the research output on neurology is covered under the Science Direct Database. Hence, the same database is selected as a source for the present study. The keyword 'neurology' has been used for extracting the number of records available in the said database. The retrieved records were examined, classified, and analyzed keeping the objectives in view. Further, the data is analyzed using MS Excel spreadsheet and SPSS software (15th version). Relative Growth Rate

(RGR) and Doubling Time (Dt.) of neurology literature have been calculated, supplementing with different growth patterns to check whether the neurology literature is fit for exponential, linear, or logistic models.

Relative Growth Rate (RGR) and Doubling Time (Dt.)

The Relative Growth Rate (RGR) is the increase in number of articles / pages per unit of time. This definition is derived from the definition of relative growth rates in the study of growth analysis of individual plants and is effectively applied in the field of botany (Hunt, 1978 & 1982; Poorter & Garnier, 1996; Hoffmann & Poorter, 2002). The mean Relative Growth Rate (RGR) over the specific period of interval can be calculated from the following equation:

$$1\text{-}2\,R = \frac{\log_{e2} W - \log_{e1} W}{2^T - 1^T}$$

Whereas

1-2 R = mean relative growth rate over the specific period of interval

$\log_{e1} W$ = log of initial number of articles

$\log_{e2} W$ = log of final number of articles after a specific period of interval

$2^T - 1^T$ = the unit difference between the initial time and the final time

Doubling Time (Dt.)

There exists a direct equivalence between the relative growth rate and the doubling time (Bradford, 1934). If the number of articles / pages of a subject double during a given period then the difference between the logarithms of numbers at the beginning and end of this period must be logarithms of number 2. If natural logarithm is used this difference has a value of 0.693. Thus, the corresponding doubling time for each specific period of interval and for both articles and pages can be calculated by the formula;

$$\text{Doubling Time (Dt.)} = \frac{0.693}{R}$$

5. RESULTS AND DISCUSSION

5.1. Year Wise Distribution of Literature (1961-2010)

Table 1 depicts the year wise distribution of papers in neurology literature. The world output in neurology literature is 286,001 (98.05 %) records and that of China is 3,730 (1.28 %), followed by India with 1,971 (0.68 %) records. A total of 291,702 records were extracted from the database for the period 1961-2010. It is observed that there is a steady growth of publications for world (except 1997) and China. A fluctuating trend was observed for India during the study period. An average of 5,720 papers were published per year at the global level, followed by China's average at 74 and India's average at 39. The maximum world contribution is observed during 2009 (20,656 publications) and those of China and India were published during 2010 (769 and 219, respectively). China took 24 years to achieve double digit numbers of publications, whereas India took twelve years to achieve the same. However, China took only 20 years to achieve three-digit numbers of publications but India took 33 years to achieve the same. The Relative Growth Rate (RGR) and Doubling Time (Dt.) of China, India, and world is calculated and presented in successive tables.

Table 1. Year-Wise Distribution of Literature (1961-2010)

Sl. No.	Year	World		India		China		Total	
		No. of articles	Percent-age	No. of articles	Percent-age	No. of articles	Percent-age	No. of articles	Percent-age
1	1961	400	0.14	5	0.26	0	0	405	0.14
2	1962	395	0.14	2	0.11	0	0	397	0.14
3	1963	473	0.17	4	0.21	0	0	477	0.17
4	1964	624	0.22	2	0.11	0	0	626	0.22
5	1965	709	0.25	2	0.11	1	0.03	712	0.25
6	1966	673	0.24	1	0.06	0	0	674	0.24
7	1967	783	0.28	0	0	1	0.03	784	0.27
8	1968	870	0.31	4	0.21	0	0	874	0.3
9	1969	926	0.33	6	0.31	0	0	932	0.32
10	1970	1,083	0.38	4	0.21	1	0.03	1,088	0.38
11	1971	1,169	0.41	5	0.26	3	0.09	1,177	0.41
12	1972	1,212	0.43	9	0.46	2	0.06	1,223	0.42
13	1973	1,351	0.48	10	0.51	1	0.03	1,362	0.47
14	1974	1,428	0.5	9	0.46	1	0.03	1,438	0.5
15	1975	1,682	0.59	12	0.61	0	0	1,694	0.59
16	1976	1,790	0.63	11	0.56	1	0.03	1,802	0.62
17	1977	1,846	0.65	11	0.56	0	0	1,857	0.64
18	1978	2,046	0.72	9	0.46	1	0.03	2,056	0.71
19	1979	2,168	0.76	10	0.51	4	0.11	2,182	0.75

20	1980	2,488	0.87	13	0.66	4	0.11	2,505	0.86
21	1981	2,839	1.00	18	0.92	3	0.09	2,860	0.99
22	1982	3,264	1.15	13	0.66	6	0.17	3,283	1.13
23	1983	3,535	1.24	15	0.77	6	0.17	3,556	1.22
24	1984	3,567	1.25	21	1.07	8	0.22	3,596	1.24
25	1985	3,962	1.39	18	0.92	17	0.46	3,997	1.38
26	1986	4,110	1.44	16	0.82	12	0.33	4,138	1.42
27	1987	4,708	1.65	25	1.27	13	0.35	4,746	1.63
28	1988	4,496	1.58	25	1.27	15	0.41	4,536	1.56
29	1989	4,852	1.7	19	0.97	16	0.43	4,887	1.68
30	1990	5,397	1.89	18	0.92	21	0.57	5,436	1.87
31	1991	5,696	2.00	25	1.27	22	0.59	5,743	1.97
32	1992	6,106	2.14	21	1.07	22	0.59	6,149	2.11
33	1993	5,708	2.00	30	1.53	27	0.73	5,765	1.98
34	1994	6,904	2.42	36	1.83	26	0.7	6,966	2.39
35	1995	6,842	2.4	36	1.83	32	0.86	6,910	2.37
36	1996	7,442	2.61	43	2.19	29	0.78	7,514	2.58
37	1997	11,698	4.1	44	2.24	39	1.05	11,781	4.04
38	1998	7,847	2.75	50	2.54	39	1.05	7,936	2.73
39	1999	8,207	2.87	39	1.98	68	1.83	8,314	2.86
40	2000	8,964	3.14	62	3.15	56	1.51	9,082	3.12
41	2001	8,692	3.04	45	2.29	69	1.85	8,806	3.02
42	2002	9,388	3.29	65	3.3	82	2.2	9,535	3.27
43	2003	11,374	3.98	71	3.61	131	3.52	11,576	3.97
44	2004	12,586	4.41	93	4.72	153	4.11	12,832	4.4
45	2005	15,115	5.29	89	4.52	203	5.45	15,407	5.29
46	2006	15,153	5.3	149	7.56	271	7.27	15,573	5.34
47	2007	16,366	5.73	163	8.27	420	11.27	16,949	5.82
48	2008	17,183	6.01	165	8.38	529	14.19	17,877	6.13
49	2009	20,656	7.23	209	10.61	606	16.25	21,471	7.37
50	2010	19,228	6.73	219	11.12	769	20.62	20,216	6.94
	Total	286,001 (98.05)	100	1,971 (0.68)	100	3,730 (1.28)	100	291,702 (100)	100

Table 2. Descriptive Statistics of Neurology Literature

Descriptive Statistics	World	India	China
Mean	5,720	39.42	74.6
Standard Error	766.51	7.5276	23.212
Standard Deviation	5420	53.228	164.13
Range	20,261	219	769
Minimum	395	0	0
Maximum	20,656	219	769
Confidence Level (95.0%)	1,540.4	15.127	46.646
Kurtosis	0.635	4.098	8.622
Skewness	1.205	2.162	2.976

5.2. Relative Growth Rate (RGR) and Doubling Time (Dt.) (India)

The Relative Growth Rate (RGR) and Doubling Time (Dt.) of publications in India have been presented in Table 3. It indicates that the value of Relative Growth Rate (RGR) of publications decreased from 0.337 in the year 1962 to 0.119 in 2010. Simultaneously, the values of Doubling Time (Dt.) increased from 2.056 in 1962 to 5.823 in 2010. It is evident from the study that research in the field of neurology in India has increased over a period of time.

5.3. Relative Growth Rate (RGR) and Doubling Time (Dt.) (China)

The Relative Growth Rate (RGR) and Doubling Time (Dt.) of publications in China have been presented in Table 4. The study reveals that the value of RGR of publications decreased from 0.693 in 1967 to 0.231 in the year 2010. However, the values of Doubling Time (Dt.) increased from 1.00 in 1967 to 3.00 in 2010. It is also observed from the study that research in the field of neurology in China has increased over a period of time.

6. GROWTH MODELS OF NEUROLOGY LITERATURE

The authors briefly introduce three growth models,

viz. the Linear Growth Model, the Exponential Growth Model, and the Logistic Growth Model, which are generally used in the literature for analyzing the growth of literature in different subjects.

6.1. Linear Growth Model

The Linear Growth Model describes growth to be constant or similar from year to year. Thus, a graphic representation of the yearly data accumulated would be a straight line.

Hypothesis 1

The growth of publications in the field of neurology literature follows the Linear Growth Model.

Testing of Hypothesis

To find out the growth pattern in the field of neurology literature, publications over the last fifty years (1961-2010) were considered as a sample for the analysis in order to fit the data to test whether the growth of literature in neurology follows the Linear Growth pattern or not. The expected numbers of publications (y) or (p) were computed using the following formula:

$Y = a + b^x$

Where a and b are constants

X is the unit of time

Inference

The results of a Chi-Square test of goodness of fit

Table 3. Relative Growth Rate (RGR) and Doubling Time (Dt.) (India)

Sl. No.	Year	No. of publications	Cumulative no. of publications	W 1	W 2	RGR	Dt. (P)
1	1961	05	05		1.609		
2	1962	02	07	1.609	1.946	0.337	2.056
3	1963	04	11	1.946	2.398	0.452	1.533
4	1964	02	13	2.398	2.565	0.167	4.149
5	1965	02	15	2.565	2.708	0.143	4.846
6	1966	01	16	2.708	2.772	0.064	10.828
7	1967	00	16	2.772	2.772	0.000	00.00
8	1968	04	20	2.772	2.995	0.223	3.107
9	1969	06	26	2.995	3.258	0.263	2.635
10	1970	04	30	3.258	3.401	0.143	4.846
11	1971	05	35	3.401	3.555	0.154	4.500
12	1972	09	44	3.555	3.784	0.229	3.026
13	1973	10	54	3.784	3.988	0.204	3.397
14	1974	09	63	3.988	4.143	0.155	4.471
15	1975	12	75	4.143	4.317	0.174	3.982
16	1976	11	86	4.317	4.454	0.137	5.058
17	1977	11	97	4.454	4.574	0.120	5.775
18	1978	09	106	4.574	4.663	0.089	7.786
19	1979	10	116	4.663	4.753	0.090	7.700
20	1980	13	129	4.753	4.859	0.106	6.537
21	1981	18	147	4.859	4.990	0.131	5.290
22	1982	13	160	4.990	5.075	0.085	8.153
23	1983	15	175	5.075	5.164	0.089	7.786
24	1984	21	196	5.164	5.278	0.114	6.078
25	1985	18	214	5.278	5.366	0.088	7.875
26	1986	16	230	5.366	5.438	0.072	9.625
27	1987	25	255	5.438	5.541	0.103	6.728
28	1988	25	280	5.541	5.634	0.093	7.451
29	1989	19	299	5.634	5.700	0.066	10.500
30	1990	18	317	5.700	5.759	0.059	11.745
31	1991	25	342	5.759	5.835	0.076	9.118
32	1992	21	363	5.835	5.894	0.059	11.745
33	1993	21	384	5.894	5.950	0.056	12.375

34	1994	30	414	5.950	6.026	0.076	9.118
35	1995	36	450	6.026	6.109	0.083	8.349
36	1996	43	493	6.109	6.200	0.091	7.615
37	1997	44	537	6.200	6.200	0.086	8.058
38	1998	50	587	6.286	6.375	0.089	7.786
39	1999	39	626	6.375	6.439	0.064	10.828
40	2000	62	688	6.439	6.534	0.095	7.294
41	2001	45	733	6.534	6.597	0.063	11.000
42	2002	65	798	6.597	6.682	0.085	8.153
43	2003	71	869	6.682	6.767	0.085	8.153
44	2004	93	962	6.767	6.869	0.102	6.794
45	2005	89	1,051	6.869	6.957	0.088	7.875
46	2006	149	1,200	6.957	7.090	0.133	5.210
47	2007	163	1,363	7.090	7.217	0.127	5.456
48	2008	165	1,528	7.217	7.332	0.115	6.026
49	2009	209	1,737	7.332	7.459	0.127	5.456
50	2010	219	1,956	7.459	7.578	0.119	5.823

Table 4. Relative Growth Rate (RGR) and Doubling Time (Dt.) (China)

Sl. No.	Year	No. of publications	Cumulative no. of publications	W 1	W 2	RGR	Dt. (P)
1	1961	00	00		00		
2	1962	00	00	00	00	00	00
3	1963	00	00	00	00	00	00
4	1964	00	00	00	00	00	00
5	1965	01	01	00	00	00	00
6	1966	00	01	00	00	00	00
7	1967	01	02	00	0.693	0.693	1.00
8	1968	00	02	0.693	0.693	00	00
9	1969	00	02	0.693	0.693	00	00
10	1970	01	03	0.693	1.098	0.405	1.711
11	1971	03	06	1.098	1.791	0.693	1.00
12	1972	02	08	1.791	2.079	0.288	2.406
13	1973	01	09	2.079	2.197	0.118	2.406
14	1974	01	10	2.197	2.302	0.105	6.600

15	1975	00	10	2.302	2.302	00	00
16	1976	01	11	2.302	2.397	0.095	7.294
17	1977	00	11	2.397	2.397	00	00
18	1978	01	12	2.397	2.485	0.088	7.875
19	1979	04	16	2.485	2.772	0.287	2.414
20	1980	04	20	2.772	2.995	0.223	3.107
21	1981	03	23	2.995	3.135	0.140	4.950
22	1982	06	29	3.135	3.367	0.232	2.987
23	1983	06	35	3.367	3.555	0.188	3.686
24	1984	08	43	3.555	3.761	0.206	3.364
25	1985	17	60	3.761	4.094	0.333	2.081
26	1986	12	72	4.094	4.276	0.182	2.807
27	1987	13	85	4.276	4.442	0.166	4.174
28	1988	15	100	4.442	4.605	0.163	4.251
29	1989	16	116	4.605	4.753	0.148	4.682
30	1990	21	137	4.753	4.919	0.166	4.174
31	1991	22	159	4.919	5.068	0.149	4.651
32	1992	22	181	5.068	5.198	0.130	5.330
33	1993	27	208	5.198	5.337	0.139	4.985
34	1994	26	234	5.337	5.455	0.118	5.872
35	1995	32	266	5.455	5.583	0.128	5.414
36	1996	29	295	5.583	5.687	0.104	6.663
37	1997	39	334	5.687	5.811	0.124	5.588
38	1998	39	373	5.811	5.921	0.110	6.300
39	1999	68	441	5.921	6.089	0.168	4.125
40	2000	56	497	6.089	6.208	0.119	5.823
41	2001	69	566	6.208	6.338	0.130	5.330
42	2002	82	648	6.338	6.474	0.136	5.095
43	2003	131	779	6.474	6.658	0.184	3.766
44	2004	153	932	6.658	6.837	0.179	3.871
45	2005	203	1,135	6.837	7.034	0.197	3.517
46	2006	271	1,406	7.034	7.248	0.214	3.238
47	2007	420	1,826	7.248	7.509	0.261	2.655
48	2008	529	2,355	7.509	7.764	0.255	2.717
49	2009	606	2,961	7.764	7.993	0.229	3.026
50	2010	769	3,730	7.993	8.224	0.231	3.000

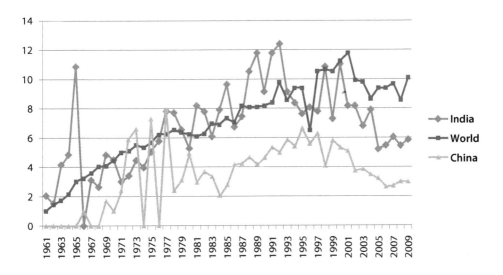

Fig. 1 Doubling time of Neurology literature

Table 5. Fit into Linear Growth of Neurology Literature

X	Year	Observed no. of publications Y (f)	XY	X^2	Expected no. of publications P $Y = a + b^x$	f-p	$(f-p)^2$	$\dfrac{(f-p)^2}{p}$
1	1961	405	405	1	-2,740.1	3,145.1	9,891,654	-3,610
2	1962	397	794	4	-2,390.2	2,787.2	7,768,484	-3,250.1
3	1963	477	1,431	9	-2,040.3	2,517.3	6,336,799	-3,105.8
4	1964	626	2,504	16	-1,690.4	2,316.4	5,365,709	-3,174.2
5	1965	712	3,560	25	-1,340.5	2,052.5	4,212,756	-3,142.7
6	1966	674	4,044	36	-990.6	1,664.6	2,770,893	-2,797.2
7	1967	784	5,488	49	-640.7	1,424.7	2,029,770	-3,168.1
8	1968	874	6,992	64	-290.8	1,164.8	1,356,759	-4,665.6
9	1969	932	8,388	81	59.1	872.9	761,954	12,892.6
10	1970	1,088	10,880	100	409	679	461,041	1,127.24
11	1971	1,177	12,947	121	758.9	418.1	174,808	230.343
12	1972	1,223	14,676	144	1,108.8	114.2	13,041.6	11.7619
13	1973	1,362	17,706	169	1,458.7	-96.7	9,350.89	6.41043
14	1974	1,438	20,132	196	1,808.6	-370.6	137,344	75.9396
15	1975	1,694	25,410	225	2,158.5	-464.5	215,760	99.9584
16	1976	1,802	28,832	256	2,508.4	-706.4	499,001	198.932
17	1977	1,857	31,569	289	2,858.3	-1,001.3	1,002,602	350.769

18	1978	2,056	37,008	324	3,208.2	-1,152.2	1,327,565	413.804
19	1979	2,182	41,458	361	3,558.1	-1,376.1	1,893,651	532.209
20	1980	2,505	50,100	400	3,908	-1,403	1,968,409	503.687
21	1981	2,860	60,060	441	4,257.9	-1,397.9	1,954,124	458.941
22	1982	3,283	72,226	484	4,607.8	-1,324.8	1,755,095	380.897
23	1983	3,556	81,788	529	4,957.7	-1,401.7	1,964,763	396.305
24	1984	3,596	86,304	576	5,307.6	-1,711.6	2,929,575	551.958
25	1985	3,997	99,925	625	5,657.5	-1,660.5	2,757,260	487.364
26	1986	4,138	107,588	676	6,007.4	-1,869.4	3,494,656	581.725
27	1987	4,746	128,142	729	6,357.3	-1,611.3	2,596,288	408.395
28	1988	4,536	127,008	784	6,707.2	-2,171.2	4,714,109	702.843
29	1989	4,887	141,723	841	7,057.1	-2,170.1	4,709,334	667.319
30	1990	5,436	163,080	900	7,407	-1,971	3,884,841	524.482
31	1991	5,743	178,033	961	7,756.9	-2,013.9	4,055,793	522.863
32	1992	6,149	196,768	1,024	8,106.8	-1,957.8	3,832,981	472.811
33	1993	5,765	190,245	1,089	8,456.7	-2,691.7	7,245,249	856.747
34	1994	6,966	236,844	1,156	8,806.6	-1,840.6	3,387,808	384.69
35	1995	6,910	241,850	1,225	9,156.5	-2,246.5	5,046,762	551.167
36	1996	7,514	270,504	1,296	9,506.4	-1,992.4	3,969,658	417.577
37	1997	11,781	435,897	1,369	9,856.3	1,924.7	3,704,470	375.848
38	1998	7,936	301,568	1,444	10,206.2	-2,270.2	5,153,808	504.968
39	1999	8,314	324,246	1,521	10,556.1	-2,242.1	5,027,012	476.219
40	2000	9,082	363,280	1,600	10,906	-1,824	3,326,976	305.059
41	2001	8,806	361,046	1,681	11,255.9	-2,449.9	6,002,010	533.232
42	2002	9,535	400,470	1,764	11,605.8	-2,070.8	4,288,213	369.489
43	2003	11,576	497,768	1,849	11,955.7	-379.7	144,172	12.0589
44	2004	12,832	564,608	1,936	12,305.6	526.4	277,097	22.518
45	2005	15,407	693,315	2,025	12,655.5	2,751.5	7,570,752	598.218
46	2006	15,573	716,358	2,116	13,005.4	2,567.6	6,592,570	506.91
47	2007	16,949	796,603	2,209	13,355.3	3,593.7	1.30E+07	967.008
48	2008	17,877	858,096	2,304	13,705.2	4,171.8	1.70E+07	1,269.88
49	2009	21,471	1,052,079	2,401	14,055.1	7,415.9	5.50E+07	3,912.86
50	2010	20,216	1,010,800	2,500	14,405	5,811	3.40E+07	2,344.17

$a = -3,090, \ b = 349.9, \ X^2 = 10,094.5$

For India: $a = -33.25, \ b = 2.85, \ X^2 = 408.399$

For China: $a = -108.9, \ b = 7.199, \ X^2 = 2,982.08$

indicated that the calculated Chi-Square value (X^2= 10,094.5) is much higher than the critical Chi-Square value of 31.41 for 49 degrees of freedom (*df*) at 0.05 (5%) level of significance. Hence, Hypothesis 1 has been rejected and it is concluded that the growth of literature in neurology does not follow the Linear Growth Model. Similar Growth Models have also been calculated for China and India. In both cases the calculated Chi-Square values (X^2= 408.399 for India, X^2 = 2,982.08 for China) are much more than the critical Chi-Square value of 31.41 for 49 degrees of freedom (*df*) at 0.05 (5%) level of significance. In both cases the growth of literature in neurology does not follow the Linear Growth Model. The application of the Linear Growth Model in terms of R^2 (0.854) is shown in Fig. 2. The fit statistics indicate a poor fit for the Linear Growth Model in the data sets. A graphical presentation of observed and estimated data values obtained is also shown in Fig. 2.

6.2. Exponential Growth Model

The Exponential Growth Model describes an unlimited exponential growth. This model not only provides a rate of growth (the exponential parameter) but also the rate at which the size of the literature doubles, and its doubling time. The exponential growth has been linked to compound interest.

Hypothesis 2

The growth of publications in the field of neurology literature better fit the Exponential Growth Model.

Testing of Hypothesis

In order to fit the data to test whether the growth of literature in neurology follows the exponential growth pattern or not, the expected number of publications (y) were computed using the following formula:

$Y= K+ab^x$

Where a and b are constants

K= is the asymptote or the upper limit

X is the unit of time

Inference

The results of a Chi-Square test of goodness of fit indicated that the calculated Chi-Square value is (X^2= 3,631.96), higher than the critical Chi-Square value of 31.41 for 49 degrees of freedom (*df*) at 0.05 level of significance. Hence, Hypothesis 2 has been rejected

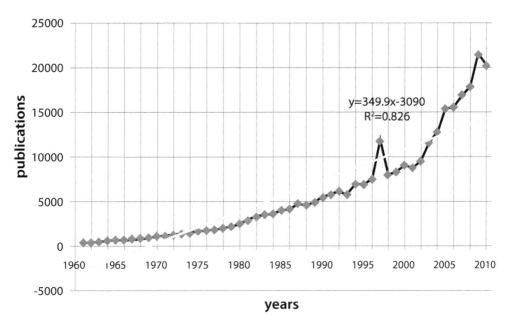

Fig. 2 Linear growth pattern of neurology literature

and it is concluded that the growth of literature in neurology does not exactly follow the Exponential Growth Model. The Exponential Growth model was also applied for China and India. In both cases the calculated Chi-Square value (X^2= 100.9477 for India, and X^2 = -5,017.79 for China) is greater than the critical Chi-Square value of 31.41 for 49 degrees of freedom (*df*) at 0.05 (5%) level of significance. In both cases, the growth of literature in neurology does not exactly follow the Exponential Growth Model. However, it nearly follows this growth model.

However, the application of the Exponential Growth Model in terms of R^2 (0.984) is shown in Fig. 3.

The fit statistics indicate that it nearly follows the Exponential Growth Model in the data sets. A graphical presentation of observed and estimated data values obtained is also shown in Fig. 3.

6.3. Logistic Growth Model

Hypothesis 3
The growth of publications in the field of neurology literature follows the Logistic Growth Model.

Testing of Hypothesis
In order to fit the data to test whether the growth

Table 6. Fit into Exponential Growth of Neurology Literature

X	Year	Observed no. of publications Y (f)	Expected no. of publication $Y=K+ab^x$	f-p	$(f-p)^2$	$\dfrac{(f-p)^2}{p}$
1	1961	405	273.27	131.73	17,354	63.505
2	1962	397	357.12	39.883	1,590.7	4.4542
3	1963	477	445.31	31.694	1,004.5	2.2557
4	1964	626	538.06	87.941	7,733.7	14.373
5	1965	712	635.61	76.39	5,835.4	9.1807
6	1966	674	738.21	-64.21	4,122.9	5.5849
7	1967	784	846.12	-62.12	3,858.5	4.5603
8	1968	874	959.61	-85.61	7,328.8	7.6373
9	1969	932	1,079	-147	21,601	20.02
10	1970	1,088	1,204.5	-116.5	13,575	11.27
11	1971	1,177	1,336.5	-159.5	25,455	19.045
12	1972	1,223	1,475.4	-252.4	63,712	43.183
13	1973	1,362	1,621.5	-259.5	67,322	41.519
14	1974	1,438	1,775.1	-337.1	113,618	64.008
15	1975	1,694	1,936.6	-242.6	58,869	30.398
16	1976	1,802	2,106.5	-304.5	92,748	44.029
17	1977	1,857	2,285.3	-428.3	183,401	80.254
	S1=	17,522				
18	1978	2,056	2,473.2	-417.2	174,062	70.379
19	1979	2,182	2,670.9	-488.9	239,011	89.487

20	1980	2,505	2,878.8	-373.8	139,723	48.535
21	1981	2,860	3,097.5	-237.5	56,387	18.204
22	1982	3,283	3,327.4	-44.44	1,974.8	0.5935
23	1983	3,556	3,569.3	-13.32	177.37	0.0497
24	1984	3,596	3,823.7	-227.7	51,853	13.561
25	1985	3,997	4,091.3	-94.27	8,886.6	2.1721
26	1986	4,138	4,372.7	-234.7	55,070	12.594
27	1987	4,746	4,668.6	77.37	5,986.1	1.2822
28	1988	4,536	4,979.9	-443.9	197,051	39.569
29	1989	4,887	5,307.3	-420.3	176,639	33.282
30	1990	5,436	5,651.6	-215.6	46,485	8.2251
31	1991	5,743	6,013.7	-270.7	73,299	12.189
32	1992	6,149	6,394.6	-245.6	60,324	9.4336
33	1993	5,765	6,795.2	-1,030	1E+06	156.18
34	1994	6,966	7,216.5	-250.5	62,748	8.6951
	S2=	72,401				
35	1995	6,910	7,659.6	-749.6	561,901	73.359
36	1996	7,514	8,125.6	-611.6	374,094	46.039
37	1997	11,781	8,615.8	3,165.2	1E+07	1162.8
38	1998	7,936	9,131.3	-1,195	1E+06	156.46
39	1999	8,314	9,673.5	-1,359	2E+06	191.05
40	2000	9,082	10,244	-1,162	1E+06	131.74
41	2001	8,806	10,843	-2,037	4E+06	382.82
42	2002	9,535	11,474	-1,939	4E+06	327.74
43	2003	11,576	12,138	-561.6	315,402	25.986
44	2004	12,832	12,835	-3.338	11.145	0.0009
45	2005	15,407	13,569	1,837.8	3E+06	248.92
46	2006	15,573	14,341	1,232	2E+06	105.84
47	2007	16,949	15,153	1,796.3	3E+06	212.94
48	2008	17,877	16,006	1,870.6	3E+06	218.6
49	2009	21,471	16,904	4,566.6	2E+07	33.7
50	2010	20,216	17,849	2,367.3	6E+06	313.97
	S3=	201,779				3,631.96

$a = 1,540.841$, $b = 1.051742$, $K = -1,347.3$, $X^2 = 3,631.96$

For India: $a = 0.77$, $b = 1.115$, $K = 3.55$, $X^2 = 100.9477$

For China: $a = -0.1768$, $b = 1.174$, $K = -160$, $X^2 = -5,017.79$

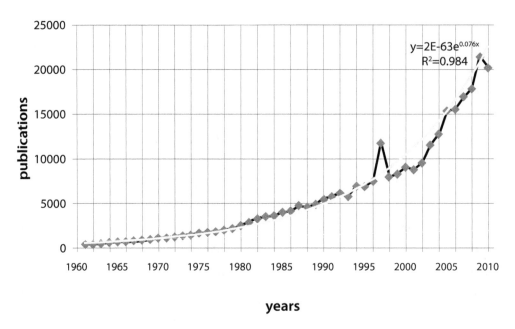

years

Fig. 3 Expontial Growth Pattern of Neurology Literature

of literature in neurology follows the logistic growth pattern or not, the expected number of publications (y) were computed using the following formula:

$1/Y= K+ab^x$

Where a and b are constants

K= is the asymptote or the upper limit

X is the unit of time

Inference

The results of the Chi-Square test of goodness of fit show that the calculated Chi-Square value is ($X^2=$ 5,821.7), much higher than the critical Chi-Square value of 31.41 for 49 degrees of freedom (*df*) at .05 level of significance. Hence, Hypothesis 3 has been rejected and it is concluded that the growth of literature in neurology does not follow the Logistic Growth Model.

The Logistic Growth model was also applied for China and India. In both cases the calculated Chi-Square value ($X^2=$ 199.669504 for India, $X^2 =$ -89,291.47204 for China) is much greater than the critical Chi-Square value of 31.41 for 49 degrees of freedom (*df*) at 0.05 (5%) level of significance. In both cases the growth of literature in neurology does not follow the Logistic Growth Model.

7. CONCLUSION

The bibliometric technique is considered as the most powerful technique for conducting such quantitative studies in this direction. An attempt was made in the present study to measure the trends in various aspects of published literature in the field of neurology literature.

The study is based on 291,702 research papers published between 1961-2010 as reflected in Science Direct, which is one of the most comprehensive databases covering all subjects. The data were collected, tabulated, and analyzed. The study reveals some factual factorial data through bibliometric analysis. Research articles have been analyzed for finding the year wise trend, Relative Growth Rate, Doubling Time, and examining the different types of growth rate models. The outcome of the present study shows that there is a steady growth of publications for world (except 1997) and China, and a fluctuating trend was observed for India during the study period. Averages of 5,720 papers were published per year at the global level, followed by China's average which is 74 and India's average at 39. The maximum world contribution is observed during 2009 (20,656 publications) and

Table 7. Fit into Logistic Growth of Model of Neurology Literature

X	Year	Y	1/Y	Expected no. of publications $1/Y=K+ab^x$	f-p	$(f-p)^2$	$\dfrac{(f-p)^2}{p}$
1	1961	405	0.00247	469.089	-64.0894	4,107.44948	8.756219
2	1962	397	0.00252	516.22	-119.22	14,213.31824	27.53347
3	1963	477	0.0021	567.969	-90.9688	8,275.322192	14.57003
4	1964	626	0.0016	624.765	1.234815	1.524767453	0.002441
5	1965	712	0.0014	687.072	24.92833	621.4217341	0.90445
6	1966	674	0.00148	755.387	-81.3875	6,623.919766	8.768903
7	1967	784	0.00128	830.25	-46.2497	2,139.03512	2.576376
8	1968	874	0.00114	912.235	-38.2347	1,461.895382	1.602543
9	1969	932	0.00107	1,001.96	-69.9592	4,894.290061	4.88472
10	1970	1,088	0.00092	1,100.08	-12.0806	145.9408986	0.132664
11	1971	1,177	0.00085	1,207.3	-30.2974	917.9336117	0.760321
12	1972	1,223	0.00082	1,324.35	-101.349	10,271.5322	7.755913
13	1973	1,362	0.00073	1,452.01	-90.012	8,102.16351	5.579956
14	1974	1,438	0.0007	1,591.1	-153.102	23,440.37362	14.73216
15	1975	1,694	0.00059	1,742.47	-48.468	2,349.148287	1.348173
16	1976	1,802	0.00055	1,906.99	-104.985	11,021.87541	5.779739
17	1977	1,857	0.00054	2,085.55	-228.553	52,236.28849	25.04674
	S1=		0.02076				
18	1978	2,056	0.00049	2,279.08	-223.083	49,766.23102	21.83607
19	1979	2,182	0.00046	2,488.5	-306.495	93,939.25715	37.74942
20	1980	2,505	0.0004	2,714.7	-209.697	43,973.00579	16.19812
21	1981	2,860	0.00035	2,958.58	-98.5786	9,717.739615	3.284597
22	1982	3,283	0.0003	3,220.99	62.01099	3,845.363017	1.193845
23	1983	3,556	0.00028	3,502.72	53.27738	2,838.479262	0.810364
24	1984	3,596	0.00028	3,804.5	-208.496	43,470.7656	11.42615
25	1985	3,997	0.00025	4,126.93	-129.928	16,881.31098	4.090527
26	1986	4,138	0.00024	4,470.51	-332.512	110,564.1821	24.73188
27	1987	4,746	0.00021	4,835.59	-89.5941	8,027.100512	1.660003
28	1988	4,536	0.00022	5,222.35	-686.347	471,072.7936	90.20327
29	1989	4,887	0.0002	5,630.75	-743.747	553,159.502	98.2391
30	1990	5,436	0.00018	6,060.55	-624.547	390,058.6262	64.3603
31	1991	5,743	0.00017	6,511.26	-768.26	590,223.1919	90.64654
32	1992	6,149	0.00016	6,982.14	-833.142	694,125.1915	99.41437

33	1993	5,765	0.00017	7,472.18	-1,707.18	2,914,460.651	390.0416
34	1994	6,966	0.00014	7,980.08	-1,014.08	1,028,367.931	128.8668
	S2=		**0.00452**				
35	1995	6,910	0.00014	8,504.3	-1,594.3	2,541,791.052	298.8831
36	1996	7,514	0.00013	9,043	-1,529	2,337,848.68	258.5257
37	1997	11,781	8.50E-05	9,594.13	2,186.871	4,782,404.508	498.472
38	1998	7,936	0.00013	10,155.4	-2,219.4	4,925,724.935	485.0352
39	1999	8,314	0.00012	10,724.3	-2,410.34	5,809,752.995	541.7351
40	2000	9,082	0.00011	11,298.4	-2,216.36	4,912,247.289	434.7753
41	2001	8,806	0.00011	11,874.7	-3,068.74	9,417,189.196	793.0436
42	2002	9,535	0.0001	12,450.8	-2,915.75	8,501,603.095	682.8185
43	2003	11,576	8.60E-05	13,023.6	-1,447.64	2,095,662.483	160.9122
44	2004	12,832	7.80E-05	13,590.7	-758.732	575,673.8623	42.35783
45	2005	15,407	6.50E-05	14,149.5	1,257.547	1,581,424.085	111.7657
46	2006	15,573	6.40E-05	14,697.4	875.6138	766,699.4442	52.1657
47	2007	16,949	5.90E-05	15,232.3	1,716.694	2,947,038.897	193.4729
48	2008	17,877	5.60E-05	15,752.2	2,124.788	4,514,724.487	286.6089
49	2009	21,471	4.70E-05	16,255.4	5,215.646	27,202,963.56	1,673.477
50	2010	20,216	4.90E-05	16,740.2	3,475.753	12,080,859.21	721.6655
	S3=		**0.00144**				

$a= 0.002304$, $b= 0.960849$, $b^n= 0.189712$, $K= 0.0000424$, $X^2= 8,451.202$

For China: $a= 0.5924$, $b= 0.929$, $K= 0.03009$, $X^2= -89,291.47204$
For India: $a= 0.5113$, $b=0.9077$, $K = 0.0025$, $X^2= 199.669504$

Table 8. Growth Models of Neurology Literature (R^2 value)

Growth models	World	China	India	Remark
Linear	0.826	0.408	0.609	Not fit
Exponential	0.984	0.861	0.765	Not fit
Logistic	0.957	0.721	0.653	Not fit

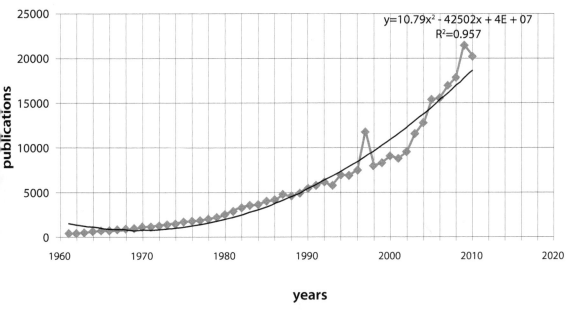

$$y=10.79x^2 - 42502x + 4E + 07$$
$$R^2=0.957$$

years

Fig. 4 Logistic Growth Model

those of China and India were published during 2010. China took 24 years to achieve double digit numbers of publications, whereas India took twelve years to achieve the same. The research in the field of neurology in India and China has increased over a period of time. The growth of literature in neurology does not follow either the Linear Growth Model or Logistic Growth Model. However, it nearly follows the Exponential Growth Model. The study concludes that there has been a consistent trend towards increased growth of literature in the field of neurology.

REFERENCES

Bouabid, H. (2011). Revisiting citation aging: A model for citation distribution and life cycle prediction. *Scientometrics, 88,* 199-211.

Bradford, S.C. (1934). Sources of information on specific subjects. *Engineering, 137,* 85-86.

Egghe, L., & Ravichandra Rao, I.K. (1992). Classification of growth models based on growth rate and its applications. *Scientometrics, 25,* 5-46.

Gilbert, G.N. (1978). Measuring the growth of science: A review of indices. *Scientometrics, 1*(1), 9-34.

Gupta, B.M., & Karisiddappa, C.R. (2000). Modeling the growth of literature in the area of theoretical population genetics. *Scientometrics, 49*(2), 321-355.

Gupta, B.M., Sharma, P., & Karisiddappa, C.R. (1997). Growth of research literature in scientific specialities: A modeling perspective. *Scientometrics, 40*(3), 507-528.

Gupta, B.M., Sharma, P., & Kumar, S. (1999). Growth of world and Indian physics literature. *Scientometrics, 44*(1), 5-16.

Gupta, B.M., Kumar, S., Sangam, S.L., & Karisiddappa, C.R. (2002). Modeling the growth of world social science literature. *Scientometrics, 53*(1), 161-164.

Hoffmann, W.A., & Poorter, H. (2002). Avoiding bias in calculations of relative growth rate. *Annals of Botany, 80,* 37-42.

Hunt, R. (1978). *Plant growth analysis.* London: Edward Arnold.

Hunt, R. (1982). Plant growth analysis: Second derivates and compounded second derivates of splined plant growth curves. *Annals of Botany, 50,* 317-328.

Karki, M.M.S., Garg, K.C., & Sharma, P. (2000). Activity and growth of organic chemistry research in India during 1971-1989. *Scientometrics, 49*(2), 279-288.

Meera, & Sangam, S.L. (2010). Indian chemical literature 1907-2005: Activity and growth. In S.L. Sangam et al. (Eds.), *Webometrics, Informetrics and Scientometrics: Measuring scientific and technological progress of India* (national seminar papers and proceedings) (pp. 47-66). Dharwad: Karnatak University.

Poorter, H., & Garnier, E. (1996). Plant growth analysis: An evaluation of experimental design and computational methods. *Journal of Experimental Botany, 47*(302), 1343-1351.

Price, D.D.S. (1966). *Little science, big science.* New York: Columbia University Press.

Price, D.D.S. (1975). *Science since Babylon.* Enlarged Edition. New Haven: Yale University Press.

Ramakrishna, N.V. (2009). Modelling the growth of ferrous metallurgy literature: A study based on iron making and steel making. *SRELS Journal of Information Management, 46*(4), 413-421.

Ravichandra Rao, I.K. (1998). Growth, obsolescence, collaboration and circulation statistics. In Ravichandra Rao, I.K. (Ed.), *Workshop on Informetrics and Scientometrics.* Bangalore: DRTC.

Sangam, S.L., Liming, L., & Ganjihal, G.A. (2010). Modeling the growth of Indian and Chinese Liquid Crystals literature as reflected in Science Citation Index (1997-2006). *Scientometrics, 84*, 49-52.

Seetharam, G., & Ravichandra Rao, I.K. (1999). Growth of food science and technology literature: A comparison of CFTRI, India and the world. *Scientometrics, 44*(1), 59-79.

Szydowski, M., & Krawiec, A. (2009). Growth cycles of knowledge. *Scientometrics, 78*(1), 99-111.

Tsay, M.G. (2008). A bibliometric analysis of hydrogen energy literature, 1965-2005. *Scientometrics, 75*(3), 421-438.

Zhao, Q., & Guan, J. (2012). Modeling the dynamic relation between science and technology in nanotechnology. *Scientometrics, 90*, 561-579.

Permissions

All chapters in this book were first published in JISTP, by Korea Institute of Science and Technology Information; hereby published with permission under the Creative Commons Attribution License or equivalent. Every chapter published in this book has been scrutinized by our experts. Their significance has been extensively debated. The topics covered herein carry significant findings which will fuel the growth of the discipline. They may even be implemented as practical applications or may be referred to as a beginning point for another development.

The contributors of this book come from diverse backgrounds, making this book a truly international effort. This book will bring forth new frontiers with its revolutionizing research information and detailed analysis of the nascent developments around the world.

We would like to thank all the contributing authors for lending their expertise to make the book truly unique. They have played a crucial role in the development of this book. Without their invaluable contributions this book wouldn't have been possible. They have made vital efforts to compile up to date information on the varied aspects of this subject to make this book a valuable addition to the collection of many professionals and students.

This book was conceptualized with the vision of imparting up-to-date information and advanced data in this field. To ensure the same, a matchless editorial board was set up. Every individual on the board went through rigorous rounds of assessment to prove their worth. After which they invested a large part of their time researching and compiling the most relevant data for our readers.

The editorial board has been involved in producing this book since its inception. They have spent rigorous hours researching and exploring the diverse topics which have resulted in the successful publishing of this book. They have passed on their knowledge of decades through this book. To expedite this challenging task, the publisher supported the team at every step. A small team of assistant editors was also appointed to further simplify the editing procedure and attain best results for the readers.

Apart from the editorial board, the designing team has also invested a significant amount of their time in understanding the subject and creating the most relevant covers. They scrutinized every image to scout for the most suitable representation of the subject and create an appropriate cover for the book.

The publishing team has been an ardent support to the editorial, designing and production team. Their endless efforts to recruit the best for this project, has resulted in the accomplishment of this book. They are a veteran in the field of academics and their pool of knowledge is as vast as their experience in printing. Their expertise and guidance has proved useful at every step. Their uncompromising quality standards have made this book an exceptional effort. Their encouragement from time to time has been an inspiration for everyone.

The publisher and the editorial board hope that this book will prove to be a valuable piece of knowledge for researchers, students, practitioners and scholars across the globe.

List of Contributors

Hui Zhang and Elin Jacob
School of Library and Information Science Indiana University, U.S.

Kiduk Yang
Department of Library and Information Science Kyungpook National University, Korea

P. Rajendran and J. Manickaraj
SRM University, India

B. Elango
IFET College of Engineering, India

Min Song
Department of Library and Information Science Yonsei University, Korea

Pia Borlund
Royal School of Library and Information Science University of Copenhagen, Denmark

Keshava and B. N. Thimmaiah
Dept. of Studies and Research in Library and Information Science Tumkur University, India

K. B. Agadi
Gujarath Central University Library, India

C. P. Uzuegbu
Department of Library and Information Science Michael Okpara University of Agriculture Nigeria

So Young YU
Department of Library and Information Science Hannam University, Republic of Korea

Jinseok Kim and Jana Diesner
Graduate School of Library and Information Science, University of Illinois at Urbana-Champaign, USA

Heejun Kim
School of Information and Library Science, University of North Carolina at Chapel Hill, USA

Gary Burnett
School of Information Florida State University Tallahassee, USA

Ramesh Pandita
BGSB University Rajouri, Jammu & Kashmir, India

Shivendra Singh
University College of Nursing Baba Farid University of Health Sciences (BFUHS), Punjab, India

Junwei Sun
WISE Lab Dalian University of Technology, China

Chunlin Jiang
Institute of Science of Science and S&T Management Dalian University of Technology, China

Abdullahi A. Bakare
Department of Library and Information Science, College of Information and Communication Technology, Kwara State University, Malete, Ilorin

Abiola A. Abioye
Department of Library, Archival and Information Studies, Faculty of Education, University of Ibadan, Ibadan

Abdulwahab Olanrewaju Issa
Department of Library and Information Science, Faculty of Communication and Information Sciences, University of Ilorin, Ilorin

M P Satija
Guru Nanak Dev University Amritsar—143005 India

Daniel Martínez-Ávila
São Paulo State University Hygino Muzzi Filho 737 17525-900 Marilia, Brazil

Gururaj S. Hadagali
Department of Library and Information Science Karnataka University, Dharwad, Karnataka, India

Gavisiddappa Anandhalli
Department of Library and Information Science Karnataka State Women's University, Bijapur, Karnataka, India

Index

Printed in the USA
CPSIA information can be obtained
at www.ICGtesting.com
JSHW051325221024
72173JS00006B/1290

9 781632 406484